Examining Human Rights at the Intersection of Digitalization and Society

Maja Pucelj
https://orcid.org/0009-0001-9063-9080
Euro-Mediterranean University, Slovenia

IGI Global
Scientific Publishing
Publishing Tomorrow's Research Today

Vice President of Editorial	Melissa Wagner
Director of Acquisitions	Mikaela Felty
Director of Book Development	Jocelynn Hessler
Production Manager	Mike Brehm
Cover Design	Jose Rosado

Published in the United States of America by
IGI Global Scientific Publishing
701 East Chocolate Avenue
Hershey, PA, 17033, USA
Tel: 717-533-8845 | Fax: 717-533-7115
Website: https://www.igi-global.com E-mail: cust@igi-global.com

Library of Congress Cataloging-in-Publication Data

LCCN: 2025024580 (CIP Data Pending)
ISBN13: 979-8-3373-3685-5
Isbn13Softcover: 979-8-3373-3686-2
EISBN13: 979-8-3373-3687-9
British Cataloguing in Publication Data
A Cataloguing in Publication record for this book is available from the British Library.

Table of Contents

Detailed Table of Contents

This chapter examines the significant importance of digital inclusion for global sustainable development and human rights in the age of rapidly expanding AI. The chapter discusses meaningful digital inclusion, which is fundamentally defined and it has been linked to both the SDGs and human rights while examining the many components of the digital divide. The chapter demonstrates how all types of digital inclusion are important and can be accelerators of economic empowerment, health, education, gender equality, governance strengthening, and sustainability on a global level. It provides critical analysis of AI's transformative promise while providing analysis of the many human rights risks that have emerged. We outline comprehensive approaches that deal with national and regional level policies, global governance capacities for AI, multi-stakeholder approaches and capacity building. The chapter ends with recommendations, recalling the vital inter-linkage among the recommendations for designing a truly human-centric, equitable and sustainable digital future for everyone.

This paper examines the complex relationship between digital media, disinformation, and human rights in postcolonial Africa. It highlights disinformation as a significant threat to civic space, democracy, health, and information rights. Through diverse case studies from the continent—covering political campaigns, public health crises, and social movements—it identifies patterns in the use and spread of disinformation via mobile technologies and social media. These practices deepen existing inequalities, erode public trust, and marginalize vulnerable voices. The analysis contextualizes the issue within historical and postcolonial frameworks, exploring African states' regulatory responses and the role of civil society organizations. The study concludes with recommendations for rights-based governance in digital environments, stressing the need for digital literacy, policy reforms, and transnational cooperation to combat disinformation and protect human rights in the digital era.

the challenges posed by fragmented enforcement and democratic oversight. The analysis emphasizes the growing need for rights-based digital governance grounded in transparency, accountability and judicial safeguards. As we advance into an era defined by digital transformation, the commitment to privacy must remain central, not only as a matter of rights, but as a means to reduce systemic inequality and promoting strong institutions and justice.

With the advent of artificial intelligence (AI), the practice of identifying exposure to risk is revolutionized which has helped businesses reshape the way they identify, assess, and address digital and physical threats. As data seems to grow exponentially and slowly gradually from the form of complex attacks, it is increasingly saturating all the old methodologies of threat detection. Today, artificial intelligence has become an integral part of modern threat detection systems because they are able to sort through huge data, point to patterns, and recognize even new forms of threats. Further, the paper looks at how artificial intelligence can be applied to evaluate risks, how it will improve cybersecurity and threat intelligence, how effective it can be in its application, and also a discussion of the emerging trends that would be anticipated in shaping this subject.

Artificial intelligence (AI) plays a transformative role in the protection and advancement of human rights within the international legal framework. Leveraging advanced analytics and automated monitoring systems, AI enables the detection, documentation, and reporting of human rights violations, thereby enhancing transparency and accountability on a global scale. International civil society

Preface

Digitalization has become one of the defining forces of the 21st century, reshaping how people communicate, work, learn, mobilize, and govern. As digital systems increasingly underpin the functioning of societies, they simultaneously generate new opportunities for empowerment and new risks of exclusion, manipulation, and rights violations. The accelerating convergence of artificial intelligence, ubiquitous data flows, digital platforms, and global communication infrastructures demands a renewed examination of what it means to protect human dignity in digitally mediated environments.

This edited volume brings together scholars and practitioners from diverse regions and disciplinary backgrounds to interrogate human rights at the critical intersection of technology and society. The chapters collectively examine how digital infrastructures influence fundamental rights, from privacy, information access, and democratic participation to equality, development, and environmental sustainability. They highlight both the enabling power of technology and the vulnerabilities born from inadequate governance, ethical oversights, and entrenched structural inequalities.

The book's contribution lies in its multidimensional approach: situating human rights concerns within socio-technical systems; analyzing concrete cases from Africa, Asia, and global digital commons; and offering normative, legal, and policy-oriented frameworks that can guide more equitable digital futures. At a moment when societies grapple with the implications of AI, disinformation, surveillance, and digital divides, this collection underscores the urgent need for holistic, rights-based digital transformation anchored in accountability, inclusivity, and global cooperation.

CHAPTER OVERVIEW

Chapter 1 – Foundations of the Digital Society (Cene Bavec)

The opening chapter provides a conceptual grounding for understanding digital society and its transformative dynamics. It emphasizes digitalization's immediate and global impact on core human rights and argues for an integrated governance approach that connects technological infrastructures to cultural, regulatory, and ethical contexts. The chapter establishes the theoretical foundation for the rest of the volume.

Chapter 2 – Digitalization and Human Rights: Navigating through Ethical and Legal Concerns (Jipson Joseph)

Chapter 2 examines digitalization through an ethical and legal lens, highlighting how misuse, rather than mere system failure, drives many contemporary human rights challenges. Through critical analysis, the chapter identifies gaps in ethical principles and legal safeguards and proposes approaches for strengthening human rights protections in digital spaces.

Chapter 3 – Digital Inclusion as a Catalyst for Sustainable Development (Pranjal Khare)

This chapter centers on digital inclusion as a prerequisite for sustainable development and human rights, especially in an AI-driven world. It links digital inclusion to the SDGs and dissects layers of the digital divide. The author provides a comprehensive review of policy, governance, and capacity-building strategies needed to ensure that digital transformation is equitable and human-centric.

Chapter 4 – Digital Media and Disinformation in Postcolonial Africa (Wafaa Taleb)

Chapter 4 analyzes the proliferation of disinformation in postcolonial African contexts, demonstrating its profound implications for democracy, civic participation, and vulnerable communities. Through diverse case studies, the chapter illustrates how disinformation exploits existing inequalities and evaluates state and civil society responses. It concludes with recommendations for rights-based digital governance.

Chapter 5 – Current Challenges of Media and Human Rights in the Digital World (Melita Zajc)

Focusing on the sociotechnical basis of digital media, this chapter explores how platform architectures shape communication rights. The author introduces epistemic rights as a potential regulatory avenue and critiques the limitations of existing mechanisms. The chapter calls for renewed approaches that reclaim the positive, rights-enhancing potential of digital technologies.

Chapter 6 – Disinformation and the Right to Access Public Information During Disasters: The 2023 Turkey Earthquake Case (Mahmut Enes Agca)

Using the 2023 Turkey earthquake as a case study, Chapter 6 examines how disinformation and restricted access to official information undermine public rights during crises. It assesses the dual responsibilities of media actors to counter falsehoods and to uphold ethical communication standards while highlighting the societal consequences of censorship and misinformation in disaster contexts.

Chapter 7 – Right to Privacy as a Digital Human Right (Hemendra Singh)

This chapter provides a comparative legal analysis of privacy as a central digital human right. It traces constitutional developments across jurisdictions and identifies critical weaknesses in oversight and enforcement. Emphasizing the need for transparent and accountable digital governance, the author argues that privacy protections are essential not only for individual rights but also for reducing structural inequality.

Chapter 8 – The Role of Artificial Intelligence in Threat Detection: Current and Future Trends (Upasana Khattri, Shiva Tiwari, Rajat Shandilya)

Chapter 8 explores how AI is reshaping threat detection across digital and physical domains. It reviews AI-driven methods for risk evaluation, cybersecurity enhancement, and threat intelligence, while also discussing emerging trends and the implications of increasingly complex computational systems for future security practices.

Chapter 9 – The Role of Artificial Intelligence in Safeguarding Human Rights: An International Legal Perspective (Saquib Ahmed et al.)

Offering an international legal analysis, this chapter investigates how AI tools aid in monitoring, documenting, and responding to human rights violations. It explores their use by civil society and enforcement bodies, including in conflict settings, and reflects on how AI's evolution intersects with broader questions of human existence, social justice, and institutional accountability.

Chapter 10 – Integrating Digital Technologies for Climate Action: Driving Innovation to Achieve SDG 13 (Anitha Kumari)

This chapter positions digital technologies as key drivers of climate resilience and sustainability. Drawing on global case studies and conceptual models, it explains how AI, IoT, blockchain, and related technologies support climate mitigation and adaptation. Practical recommendations guide policymakers and organizations working to align climate strategies with digital innovation.

Chapter 11 – The Sesame Social Credit System and Human Rights Impacts in China's Social Commerce Marketplace (Yowei Kang & Kenneth C. C. Yang)

The final chapter investigates China's Sesame Social Credit System through mixed methods, analyzing its surveillance architecture, government rationales, and public responses. Identifying recurring themes in media and user narratives, the chapter evaluates the broader implications of such systems for privacy, autonomy, and rights in digital marketplaces, concluding with managerial and policy insights.

Together, the chapters in this volume illuminate the multifaceted challenges and possibilities at the nexus of digitalization and human rights. They provide analytical depth, empirical grounding, and practical guidance—supporting scholars, policymakers, and practitioners committed to building fair, inclusive, and accountable digital societies.

Chapter 1
Foundations of the Digital Society

Cene Bavec
https://orcid.org/0009-0006-5227-825X
Euro-Mediterranean University, Slovenia

ABSTRACT

This chapter outlines the foundational concepts of the digital society, with particular attention to the transformative role of digital technologies. This chapter offers a framework for interpreting both the unprecedented opportunities and the profound risks that digitalization presents, emphasizing that meaningful protection of human rights requires an integrated approach - one that balances innovation with ethical governance, inclusivity, and cross-cultural awareness. Unlike previous technological revolutions, whose societal effects were often indirect and unfolded over decades, digital transformation exerts an immediate, direct, and global influence on rights such as privacy, freedom of expression, non-discrimination, and access to information. By situating human rights concerns within the broader socio-technical ecosystem, the discussion links technological infrastructures - such as data networks, artificial intelligence, and digital communication platforms - with their governance, regulatory, and cultural contexts.

INTRODUCTION

The article offers a broad, introductory examination of the digital society, integrating technological, social, legal, and ethical perspectives. It establishes the foundational concepts and contextual background necessary for understanding how human rights are shaped, challenged, and redefined in the digital age. By explaining the technological foundations - such as data infrastructures, AI, and digital commu-

DOI: 10.4018/979-8-3373-3685-5.ch001

nication networks - alongside their societal, political, and cultural implications, the chapter provides a framework that supports and contextualizes the more specialized analyses presented in subsequent contributions to this volume.

This chapter focuses on several critical aspects of the digital society:

- Technological and data infrastructure enabling information connectivity and data accessibility.
- Economic and organizational changes stemming from digital innovations, process automation, and data-driven business models.
- Social and cultural environments supporting harmonious development with technology.
- Legal and political frameworks safeguarding rights, protection, and security for individuals and society.
- Ethics and values critical for responsible data management.

The central argument is that the sustainable and equitable development of the digital society depends on a carefully maintained balance between technological innovation and governance grounded in ethical, inclusive, and cross-culturally sensitive principles. While digital transformation brings unprecedented opportunities for connectivity, efficiency, and innovation, it also reshapes power relations, labour markets, and cultural norms. Addressing these shifts requires proactive, evidence-based measures to safeguard human rights, prevent monopolistic dominance, and bridge persistent global digital divides. The digital society should therefore be understood not merely as a technical system, but as a socio-technical ecosystem in which human values, institutional arrangements, and technological infrastructures continuously co-evolve (Van Dijk, 2020).

Human societies are inherently complex and dynamic systems that adapt to shifting environmental, economic, and cultural conditions. Technological development has historically been one of the primary drivers of structural and functional transformations in these systems, from the mechanization of production to the globalization of communication networks. Today, the world is undergoing a critical transformation from a post-industrial society to a digital society, in which advanced information and communication technologies are deeply embedded in every sphere of life. Understanding this transition requires attention to both the technological enablers and the social structures that adopt, resist, or reshape them.

The digital society is not merely a technological phenomenon, but also a profound social and political project, whose outcomes are shaped by institutional choices, cultural contexts, and global inequalities. As a result, its study requires a distinctly interdisciplinary approach (Van Dijk, 2020). Such an approach situates technological change within broader frameworks of economics, sociology, political science, law, and psychology, recognizing that technological artefacts are never neutral but carry embedded values and societal consequences (Khazieva at al, 2018, Kudina, van de Poel, 2024). This perspective is increasingly reflected in recent empirical work that explores socio-technical dynamics, such as how digital transformation fuels social innovation across economies (Nagy & Somosi, 2022) and reshapes digital inclusion through platform affordances (Yang & Zhang, 2023). These studies reinforce the view that technology and society are mutually constitutive - constantly influencing each other's trajectories and outcomes.

Even definitions of society have evolved alongside technological advancement, from the post-industrial society in the 1970s, through the information society at the turn of the millennium, to today's concept of the digital society. Emerging terms, such as algorithmic society (a social structure where algorithms significantly shape decision-making, governance, and daily life) and the metaverse (a persistent, shared 3D virtual space merging physical and digital realities), reflect an even higher level of integration between our physical and digital worlds. Generative AI further exemplifies this duality, offering new possibilities for information access while raising systemic risks related to bias, misinformation, and democratic resilience (Mitra et al., 2024).

Although the digital society exceeds technology alone, its dynamics cannot be fully understood without examining the foundational technological architectures that enable its functionality alongside the human, institutional, and political contexts in which these structures operate. The digital infrastructure of today forms a multilayered socio-technical ecosystem, comprising physical networks (fixed, mobile, satellite), data centers, cloud platforms, diverse devices (e.g. smartphones, Internet of Things - IoT sensors), and software protocols optimized for efficient communication. Critically, these infrastructures are shaped by policies, organizational cultures, and user practices that determine how technologies are implemented and experienced (Avtalion et al., 2024).

A socio-technical perspective underlines that the digital society is co-constructed through engineered systems and the societal structures that enable or constrain them (Kudina & van der Poel, 2024, Iden & Bygstad, 2025). Integrating digital and social infrastructures also poses challenges for ensuring social cohesion and equity, especially in underserved contexts (Giest, 2025). The development of the digital society brings numerous opportunities but also a range of legal and ethical challenges and dilemmas that must be addressed in parallel with technological advancement, as the boundaries between the virtual and physical worlds are becoming increasingly blurred.

The digital economy, encompassing all economic and business sectors reliant on digital technologies - from online sales and marketing to data services and innovative financing models - serves as the driving force of the digital society (Martynov et al., 2019, OECD, 2020). In contrast to the traditional economy, which is founded on physical products and distribution chains, the digital economy enables the development of entirely new business and production models previously unknown in the classical economy. The digitalization of work processes and services influences employment trends, the balance of power between providers and consumers, and the availability and accessibility of services. The transformed business models and relationships between business partners allow for significantly faster business processes and, consequently, rapid growth, which is particularly evident among large technology corporations.

While much of the existing scholarship highlights the transformative potential of digital innovation, it is equally important to acknowledge the systemic risks and long-term vulnerabilities it entails. Beyond technical and regulatory challenges, digital societies may enter structural conditions of dependence that are difficult—if not impossible—to reverse. This raises fundamental questions about resilience, freedom, and human activity in an increasingly digitized world. A defining, yet often underexplored, characteristic of the digital society is its irreversibility.

Once infrastructures, institutions, and everyday practices become fully digitized, the option of returning to analog alternatives effectively disappears. This process is more than technological progress; it marks a civilizational point of no return. Artificial intelligence illustrates this irreversibility even more clearly: once adopted, its learning capabilities, economic advantages, and geopolitical stakes make retreat virtually unthinkable. Moreover, once a digital trajectory is established, it tends to persist with great inertia, making redirection slow, costly, and uncertain. The challenge is therefore not only the impossibility of disconnection but also the extreme difficulty of altering technological pathways once they have been implemented.

INDICATORS OF THE DIGITAL SOCIETY

EU Digital Economy and Society Index (DESI)

As the definition of digital society encompasses both measurable and intangible factors, assessing its effectiveness or developmental stage poses significant methodological challenges. Its assessment is possible only through indirect indicators covering technological infrastructure, digital services, user skills, and the impact of digitalization on the economy and society. Each of these indicators helps elucidate a part of how digital technologies integrate into everyday life, the effectiveness of digital services, and the capability of individuals, society, and the economy to utilize them optimally. Such an approach allows comparisons across different regions and countries, serving as an essential tool for policy planning and investments in digital transformation.

Figure 1. Selected indicators from the State of the Digital Decade report, 2023 (Source: European Commission, 2024)

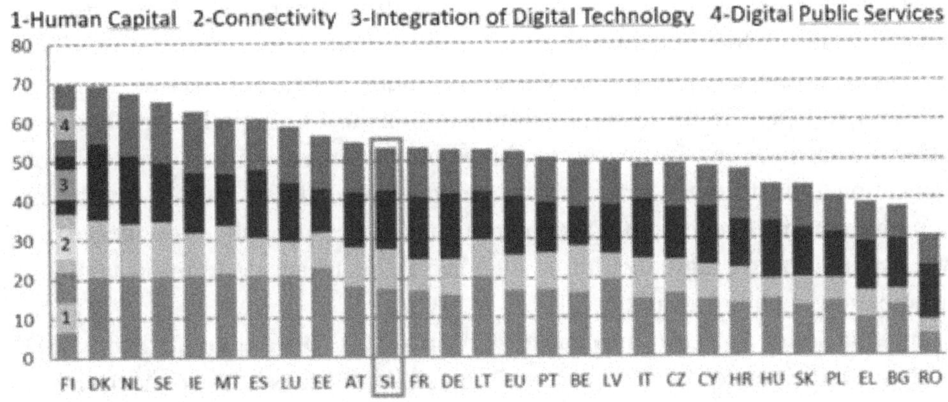

At the EU level, the Digital Economy and Society Index (DESI) has for years served as the key tool to benchmark Member States' progress in digitalization. It was used by the European Commission to track digital progress across four key areas: connectivity, digital skills, integration of digital technologies by businesses, and digital public services. Figure 1 presents all four indicators (according to the former DESI methodology) combined into a single graph for all EU Member States. It provided a clear comparative overview, enabling the EU to monitor convergence and highlight areas requiring additional investment or regulatory intervention.

In 2023, DESI was formally integrated into the State of the Digital Decade framework, which tracks progress toward the EU's 2030 digital targets through a refined set of Key Performance Indicators (European Commission, 2024). These continue to cover four central dimensions - connectivity, digital skills, business digitalization, and digital public services - ensuring continuity with DESI while aligning more directly with long-term policy objectives. The updated framework This updated framework continues the multi-dimensional logic of DESI, while offering enhanced alignment with long-term policy objectives. It enables benchmarking between EU countries and informs national strategies and investment decisions in the digital domain.

Indicators of the Digital Society: International Approaches

While the European Commission's Digital Economy and Society Index (DESI) has become a benchmark within the EU, other regions and international organizations have also developed their own frameworks to measure digital transformation. Placing DESI alongside these international indicators shows that measuring the digital society is not a purely technical exercise, but also reflects broader cultural, political, and normative choices. Recognizing these differences is essential for understanding how digital progress interacts with human rights, governance, and societal values in diverse contexts.

United Nations E-Government Development Index (EGDI) measures the readiness and capacity of national administrations to use digital technologies for public service delivery. It is based on three components: online services, telecommunication infrastructure, and human capital. Unlike DESI, which emphasizes economic competitiveness, EGDI reflects a governance and public service perspective, directly linking digitalization to citizens' rights of access to information and participation in public affairs.

International Telecommunication Union – ICT Development Index (IDI) combines indicators on ICT access, use, and skills. It focuses on connectivity and capacity, providing a global comparison across developed and developing countries. This index is crucial for monitoring the digital divide at a global scale, particularly in relation to equality and non-discrimination in access to digital infrastructures.

OECD – Digital Government Index (DGI) evaluates how governments design and deliver policies in the digital age. Its pillars - digital by design, data-driven public sector, proactiveness, openness, and user-driven approaches - emphasize governance culture and institutional change rather than infrastructure alone. This makes it particularly relevant from a human rights and accountability perspective.

United States – Digital Nation Data & Broadband Indicators are no single composite index equivalent to DESI. Instead, agencies like the National Telecommunications and Information Administration (NTIA) and the Federal Communications Commission (FCC) publish data sets on broadband access, digital inclusion, and adoption. These focus on market-driven infrastructure and access disparities, especially rural–urban divides, rather than a comprehensive rights-based framework.

China – Digital Economy Development Index (DEDI) has introduced the *DEDI*, published annually by the China Academy of Information and Communications Technology (CAICT). It measures the scale, structure, and efficiency of the digital economy, emphasizing industrial transformation and state-driven innovation. However, unlike DESI or OECD's DGI, this index pays little attention to individual rights such as privacy or freedom of expression, reflecting a distinct regulatory philosophy.

AN OVERVIEW OF TECHNOLOGICAL FOUNDATIONS OF THE DIGITAL SOCIETY

Development of Digital Technologies and Services: Social Implications

The technological foundations of the digital society were laid in the second half of the twentieth century, when computing and networking advanced at an unprecedented pace (Zaagsma, 2013). This trajectory - often described by Moore's Law of exponential development - was characterized by cycles of innovation in which the limits of one paradigm rapidly gave way to another. Unlike earlier industrial revolutions, digital innovations have had immediate and global consequences, directly reshaping access to information, privacy, and freedom of expression.

Since the 1960s, the pace of technological progress has been not only linear but exponential, combining miniaturization of hardware, standardization of internet protocols, and expansion of network capacity (Giest, 2025). This evolution narrowed - but did not eliminate - the digital divide, making access to information and digital services a core dimension of equality and non-discrimination. Yet many breakthroughs, such as the indexed internet in the early 1990s or the sudden emergence of generative AI after 2020, were largely unforeseen, leaving little time for legal systems and societies to prepare. This pattern highlights a structural dynamic: societies will continue to "chase" technological innovation, with governance and regulation persistently lagging behind.

Two milestones illustrate the profound impact of technological disruption. The introduction of the indexed internet democratized access to knowledge, transforming the exercise of freedom of information and expression (Berners-Lee, 2019). More recently, generative AI has introduced unprecedented opportunities - and risks - for social, economic, and cultural transformation (Kudina & van de Poel, 2024). In both cases, technological breakthroughs required urgent reconsideration of legal frameworks concerning privacy, intellectual property, and accountability.

Equally significant as the development of core technologies has been the evolution of user-oriented services. While early applications were largely institutional (e.g., government administration and banking), the post-1990s era saw digital technologies embedded in everyday life, transforming markets, communication, and civic participation (Dufva & Dufva, 2019; Van Dijk, 2020).

Figure 2. Timeline of the Development of Key Applications and Services (Author's elaboration)

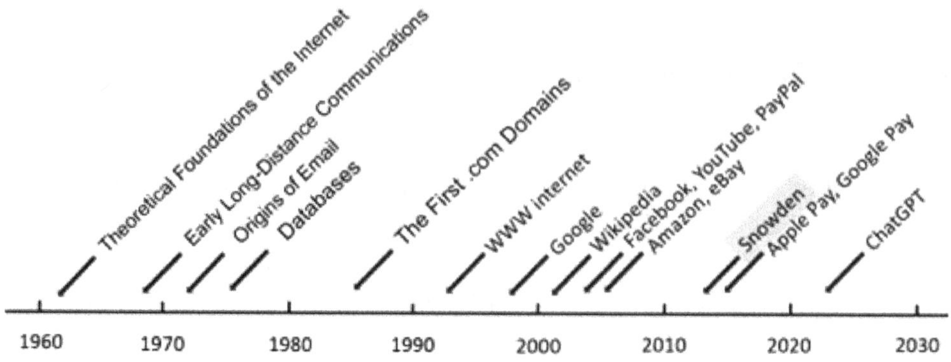

This timeline illustrates how the diffusion of services - ranging from early network applications and email, to the rise of social media, the mobile revolution, and, most recently, generative AI - has repeatedly reshaped the conditions under which fundamental rights are exercised. Social media amplified individual voices and enabled new forms of participation, yet also facilitated disinformation and surveillance. The mobile revolution extended connectivity across populations, but simultaneously deepened dependencies on private infrastructures. Generative AI now raises complex questions about intellectual property, freedom of expression, and the right to truth in an environment where synthetic content is indistinguishable from human-created material (UNESCO, 2023; Sag & Yu, 2025).

Taken together, these developments underscore a central feature of the digital society: technological innovation is not only an economic or technical process but also a continuous reconfiguration of rights. The speed, unpredictability, and disruptive nature of digital change ensure that societies will remain in a state of legal and normative "catch-up," balancing innovation with the protection of human dignity and fundamental freedoms.

Data Infrastructure

Data has become the cornerstone of the digital economy, functioning as the most valuable resource for innovation and transformation. Much like oil in the industrial era, data fuels today's digital society. Infrastructural and publicly accessible datasets underpin services ranging from e-commerce to e-government, enabling communication and decision-making across all societal levels. Initially developed for operational purposes, data has become essential for transparency, accountability, and democratic participation.

At the policy level, the European Union has advanced frameworks such as the Data Governance Act (2022) and European Data Spaces, emphasizing sovereignty, interoperability, and public trust. The U.S., by contrast, follows a more market-driven approach, with open access policies shaped primarily by private corporations, while China has centralized state control (Yang, & Chen, 2022) through initiatives like the Data Security Law (2021). These diverging models illustrate how data infrastructure is not merely technical but also geopolitical, reflecting competing values of openness, competition, and control.

Data infrastructure and public internet access are two sides of the same ecosystem: on one side, extensive networks, data centers, and communication protocols; on the other, user tools such as browsers enabling access to online content and services. Their interplay defines who has the ability to access information, how securely, and under which conditions of oversight.

Communication Infrastructure

Data transmission networks are a foundational technology of the digital society. Beyond coverage and accessibility, transmission speed has become critical, enabling latency-free applications such as industrial automation and real-time medical monitoring. Increasingly, connectivity extends to devices and sensors through the Internet of Things (IoT). Built on high-speed connections (5G), IoT already links more than 15 billion devices worldwide, far outnumbering human users (Statista, 2024). Emerging 6G standards and low-earth orbit satellite constellations (e.g., Starlink, OneWeb) further transform global connectivity. For instance, the deployment of satellite internet in Ukraine during the 2022 Russian invasion demonstrated how communication infrastructure has become vital for not only military operations but also the protection of human rights, freedom of expression, and access to information in crisis contexts.

Fiber optic and satellite connections complement each other: while satellites extend access to remote areas, fiber optic networks offer reliability and capacity for densely connected regions. These infrastructures are now recognized as critical components of digital sovereignty, as states seek to reduce dependence on foreign providers while ensuring resilience against cyber threats.

Cloud Computing and Service Platforms

Cloud computing rationalizes the use of computing resources by replacing expensive proprietary systems with scalable, on-demand services. Users, from individuals to corporations, can access data and applications from anywhere, reducing costs and enhancing flexibility.

Three main models are distinguished:

- **Infrastructure as a Service (IaaS):** provision of servers, networks, and storage (e.g., AWS, Azure, Google Cloud).
- **Platform as a Service (PaaS):** development environments enabling deployment of applications without managing infrastructure.
- **Software as a Service (SaaS):** ready-to-use applications delivered over the internet.

Yet, cloud platforms also raise new vulnerabilities. The market is highly concentrated, with three U.S. companies (Amazon Web Services, Google Cloud, and Microsoft Azure) controlling over two-thirds of global capacity. This concentration creates systemic risks: failures or breaches may affect millions of users simultaneously. From a legal perspective, data localization and privacy concerns have prompted initiatives like the EU-US Data Privacy Framework (2023). In response, Europe invests in alternative solutions (e.g., GAIA-X), while China fosters domestic providers under strict state oversight. These developments highlight how cloud services sit at the intersection of innovation, dependency, and sovereignty.

Blockchain and Distributed Ledger Technologies

Blockchain enables secure and transparent data storage through distributed ledgers (Niranjanamurthy et. al, 2019). Its potential spans industries including finance, healthcare, and logistics (Reddy et al., 2020). Cryptocurrencies such as Bitcoin and Ethereum, based on blockchain, embody decentralized alternatives to state-backed currencies. Smart contracts extend this principle by automatically executing agreements when predefined conditions are met, reducing intermediaries and enhancing transparency.

While blockchain promises efficiency and traceability, it also introduces significant challenges. Its energy consumption raises sustainability concerns, while pseudonymity creates opportunities for criminal misuse, including money laundering. Regulatory responses diverge sharply: the EU adopted the Markets in Crypto-Assets Regulation (MiCA, 2023) to establish clear rules, the U.S. remains fragmented between federal agencies, and China has banned cryptocurrency trading but actively develops state-backed digital currencies. Importantly, blockchain has also been tested in human rights contexts - for instance, to record evidence of war crimes or trace humanitarian aid.

Virtual and Augmented Reality (VR/AR)

VR, AR, and the broader concept of the metaverse are reshaping education, tourism, and work (Dwivedi et al., 2022). In education, immersive simulations enhance accessibility and retention, supporting personalized learning, including for students with special needs. In tourism, AR overlays enrich cultural experiences while potentially reducing environmental pressures of mass travel. The metaverse integrates VR, AR, and other technologies into a persistent 3D environment for social and professional interaction.

Combined with AI, these technologies may profoundly affect cultural participation and labor markets, raising questions of access, equity, and digital well-being. Yet they also raise new dilemmas: harassment in virtual environments, the collection of sensitive biometric data, and blurred boundaries between public and private spaces. These issues highlight the importance of anticipating not only technological potential but also social risks.

Algorithms

Algorithms have moved far beyond fixed sets of instructions. Increasingly, they adapt through learning from data, with deep learning standing out as a prominent example. Built on multilayered neural networks, these methods detect intricate patterns that enable image recognition, natural language processing, and autonomous decision-making. Their role is not limited to advanced systems; algorithms also shape everyday experiences, from social media feeds to video recommendations and targeted advertising.

However, algorithmic governance extends well beyond consumer services. Predictive policing systems COMPAS in the U.S. is the algorithm that has been used to assess the likelihood of criminal reoffending. While intended to support judicial decisions, it has raised serious concerns about bias, transparency, and accountability—illustrating that algorithms are not neutral tools but reflect the data and assumptions on which they are built. The recruitment tools at Amazon, which systematically downgraded applications from women for technical positions, also illustrate risks of algorithmic bias and opacity. These cases show how algorithms can reinforce discrimination, erode trust, and raise questions under legal frameworks such as GDPR Article 22 on automated decision-making.

Artificial Intelligence (AI)

Artificial intelligence refers to systems capable of simulating human cognitive functions such as learning, reasoning, and problem-solving. Today, AI is embedded across daily life - from search engines to healthcare - while simultaneously shaping global economic and political processes (Jobin et.al, 2019).

A technical breakthrough was the development of transformer models, built from multiple layers of artificial neurons. Originally designed for natural language processing, transformers now power systems in vision, music generation, and drug discovery. Their "attention mechanism" enables context-sensitive processing, mimicking human selective focus.

Figure 3. Generative AI as a Subfield of AI (Source: Wagh, 2023)

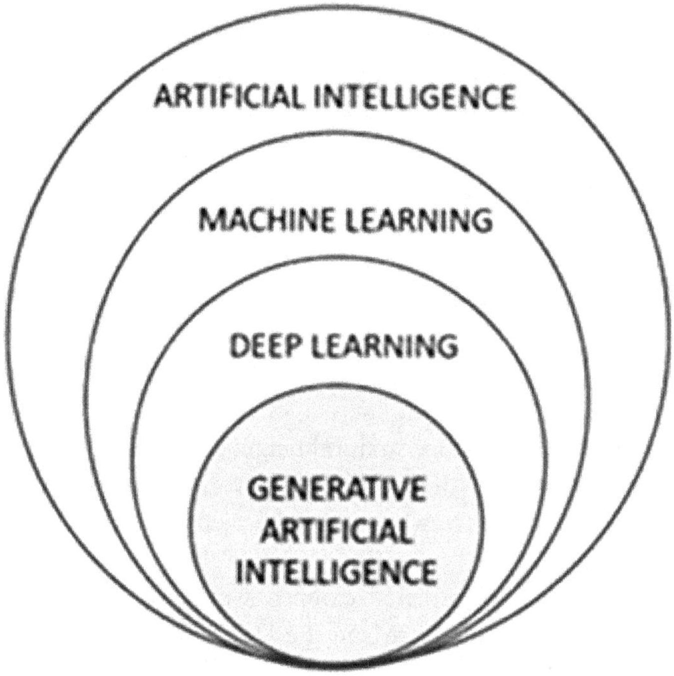

A rapidly expanding branch of AI is Generative AI (GenAI), designed not only to analyze data but to create new content. Examples include GPT systems generating text, images, or music. It is crucial to distinguish between:

- **AI** – systems solving defined tasks,
- **GenAI** – systems producing new content,
- **AGI (Artificial General Intelligence)** – hypothetical human-level systems, still speculative.

Generative AI is rapidly moving from experimental applications into critical domains of society. It already supports document drafting, logistics optimization, fraud detection, and personalized education. In healthcare, it assists in diagnosis, therapy design, and even drug discovery, while in scientific research it helps analyze vast datasets, generate hypotheses, and accelerate the pace of innovation. Creative industries increasingly rely on GenAI to produce text, images, and music, reshaping notions of authorship and originality.

At the same time, governments and businesses employ such systems to monitor patterns of consumption, optimize supply chains, and provide adaptive digital services. These broad applications illustrate both the promise of enhanced efficiency and creativity, and the risks of overreliance on technologies that are often poorly understood by their users. The ethical and legal concerns are far-reaching: misinformation and deepfakes threaten public trust, disputes over intellectual property challenge existing legal frameworks, and the blurred boundary between authentic and synthetic content complicates cultural and political communication (Jobin et al., 2019; UNESCO, 2023; Floridi, 2023).

These challenges have triggered divergent governance responses worldwide. The EU AI Act (2024) represents the most comprehensive attempt to date, applying a risk-based framework that restricts certain high-risk applications while promoting transparency and accountability. The United States maintains a fragmented, largely sectoral approach, shaped by industry self-regulation and selective federal interventions, which reflects its market-driven innovation culture. China, by contrast, embeds AI regulation within the framework of "socialist values" and exerts strict content controls, aligning technological development with political stability and state priorities (Kostka & Antoine, 2020; Creemers, 2023).

Other regions, such as India and Africa, are developing hybrid strategies that emphasize capacity-building and adaptation to local contexts. This diversity underlines that AI is not merely a technological challenge but a global contest of political priorities, economic strategies, and social values. The trajectory of AI governance will therefore play a decisive role in determining whether its benefits are widely shared or concentrated in the hands of a few powerful actors.

Concluding Remarks

Technological progress has always been a driver of social change, but the digital society is unique in its speed, unpredictability, and global reach. Each innovation - from internet protocols to generative AI - has redefined not only economic opportunities but also the ways in which fundamental rights are exercised and contested.

As technologies evolve, legal and regulatory systems face the constant challenge of balancing innovation with the protection of human dignity. The digital society thus remains a space of continuous negotiation between technological capabilities and the ethical, social, and legal frameworks that seek to guide their use.

PRIVACY, DATA PROTECTION, AND COPYRIGHT IN THE DIGITAL ENVIRONMENT

Interplay of rights and interests

The digital environment is transforming how fundamental human rights are defined, protected, and contested. In this context, privacy, data protection, and intellectual property often intersect - and sometimes collide - at the point where decisions must be made between competing values. The central challenge is to find mechanisms that balance these rights without giving disproportionate weight to one at the expense of others. Balancing these legitimate but sometimes conflicting values - ranging from the protection of creativity and privacy to freedom of expression and economic development - requires ongoing negotiation and careful governance.

One recurring dilemma is regulation itself. Too much regulation of data protection can restrict scientific research and technological innovation. Too little regulation, by contrast, allows unethical or illegal practices, such as mass user profiling or the unauthorized use of copyrighted works. The rise of artificial intelligence adds further complexity, especially in the field of intellectual property. AI-generated content raises questions about authorship, ownership, and fair use (EU, 2019; UNESCO, 2023; Sag & Yu, 2025).

These challenges are amplified by the global nature of the digital world. Legal frameworks and cultural values differ sharply across regions. Even between close partners such as the European Union and the United States, approaches diverge significantly. The EU's General Data Protection Regulation (GDPR) has become a global benchmark, while the U.S. relies on a fragmented, sector-specific model (such as the California Consumer Privacy Act). China, in contrast, has enacted comprehensive data protection rules through its Personal Information Protection Law (2021), yet these coexist with extensive state access and surveillance powers (Calzada, 2022).

Other jurisdictions are moving quickly as well. Australia's Human Rights Commission (2025) has warned that AI systems risk perpetuating racism and sexism unless trained on representative datasets. The UK's Data Use and Access Act (2025) introduces broad "smart data" provisions with significant implications for AI governance. On the international stage, UNESCO's Recommendation on the Ethics of AI (2023) and the Council of Europe's Framework Convention on Artificial Intelligence (2024, draft) represent key efforts to create globally coherent principles that protect human rights while acknowledging diverse cultural and political contexts.

Privacy and data protection

Privacy refers to the individual's right to control how their personal data is collected, stored, and used, and to regulate access to information about themselves. In the digital society, this notion extends to include online tracking, user behavior analytics, and profiling - for example, for advertising or political targeting (Taddeo & Floridi, 2025). Key challenges include:

- **Algorithmic surveillance and tracking**: Online companies and platforms collect vast amounts of data (e.g., location, behavior patterns, search history). These are often used for targeted advertising or content personalization, raising significant ethical concerns.
- **Smart devices and the Internet of Things (IoT)**: Smartphones, smartwatches, and household appliances collect personal data (e.g., health, location, consumption habits), often without users being fully aware of the extent or purpose of the data collection.
- **State surveillance**: In many countries, large-scale population monitoring practices are implemented without adequate legal regulation or alignment with democratic standards.
- **Cyberattacks, ransomware, and data breaches**: These pose serious threats to individual privacy and institutional credibility.

Legal frameworks governing the digital society must guarantee individuals a set of fundamental rights, as outlined in the European Union's approach:

- **Right of access and rectification**: Individuals have the right to know what data an organization holds about them (with limited exceptions defined by law) and to request corrections if the data are inaccurate.
- **Right to be forgotten**: Defined by the GDPR, this allows individuals to request the deletion of their personal data when no legal basis exists for their continued storage.
- **Right to data portability**: Individuals have the right to "take" their data from one service provider and transfer it to another.

The General Data Protection Regulation (EU, 2016) introduces principles such as informed consent and purpose limitation, and imposes substantial penalties for non-compliance. Similar protections are emerging elsewhere - such as Brazil's

General Data Protection Law (LGPD, 2020) and Japan's amendments to the Act on the Protection of Personal Information (APPI, 2022) - demonstrating a growing convergence on privacy norms, albeit with local variations.

Copyright

In the digital environment, copyright applies to online content - including texts, images, videos, music, and software - yet the system becomes increasingly complex due to the ease of copying and the global accessibility of copyrighted works. The ease of duplicating and sharing digital content facilitates unauthorized use, such as the illegal downloading of movies, music, images, or books. This ongoing tension between rights holders, service providers, and users remains a core challenge in digital copyright enforcement. Emerging technologies, such as blockchain, may offer partial solutions to issues related to tracking and verifying ownership.

Platforms like YouTube allow users to create derivative content based on existing works, raising legal ambiguities about what constitutes copyright infringement. Generative AI further complicates this landscape, as it can be trained on vast collections of copyrighted materials and produce novel outputs without clear attribution. In the United States, the proposed Generative AI Copyright Disclosure Act (2024) seeks to mandate transparency in AI model training datasets, directly addressing the need to protect creators while enabling innovation. This raises fundamental questions: how can original authors be protected, and who should be recognized as the creator of AI-generated content? The development of the metaverse - a persistent, shared 3D virtual space merging physical and digital realities - adds yet another layer of complexity, where the intersection of virtual and physical environments introduces new challenges concerning the use of copyrighted material, personal data collection, and privacy.

European Union Initiatives

The European Union is pursuing a comprehensive approach to digital transformation - one that prioritizes not only technological progress, but also the creation of a fair, secure, and inclusive digital society. In 2020, the EU adopted its Digital Strategy for the Digital Decade, which outlines a vision for digital development (European Commission, 2024). As part of this agenda, the Union has committed to investing in digital infrastructure and advanced technologies to accelerate the digital transition and strengthen its resilience against future crises.

The European Union has taken a leading role in shaping the global debate on how to regulate digital technologies and artificial intelligence. It is currently finalizing the AI Act, the world's first comprehensive attempt to create binding rules for the development and use of AI. The goal is to ensure that AI systems are not only innovative but also ethical, transparent, and safe for citizens. Alongside this, the General Data Protection Regulation (GDPR) remains the cornerstone of European digital policy. Since its adoption in 2016, the GDPR has become a global benchmark for personal data protection, inspiring similar legislation in regions as diverse as Latin America, Africa, and Asia.

To strengthen its digital governance framework, the EU has also introduced two complementary instruments: the Digital Services Act (DSA, 2022) and the Digital Markets Act (DMA, 2022). The DSA sets out clear responsibilities for digital platforms, requiring them to remove illegal content more effectively, protect users from harmful practices, and increase transparency in how online services operate. The DMA, by contrast, focuses on competition, aiming to curb the dominance of the largest technology companies - often referred to as "gatekeepers" - and to ensure fair and open digital markets where smaller innovators also have a chance to thrive.

Initiatives Beyond Europe: The United States and Global Frameworks

While the European Union has positioned itself as the global leader in setting binding digital regulations, the United States and China follows a markedly different path. The American approach to digital governance is largely market-driven and sectoral, with regulation often left to industry self-regulation or to state-level initiatives rather than comprehensive federal frameworks. This results in a less restrictive environment for businesses but often leaves individuals with weaker protections compared to their European counterparts. China, by contrast, represents a state-centered and security-focused model.

In the field of artificial intelligence, U.S. policy emphasizes innovation and competitiveness, prioritizing leadership in AI development to maintain global economic and strategic advantage. The AI Bill of Rights (White House, 2022) outlines principles such as safe and effective systems, protection against algorithmic discrimination, and data privacy, but it is non-binding and primarily serves as guidance rather than enforceable law. This reflects a governance philosophy that favors flexibility and rapid innovation, but critics argue that it risks insufficient oversight of the societal and ethical implications of AI. The contrast between the EU and U.S. approaches thus reflects broader cultural and political differences: Europe prioritizes rights and collective protections, while the United States emphasizes market freedom and technological leadership.

China's data protection regime - anchored in the Personal Information Protection Law (PIPL, 2021) bears some resemblance to the GDPR in terms of individual rights, but its enforcement is embedded in a broader system of state control. The government retains wide access to personal and corporate data, both for regulatory oversight and national security purposes. At the same time, China pursues an aggressive AI development strategy, aiming to become the global leader in AI by 2030. Digital governance in China thus combines strict state intervention, industrial policy, and surveillance practices, creating a model that prioritizes national stability and technological sovereignty over individual freedoms.

Taken together, the three models highlight the global divergence in digital governance philosophies:

- EU: Rights-first, regulation-driven, strong emphasis on human rights and ethics.
- U.S.: Market-first, innovation-driven, fragmented protections.
- China: State-first, security-driven, prioritizing national control and industrial strategy.

Beyond Europe, U.S. and China, global initiatives highlight both convergence and divergence in approaches to digital governance. UNESCO's Recommendation on the Ethics of AI (2021) provides a soft-law framework encouraging countries worldwide to adopt ethical standards for AI. Taken together, these efforts reflect a growing recognition that the governance of privacy, data protection, and intellectual property in the digital society cannot be addressed in isolation but must be coordinated across borders - while still accommodating diverse cultural values and political systems.

ETHICS AND SOCIAL VALUES IN THE DIGITAL SOCIETY

Ethical principles and social values form a cornerstone of the digital society, shaping how technologies are designed, deployed, and experienced. The central challenge is not only technological but deeply human: how can digital innovation enhance well-being and collective prosperity without enabling data misuse, deepening inequalities, or undermining fundamental rights? (Floridi, 2020).

Social and ethical challenges of AI and algorithmic automation

Generative AI raises novel dilemmas concerning authenticity, authorship, and accountability - especially in social media contexts where synthetic content is easily confused with human-created material. Legal systems struggle to keep pace, as illustrated by ongoing debates about training data, transparency, and recursive models trained on AI-generated outputs.

While AI offers opportunities for creativity and innovation, its risks require robust ethical and legal frameworks. How do we distinguish human-generated content from that produced by machines? This question becomes especially urgent in the context of fake news and disinformation. Furthermore, who should be recognized as the author of AI-generated content - the programmer, the system operator, or the AI model itself?

Core dilemmas include:

- **Algorithmic bias**: Algorithms trained on historical data may reproduce or amplify biased patterns, leading to discriminatory outcomes against certain groups - based on gender, race, age, or other characteristics.
- **Lack of transparency**: Many advanced AI models, particularly those based on deep learning, function as "black boxes," making it difficult to understand or audit how decisions are made.
- **Accountability**: When an algorithm causes harm or leads to a poor decision, it is often unclear who holds responsibility - the developer, the operator, or the algorithm itself. This complicates legal and ethical accountability.
- **Cybersecurity threats**: AI-driven systems are vulnerable to cyberattacks. Malicious actors can exploit software vulnerabilities to gain access to sensitive data or manipulate system outputs.
- **Privacy**: The extensive data collection required to train AI models may violate individuals' privacy, especially when data are gathered without adequate oversight or consent.
- **Deepfakes**: Generative AI can produce highly convincing fake videos, images, or audio recordings, which may be used to spread misinformation, conduct political manipulation, or launch harmful campaigns.
- **Algorithmically shaped content**: Social media algorithms that personalize content may create so-called "filter bubbles," where users are exposed only to information that aligns with their existing beliefs - thus reinforcing societal polarization.

Together, these issues highlight the urgent need for transparency, accountability, and intercultural dialogue to avoid narrow, unilateral ethical frameworks.

Digital Technologies, Political Processes, and Civic Participation

Digital technologies have profoundly reshaped politics and civic participation. On the positive side, they remove informational barriers, enhance transparency, and facilitate civic organization and responsiveness of authorities. Political actors increasingly rely on social media platforms to communicate directly with citizens, while some states experiment with e-voting to improve accessibility.

Yet these same technologies introduce serious risks. Social media personalization fosters polarization and echo chambers, while bots and automated accounts spread disinformation and extremist narratives, undermining democratic integrity. Cyberattacks on campaigns and institutions further erode public trust. Moreover, the influence of large technology corporations - whose platforms control the flow of political discourse - raises concerns about accountability and concentration of power.

Addressing these challenges requires a multi-pronged approach: technological solutions for detecting fake content, political and regulatory measures to ensure transparency in campaigning and e-government, and, crucially, investment in media literacy to empower citizens to recognize manipulation and bias.

Technologies for the Protection of Human Rights

Technologies designed to protect human rights in the digital society encompass innovations and tools that enable individuals and organizations to express themselves freely, share data securely and anonymously, and participate in social and political activities without unlawful surveillance, censorship, or abuse (EU, 2024). Especially in contexts where human rights are threatened by state or corporate surveillance, tools such as encryption, Tor in Dark Web, or VPNs serve as vital foundations for secure communication, evidence gathering, and the expression of dissent without fear of retribution.

Key technologies available to individuals for self-protection include:

- **Encryption and secure communication**: End-to-end encryption ensures that messages are encrypted by the sender and can only be decrypted by the intended recipient, making the content inaccessible to service providers or third parties.
- **Anonymity and identity protection**: The Tor network (The Onion Router) routes internet traffic through multiple intermediary nodes, encrypting each layer of the transmission. As a result, neither the intermediary servers nor the destination site can identify the full path or origin of the traffic. This provides

a high level of anonymity and protects users' identities. In addition to Tor, privacy-focused browsers also limit tracking, data collection, and cookie use.

- **Digital forensics**: Forensic tools are used to verify the authenticity of photos, videos, and documents. These tools are critical for documenting human rights violations, helping to establish whether evidence is genuine or has been manipulated (e.g., deepfakes).
- **Blockchain technology**: Blockchain can function as a tamper-proof ledger - for instance, to store indelible records related to human rights violations, property ownership, or election results. It provides transparency, traceability, and reduces the risk of data falsification.
- **E-government and e-voting**: Cryptographic and blockchain-based solutions in electronic voting systems can strengthen public trust in electoral processes - provided they are implemented transparently and responsibly.

There are many additional digital technologies that can support the protection of human rights. However, they often require advanced technical knowledge and, in some cases, specialized equipment. It is also important to emphasize that many of these same technologies are frequently misused - for example, by criminal networks seeking to avoid detection - illustrating the dual-use nature of privacy-enhancing tools.

CASE STUDIES IN DIGITAL GOVERNANCE

Digital technologies evolve globally, but their ethical and legal implications are mediated by the political, economic, and cultural environments in which they are deployed. Comparing case studies from the European Union, the United States, and China reveals three contrasting governance models - rights-driven, market-driven, and state-driven - each with profound consequences for human rights and democratic accountability.

The importance of examining these models lies in the inherently transnational nature of the digital society. Digital infrastructures, algorithms, and AI systems are not confined by national borders; a platform developed in one jurisdiction operates across many others, often exporting its governance assumptions along with its technical design. This raises a fundamental question: can the digital society truly function if governance frameworks remain fragmented, or does its global nature demand at least partial convergence of regulatory and ethical standards?

Artificial intelligence illustrates this dilemma most vividly. Training large-scale AI models requires global data flows and computing resources, yet the interpretation of rights such as privacy, authorship, or accountability differs sharply between jurisdictions. A lack of harmonization risks producing regulatory arbitrage, where companies shift operations to less restrictive environments, undermining protections elsewhere. At the same time, competing models can escalate into technological conflicts—what some describe as a "digital cold war" - in which infrastructure, standards, and platforms become instruments of geopolitical rivalry rather than public goods.

Despite these tensions, complete fragmentation is neither sustainable nor desirable. Without at least partial alignment on issues such as data protection, cybersecurity, and AI ethics, the digital society risks devolving into incompatible islands of regulation, limiting innovation and creating uncertainty for citizens and businesses alike. More importantly, the stakes are profoundly human: questions of privacy, freedom of expression, and the right to truth cannot be meaningfully addressed within purely local frameworks when technologies operate globally.

Thus, these case studies are not only about contrasting governance models but also about the urgent need to explore possibilities for convergence. Whether through multilateral organizations, bilateral agreements, or industry-driven standards, the search for shared principles will determine whether the digital society evolves as a space of cooperation and rights protection—or as an arena of conflict where technological power dictates the boundaries of freedom.

The European Union: A Rights-Centered Approach

The EU has positioned itself as the most ambitious global regulator of the digital environment. Its regulatory philosophy is grounded in the view that privacy and data protection are fundamental rights rather than consumer preferences.

One quite old landmark case is the Google versus Agencia Española de Protección de Datos (AEPD) and Mario Costeja González (EUR-Lex, 2014), an individual requested that Google remove links to newspaper articles containing outdated information about his past debt, which still appeared prominently in search results. The Court of Justice of the EU recognized the "right to be forgotten." This decision redefined the balance between freedom of expression and privacy by obliging search engines to delist personal information deemed outdated or irrelevant. It established the principle that individuals can exercise agency over their digital identities.

More recently, the EU's enforcement of the General Data Protection Regulation (GDPR) against Meta resulted in a record €1.2 billion fine in 2023 for unlawful transfers of personal data to the United States (EDPB, 2023). This case illustrates the EU's willingness to confront powerful global corporations and enforce its rights-based digital order beyond its territorial borders.

These examples highlight the EU's preventive approach: law is not only a corrective tool but a structural framework for embedding human rights into the digital society.

The United States: Market-Driven and Reactive Regulation

The U.S. model underscores the risks of reactive governance: rights protections are often formulated in response to technological misuse rather than proactively integrated into digital infrastructures.

The Cambridge Analytica scandal (2016), where millions of Facebook users' data were harvested without consent for political profiling and electoral manipulation, exemplifies the fragility of privacy in a lightly regulated market (Cadwalladr & Graham-Harrison, 2018). It demonstrated how algorithmic tools could undermine democratic integrity by microtargeting voters with manipulative content.

Another ongoing controversy concerns TikTok and national security. U.S. policy-makers argue that TikTok's ownership structure poses risks of foreign surveillance, leading to calls for bans or forced divestiture. Yet, critics view such measures as veiled restrictions on freedom of expression and cultural exchange (Pew Research Center, 2023). The debate reflects the U.S. struggle to balance open digital markets with geopolitical and security concerns.

China: State-Driven Surveillance and Social Control

China represents a radically different model in which digital technologies are fully integrated into governance mechanisms. The state exercises broad control over both infrastructures and platforms, using them as tools of social management and surveillance. In this model, data governance prioritizes social stability and political authority over individual autonomy.

The most emblematic case is the Social Credit System, which aggregates financial, social, and political behavior into "trustworthiness" scores. While initially framed as a way to enhance economic reliability and combat fraud, the system also functions as a political tool, restricting access to transport, education, or employment for individuals deemed "untrustworthy" (Creemers, 2018).

FACING THE FUTURE OF THE DIGITAL SOCIETY

Technology

The trajectory of the digital society will be determined by two intertwined dynamics: on the one hand, the pursuit of benefits such as efficiency, innovation, and broader accessibility; on the other, the need to confront risks ranging from manipulation and discrimination to pervasive surveillance. Nowhere is this tension more visible than in the field of artificial intelligence, whose future impact remains profoundly uncertain. Current projections diverge widely - from scenarios of unprecedented progress to those raising deep concerns about societal disruption.

The advancement of **digital technologies** is expected to continue unabated, driven by miniaturization and ever-increasing computational capabilities. By the end of the decade, the full transition to 5G and the early deployment of 6G networks are anticipated. Quantum computing - based on qubits rather than bits - will gradually emerge, enabling exponential acceleration in data processing. Yet this same computational power threatens to render today's cryptographic systems obsolete, making the design of entirely new security protocols imperative.

At the same time, the environmental footprint of digitalization is becoming an increasingly pressing concern. Energy consumption from data centers-driven in large part by AI and cloud computing could reach as much as 3% of global electricity production by 2030 (International Energy Agency, 2025). A shift toward "green" digitalization will require more energy-efficient hardware, software, and data management practices, as well as large-scale investment in sustainable energy sources.

Generative AI models are developing rapidly and are becoming capable of performing creative tasks previously reserved for highly skilled human professionals. This shift will significantly affect labor markets, potentially reducing demand for certain creative and expert roles while simultaneously creating new jobs related to AI management and oversight. The growth of AI will also require profound changes in education systems, which will increasingly emphasize algorithmic literacy, interpretation of AI-generated outputs, and, above all, critical thinking - skills that complement rather than compete with AI.

There will be increasing demands for explainable AI (XAI), particularly in high-stakes domains such as healthcare, law, and financial management, where individuals must be able to access and understand the reasoning behind algorithmic decisions.

The challenges will intensify with the emergence of Artificial General Intelligence (AGI), which surpasses narrow, task-specific algorithms and demonstrates autonomous learning and reasoning in complex, unstructured environments. In such systems, human oversight, interpretability, and traceability of decision-making processes may become nearly impossible, as the AI could develop its own internal logic. This raises a host of unprecedented ethical, safety, and regulatory questions for society at large.

Social Implications

Privacy, data protection, and copyright will remain central challenges of the digital society, shaping not only technological development but also the protection of fundamental rights and the balance between innovation and regulation in the years ahead. Existing legal frameworks such as the GDPR will be supplemented with new provisions on biometric data and international data transfers. As data continues to grow in value, threats such as cyberattacks, ransomware, and identity theft will become more severe. Both private and public sectors will invest heavily in cybersecurity and vulnerability management, while attackers - often aided by AI - will employ increasingly sophisticated techniques.

With the exponential growth of generative AI systems, copyright protection will become a central concern. New legal mechanisms will need to address content generated by algorithms while ensuring that creators are protected without stifling knowledge exchange or hybrid forms of authorship (involving both human and machine contributions). The European Union's directives and other international agreements will need to evolve accordingly.

Ethics and human rights protection will remain fundamental pillars of the digital society, as the rapid deployment of information technologies directly affects individual freedoms, equality, and dignity. Societal approaches to these principles differ significantly - for example, between the European, American, and Chinese models. Despite these divergences, global agreements on AI ethics are both challenging and essential, as technological progress transcends national borders.

Ethical discussions will focus on the proportional use of algorithms, ensuring they do not excessively infringe upon individual privacy or autonomy. Therefore, ethical principles must be embedded early in the design and training phases of AI systems and digital services. Transparency and accountability mechanisms - such as clearly defined responsibility for algorithmic decisions - will be crucial in sustaining public trust.

Social systems and politics will inevitably adapt to the development of the digital society, yet this adaptation will itself shape the very contours of digital transformation. Digitalization will increasingly influence the foundational structures of social and political systems, reshaping governance models and the relationship between citizens and the state. Ideological divisions may become more pronounced. A growing global competition among major powers (e.g., the US, China, EU) could lead to a fragmented internet ecosystem and divergent regulatory environments, complicating cross-border cooperation.

Both major corporations that control social media platforms and government institutions will need to assume greater social responsibility and steer digital development toward the common good. Governments are expected to establish additional regulatory frameworks to oversee tech corporations and promote local innovation in digital technologies, which are currently heavily centralized in the United States.

Irreversibility and the Impossibility of Disconnection

Most scholarship on the digital society highlights opportunities—efficiency, innovation, connectivity—while devoting far less attention to the darker scenarios implied by irreversible dependence. A central, yet underexplored, feature of digital transformation is the gradual loss of the ability to disconnect or even change the course of its development. This is not simply a technical matter of shutting down servers or suspending networks; it represents a deeper civilizational entrapment. Once core functions such as identity, payments, healthcare, and communication operate exclusively in digital form, alternatives vanish. Opting out, individually or collectively, becomes infeasible (Bucher, 2020). The digital society thus advances along a trajectory from which retreat is impossible, moving forward into a future that is uncertain yet inescapable.

What proves irreversible is the embedding of digital infrastructures into the very fabric of daily life. When societies come to depend on digital identity to prove legal existence, digital banking to conduct economic exchange, digital communication to maintain social relations, and digital platforms to access information and services, there is no viable return to purely analog systems. Disconnection ceases to be an act of personal choice and becomes structurally impossible, because the surrounding environment—administration, commerce, medicine, education, even culture—presupposes continuous digital participation. In this sense, irreversibility means that entire societies are locked into infrastructures that can neither be abandoned nor meaningfully replaced (Albris et al., 2024). Even the imagination of life outside the digital sphere gradually fades. Yet the problem lies not only in the impossibility of disconnection. Once a digital path is chosen, altering its direction becomes exceedingly difficult. Like a supertanker that requires vast time and energy to change course, technological systems, once implemented, create path dependencies that lock societies into specific trajectories for decades to come.

Among these technologies, artificial intelligence stands out as the most irreversible of all. Unlike other digital tools, AI systems do not merely store or transmit information—they learn, adapt, and integrate themselves into decision-making structures. Once implemented in critical domains such as medicine, security, law, or education, withdrawal becomes almost inconceivable. Each cycle of use generates new data and feedback that strengthen the system's capabilities and deepen society's dependency. Moreover, economic competition and geopolitical rivalry accelerate the diffusion of AI, making any collective pause or reversal nearly impossible. For this reason, AI does not simply illustrate irreversibility; it intensifies it, locking humanity into trajectories that extend far beyond the digital infrastructures of previous decades.

The philosophy of technology has long anticipated this dynamic. Ellul, already in 1964, warned that technological systems evolve according to their own internal logic of efficiency, beyond the reach of social control. Likewise, Heidegger, in 1977, described technology as a mode of "enframing" that reshapes how humans perceive and inhabit the world. Contemporary authors extend these insights into the digital domain: Malgieri (2025), for instance, conceptualizes digital infrastructures as systems of dependency that eliminate meaningful alternatives to participation.

This irreversibility carries profound implications. In earlier stages of modernization, analog substitutes remained available as fallback options in times of disruption. In the digital society, however, crises of any kind automatically become digital crises. The failure of electronic banking undermines the exchange of value, while the collapse of registries or communication infrastructures destabilizes entire social systems. Resilience is gradually eroded.

The impossibility of disconnection also raises political and ethical concerns. Global infrastructures are interconnected but controlled neither uniformly nor transparently. States, corporations, and individuals all depend on a system that no one can fully govern and from which no one can exit without harm (Stilgoe, 2020). For individuals, freedom narrows to choosing among alternatives within the system, while the option of withdrawal disappears.

The most unsettling prospect is that this condition may not be solvable. Economic pressures, geopolitical competition, and generational habits all drive further digitalization while discouraging investment in costly analog alternatives. Those who control infrastructures lack incentives to preserve exit strategies. In this sense, the digital society is not merely a technological evolution but a civilizational trajectory with no return. It is to confront the possibility that humanity is entering a condition of permanent vulnerability without exit—a future we cannot fully foresee, yet cannot refuse.

CONCLUSIONS

The digital society is already transforming the foundations of modern life. Today, individuals, economies, and political systems depend on advanced digital infrastructures, global data flows, and algorithmic decision-making. Yet these same systems raise urgent concerns: the misuse of personal data, market concentration by a handful of global actors, the spread of misinformation, and widening digital divides within and between societies. Energy demand from data centers and the environmental footprint of digitalization further underscores the material costs of progress.

At the same time, digital technologies offer substantial benefits. They expand access to information, enhance efficiency and innovation, and create new opportunities for participation and connectivity across the globe. The challenge is not technological capacity itself, but how societies govern and direct it. Governance frameworks, cultural contexts, and institutional choices determine whether digitalization strengthens or undermines democratic values, human rights, and social equity.

Looking forward, the next decade will be decisive. The rollout of 5G and 6G, advances in quantum computing, and the accelerating integration of AI systems will amplify both opportunities and risks. Among these forces, AI stands apart: its potential benefits are extraordinary, but its impacts remain deeply unpredictable and may rival or surpass the Industrial Revolution in speed, scale, and scope.

No single jurisdiction can address the borderless challenges of digital technologies. Effective governance requires international collaboration on cybercrime, misinformation, and AI ethics - anchored in fairness, accountability, and transparency - while respecting local contexts, particularly in the Global South. To succeed, digital transformation must be accompanied by resilient education systems, sustainable energy strategies, and robust cross-border institutions.

In sum, the digital society is at a crossroads. Its trajectory will not be determined by technology alone, but by our collective ability to align innovation with democratic values, human rights, and sustainability. Meeting current challenges while preparing for an uncertain future demands bold policymaking, continuous dialogue between technology and society, and a shared commitment to ensuring that digital progress serves the common good - globally, equitably, and for generations to come.

The digital society compels us to confront an unprecedented paradox: the faster technology advances, the more urgent it becomes to slow down and reflect on its human consequences. Every technical design is also a normative choice - about what kind of society we wish to build and whose values it will embody. History will not judge the digital age by its innovations alone, but by whether humanity succeeded in steering them toward dignity, justice, and sustainability.

Ultimately, the digital society represents a point of no return. Acknowledging its irreversibility is essential if we are to prepare not only for its opportunities but also for its risks, ensuring that humanity does not lose freedom and resilience in the very systems designed to enhance them. The challenge lies not only in the impossibility of exit but also in the inertia of direction: once digital infrastructures are entrenched, altering their course demands extraordinary effort, if it is possible at all. Among these infrastructures, artificial intelligence embodies the most pronounced form of irreversibility. Its capacity to learn, adapt, and embed itself into decision-making accelerates dependency far beyond previous technologies. Once adopted, AI rapidly becomes indispensable, while geopolitical rivalry and economic incentives make reversal or withdrawal nearly unthinkable. This suggests that the future of digital society will be shaped not only by irreversibility in general, but increasingly by the specific, deep, and self-reinforcing irreversibility of artificial intelligence.

REFERENCES

Albris, K., Fast, K., Karlsen, F., Kaun, A., Lomborg, S., & Syvertsen, T. (2024). The Digital Backlash and the Paradoxes of Disconnection: An Overview

Australian Human Rights Commission. (2025). Artificial intelligence and human rights. https://humanrights.gov.au

Avtalion, Z., Aviv, I., Hadar, I., Luria, G., & Bar-Gil, O. (2024). Digital infrastructure as a new organizational digital climate dimension. *Applied Sciences (Basel, Switzerland), 14*(19), 8592. DOI: 10.3390/app14198592

Berners-Lee, T. (2019, November 24). I invented the World Wide Web. Here's how we can fix it. The New York Times. https://www.nytimes.com

Bucher, T. (2020). Nothing to disconnect from? Being singular plural in an age of machine learning. *Media Culture & Society*, *42*(4), 610–617.

Cadwalladr, C., & Graham-Harrison, E. (2018). *Revealed: 50 million Facebook profiles harvested for Cambridge Analytica in major data breach.* The Guardian

Calzada, I. (2022). Citizens' data privacy in China: The state of the art of the Personal Information Protection Law (PIPL). *Smart Cities*, *5*(3), 1129–1150. DOI: 10.3390/smartcities5030058

Creemers, R. (2018). *China's Social Credit System: An Evolving Practice of Control.* MERICS.

Dufva, T., & Dufva, M. (2019). Grasping the future of the digital society. *Futures*, *107*, 17–28. DOI: 10.1016/j.futures.2018.11.001

Dwivedi, Y. K., Hughes, L., Baabdullah, A. M., Ribeiro-Navarrete, S., Giannakis, M., Al-Debei, M. M., & Wamba, S. F. (2022). Metaverse beyond the hype: Multidisciplinary perspectives on emerging challenges, opportunities, and agenda for research, practice and policy. *International Journal of Information Management*, *66*, 102542.

EDPB. 2023, EDPB binding decision on Meta. https://www.edpb.europa.eu/news/news/2023/12-billion-euro-fine-facebook-result-edpb-binding-decision_en

. EUR-Lex. (2014). Document 62012CJ0131

European Commission. (2024). State of the Digital Decade 2024: DESI indicators. https://digital-strategy.ec.europa.eu/en/policies/desi

European Commission. (2024). Regulation (EU) 2024/1689 of the European Parliament and of the Council on artificial intelligence (EU AI Act). EUR-Lex. https://eur-lex.europa.eu/eli/reg/2024/1689/oj

European Union. (2016). Regulation (EU) 2016/679 of the European Parliament and of the Council on the protection of natural persons with regard to the processing of personal data (GDPR). EUR-Lex. https://eur-lex.europa.eu/eli/reg/2016/679/oj

European Union. (2019). Directive (EU) 2019/790 on copyright and related rights in the Digital Single Market. EUR-Lex. https://eur-lex.europa.eu/eli/dir/2019/790/oj

Floridi, L. (2020). What the near future of artificial intelligence could be. In Floridi, L. (Ed.), *The 2019 yearbook of the digital ethics lab* (pp. 127–142). Springer., DOI: 10.1007/978-3-030-29145-7_9

Giest, S. (2025). The intersection of digital and social infrastructures in (a) spatial policymaking. *Policy Sciences*. Advance online publication. DOI: 10.1007/s11077-025-09516-3

Iden, J., & Bygstad, B. (2025). Sociotechnical micro-foundations for digital transformation. *European Journal of Information Systems*, *34*(2), 367–382. DOI: 10.1080/0960085X.2024.2404197

International Energy Agency. (2024). Electricity 2024: Analysis and forecast to 2026. https://www.iea.org/reports/electricity-2024

Jobin, A., Ienca, M., & Vayena, E. (2019). The global landscape of AI ethics guidelines. *Nature Machine Intelligence*, *1*(9), 389–399.

Khazieva, N. O., Khaziev, A., & Klyushina, E. (2018). Digital society: The experience of the philosophical understanding of a problem. *Tarih Kültür ve Sanat Arastirmalari Dergisi*, *7*(4), 347–353. DOI: 10.7596/taksad.v7i4.1832

Kostka, G., & Antoine, L. (2020). Fostering model citizenship: Behavioral responses to China's emerging social credit systems. *Policy and Internet*, *12*(3), 256–289.

Kudina, O., & van de Poel, I. (2024). A sociotechnical system perspective on AI. *Minds and Machines*, *34*(3), 21. DOI: 10.1007/s11023-024-09693-1

Malgieri, G. (2025). Digital Dependency: Needs, Vulnerability, and Power in the Digital Society. *SSRN*

Martynov, V. V., Shavaleeva, D. N., & Zaytseva, A. A. (2019). Information technology as the basis for transformation into a digital society and Industry 5.0. In 2019 International Conference on Quality Management, Transport and Information Security, Information Technologies (IT&QM&IS) (pp. 539–543). IEEE. https://doi.org/DOI: 10.1109/ITQMIS.2019.8928362

Mitra, B., Cramer, H., & Gurevich, O. (2024). Sociotechnical implications of generative artificial intelligence for information access. In Ekstrand, M. D., Potthast, M., & Ferro, N. (Eds.), *Information access in the era of generative AI* (pp. 161–200). Springer Nature., DOI: 10.1007/978-3-031-45432-5_8

Nagy, S., & Somosi, M. V. (2022). The relationship between social innovation and digital economy and society. arXiv. https://arxiv.org/abs/2212.13840

Niranjanamurthy, M., Nithya, B. N., & Jagannatha, S. J. C. C. (2019). Analysis of Blockchain technology: Pros, cons and SWOT. *Cluster Computing*, *22*(Suppl 6), 14743–14757.

OECD. (2020). *Digital economy outlook 2020*. OECD Publishing., DOI: 10.1787/2617653f-

Parliament, U. K. (2025). *Data (Use and Access) Act 2025*. UK Government.

. Pew Research Center. (2023). *Key facts about Americans and TikTok*

Reddy, S., Allan, S., Coghlan, S., & Cooper, P. (2020). A governance model for the application of AI in health care. *Journal of the American Medical Informatics Association : JAMIA*, *27*(3), 491–497. DOI: 10.1093/jamia/ocz192 PMID: 31682262

Sag, M., & Yu, P. K. (2025). The globalization of copyright exceptions for AI training. *Emory Law Journal*, *74*(5), 1163–1218.

Statista. (2024). Number of Internet of Things (IoT) connected devices worldwide from 2019 to 2030. https://www.statista.com/statistics/1183457/iot-connected-devices-worldwide/

Stilgoe, J. (2020). *Who's Driving Innovation?* New Technologies and the Collaborative State. Palgrave Macmillan.

Taddeo, M., & Floridi, L. (2025). Digital ethics. In Wareham, C. (Ed.), *A companion to digital ethics* (pp. 1–9). Routledge., DOI: 10.4324/9781003241297-1

UNESCO. (2023). Recommendation on the ethics of artificial intelligence. UNESCO Publishing. https://unesdoc.unesco.org/ark:/48223/pf0000381137

U.S. Congress. (2024). *Generative AI Copyright Disclosure Act of 2024*. U.S. Government Publishing Office.

Van Dijk, J. (2020). *The network society* (4th ed.). SAGE.

Wagh, A. (2023). What's generative AI? Explore underlying layers of machine learning and deep learning. Medium. https://medium.com/@amol-wagh

Yang, H., & Chen, Y. (2022). China's Data Security Law: Governance, regulation, and global implications. *Journal of Cyber Policy*, *7*(2), 163–182.

Yang, J., & Zhang, M. (2023). Beyond structural inequality: A socio-technical approach to the digital divide in the platform environment. *Humanities & Social Sciences Communications*, *10*(1), 1–12. DOI: 10.1057/s41599-023-01640-9

Zaagsma, G. (2013). On digital history. *Bijdragen en Mededelingen Betreffende de Geschiedenis der Nederlanden*, *128*(4), 3–29. DOI: 10.18352/bmgn-lchr.9353

Zhang, Y., Zhao, W., & Chen, L. (2024). From narrow AI to AGI: Technical, ethical, and governance perspectives. *AI & Society*. Advance online publication. DOI: 10.1007/s00146-024-01712-5

Chapter 2
Digitalization and Human Rights:
Navigating through Ethical and Legal Concerns

Jipson Joseph
https://orcid.org/0009-0005-1795-5051
Christ University, India

ABSTRACT

Digitalization became popular with the digital revolution of the late 20th century, propelling the shift from mechanical and analog electronic technology to digital electronics. It significantly contributed to all fields of human interactions, ensuring sustainable development, human well-being, and societal welfare. The latest innovations and constant changes in the technological world have broadened the scope of digitalization. Along with the many advantages, digitalization poses some particular challenges to global society. Although these complexities can be attributed to system failures, they are primarily due to the misuse of digital technologies. Some people fraudulently use digitalization to satisfy their egoistic and profit-oriented motives, neglecting the fundamental claims of others. This shows that ethical principles and legal standards have not been adequately respected in the digital space. From this perspective, this chapter, using the critical analytical method, examines the required ethical and legal concerns to protect human rights in the digital space.

1 INTRODUCTION

Scientific and technological advancements with the support of computers and the Internet provided many opportunities and possibilities for fast and easy interac-

DOI: 10.4018/979-8-3373-3685-5.ch002

tion between people, communication of ideas, and enhanced provisions of business activities. With digital technologies, the present globe has broadened the horizon of business models and customer interactions, strengthening economic development. Digitalization refers to incorporating digital technologies in various fields of human interaction and financial activities. It started in the late 20th century and is often termed the digital revolution (Petrov et al., 2024). Almost all areas of human life are digitalized, such as education, healthcare, transportation and communication, supply chain management, and banking. The widespread growth of digitalization has immense scope to promote sustainable development and inclusive growth. However, it also brings specific threats and challenges (European Commission, 2017). Along with the increased digitalization, society faces specific human rights concerns since digitalization's speed and complexity do not respectfully acknowledge human dignity but prioritize profit and other benefits (Pūraitė et al., 2020). Human dignity and human rights are intimately connected. Accordingly, challenges to human dignity become concerns of human rights as well.

Human rights are innate claims of human beings. They originate from their human nature and are not awarded by external agents. Human rights are inborn rights, and the UDHR (1948) provided an international framework stating that the rights listed in the declaration should be protected and guaranteed by all member states. Human rights demand that an individual's dignity always be respected and protected. Humans should never be used as a means but as an end (Smith, 2022). Digitalization is appreciable, but it cannot be allowed to violate fundamental human rights. It is in no way superior to the demands and concerns of human rights. However, most fundamental human rights standards were formally recognized in the first few decades of the second half of the last century. In contrast, digitalization became prominent only in the present century (Amelicheva et al., 2021). Although some regional and national initiatives addressed human rights in the digital space, a universal and formal legal framework has not yet been finalized. It creates confusion and apprehension about safeguarding human rights in the digital era.

From this perspective, this chapter critically examines digitalization through the lens of human rights to verify whether ethical and legal concerns are respected, affirming human dignity. The chapter does not criticize digitalization but argues that it should respect and value human rights. It thus suggests some ethical and legal concerns that should guide the digitalization process in any field of activity. The chapter underlines that promoting human rights in the digital space is essential for the global march toward a sustainable future.

2 SIGNIFICANCE OF THE STUDY

The 21st century has given significant attention to digitalization. Realizing the scope of digitalization, the UN's (2015) 2030 Agenda for Sustainable Development underlined that international institutions and national governments should prioritize building "resilient infrastructure, promote inclusive and sustainable industrialization and foster innovation" (SDG9). Digitalization, as such, is neither a problem nor a solution. The main concerns are how digitalization is used in human interactions and how human rights are affected by the interaction between people and digital technologies. With its speed, precision, productivity, and efficiency, digitalization helps humans in many ways (Duan et al., 2019). However, balancing human reflection's glacial pace and digitalization's fast-moving nature has become difficult. Even when society appreciates the advantages of digitalization, it finds it difficult to fully grasp its possible impacts and consequences on human rights and security (Pūraitė et al., 2020).

Digitalization has significantly changed society and business models in the last few decades (Parviainen et al., 2017). However, the present globe testifies that many human rights violations occur as side effects of digitalization (Petrov et al., 2024). For instance, the e-commerce giants like Amazon, Flipkart, and Alibaba have provided many purchasing opportunities for customers. However, it adversely affects the retailers' right to life and employment. It also questions the customer's right to privacy by sharing information about the purchase with others and sending advertisements without their prior consent (Petryshyn & Hyliaka, 2021). It shows that, along with the advantages of digitalization, the rights of vulnerable sections of society will be at risk. Such a scenario necessitates focusing more on ethical and legal concerns to guarantee and protect human rights within digitalization.

Many people utilize the benefits of digital technologies to violate others' fundamental rights. Their egoistic, profit-oriented, and harmful orientations and behaviors are causing problems and human rights violations in the digital space. Wagner et al. (2015) state that human rights violations in the digital arena have become more common in the present times. Since digitalization causes unlimited possibilities for human rights violations without revealing the identity of the violators, scholars argue the importance of promoting the fourth generation of human rights (the right to privacy, security, and confidentiality on the Internet) that can address rapid technological advancements and evolving complex social realities (Panova et al., 2022). When 'digits' guide the world and social interactions, they may not align with the values and principles that should design people's dignified lives. Accordingly, this chapter examines the benefits and challenges of digitalization through the human rights lens, proposing some specific ethical and legal considerations for a more significant perspective of digitalization.

3 THEORETICAL FRAMEWORK AND LITERATURE REVIEW

The present globe is witnessing the new digitalized era and undergoing fundamental changes caused by digitalization in almost all fields of societal life and economic interactions (Pūraitė et al., 2020). Digitalization has changed the global scenario by bringing more positivity and efficiency. Digitalization counts everything in digits and does not bother about human rights. The world of technology is different. However, the makers and users of technology should design and use them to benefit people and protect their rights. In contrast, the reality shows that many human rights violations occur by taking advantage of technological advancements like digitalization. It shows that there is an intimate interconnection between digitalization and human rights.

3.1 Digitalization

Digitalization evolved from the term 'digital,' which refers to the progress in electronic technology that generates, stores, and uses data in positive (using the digit 1) or nonpositive (using the digit 0) states. Digital also refers to progress or change with existing knowledge, ideas, technologies, or functioning systems. It functions as a modifier. For instance, literacy or human rights are fixed properties. When the term 'digital' is added to literacy, it affirms that some progress has been made in this fixed property (Pangrazio & Sefton-Green, 2021). Digitization and digitalization are closely interrelated. The Oxford English Dictionary makes the first reference to digitization in association with computers in the mid-1950s. It defines digitization as the process by which analog data is converted to digital forms. On the other hand, digitalization points to the adoption and increased use of digital or computer technology by an institution, country, or organization. The first contemporary use of digitalization is attributed to Robert Wachal's 1971 essay in the *North American Review* (Brennen & Kreiss, 2016). Digitalization is the process of converting information to a digital format. It is also understood as integrating "an increasing number of digital computing devices into everyday life to solve varying degrees of complexity" (Panova et al., 2022, p.322). It increases the accessibility of various services to empower people with more possibilities and opportunities (Petrov et al., 2024). Accordingly, digitalization invites humans to a new horizon of values, meanings, opportunities, and challenges.

Digitalization is associated with digital transformation, which means "changes in ways of working, roles, and business offering caused by adoption of digital technologies in an organization, or in the operation environment of the organization" (Parviainen et al., 2017, p.64). It brings digital transformation on many levels, such as process, organization, business domain, and society. By transforming conventional processes, digitalization aims to make substantial changes in society. Digital technologies transform a business model that promotes more revenue generation and value-producing opportunities (Ruud, 2018). Digitalization helps people "to seek, receive, and impart information and ideas of all kinds, regardless of frontiers, either orally, in writing, or in print" (ICCPR, Art. 19). The whole range of new digital technologies helps to access information on an unprecedented scale (Wagner et al., 2015). Digitalization has changed the global setting of social relations, economic interactions, industrial productivity, and legal foundations (Petryshyn & Hyliaka, 2021). Accordingly, the ultimate objective of digitalization is to realize a sustainable future for the global community.

3.2 Human Rights

Human rights are inborn claims of people. They are not imposed on them by any authority, but evolved from their human nature. Since they are inalienable, no one can give away these rights, and no external authority can take them away. They evolved from the philosophical background of natural rights and natural law theory (Finnis, 2015). However, the universal acceptance of human rights occurred through the Universal Declaration of Human Rights (UDHR) in 1948. Human rights are "broad, universally applicable rights recognized and protected under international law" (Petrov et al., 2024, p.345). Implementing and complying with the standards and principles of human rights is a moral and legal imperative. Although digital rights evolved from the broader horizon of human rights, their legal framework is a relatively new field. A systematic and well-defined area of concern for digital human rights has not yet been defined (Amelicheva et al., 2021).

Making specifically defined digital human rights is unnecessary, as it is only an extended application of human rights into the digital space. However, Amelicheva et al. (2021) argue that such a separation is advantageous as it helps to address individual claims in the cyber world. They state that the Internet plays a vital role in modern interactions. Accordingly, conventional human rights may not address the changed scenario. They may fail to confront the virtual world violations and complexities. Panova et al. (2022) thus claim that the previous generations of human rights do not work with the latest technological complexities like the IoT, blockchain, cryptocurrency, social networks, etc. However, a fourth generation of human rights can substantially address these concerns. From this perspective, Bochkov (2019) states that digital rights are citizens' right to use, access, create, and publish digital works in any form and access the Internet and other communication devices using computers and other electronic devices. If this understanding is accepted, digital rights are an extension of the right to access information, freedom of speech and expression, and education. There is no difference between the offline and online worlds concerning human rights (Vincent, 2016). Whatever the nature of the world, its ultimate objective is to safeguard human rights. Accordingly, society needs a broader application of human rights to cover the digital space rather than demanding a separate set of digital rights.

The UN has acknowledged the right to the Internet as a universal and inalienable right. The right to the Internet is vital for realizing the right to development. However, while promoting this right, the international community cannot neglect people's right to privacy in the digital world. Amelicheva et al. (2021) argue that, based on the global promotion of the right to the Internet and other digital rights, the national constitutions should incorporate such a provision for guaranteeing these unique rights. The constitutions of Greece and Giorgia have already incorporated the right to the Internet. They also suggest that countries must interpret certain constitutional norms within digitalization or design specific laws based on constitutional rights to guarantee people's rights in the digital space. The examples of France and Germany affirm the importance of progressively interpreting constitutional provisions while considering the new ambit of digital technological advancements. Agreeing with them, I also believe that the current society needs a progressive interpretation of human rights and constitutional provisions to apply them to the new horizon of digitalization.

3.3 Interplay between Digitalization and Human Rights

Digitalization and human rights were separate denominations. However, digitalization has impacted every aspect of human life in the present times. It is an undeniable fact that human life has become thoroughly digitalized. Along with the advent of digital technologies, human rights have also transitioned to the digital sphere. People's offline human rights should also be protected in the digital space (Wagner et al., 2015). Digitalization broadens people's choices and claims. Nevertheless, if it does not adhere to international human rights principles and guidelines, it can harm the functioning of human rights. For instance, the use of biometric data has many advantages. However, collecting and using it without an individual's consent breaches privacy rights (Petrov et al., 2024). Piccone (2018, p.30) notes that "the Internet can be a tool for both protecting and violating human rights, with direct implications for individuals' cyber and physical security." The digital world can protect, promote, violate, or degrade people's fundamental rights. The digital environment advances new forms of rights, which require additional guarantees and adequate protection (Petrov et al., 2024). It also provides new opportunities to exercise human and civil rights on a broader horizon.

Digital technologies are not against individual well-being and societal welfare. Although they have a few disadvantages, they benefit people and society in many ways. The primary concern of using digital technologies should be to align them with people's rights and fundamental freedoms. If digital technologies adhere to international human rights standards and principles, they can substantially influence society and promote its welfare (Chirkov et al., 2022). The transformation and growth of digital technologies have become so powerful that they even require new forms of civil and human rights for substantial interaction in the digital space (Petryshyn & Hyliaka, 2021). The concept of human rights within digitalization leads to the evolution of digital human rights. They evolve from universally accepted fundamental human rights. However, they focus more on the digital environment's concerns, interests, and challenges. These rights primarily address the challenges and vulnerabilities of individuals in the digital age (Petrov et al., 2024). The main problem human rights face in the digitalized world is people's behavioral differences in different jurisdictions and legal and political cultures (Petryshyn & Hyliaka, 2021). These cause challenges to the realization of human rights.

The UDHR affirms the universal recognition of human rights. The rights enshrined in the UDHR apply to everyone regardless of nationality, sex, gender, color, or other differentiating parameters. The International Human Rights Law (IHRL) provides the basic framework of universally accepted human rights and the importance of their implementation. The UN Office of the High Commissioner for Human Rights (OHCHR) coordinates these initiatives. The UN Human Rights Council, the OHCHR, and the International Criminal Court address the violations of IHRL. The National Human Rights Commission and the judicial system also deal with human rights offenders. Although there is a significant international framework, the ultimate responsibility to protect people's fundamental rights is bestowed on national governments. However, states have limitations concerning extraterritorial operations (Kanalan, 2018). With the advancement of digitalization, many human rights violations happen without territorial limitations. When the holders of human rights belong to one country and the violators belong to and operate from another, how can a state address such violations? Since digital rights have not yet received universal acceptance, the situation has become more complex (Petryshyn & Hyliaka, 2021). Although states have some extraterritorial jurisdiction concerning the protection of human rights, the question of its applicability to the digital space is still disputable (Kanalan, 2018). The UN Resolutions, the EU's General Data Protection Regulation (GDPR), various countries' data protection initiatives, and private bodies' initiatives like the Global Network Initiative (GNI) provide an ample framework for digital data protection. However, considering the vast possibilities of digital human rights violations, these frameworks and the options to punish the violators are minimal, depending on many factors. To ensure a perfect balance between human rights and digitalization, there is an urgent requirement for an internationally agreed set of digital rights and enforcement mechanisms.

Digitalization brings forth the possibility of positive, transparent, and fair interaction between people and public authorities. When every governmental activity becomes digital, it increases speed and objectivity for better results and reduces corruption. However, the government receives a large amount of personal information, which is a unique claim of an individual. When states fail to protect their citizens' personal information, it becomes a human rights issue. If governments misuse personal information, it jeopardizes the possibility of a fair election, complicates freedom of expression, and reduces freedom of information. For instance, there were strong allegations by the opposition party leaders and some media claiming that misuse of citizens' personal information occurred in the US Presidential election, the Indian Parliament election, the Brexit Referendum, and the elections in Brazil and Kenya. The same ethical and legal complexity arises when international institutions, multinational and transnational corporations, and commercial organizations collect and keep the personal information of billions of people (Amelicheva et al., 2021). Regardless of the differences, the commercial sector, financial institutions, healthcare sector, transport and communication field, e-government services, entertainment sector, and various chatbots and engines collect, keep, and manage their customers' information. Such a wide range of personal information can end up in the hands of third parties, fraudulent people, or terrorist groups, causing serious human rights concerns. All these factors underline the undeniable interaction between digitalization and human rights.

4 DIGITALIZATION: AN ANALYSIS THROUGH THE LENS OF SDGS

The UN's (2015) aspirations for a sustainable future by transforming the world revolve around realizing the SDGs. These seventeen goals with 169 specific targets provide a global action framework prioritizing economic, social, and environmental sustainability. These goals underline that the globe should focus on people, planet, prosperity, peace, and partnerships. Digitalization and new technologies are crucial for a concentrated approach toward a global transformation objective of sustainability (Meskic et al., 2022; Amelicheva et al., 2021). For instance, digital technologies help women's active engagement in education, social activities, and the workforce. The gender equality objective (SDG5) thus becomes realizable. These things would be possible only when strong broadband connectivity and properly trained people exist. On the one hand, there is immense growth in digitalization. On the other side, there is a wide requirement for adequate awareness mechanisms that promote the importance of digitalization. Public and private sector actors should take up the responsibility to train people, regardless of gender or other differentiating barriers, and conscientize them about the importance of digitalization for the smooth realization of SDGs and other meaningful objectives. The digital divide between people and nations should be reduced to achieve the full potential of SDGs (European Commission, 2017). The following points examine how digitalization has caused significant changes in various fields regarding SDGs. This section also analyses the benefits and challenges of digitalization to pinpoint its importance in human lives.

4.1 Digitalization: Some Essential Fields

The present global experience affirms that digitalization covers a wide range of areas, such as governance, the fight against corruption, environmental protection, increased access to services, the promotion of education, quality healthcare facilities, and sustainable agriculture (European Commission, 2017). Smart homes, e-healthcare, e-government services, smart mobilities, and smart cities are other examples of increased digitalization. The new developments in digitalization help to make everything smart by improving the quality and efficiency of the field. Applying new technologies in various fields and promoting digitalization are key factors for increasing productivity, collaboration, and efficiency (Ruud, 2018). Digitalization has entered almost all fields of economic activity, and the present economic life cannot survive without digitalization. It improves employee performance in the workplace by providing possibilities for flexible timings, time and cost management, and sustainable innovation (Meskic et al., 2022). The following fields are some examples where digitalization has made momentous progress. However, digitalization in any of the fields mentioned below also causes issues with data privacy and employment opportunities.

4.1.1 Education

Education is one of the major areas that is thoroughly digitalized. Digital classrooms that use computers, interactive whiteboards, various educational software, and other technologies have become common parlance in the present century. The realization of quality education (SDG4) becomes easy with the support of widespread digitalization. During the COVID-19 pandemic, the globe has witnessed the significance of digitalization as it helped students continue their education through online platforms. E-teaching and e-learning possibilities help teachers and students widen their teaching and learning horizons (European Commission, 2017). Digitalization provides the facilities for personalized learning. Some students require special attention. Teachers may not be able to assist them efficiently in the classrooms. However, digital educational platforms provide the possibility of personal trainers and teachers who can concentrate more on the concerns and needs of the students

(Amelicheva et al., 2021). Education and academic research are increasingly utilizing the benefits of digitalization. The increased online collaborations for research, the growing number of academic search engines, online publication agencies, and literature recommendation engines have eased the efforts of scholars to make significant contributions in the academic field. All these necessitated the evolution of some guiding principles. Accordingly, the FAIR principles evolved to optimize data reuse based on four principles: findability, accessibility, interoperability, and reusability (Wilkinson et al., 2016).

4.1.2 Healthcare

Digital services and technologies can leverage global attempts towards quality healthcare facilities (SDG3). The latest digital technologies help make diagnoses easier and swiftly increase the quality of the entire healthcare sector. For instance, a few decades back, an MRI scan or X-ray images were uncommon in healthcare, especially in developing countries. The lack of such digital technologies made diagnosis difficult. Even when they were available, finishing the process and bringing the printed copy to the consultant took long hours. However, with the growth of digitalization, all these have become quite common, and within seconds, the images are loaded on the consultant's computer screen. It shows that data transmission within and between hospitals has become easier. Such a system helps patients save time and energy and receive good healthcare facilities. The increased digitalization in the healthcare sector also supports the rural population, as they can easily consult doctors with telemedicine support. mHealth and eHealth possibilities have promoted the scope of healthcare services in developing countries. They support epidemiological surveillance programs, training of healthcare workers, and systematic management of healthcare services (European Commission, 2017). Such latest technological advancements help people to consult with registered medical practitioners (RMPs) routinely and take advantage of a sound healthcare support system at their convenience. They also increase the quality of healthcare service management through routine interaction with customers (Cobelli & Chiarini, 2020). Digitalization of healthcare benefits people in many ways, as it can detect disease at an early stage, provide better consultation with the support of advanced technologies, and prevent epidemics. Nevertheless, it is also not without any drawbacks. Since everything is digitalized, any hacker can access medical records, violating confidentiality (Amelicheva et al., 2021).

4.1.3 Agriculture

Digitalization also benefits the agricultural sector (SDGs 8 & 12). Traditional farming methods have limitations concerning the workload, timely attention to crops, and productivity. Various digital initiatives like smart farms and smart greenhouses increase agricultural productivity (Amelicheva et al., 2021). The farm sector has been thoroughly digitalized due to the incorporation of digital agricultural tools and smart farming. Technological advancements in communication, information, supply chain management, and spatial analysis have transformed the agricultural sector into a digital one. Precision agriculture, remote sensing, data analytics, IoT applications and connectivity solutions, cloud computing, artificial intelligence, blockchain, and global positioning systems help farmers to plan, efficiently monitor, and prudently manage agricultural productivity (Papadopoulos et al., 2024). Digital technologies also help farmers sell their goods conveniently without the involvement of intermediaries. E-farming methods provide a better scope for farmers to earn more profit from farming.

4.1.4 Banking and E-Commerce

The digitalization of the banking sector started with the first ATM opened in London in 1967. In 1985, the Bank of Scotland provided electronic home banking services to its clients. When the Stanford Credit Union launched the first banking website in 1994 to provide services, it became an energizer for the digital banking sector (UBS, 2022). Thereafter, mobile banking became popular. First, it started with SMS banking, which the European banks widely promoted in the late 1990s. With the advancement of IOS and Android technologies around 2010, the digital banking sector entered into a new phase of active and fast interaction (CFI, n.d.). The COVID-19 crisis further broadened the scope of digital banking. Various researchers affirm that digital banking has increased the banking sector's security, reliability, speed, and efficiency. It reduced the use of paper money and the frequency of customers' bank visits. Besides, they also claim that although the number of branches was considered a prerequisite for attracting customers' confidence, the scenario has entirely changed with the increase in digital banking. Present banking activities can be done easily without the support of banking staff. Blockchain technology and smart contracts help reduce fraudulent activities in the banking sector. Artificial intelligence and cloud technologies also optimized the banking processes (Havryliuk et al., 2021). Digitalization in the banking sector has reached almost all parts of the globe, and it has helped to increase people's confidence and financial engagement.

E-commerce is different from traditional commerce in terms of the exchange and processing of information. Direct personal contact was the mode of information exchange in the past. But e-commerce is done through a digital networking system (Mihaila et al., 2021). The history of e-commerce began with CompuServe in 1969. However, full-fledged e-commerce activities started only after the invention of the World Wide Web (www) in 1990. With the launch of Amazon in 1995, e-commerce interactions began to grow in size and value. Statista (2025) states that the global retail e-commerce market reached a record business of US$ 6 trillion in 2024. It also affirms that Amazon leads the e-commerce sector with a merchandise value of US$ 800 million. SellersCommerce (2025) provides some interesting data about the current e-commerce activities. Almost 33% of the global population (2.77 billion) purchases online from around 28 million e-commerce platforms and social media stores worldwide. The e-commerce industry is supposed to reach US$ 8 trillion by 2027. E-commerce has provided plenty of opportunities for farmers, industrialists, and businesspeople to attract more consumers, address supply chain management effectively, and earn more profits.

4.2 Digitalization: Benefits

Digitalization is considered positive and highly influential for the substantial growth of society. Digital technologies help to promote the aspirations of sustainable development and inclusive growth (European Commission, 2017). Digitalization cannot be merely considered a possibility like many others; it has become almost a vital condition to improve public services. It helps to modernize, simplify, and improve the public sector, oriented on improving the quality and velocity of services (Pūraitė et al., 2020). It helps organizations and institutions to reduce costs and increase productivity (Meskic et al., 2022). Digitalization helps people expand their possibilities to exercise their rights more freely, participate actively in civic life, and hold human rights violators accountable. It also helps to augment a detailed awareness of global human rights violations (Piccone, 2018). Digitalization has opened many opportunities for protecting human rights, which otherwise would not have been possible. For instance, the satellite images help human rights activists examine and understand the abuses that take place in North Korean political prisons, the ethnical cleansings of Myanmar that touch the global conscience, and the alarming human insecurities in Gaza. Digital technologies also help to uncover specific historical human rights violations like the mass killings that took place in 1965, 1969, 1972, 1988, and 1993 in Burundi (Piccone, 2018). Digital technologies are helpful in rapidly realizing the SDGs and strengthening the global march towards a sustainable future. The international and national efforts to eradicate poverty and hunger, improve humanitarian and developmental activities for better growth, and manage the issues of migration and climate change become easier with digitalization (European Commission, 2017). Digitalization advances new forms and methods of cultural and knowledge production, political participation, and collective action (Brennen & Kreiss, 2016). It empowers civil society to express its opinions and concerns against authoritarian governments by circulating ideas within seconds and reducing mobilization costs. There are many examples where activists and freedom seekers have used digital and social media platforms to coordinate their non-violent fights for justice against authoritarian governments (Dragu & Lupu, 2021). This section briefly explains the advantages of digitalization in terms of a sustainable global future.

4.2.1 Economic Growth

Economic growth depends on increased productivity. Digital technologies support human endeavors for more productivity. Digitalization has increased employment opportunities directly or indirectly, leading to economic growth (European Commission, 2017). There is unprecedented economic growth in the 21st century, mainly due to the contributions of digital technologies. Digitalization reduces paper use, easily addresses environmental degradation causes, and promotes sustainable economic growth. It helps managers address issues by easily accessing real-time reports and dashboards on digital process performance. Studies reveal that countries with advanced digitalization have better economic outcomes than those in the initial stages (Parviainen et al., 2017). It necessitates that digitalization become a global initiative and that the more developed and digitalized countries support the digitalization programs of the less developed countries. The true benefit of digitalization will be achievable only when there is an equitable distribution of its benefits to all sections of people.

4.2.2 Data-Driven Decision-Making

Decision-making is essential for increasing global productivity and strengthening global efforts toward sustainable development. Decision-making is a prerogative of humans. Digitalization provides more vibrant data on a specific area of concern, helps with analysis and evaluation, and promotes meaningful decision-making processes. The data is analyzed with the support of artificial intelligence for more accurate results. Today, most companies and institutions prefer a data-driven decision-making system that uses the latest digital technologies for accuracy and efficiency (Korherr et al., 2022). Duan et al. (2019) affirm that digitalized data-driven decision-making has significantly improved decision quality.

4.2.3 Improved Customer Satisfaction

Digitalization systematically improves the customer satisfaction level. For instance, the e-commerce purchaser of any product or service prefers to examine customer reviews first to ensure whether the product is worth purchasing (Mihaila et al., 2021). The vast number of e-commerce, e-health, and other digital goods and services purchasing platforms provides customers with ample opportunities and possibilities for choice-making. It forces such platforms to ensure customer satisfaction by addressing their queries and apprehensions by providing 24*7 customer service. Improvements in the customer service field underline the changed perspective of multinational and transnational companies. Although their priority is profit-making, they cannot neglect the interests and satisfaction of customers due to the availability of many choices. Compared to conventional methods of business and other activities, the present globe focuses on customer-oriented activities (Cobelli & Chiarini, 2020).

4.3 Digitalization: Challenges

Digitalization, though advantageous to society in many aspects, puts forward specific challenges and risks that public and private sectors try to tackle (Pūraitė et al., 2020). Digital technologies function with the support of data. Currently, society collects an enormous amount of data than ever. Although the increased amount of data benefits many ways, it also causes several challenges. People still face issues with digital competence even when society has made significant progress in digitalization. People from rural areas and developing countries face more problems with digital expertise. Women and the aged population also face the same challenges in many countries. Lack of awareness and digital competence has become a barrier to realizing digitalization's full potential (Ruud, 2018). Digitalization also supports authoritarian governments in taking preventive measures against potential opposition so that they can continue to remain in power and exploit people. Since the opposition groups circulate ideas and convene meetings through digital technologies, the shutdown of the Internet, the blocking of social networks, or the monitoring of social media accounts help authoritarian governments to oppress such freedom initiatives (Dragu & Lupu, 2021).

Digitalization benefits society through the effective coordination and management of digital technologies. However, most developing countries face issues managing and coordinating the digitalization process. Lithuania is one of the most digitalized countries in the world. More than 90% of its governmental services are available to the public on digital platforms, and 80% of its citizens use e-government services, reducing the time and long queues for getting the services done. However, there are criticisms of its management and coordination. The digitalization system and process function well and are in tune with the needs of the time. However, the lack of coordination makes it difficult to manage the system. It insists that the digitalization process's performance and efficiency depend on its management (Pūraitė et al., 2020).

4.3.1 Insecurity

Digitalizing public services has already raised security concerns in many parts of the world (Pūraitė et al., 2020). Digitalization is constantly challenging cybersecurity. Although digitalization benefits socioeconomic development, it fails to address cybercrimes systematically. Cyberspace provides an immense scope for sustainable development. However, it poses various threats and challenges that could never be imagined. Cybercrimes range from attacks on information systems, hacking, online fraud activities, and child and women sexual exploitation to cyber terrorism and drug trafficking. Cyberattacks can complicate critical infrastructure facilities, adversely affecting people's daily interactions (European Commission, 2017). Many countries have not yet incorporated cyberspace criminal activities into their justice delivery system. It gives such criminals more freedom to broaden their range of criminal activities. Besides, installing effective cybersecurity software is costly and difficult for developing countries. When cybersecurity is weak, the country's digital and cyberspace become a target of constant attack.

4.3.2 Complexity

Digitalization also faces challenges concerning its implementation in the public sector. The private sector widely makes use of the possibilities of digitalization. However, the public sector is yet reluctant to squeeze the full potential of digital technologies. The public sector's cultural, legal, and bureaucratic barriers do not promote the replacement of its conventional mentality, which does not support digitalization techniques (Pūraitė et al., 2020). Many workers in the public sector, especially in developing countries, are not adequately trained in digital technologies. They prefer conventional methods and insist that people follow such methods for effectiveness. Since most people are also not aware of the possibilities and advantages of digitalization, they prefer traditional methods. For instance, many online government portals allow people to complain against a public servant. The complainant may not be aware of such systems. When the complainant approaches another officer, proper guidance may not be given. There are possibilities, but the desired benefits are not achieved since awareness and conscientization are lacking. It creates confusion among the public concerning the benefits of digitalization. The free flow of data is essential for taking full advantage of digitalization. However, many countries restrict data access for many reasons. When access to data is limited, it affects people's possibilities to take maximum benefits (European Commission, 2017). The same scenario happens when there is no fast network for easy access.

5 DIGITALIZATION AND HUMAN RIGHTS CONCERNS

The fast growth of technology and digitalization causes threats to the realization of human rights. Digitalization is famous for its quantification and immediate results. The logic of quantification is evaluated through monetary benefits. In contrast, human rights focus on long-term benefits that affirm people's dignity and rightful claims. While digitalization emphasizes the possibilities for living a comfortable life, human rights underline the importance of having a quality life (Pūraitė et al., 2020). The assessment of digitalization's risks to human rights is mainly concentrated on privacy, bias, and accountability (Kemper & Kolkman, 2018). Rapid access to the Internet, reliability of information and data, consistency, and security are essential components for improved digitalization. When these crucial elements are not adequately satisfied, it creates confusion and complexities. The importance of technologies in human life has become so explicit as people widely use them for accessing goods and services, maintaining easy and rapid networking with others, balancing both household activities and office workloads by utilizing the possibilities of working from home, and pursuing education even when engaged in other activities (Sanders & Scanion, 2021). However, Pūraitė et al. (2020) state that the expansion and use of artificial intelligence tools and the increased implementation of digitalization in almost all areas of human life have caused concerns about people's right to equality, non-discrimination, and privacy. The human rights lens underlines that promoting and protecting universal human rights and fundamental freedoms in physical and digital spaces are essential for a sustainable future.

Digitalization has many challenges, but neglecting it will create more challenges, as no society can meaningfully survive without digitalization in the present times. What society needs is to curb the challenges that complicate the digitalization process. Its priority should be to protect human interests concerning their rights and security. Identification of the new threats to human rights within the context of digitalization is crucial for initiating actions to eliminate them. The human rights concerns within the context of digitalization should address both fundamental and specific human rights. The basic human rights, in this context, include the right to adequate information, the right to freedom of speech and expression, the right to privacy, and the right to access the Internet. The human rights that evolved from the digital landscape are the right to digital sovereignty, the right to manage and protect a digital profile, the right to protect biometric data, and the right to safety on the Internet (Petrov et al., 2024). Although a detailed evaluation of the protection of fundamental and specific human rights in the digital space may not be possible, this section critically analyzes some human rights in terms of digitalization.

5.1 Right to Privacy

Digital platforms are on the rise. They collect people's data to make a profit. It can also cause data leakage, as well as data being used for fraudulent activities. Such activities invade people's privacy rights (Petrov et al., 2024). In the digitalized world, many agencies collect people's data for tracking and surveillance purposes, which is against the logic of the right to privacy. If surveillance mechanisms follow international human rights standards, it can lead to effective governance. Otherwise, it will create chaos in society. This issue is more complex with targeted and mass surveillance (Pūraitė et al., 2020). Targeted surveillance focuses on a specific individual or a group of individuals. It is done through hacking digital devices and continuous online monitoring (La Rue, 2013). Meanwhile, mass surveillance focuses on "collecting all information possible from the digital sources," which is against the core of ICCPR Art. 17 (Pūraitė et al., 2020). Article 12 of the UDHR protects people from arbitrary interference with their privacy. Digital technology users provide their personal information to access such services. They should have control over such information, as it should not be shared with any third parties without their consent (Yerkinbayeva et al., 2022). For instance, if an insurance agency shares a patient's medical records with others without the patient's consent, it breaches the patient's right to privacy. It applies to other matters like passport, bank account, and credit card details. In many developing countries like India, shopkeepers collect mobile numbers or email IDs when people purchase certain items. Thereafter, customers receive many advertisements through messages and emails. They have not consented to use their personal information for marketing purposes. But it happens. It violates people's right to privacy. The main problem with data collection and misuse is that many are unaware that their personal information is collected and misused. Some agencies indirectly collect personal data and share it with others. It poses serious security concerns (Petrov et al., 2024).

Personal information is an individual's biggest asset. However, for some fraudulent people, it is only a commodity that can increase their profit. Realizing online data privacy infringement, governments and various agencies have incorporated many protective measures. Two-factor verification, setting passwords, compulsory routine changes of passwords, and guidelines not to share personal information on unauthentic sites are some directives that prioritize people's right to privacy (Petrov et al., 2024). However, with the ever-growing digitalization in the modern world, states find it difficult to protect people's right to privacy (Petryshyn & Hyliaka, 2021). The ruling of a Dutch court is interesting as it prohibited the government from taking support from artificial intelligence to identify potential welfare fraudsters. The government wanted to use algorithms that could predict the possibility of an individual committing fraud by collecting an enormous amount of personal data in various ways. The court said that such an initiative of the government would violate people's fundamental right to privacy (Jacobson, 2020). The Mexican government's infringement of the right to privacy of some human rights activists, journalists, and anti-corruption movement leaders using the Pegasus software has also been widely criticized as unethical and illegal (Pūraitė et al., 2020). All these underline that any digital activity that infringes on an individual's right to privacy, whether done by government or private actors, violates human rights in the digital space.

5.2 Right to Adequate Information

The Internet and cyberspace have ample amounts of information. People should be able to access such information to increase their understanding of various factors. They have a specific right to access information and resources available in cyberspace. This unique right of people should always be respected, except when limited in conformity with the law to protect genuine security demands (Petrov et al., 2024). Access to information also includes the right to share information. It is not an absolute right, as one cannot share information using digital technologies. The government may enact specific guidelines concerning the content, method, and form of the information intended to be shared, as it cannot curtail the freedoms and rights of other people (Smith, 2013). Furthermore, the right to adequate information is closely associated with the right to education, which is recognized as a universal human right (UDHR, art. 25). Some constitutions have specifically identified it as part of fundamental rights. For instance, the Constitution of India has recognized the right to education for all children between 6 and 14 (Art. 21A). The right to digital education is also an extended part of the right to education. Such a digital education is essential to improve people's digital competence and the capacity to have adequate information.

Some governments monitor and archive the digital data of their citizens to scrutinize their involvement in the digital world. Although citizens have the right to freedom of speech and expression, governments monitor their social media interactions to examine whether they criticize governmental policies and programs. The continuous criticisms against governments are not accepted in some countries. Such governments restrict the freedom and security of their citizens by misusing digital data (Donahoe, 2014). When governments unnecessarily interfere with the free circulation of ideas and expression, it curtails people's right to adequate information. This is visible in the internet restrictions and shutdowns practiced in many countries. People across the globe face many denials concerning their right to information. When the public protests against such authoritarian actions, governments use the excuse of security reasons. However, when such instances increase, it creates uncertainty, panic, and distrust among the citizens against the government (Pūraitė et al., 2020).

The government is a trusteeship. It must respond positively to citizens' trust in the governance system. When people elect a government, they believe it will protect their rights rather than restrict them. Restricting the circulation of news and ideas that can endanger a country's integrity, security, and harmonious living is not a violation of fundamental rights. However, it should be done based on significant and transparent legal grounds. Piccone (2018) states that governmental actions against freedom of speech and expression and the right to adequate information should not subscribe to the narrow view of security. Governments should adhere to the broader security paradigm that prioritizes people's genuine concerns over abstract territories. Restricting human security concerns and interests for territorial security can not always be justified. Policies restricting internet usage should be framed in consultation with all the stakeholders. European Commission (2017) claims that digitalization has grown to such extremes that judicial and democratic oversight has become challenging. Such a scenario anticipates some forms of censorship, surveillance, tracing, and tracking threats. All these misuses of data endanger people's security and meaningful lives. Digitalization helps increase people's awareness in many areas by giving adequate information. This possibility should not be restricted, imposing unnecessary barriers. The right to sufficient information in the digital space underlines this prerogative.

5.3 Right to Equality

A sustainable society has the responsibility to treat all its members equally. It should share the benefits and burdens equally among all its members. Besides, all deserve equal treatment before the law. When we examine the beneficiaries of digitalization, we see that discrimination exists among people and countries. Some people and areas are not aware of the advantages of digitalization. Some do not even have smartphones, digital technologies, or the Internet to reap the benefits of digitalization (Petrov et al., 2024). While the developed countries enjoy the advantage of 5G connectivity, many areas in the developing world do not even have 3G connectivity. It limits their access to information and other digital services. People can access the Internet when the State provides essential infrastructure facilities. Cables, communication towers, servers, and other technical devices are integral to improving and spreading digitalization across the globe (Belyanskaya et al., 2022). Secured access to broadband internet and protection of internet users' data must be promoted nationwide to ensure all people have access to digitalization (Meskic et al., 2022).

The digital divide is a crucial concern from the perspective of the right to equality. The digital divide refers to the gap between those who can easily access digital technologies and those who cannot. It refers to the haves and have-nots concerning digital technology and competence (West, 2011). Some people have all the benefits of digitalization due to factors like digital literacy, access to broadband connectivity, people-centered development, and a supportive government. In contrast, others have not even heard of the latest technological changes. It creates inequality in society. When the digital divide is enormously vast, it establishes two diverse categories of people across the globe. People with digital literacy reap all the fruits of economic growth. On the other hand, those who fail to cope with technological advancements become unsuccessful in civil, political, and economic interactions (Sanders & Scanion, 2021). Accordingly, the digital divide has led to an amplification of the socioeconomic divide. Besides, if digital technologies are used to "incorrectly identify certain minority groups, consolidating existing stereotypes in society, and increase the probability that representatives of marginalized groups and minority communities will face discrimination more often," it challenges the very core of the right to equality (Petryshyn & Hyliaka, 2021, p.17). Digitalization and its advantages can cause societal inequalities if not adequately addressed and used.

6 AN ETHICO-LEGAL POLICY-PERSPECTIVE FOR EFFICIENT DIGITALIZATION

The wide use of digital algorithms in public governance and decision-making areas raises significant ethical, legal, and regulatory concerns across the globe (Babuta et al., 2018). Kemper and Kolkman (2018) state that the moral and legal considerations for an efficient digitalization process mainly concentrate on transparency, accountability, fairness, ethics, and intelligibility. Digitalization should be promoted for the socioeconomic growth of the country. However, effective measures should be taken to ensure this process aligns with transparency, accountability, and fairness demands. Neglecting these ethical values and principles of justice will cause insecurities and violations of human rights in society. There is every possibility of prioritizing profit and efficiency in digitalization. As such, it is not against the logic of justice. However, digitalization should prioritize ethical and legal parameters to become a more people-centered developmental model. Wagner et al. (2015) note that making laws or guidelines that can systematically address all the changes caused by digital technological developments to protect people's digital rights is impractical. However, if countries cooperate and develop comprehensive policy guidelines according to internationally agreed laws and standards, they can somehow fulfill their obligations towards people's rights. The ultimate objective of any national or international governance system should be to protect people's fundamental rights and promote people-centered development. Since national governments will have their peculiar interests, the reputed global institutions and NGOs should coordinate the initiatives to ensure privacy in the digitalization process. They should influence national governments to promote the protection of digital human rights and make the violators liable. It can be done through appropriate legislation that adheres to the common standards and principles of international human rights law (Pūraitė et al., 2020).

To address cyberattacks and cybercrimes, countries must prioritize developing a group of experts to handle such activities. Extraterritorial and international co-operation is also necessary to confront cyber criminals as they engage in criminal activities beyond their territories. The globe requires a multi-stakeholder approach to confront these virtual criminal activities (European Commission, 2017). Cyber-attacks and cybercrimes are uncontrollably increasing. They harm personal data, plunder people's money, spoil their reputation by circulating morphed images and falsified stories, endanger traffic, communication, energy, and supply chain systems, and even challenge national security, integrity, and sovereignty. Accordingly, the global community requires effective legal frameworks to protect the interests of people and independent countries.

Digitalization will be effective only when transparency and accountability are strictly practiced. Digitalization is a process that is intimately connected with the use of digital technologies and data. Digitalization is a data-driven process. Accordingly, digitalization's efficiency is based on the authenticity of the data. People should be able to trust the provided data to infer and evaluate it. It happens only when the data is transparent. The journey from raw data to meaningful conclusions is a significant process that involves various actors and steps. Accordingly, comprehensibility and accountability are required to ensure increased transparency (Kemper & Kolkman, 2019).

In the present times, many governments and institutions encourage the digitalization of personal documents. The digital documents are accepted as valid proof in many countries. For instance, an Indian citizen traveling domestically must not carry an Aadhaar ID or other ID cards. They need to show it from the DigiLocker, a government initiative for paperless governance. However, it can cause data leakage due to software failures and other technical issues. Since many people are unaware of data misuse, it can cause insecurities if these documents end up in the hands of mischievous people (Petrov et al., 2024). When citizens' data are collected, proper care should be given to ensure security. The public authorities should revolve around ethical principles like transparency and accountability and design effective legal frameworks when they deal with citizens' personal information in the digital space.

The problem with increasing cybercrimes and misuse of digital technologies is that the legislators are running behind technological advancements (Meskic et al., 2022). When they develop some legislation, the digital landscape will have already progressed, producing more complicated human rights violations. When the legal framework lags, human rights violations using digital technologies become more severe. Regulation, implementation, and protection of human rights will become an unrealizable dream if the legal framework fails to progress along with the changes in the digital world. Legal regulation is an effective mechanism to confront data breaches and digital rights violations. The legislators must enact rules and regulations that address human rights violations in the digital space. They must also make timely revisions to the legal regime to keep up with the changes in digital technologies. A minimized set of legal provisions cannot significantly guarantee the protection of human rights in the digital space. Reviewing legal regulation mechanisms and increasing professional legal awareness are essential for establishing a protective framework in the digital space (Petryshyn & Hyliaka, 2021).

7 CONCLUSION

Globalization and neoliberalism have fortified digitalization to permeate all areas of human interaction, making them more successful and effective (Amelicheva et al., 2021). The countless benefits of digitalization support the global march towards economic sustainability by facilitating the realization of SDGs. However, some people misuse the vast possibilities of digitalization for their egoistic and profit-oriented motives. It adversely affects the human rights of many others. Even when the globe is proud of the constant improvements in digitalization, it feels helpless when many human rights violations are reported. Advancements in digitalization are to facilitate human well-being and societal welfare. Digitalization must be people-centric, adhering to human rights and promoting ethical and legal considerations for a sustainable future. Care should be taken to ensure that digitalization does not endanger human rights and people-centered sustainable development. The loopholes of digitalization, which are misused for fraudulent activities, should be addressed with systematic and well-defined international and national legal standards. To achieve this objective, an effective coordination of international institutions, national governments, NGOs, multinational and transnational corporations, and civil society is required. As SDG 17 underlines, global partnerships are the best available mechanisms to confront insecurities, like human rights violations in the digital space, in view of a sustainable future. Besides, the globe must consider convening an international binding covenant on applying human rights in the digital space to ensure global accountability.

REFERENCES

Amelicheva, L., Martyniuk, O., Pyroha, I., Qaracayev, C., & Myroshnychenko, V. (2021). Implementation of Constitutional Human Rights and Social Guarantees of Security in the Context of Digitalization. *Amazonia Investiga*, 10(45), 265-271. https://amazoniainvestiga.info/check/45/26-265-271.pdf

Babuta, A., Oswald, M., & Rinik, C. (2018). Machine Learning Algorithms and Police Decision-Making: Legal, Ethical, and Regulatory Challenges. *Whitehall Report 3-18*. https://researchportal.northumbria.ac.uk/ws/portalfiles/portal/21461394/Babuta_et_al_Machine_Learning_Algorithms_and_Police_Decision_Making_OA.pdf

Belyanskaya, O. V., Kazanovskaya, J. A., & Strutinskaya, T. A. (2022). Updating Human Rights and Freedoms in a Digitalized Society. In E.G. Popkova (Ed.), *Business 4.0 as a Subject of the Digital Economy: Advances in Science, Technology, & Innovation* (PP. 225-228). Springer. https://link.springer.com/chapter/10.1007/978-3-030-90324-4_37

Bochkov, A. A. (2019). Modern State and Law in the Context of Digital Reality. *Law, Economics. Psychology (Irvine, Calif.)*, *1*(13), 3–9. https://rep.vsu.by/handle/123456789/17978

Brennen, J. S., & Kreiss, D. (2016). Digitalization. In *The International Encyclopedia of Communication Theory and Philosophy* (pp. 1-11). https://onlinelibrary.wiley.com/doi/epdf/10.1002/9781118766804.wbiect111

CFI. (n.d.). Mobile Banking. https://corporatefinanceinstitute.com/resources/wealth-management/mobile-banking/

Chirkov, D., Plohih, G., Kapustina, D., & Vasyukov, V. (2022). Opportunities for Using Digital Data in Evidence for Criminal Cases. *Revista Juridica*, 4(71), 364-380. https://revista.unicuritiba.edu.br/index.php/RevJur/article/view/5782/0

Cobelli, N., & Chiarini, A. (2020). Improving Customer Satisfaction and Loyalty through m-Health Service Digitalization: New Challenges for Italian Pharmacists. *The TQM Journal*, *32*(6), 1541–1560. https://www.emerald.com/insight/content/doi/10.1108/tqm-10-2019-0252/full/html

Donahoe, E. (2014). Human Rights in the Digital Age. *Just Security*. https://www.justsecurity.org/18651/human-rights-digital-age/

Dragu, T., & Lupu, Y. (2021). Digital Authoritarianism and the Future of Human Rights. *International Organization*, *75*(4), 991–1017. DOI: 10.1017/S0020818320000624

Duan, Y., Edwards, J. S., & Dwivedi, Y. K. (2019). Artificial Intelligence for Decision-Making in the Era of Big Data—Evolution, Challenges, and Research Agenda. *International Journal of Information Management*, *48*, 63–71. https://www.sciencedirect.com/science/article/abs/pii/S0268401219300581

European Commission. (2017). Digital4Development: Mainstreaming Digital Technologies and Services into EU Development Policy. https://digital-strategy.ec.europa.eu/en/library/digital4development-mainstreaming-digital-technologies-and-services-eu-development-policy

Finnis, J. (2015). Grounding Human Rights in Natural Law. *The American Journal of Jurisprudence*, *60*(2), 199–225. https://academic.oup.com/ajj/article-abstract/60/2/199/83306

Havryliuk, O., Yakushev, O., Prodanova, L., Yakusheva, O., & Kozlovska, S. (2021). Digital Banking and E-commerce in the Context of Digitalization of Business Management. *Financial and Credit Activities: Problems of Theory and Practice*, 5(40), 4-15. https://fkd.net.ua/index.php/fkd/article/view/3465/3341

Jacobson, D. (2020). Dutch Anti-Fraud System Violates Human Rights, Court Rules. *UPI*. https://www.upi.com/Top_News/World-News/2020/02/05/Dutch-anti-fraud-system-violates-human-rights-court-rules/6051580914081/#google_vignette

Kanalan, I. (2018). Extraterritorial State Obligations Beyond the Concept of Jurisdiction. *German Law Journal*, *19*(1), 43–64. DOI: 10.1017/S2071832200022598

Kemper, J., & Kolkman, D. (2019). Transparent to Whom? No Algorithmic Accountability without a Critical Audience. *Information Communication and Society*, *22*(14), 2081–2096. https://www.tandfonline.com/doi/epdf/10.1080/1369118X.2018.1477967?needAccess=true

Korherr, P., Kanbach, D. K., Kraus, S., & Mikalef, P. (2022). From Intuitive to Data-Driven Decision-Making in Digital Transformation: A Framework of Prevalent Managerial Archetypes. *Digital Business*, 2(2), 100045. https://www.sciencedirect.com/science/article/pii/S2666954422000254

La Rue, F. (2013). Report of the Special Rapporteur on the Promotion and Protection of the Right to Freedom of Opinion and Expression. *A/HRC/23/40*. https://www.right-docs.org/doc/a-hrc-23-40/

Meskic, Z., Albakjaji, M., Jevremovic, N., Omerovic, E., & Adams, J. (2022). Digitalization and Innovation in Achieving SDGs—Impacts on Legislation and Practice. *IOP Conference Series. Earth and Environmental Science*, *1026*(1), 012061. https://iopscience.iop.org/article/10.1088/1755-1315/1026/1/012061

Mihaila, S., Bădicu, G., Codrean, V., & Dascălu, I. (2021). E-Commerce in the Context of Globalization and Digitalization: Opportunities, Challenges, and Perspectives. *European Journal of Accounting, Finance, &. Business (Atlanta, Ga.), 16*(26), 1–9. https://ibn.idsi.md/vizualizare_articol/202031

Pangrazio, L., & Sefton-Green, J. (2021). Digital Rights, Digital Citizenship, and Digital Literacy: What's the Difference? *Journal of New Approaches in Educational Research, 10*, 15–27. https://link.springer.com/article/10.7821/naer.2021.1.616

Panova, L., Gramartskyy, E., Kryvosheyina, I., & Makoda, V. (2022). Human Rights in the Context of Digitalization: International-Legal Analysis. *International Journal of Computer Science and Network Security, 22*(5), 320–326. https://koreascience.kr/article/JAKO202221358522908.page

Papadopoulos, G., Arduini, S., Uyar, H., Psiroukis, V., Kasimati, A., & Fountas, S. (2024). Economic and Environmental Benefits of Digital Agricultural Technologies in Crop Production: A Review. *Smart Agricultural Technology, 8*, 100441. https://www.sciencedirect.com/science/article/pii/S2772375524000467

Parviainen, P., Tihinen, M., Kääriäinen, J., & Teppola, S. (2017). Tackling the Digitalization Challenge: How to Benefit from Digitalization in Practice. *International Journal of Information Systems and Project Management, 5*(1), 63–77. https://aisel.aisnet.org/ijispm/vol5/iss1/5/

Petrov, A., Kuraev, A., Mirzagitova, A., & Kirillova, E. (2024). Main Threats to Human Rights and Freedoms in the Context of Digitalization. *Jurídicas CUC*, 20(1), 343-357. https://revistascientificas.cuc.edu.co/juridicascuc/article/view/5330

Petryshyn, O. V., & Hyliaka, O. S. (2021). Human Rights in the Digital Ages: Challenges, Threats, and Prospects. *Journal of the National Academy of Legal Sciences of Ukraine, 28*(1), 16–23. https://visnyk.kh.ua/web/uploads/journals_pdf/%D0%92%D1%96%D1%81%D0%BD%D0%B8%D0%BA%20%D0%9D%D0%90%D0%9F%D1%80%D0%9D%D0%A3_%D0%A2%D0%BE%D0%BC%2028(1)_2021.pdf#page=16

Piccone, T. (2018). Democracy and Digital Technology. *International Journal of Human Rights, 15*(27), 29–38. https://sur.conectas.org/wp-content/uploads/2018/07/sur-27-ingles-ted-piccone.pdf

Pūraitė, A., Adamonienė, R., & Žemeckė, A. (2020). Sustainable Digitalization in Public Institutions: Challenges for Human Rights. *European Journal of Sustainable Development, 9*(3), 91–102. https://ecsdev.org/ojs/index.php/ejsd/article/view/1072/1054

Ruud, O. (2018). How to Succeed with Digital Transformation Projects in Public Sector with Focus on Municipalities (Research in Progress). *Central and Eastern European EDem and EGov Days*, 325, 425-436. https://ejournals.facultas.at/index.php/ocgcp/article/view/1575

Sanders, C. K., & Scanlon, E. (2021). The Digital Divide is a Human Rights Issue: Advancing Social Inclusion through Social Work Advocacy. *Journal of Human Rights and Social Work*, *6*, 130–143. https://link.springer.com/article/10.1007/s41134-020-00147-9 PMID: 33758780

SellersCommerce. (2025). 51 e-Commerce [Global and U.S. Data] [. https://www.sellerscommerce.com/blog/ecommerce-statistics/.]. *Statistics in*, *2025*, •••.

Smith, P. S. (2013). Imprisonment and Internet-Access-Human Rights, the Principle of Normalization and the Question of Prisoners' Access to Digital Communications Technology. *Nordic Journal of Human Rights*, *30*(4), 454–482. https://www.scup.com/doi/10.18261/ISSN1891-814X-2012-04-04

Smith, R. K. M. (2022). *International Human Rights Law* (10th ed.). Oxford University Press.

Statista. (2025). Retail E-Commerce Sales Worldwide from 2022 to 2028. https://www.statista.com/statistics/379046/worldwide-retail-e-commerce-sales/

UBS. (2022). The History of Digital Banking. https://www.ubs.com/ch/en/wealth-management/womens-wealth/magazine/articles/history-of-digital-banking.html

Vincent, J. (2016). UN Condemns Internet Access Disruption as a Human Rights Violation.

Wagner, B., Bronowicka, J., Berger, C., & Behrndt, T. (2015). Surveillance and Censorship: The Impact of Technologies on Human Rights. European Parliament. https://www.europarl.europa.eu/RegData/etudes/STUD/2015/549034/EXPO_STU(2015)549034_EN.pdf

West, J. C. (2011). *Without a Net: Librarians Bridging the Digital Divide*. Libraries Unlimited. *The Verge*. https://www.theverge.com/2016/7/4/12092740/un-resolution-condemns-disrupting-internet-access

Wilkinson, M. D., Dumontier, M., Aalbersberg, I. J., & Mons, B. (2016). The FAIR Guiding Principles for Scientific Data Management and Stewardship. *Scientific Data*, *3*, 160018. https://www.nature.com/articles/sdata201618 PMID: 26978244

Yerkinbayeva, L., Nurmukhankyzy, D., Kalymbek, B., Ozenbayeva, A., & Kalymbekova, Z. (2022). Digitalization of Environmental Information in the Republic of Kazakhstan: Issues of Legal Regulation. *Journal of Environmental Management and Tourism*, *13*(1), 115–127. https://journals.aserspublishing.eu/jemt/article/view/6815

KEY TERMS AND DEFINITIONS

Accountability: Accountability is the virtuous willingness and commitment to take responsibility for one's actions.

Human Security: Human Security is the UNDP-framed international people-centered policy design, based on the human rights standards, to address freedom from want, fear, and indignity across the globe.

Right to Adequate Information: The right to adequate information refers to people's fundamental right to receive vital information concerning technological advancements and digitalization.

Right to Privacy: Right to privacy in the digital space refers to the fundamental right to be secure in online interactions and information.

Sustainable Development: Sustainable development means that the developmental and environmental needs of the present and future generations should be equally considered in designing developmental policies.

Technological Advancements: Technological advancements refer to the significant growth achieved by humans in making machines more productive and efficient to facilitate and substitute many human activities, enhancing the possibilities of humans.

Transparency: Transparency is the value or quality that combines openness and sincerity in human interactions, intending not to cheat anyone for individual benefits.

Chapter 3

Digital Inclusion as a Catalyst for Sustainable Development:
Bridging the Human Rights Divide in the Age of AI

Pranjal Khare
https://orcid.org/0000-0002-9937-9588
Jindal Global Law School, O.P. Jindal Global University, India

ABSTRACT

This chapter examines the significant importance of digital inclusion for global sustainable development and human rights in the age of rapidly expanding AI. The chapter discusses meaningful digital inclusion, which is fundamentally defined and it has been linked to both the SDGs and human rights while examining the many components of the digital divide. The chapter demonstrates how all types of digital inclusion are important and can be accelerators of economic empowerment, health, education, gender equality, governance strengthening, and sustainability on a global level. It provides critical analysis of AI's transformative promise while providing analysis of the many human rights risks that have emerged. We outline comprehensive approaches that deal with national and regional level policies, global governance capacities for AI, multi-stakeholder approaches and capacity building. The chapter ends with recommendations, recalling the vital inter-linkage among the recommendations for designing a truly human-centric, equitable and sustainable digital future for everyone.

DOI: 10.4018/979-8-3373-3685-5.ch003

INTRODUCTION

As we progress through the first two decades of the 21st Century, one thing has become clear that we are living in the midst of a global technological revolution that is transforming nearly every aspect of human life. Digital technologies have become entrenched in how we communicate, learn, work, govern, and interact with the world around us. This transformation offers tremendous upside, allowing for unparalleled opportunities for advancement, innovation, and global exchange. However, it presents a powerful current of change that also creates real challenges, particularly the danger that inequities are exacerbated unless access to meaningful engagement in this digital ecosystem remains broadly and inclusive. Technology development and deployment considerations around social and digital inclusion will be critical if public, private, and civil society hope to leverage these advances in sustainable ways. In this chapter, the author argue that digital inclusion is not simply something society strives for but rather, a requirement that is foundational in nature, and essential to achieving the ambitious Sustainable Development Goals (SDGs) that we have collectively committed ourselves to by virtue of being member states of the United Nations (UN) and universal human rights agreements and treaties. In fact, the enduring relevance of our premise is amplified when viewed from the lens of Artificial Intelligence (AI), which has the potential to greatly advance human progress or further enhance societal barriers and inequities depending on whether this digital ecosystem evolves to include physical and virtual human rights for all, rather than just enforced norms or intentions (Ho et al., 2025).

As we advance further into the 21st century, it is becoming increasingly evident that digital inclusion is foundational to sustainable development and to advancing human rights, especially in the age of AI. Recent research has shown that not only does a lack of access to, but literacy in, digital technologies exacerbate social inequality and stymie progress towards global equity. Foundational papers such as the UNESCO's Recommendation on the Ethics of AI (2021) and the World Bank's Digital Development Reports (2023), recognize the multifaceted nature of digital inclusion, acknowledging that it goes beyond access to also include affordability, digital literacy, content available in digital form, and protections around data and privacy. These facets contribute to measurable advancement towards the SDGs on poverty reduction, quality education, gender equality, and reduced inequality.

This chapter sets the groundwork by defining digital inclusion, exploring the complex links between digital transformation, sustainable development and human rights, and critically reviewing the continuing digital divide that could leave billions behind as the world becomes more connected. The author contends that a strong, human-centered, digital inclusion approach is essential to building a truly sustainable and human rights-respecting future in the AI Age.

For many years, the "digital divide" concept was primarily considered a binary problem. Those who have access to the internet and digital devices, versus those who do not. As a result, "digital inclusion" was largely defined as connecting users to a network and providing digital devices. Though this was a strong starting point, this is not enough. True digital inclusion goes well beyond access as it has a nuanced framework, ensuring that individuals and communities can access digital technologies, as well. However, they can use, understand, and benefit from them to improve their lives and realize their empowerment (Nguyen, 2020).

To understand this evolving definition, several key issues must be factored in. At the most basic level of being included is the availability of the required infrastructure that is, broadband internet, mobile networks, and community access points such as public Wi-Fi or community centers, there can be no inclusion of any type without basic infrastructure. Additionally, even where infrastructure is present, often the cost of internet services, keeping up with data plans, and purchasing digital consumer devices such as smartphones and computers is prohibitive. Therefore, affordability is another prerequisite to bridge the economic divide. Digital inclusion also requires that technologies are designed and implemented in a usable way for all people. It includes people with disabilities, older adults, and people with varying abilities to engagement including those with limited literacy and tech skills, demonstrating the importance of accessibility through accessible web design, assistive technologies, and interfaces that are easy to use. Having a device and internet connection does not matter at all without the knowledge and skills to independently navigate the digital landscape safely and effectively. This is also what is meant by digital literacy and skills, indeed with a range from basic operable skills, through critical thinking, being able to evaluate online information, know basic privacy settings and understand misinformation, while also managing the awareness of the ramifications of online actions, and the ethical use of technology (Perez-Escolar & Canet, 2022).

Moreover, the digital world must provide relevant content and services that are meaningful, culturally relevant, and available in the local language, because when online resources do not meet the needs or interests of a community or are only available in an inaccessible language, connected people, and, by extension, e-governance, online education, health information, or economic opportunities will not be considered life-affirming or empowering; and importantly, culturally interesting. Finally, trust and safety are of the utmost importance, as individuals' fears of online crime, violation of privacy, harassment, and disinformation are barriers to the potential of digital platforms, and thus require not just trust in robust cybersecurity measures, but sustainable downloads, consideration of reasonable data protection practices, and consideration in eliminating harmful content and activities to encourage long-term digital confidence (Khare & Raghuwanshi, 2024). In the end, meaningful digital inclusion is about equitable engagement with the promise of the digital society for everyone, regardless of socio-economic status, geography, age, gender or physical ability, and the potential for using digital technologies to improve education, health, economic and civic engagement, and human flourishing. When all these areas of meaningful digital inclusion are adequately met, digital inclusion becomes more than just a technical provision; it becomes a means for empowerment of both individuals and communities (Hariyani et al., 2025).

In 2015, the 2030 Agenda for Sustainable Development was adopted unanimously by the UN. It provides a common vision for peace and prosperity for people and the planet. At the heart of the 2030 Agenda are the 17 (SDGs), which present an urgent call for action for countries to work in global cooperation, regardless of whether they are developed or developing countries. The SDGs are to be pursued in a manner that simultaneously ends poverty in all its forms and dimensions and seek to eliminate other deprivations through strategies that improve health and education, reduce inequality and promote economic growth, all while tackling climate change and preserving and managing our oceans and forests. The last decade since adoption has demonstrated, very clearly, that digital transformation is not only a parallel activity, but a transformative, critical, cross-cutting action which has today impacted the practical realization of all of the SDGs. Digital technologies, established as powerful enablers, have also provided many new solutions for many of the complex challenges of developing countries' development (Alhassan & Adam, 2024).

Digital technologies can be extremely powerful. However, the uneven digital poverty that exists and the absence of substantive inclusion can also deepen and widen inequalities, creating new exclusion "spaces". Without our deliberate efforts to digitally include everyone, particularly those populations that the SDGs are striving to support, the digital revolution will inadvertently create conditions for further exclusion.

In addition, the "digital divide" is a term that has changed dramatically since its emergence in the late 1990s. The term was first used as a descriptor of the gap between individuals or groups on the basis of access to the internet. Today, the digital divide is recognized as a multifaceted phenomenon, with a nature that is much more complex than mere connectivity. Understanding the digital divide in a nuanced way is important because it has real-world socioeconomic consequences that reinforce and extend the socio-economic gap amongst individuals and groups. The current digital divide consists of numerous, interleaved layers. For example, there is often an overall geographic divide between urban and rural areas, as cities in the wealthiest countries may have fibred optic networks with speeds measured in gigabits per second, where many remote and rural communities, in the wealthiest as well as in most developing countries, have inadequate internet infrastructure or only slow and unreliable internet, significantly limiting one's ability to access digital possibilities. A second reality is the wealth gap between and amongst individuals and groups, income and educational attainment shape levels of digital inclusion, and form a socioeconomic divide as many lower-income households do not have the ability to pay for devices or internet subscriptions/data plans; even with infrastructure in place, lower incomes create a barrier to digital engagement; lower education often relates to lower levels of digital literacy, creating a double barrier to meaningful engagement (Dastyari & Jose, 2024).

Worldwide, and specifically in many developing countries, women and girls experience serious inequalities in digital access and use, creating a gender divide, where culture, economic factors, and safety sometimes inhibit their ability to own devices, connect to the internet, or participate equally in online spaces negatively affecting their access to educational, economic, and critical information. The two ends of the age spectrum experience inequalities, creating an age divide, whereby older populations may have less access to digital services or are unable to participate in the increasingly digitized services due to the inability to adapt to new technologies, and the younger generations may be able to access online services, but may encounter risks associated with online safety, misinformation, and digital addiction without guidance. People with disabilities are often excluded from digital inclusion due to many barriers, including inaccessible hardware and software, non-conforming websites, and lack of assistive technologies, creating a disability divide that inhibits their opportunities for engagement in education, employment, and social life (Mohan et al., 2024).

Furthermore, the Universal Declaration of Human Rights (UDHR), adopted in 1948, expresses the inalienable rights possessed by all human beings. These rights, including the rights to privacy, freedom of expression, access to information, education, work, and rights to freedom from discrimination, are the foundation of equity and justice. During the early period of digital transformation, the internet was heralded as a liberating force for individuals, for democracy, and for access to information. Digital technologies have increased the capacity of many human rights; however, they have also introduced some novel challenges and require an examination and reaffirmation of these rights within the digital environment. In the positive sense, digital technologies have increased the number of human rights. Social media and online news have allowed for ordinary citizens to express their views and access viewpoints like they never could have previously, while bypassing traditional gatekeepers, which has enhanced the right to freedom of expression and the right of access to information. This capacity is abundantly visible in social movements and political uprisings (Reed & Thompson, 2021).

Hence, digital inclusion, now defined as equitable and meaningful engagement in the digital realm, is a fundamental condition for achieving SDGs and other universal human rights. The digital revolution has the potential to boost all development measures, despite the monumental inequalities on the same global stage. However, without equitable access to the opportunity for digital engagement, the digital revolution carries the potential of deepening existing divides. With the introduction of Artificial Intelligence comes a new and powerful dimension to this discussion. AI can, and will, change entire economic sectors, deliver health care innovations, provide personalized education, and reshape governance, thereby allowing the potential for dramatic accelerations on the journey to the SDGs. For example, AI can help ensure the efficient allocation of resources targeted for poverty alleviation action (SDG 1), personalized learning (SDG 4), guide a more accurate disease diagnosis pathway (SDG 3), and streamline public sector services (SDG 16). But if communities are digitally excluded, they will never benefit from artificial intelligence and other meaningful technological innovations. The moment a population lacks access to the basic infrastructure of internet connectivity, the affordability of devices, or the digital literacy to interact with artificial intelligence tools, they are incapable of accessing any interventional advancements.

Moreover, the nature of artificial intelligence poses new and complicated human rights dilemmas. AI systems can embed or scale societal biases leading to discrimination; threaten people's privacy through the gathering of their data with the extensive processing of that data (on privacy rights); and raise questions of accountability and due process concerning decision-making which affects fair trial rights. If these AI systems are conceived and deployed without a strong ethical stance, transparency, and a human-centered approach, then they might reinforce the already widening human rights gaps, and create a new level of exclusion and injustice. Thus, the need is two-fold: first to continue to strive to comprehensively address digital inclusion, so that all people, all communities are able to access and meaningfully participate in the digital economy and society; and that this fundamental first stage is needed before we can fully take advantage of AI's potential for sustainable development. Second, we also need to make space to safely create policy frameworks and ethical protocols around the development and deployment of AI and technological innovation, while ensuring these power technologies do no harm, respect, protect, and uphold human rights (Ochoa-Daderska et al., 2024).

DIGITAL INCLUSION AS AN ACCELERATOR FOR SUSTAINABLE DEVELOPMENT

The global effort represented by the 17 SDGs constitutes a universal call to action to end poverty in its many forms, protect the planet, and ensure that all people enjoy peace and prosperity by 2030. Although the SDGs address challenging and interrelated issues, there exists a potentially powerful but often underappreciated enabler of their achievement that takes place in the realm of digital inclusion. This subchapter examines how equitable access to, and meaningful use of the digital world can be leveraged as a powerful accelerator to help meet several SDGs by reframing traditional development paradigms to drive inclusive developmental growth.

Digital Literacy, E-commerce, Fintech, and the Gig Economy for Inclusive Growth

Digital inclusion is a key engine for economic empowerment and poverty eradication, directly contributing to SDG 1 (No Poverty) and SDG 8 (Decent Work and Economic Growth). At its core, meaningful digital engagement gives users the tools and knowledge to access new economic opportunities, work more productively, and engage more in the global economy. To access all this empowerment, the individual must have digital literacy. Digital literacy involves much more than simply knowing how to operate devices. The individual should know how to use digital tools to manage their finances, learn new skills, and access markets. Once the individual possesses digital literacy, they will use job boards to find work, use e-learning courses to upgrade skills, and they will not only see local entrepreneurship opportunities that they would not have otherwise, but not be afraid to use them (Lee et al, 2023).

The emergence of e-commerce platforms has created democratized access for entrepreneurs who are starting small and medium enterprises (SMEs), and for individual entrepreneurs. This is especially significant for civil society in developing countries. Artisans in remote villages, for example, can now sell their crafts directly to a worldwide audience, avoiding intermediaries, and ensuring they get a fairer share of the profits. This is having a positive economic impact at the village level, while also supporting traditional skills and cultural heritage. Digital marketplaces diminish geographic barriers, expand access to new customers, and frequently have a lower cost of doing business than physical locations, reducing barriers for those needing to start with limited capital (Ozturk et al., 2024).

Fintech (i.e. financial technology) is changing access to financial services for millions who were once unbanked or underserved by traditional financial institutions. Many of the previous tasks, taking weeks or months, are now handled in seconds and at lower costs. Mobile banking, digital wallets like PayPal, Venmo, and Cash App, and peer-to-peer lending services like Kiva allow individuals to save, transfer money, access micro-loans, purchase insurance, and much more, faster and cheaper than before. In many parts of Africa and Asia, mobile money services are a part of everyday life, which enables remittances from migrant workers, payments for goods and services, and safer cashless transactions. Financial inclusion offers individuals decision-making capacity around their money, the ability to invest in a small business, and the means to build resilience against economic shocks, while also contributing to a financially inclusive economy (Abdulkareem et al., 2024).

Again, despite the challenges of the gig economy and labor rights, it has created job opportunities for many, often in urban centers but increasingly appearing in semi-urban parts of many cities. Ride-share services like Uber and Lyft deliver services on-demand via computer applications, connecting workers to consumers. Food delivery services like Door Dash, Skip the Dishes, etc., and freelance services like Fiverr and Upwork offer supplemental income opportunities apart from traditional employment. The gig economy has removed barriers to income, as all one needs to receive an income stream is a smartphone and basic digital skills.

Telemedicine, E-learning Platforms, Digital Tools for Women's Empowerment, and their Role in Improving Social Indicators

In the area of health and well-being (SDG 3), digital inclusion has enabled an age of telemedicine and mobile health (mHealth). For millions living in remote or rural areas, access to medical professionals is often a huge barrier. Telemedicine helps bridge this gap by allowing patients to speak with doctors via an online video call, receive a diagnosis, and receive a prescription without the need for lengthy and expensive travel. This is impactful for routine care management of chronic diseases, mental health support, and routine check-ups.

Digital health records also improve coordination and better patient care, reduce medical errors, and simplify administrative processes of care delivery. For example, in some areas across India, mobile phones are being used to disseminate important information about maternal and child health, connecting pregnant women to health care providers, and tracking immunizations. As a result, health outcomes have improved significantly for at-risk populations (Xie et al., 2025).

For quality education (SDG 4), digital inclusion creates unprecedented opportunities to democratize and improve educational outcomes. E-learning platforms have transformed access to knowledge, enabling access to quality educational resources, courses, and vocational training for anyone with access to the internet. This is particularly transformative for students who reside in rural areas and do not have access to schools with sufficient resources or qualified teachers. During global crises, like the recent pandemic, it has become evident that digital learning was critical, enabling continuity of education when physical schools were closed.

Importantly, digital inclusion is a major lever for gender equality (SDG 5). Globally, women and girls tend to have disproportionate barriers to digital access due to socio-economic barriers, cultural norms, and safety. Addressing the digital gender gap identity is critical for women empowerment. When women have access to smartphones, affordable data, and digital literacy, it creates pathways to opportunities. These digitally empowered women will have access to information about reproductive health; they may also engage with their support networks, do online advocacy, and participate in e-commerce or online freelancing. In turn, all of these will enable a woman to gain economic independence and political voice in her community. Digital technologies can also serve as platforms for women entrepreneurs to sell their goods, access financial services, and break into traditional markets. Additionally, digital learning experiences can provide girls with the skills to find work in the future, while challenging gender stereotypes in education and work. By ensuring women equitably access and meaningfully use digital technologies in these ways, societies can unlock women's potential, foster their leadership, and speed up the gender equality agenda across all aspects of society, including level of political participation and economic independence (Srinivasan et al., 2024).

Digital Public Services, E-governance, Citizen Participation, and Data-driven Policymaking for More Equitable Societies

The digital transformation of public services (e-governance) is an essential pillar of this paradigm shift. Governments around the world are expanding digital service delivery of a multitude of services including identity verification, registering births and deaths, tax returns, payments for social support, and applying for permits and licenses. When transitioning services online, and enabling citizens to access them, we are mitigating the burden on citizens traveling, waiting in long lines, and dealing with complex bureaucratic systems. Saving citizens time and money from the costs of inconvenience, especially for citizens in rural locations or those with limited mobility or skills and further purchasing power to protect from corruption (Djatmiko et al., 2025).

An example would be digital identity systems in India, that are linked to welfare schemes like India's Aadhaar specifically designed to prevent gaps in ensuring, that subsidies and welfare benefits reach an intended beneficiary directly and mitigates leakage and makes public expenditure transparent. Although the success of a digital identity depends on ensuring digital inclusion, those that do not digitally connect or digitally literate or otherwise lack any skills will be at risk of being excluded from services.

In addition to service delivery functions, digital technologies also improve citizen participation and support civic engagement using digital technology, as there are online public consultations, feedback channels, and communication with elected representatives shaping effective and potentially more participatory democratic processes giving citizens a seat at the table in policymaking (Liu et al., 2025).

Social media and online platforms can serve as a key advocacy tool for citizens to organize, bring attention to issues, and hold their governments accountable. With the potential for more transparency and opportunity for engagement, social media can lead to governance that is broader, more inclusive, and more responsive to the needs of different groups, giving voice and responding to their needs instead of letting them feel alienated or marginalized. Digital tools have not only provided new means for organizations to monitor elections, and technologies that support voter registration, but they are also providing transparency in elections, contributing to the strength of democratic institutions.

Most importantly, connection to the internet, as what enables digital inclusion, provides the basis for data-driven policy provision for other equitable and more equitable societies. As governments phase in the digitization of public services, digital means will generate billions of data points that, if ethically collected and analyzed, will be a content laboratory of data enabled to provide governments real-time information about the needs of citizens, the effectiveness of resources allocated to the needs assessed for improved development. The introduction of this data enables evidence-based policies to be developed, where the governments can identify underrepresented populations, where residents are in greatest need of assistance, and develop interventions to address their needs to a higher degree of specificity. For example, anonymized data of transactions on a digital payments service can provide a pattern of economic activity for a geographical region allowing to develop programs, or program type aimed at the greatest area of need. Data analytics can also provide opportunities to identify and address system inequality in service provision to assure the sheer number of resources are distributed proportionately, and so no community is eluded from the resource provision (Indar et al., 2024).

Successful Digital Inclusion Initiatives and their Impact on Specific SDG Targets

To show the measurable effect of digital inclusion as an important accelerator of sustainable development, it is helpful to review exemplary initiatives from around the world that illustrate best practice examples and the many ways digital tools can be used to advance the SDGs. These case studies demonstrate the importance of multi-stakeholder partnerships, context-specific responses, and meaningful access versus mere access.

One major example is India's Digital India program, which has made remarkable strides towards financial inclusion (SDG 1 & 8) through its Jan Dhan-Aadhaar-Mobile (JAM) (trinity). The JAM method created a digital public infrastructure which connects universal identity (Aadhaar) with bank accounts (Jan Dhan Yojana) and a mobile phone. The Indian government can now transfer benefits directly eliminating petty corruption and laying the groundwork for systems in which subsidies reach the poor. The JAM initiative created access for millions of previously unbanked people in India to make deposits and receive payments to build histories which can be used to further mitigate poverty and create opportunities for inclusive economic growth. This is an example of scale and a demonstration of the effectiveness of an integrated digital system used alongside real political will, and therefore, the largest outreach campaign in India's history (Sindakis & Showkat, 2024).

In terms of health and education (SDG 3 & 4) occasions such as the rise of M-Pesa in Kenya make for an amazing example of a non-intended effect that is quite powerful. While M-Pesa is a mobile money transfer system, the way in which citizens have adopted M-Pesa has allowed for the payment of health services and school fees in rural areas more easily and, as a result, is releasing some financial pressure to provide access to services for citizens. M-Pesa has also indirectly increased the development of the mobile application ecosystem by allowing a payment infrastructure, that includes payments for health services and education, to ease consumer behavior. It has allowed for health platforms that can provide citizens with remote consultations, and applications for educational activities supported and based on M-Pesa. What this example demonstrates is how digital inclusion in a fundamental service can create a ripple of other innovations that have effects on other SDGs (Mabelle et al., 2023).

As for improvements in governance and reducing inequalities (SDG 10 & 16) Estonia's e-Residency and digital governance is a clear example that should be highlighted. They have developed to be one of the strongest digital societies globally and not only can citizens do nearly all government functions online, from voting to paying taxes, starting a business, and accessing their medical records, but how this has vastly improved efficiency, and transparency, and citizens are engaged. Estonia has developed its particular approach to secure digital identity, interoperable government databases, and a "digital-first" culture, which illustrates how digital inclusion can create strong and transparent institutions with reduced bureaucracy, ultimately creating a fairer society based on easily available services for all citizens, that minimizes accessibility based on relative position in physical space.

With relation to innovation, infrastructure, and sustainable communities (SDG 9 & 11), examples in Rwanda show how countries are making substantial improvements. Through an energetic government commitment to digital infrastructure, which includes their wide-ranging fiber optic networks and affordable mobile broadband, Rwanda has supported tech ecosystems to grow around their digital infrastructure and regulations. A spate of innovations has developed in other sectors off the back of this investment, including drone technology to distribute medical supplies to remote areas, and digital agricultural services for farmers to increase productivity and sustainability. Finally, Rwanda's focus on digital literacy training, perhaps especially for youth and women, similarly facilitates capability of the population to contribute to the new infrastructure and helps to shift economies to develop knowledge-based industries and more sustainable urban and rural communities (Ahishakiye & Nizeyimana, 2024).

The common thread among these varied case studies from India's wide-ranging financial inclusion program to Kenya's mobile money revolution, then Estonia's robust digital governance, finally, Rwanda's transformative infrastructure and innovation initiatives, sends a very important message. That is digital inclusion is not a singular offer, but rather a permissive force. The strength of digital inclusion is found in the variety it can accommodate to the local context as well as its ability to address an array of development challenges by ensuring that the tools are usable and accessible, information is timely and relevant, and pathways to participate and empowerment are clear and open. The challenges and opportunities faced by the initiatives are complicated by the multifaceted nature of the digital divide, which need to be understood and addressed holistically to ensure that all citizens can have these opportunities and that the digital space engages them beyond basic connectivity.

EXPLORING THE NEXUS OF ARTIFICIAL INTELLIGENCE AND HUMAN RIGHTS

The digital world we now inhabit is in the midst of a rapid shift to an AI world. AI is capable of impacting societies at an unprecedented speed and scale. AI may be one of the most impactful technologies humanities has ever created. AI is often defined as the imitation of human intelligence processes by machines, especially computer systems, and is made up of a wide range of technologies from machine learning algorithms that can find patterns in data to the natural language processing that allows humans to interact with computers and computer vision that allows computers to identify and interpret images. AI is already used for a diverse set of applications and is reshaping more and more industries. While the opportunities powered by AI are exciting, they often come along with complex challenges, particularly the issues related to human rights and sustainable development. This subchapter will outline the complexities of AI, offer some of the exciting potential and also consider the dual nature of the technology it has the potential either to inhibit or accelerate achievement of societal aims and also examine some of the human rights concerns that accompany the growing presence of AI in our lives. Ultimately, we want to drive home the unambiguous call for ethical development and use of AI grounded in values that privilege human dignity and rights (Adetomiwa, 2021).

Artificial intelligence is not one single technology, but a group of sophisticated computing methods aimed at enabling machines to perform tasks that would require human intelligence. This entails learning from data (machine learning), being able to understand and produce human language (natural language processing), distinguishing objects and faces (computer vision), and being able to make decisions or predictions from complex and sophisticated patterns (Khare, 2025). These capabilities are causing enormous changes across almost every sector that you can imagine. In the healthcare sector, AI is revolutionizing diagnostics by identifying and recognizing patterns in medical images more accurately than human professionals, expediting drug discovery via simulations of molecular interactions, and implementing individualized treatment plans via personalizing the treatment and care based off each patient's data. AI-based applications for healthcare assist in predicting when diseases will occur, managing hospital logistics, and delivering mental health support via chatbot simulations, greatly improving both the efficiency of care and accessibility of medical services (Temperman & Quintavalla, 2023).

In education, AI allows for truly personalized learning experiences by using adaptive learning trajectory and adaptive learning content to meet the needs of individual students. In addition to being able to tailor feedback as an AI tutor, AI will allow for the automation of grading on lower-level assignments, thereby giving educators the opportunity to invest their time into higher-order teaching strategies and pedagogies. AI will complement education by expanding access to education for learners who are in remote areas utilizing intelligent and adaptive English to Chinese and vice versa translation services and intelligent adaptive learning systems free of geographical or language constraints. In finance, AI will allow for some of the most necessary tasks, from fraud detection, algorithmic trading, and credit-scoring to customer service through virtual assistants.

In addition, AI-enabled analytics can refine investment strategies, resulting in enhanced efficiency of capital allocation. For its part in governance, AI has the potential to improve the quality of public service delivery, urban planning, and law enforcement. AI-enabled systems can sift through large amounts of data that can reveal many patterns relating to public demands, and to optimize resource allocation, along with identifying potential bottlenecks in relation to the provision of public services, ultimately making administrations more effective. Smart city initiatives relating to traffic management, waste optimization, and energy efficiency demonstrate how AI can support sustainability initiatives in urban areas. For justice systems, AI has been introduced as a means to process a large number of legal documents, developing pre-civilian, and streamlining judicial processes, albeit controversially. Addressing and discussing the role of AI in governance is understudied because of the long-term promise of improving public service delivery and augmenting human decision-making that would lead to more informed evidence-based policies for enacting better policy for citizens improving their overall quality of life. In these examples, AI can show its enormous capability to drive innovations and progress that have never been witnessed on a global scale (Dias & Satiro, 2024).

While AI describes transformative technology, it is paradoxical in nature and traits promoting rapid advancements. On the one hand, AI can lead to accelerated advancement towards SDGs. For example, AI algorithms can enhance agricultural yields and supply chains, thereby working towards Zero Hunger (SDG 2), or predict where outbreaks of diseases will occur and personalize health actions, advancing Good Health and Well-being (SDG 3). Its ability to interpret massive amounts of data also offers opportunities for new insights that directly relate to Climate Action (SDG 13). For example, improved climate models or better ways to optimize energy use. AI can enhance efficiency with our resources in different sectors and urban cities, facilitating Responsible Consumption and Production (SDG 12) and Sustainable Cities and Communities (SDG 11). In this perspective, AI can be an intelligent assistant that will allow humans to think and act together to address the complex globally shared challenges we face. However, the very strengths that create opportunities with AI create risk. The future impact of AI may be substantial, but unless AI systems are well-considered in terms of ethics and governed thoroughly, it could exacerbate inequality and undermine fundamental human rights. AI requires a lot of data, which means that existing social inequalities may be enshrined in historical datasets; if they enter algorithms, the outcomes may soon contradict Reduced Inequalities (SDG 10) in a supportive policy environment. Depending on the nature of the system, increased automation could also alter workforce availability and demand and put workers at the risk of losing job opportunities entirely as new technologies take their place as AI-directed solutions shift. Consequently, the promise for Decent Work and Economic Growth (SDG 8) may be compromised if such scenarios emerge without the support of reskilling programs and social safety nets (Teo, 2024).

The wide-ranging use of AI in societal systems presents a new category of human rights challenges, requiring a critical evaluation and strengthening of existing legal and ethical frameworks. If we consider privacy and data protection, AI systems are fundamentally data-driven and need huge volumes of personal data to learn and work. Moreover, AI uses ubiquitous data collection often without explicit and informed consent, and increasingly sophisticated analytical frameworks, to make surveillance and profiling by state and corporate actors an everyday consideration that complicates our ability to enforce our right to be forgotten. Similarly, freedom of expression and information is threatened by AI's ability to undertake algorithmic content moderation, create disinformation, and censor, where the algorithms may be opaque, biased or inaccurate, and, unknowingly, silence legitimate speech or promote misinformation (Khare & Raghuwanshi, 2025).

Given the power of AI and its potential to affect human rights and sustainable development, the need for ethical AI is urgent and critical, and not simply an academic question, but a practical necessity to ensure AI has humanity's best interests in mind. There are several key principles that will guide the development, deployment, and governance of AI systems. First is Fairness; AI technologies should not be introduced with bias and discrimination. This depends on careful consideration of training data, use of bias-reducing techniques, and regular audits to ensure fairness, as well as equitable access to the advantages of AI that do not widen the digital divide. Second is Transparency; many AI algorithms are "black boxes," and a noticeable level of explainability is required that allows all stakeholders to understand how particular decisions came about, especially when human impacts are substantial, to increase trust and compliance. This also means identifying when someone is interacting with an AI system instead of a human agent to increase trust. Third is accountability; mechanisms should be available to identify who caused harm or made unfair decisions from an AI system, and procedures should identify who is responsible, also legally and ethically, and provide mechanisms for redress. Auditing and regulatory compliance should be instituted as well. Finally, and importantly, is human oversight; while AI can take over and augment, humans will need to decide critical decisions, particularly ones impacting human rights, so it is important that AI systems should support not replace human decision-making, and allow for human override or challenge algorithm decisions to reintegrate ethical, moral and empirical humanity into the AI assessment process (Rodrigues, 2020).

FACETS OF HUMAN RIGHTS IN THE AGE OF AI AND EMERGING NORMS

The emergence of AI has created a new era, fundamentally changing the way human rights are experienced, safeguarded, and threatened. While other forms of digital transformation in the past have displaced rights that already existed, AI is unique in its autonomous form of decision-making, advanced patterns of data analysis, and how it permeates all levels of society in the most extensive ways imaginable. The vast complexities AI brings into play are as unprecedented as the challenges and rights they create. This chapter takes a systematic approach to examine the new challenges that AI introduces to the basic human rights discussed here, whether from the intimate realm of privacy, more structural concepts of democracy, and what new concepts and laws these transformative technologies will bring. The very concept of humanity in the age of AI needs a prescriptive and rights-based approach to technological governance to ensure dignity and freedom and to innovate and inspire, rather than undermine, humanity and autonomy.

Right to Privacy and Data Protection

From a rights perspective, one of the most acute and wide-ranging challenges raised by an AI-driven world relates to the right to privacy and data protection. AI systems are voracious consumers of data and require significant amounts of personal information for training and operation, which requires levels of data collection that have never been reached before, and often without explicit and informed consent (Martin & Zimmermann, 2024). This is producing an environment of constant surveillance, hyper-targeted profiling, and loss of individual autonomy. The idea of a "right to be forgotten," which allows individuals to remove their data, becomes extremely convoluted when AI is constantly processing, analyzing, and linking forms of information on a global scale across an infinite number of platforms. The amount of data and extent of linking also means that the risk of data breaches, misuse, and unauthorized access become more profound, and may result in identity theft, targeted discrimination, or even manipulation, fundamentally redefining how we define personal privacy in an increasingly interconnected society where data has become currency (Bag et al., 2024).

Freedom of Expression and Access to Information

Along with privacy, freedom of expression and access to information also comes under great new pressures from AI. Algorithmic content moderation, used by social media platforms to filter out harmful speech, can limit or eliminate legitimate speech, and solely eradicate underrepresented voices, or further enhance echo chambers and limit exposure to diverse perspectives. AI also produces "deepfakes," and deepfakes have proven capable of fooling even the most critical observer. AI can also create sophisticated disinformation campaigns that are difficult for anyone to recognize as unreliable, meaning that we increasingly have less ability to tell facts from fiction. While some governments suppress easy access to information, authoritarian governments are using advanced AI for censorship and surveillance to suppress any form of dissent and monitor people and information flows on a scale and efficiency that has never been possible before. Such countries could employ AI and even use this information to improve the regulation of ideas and suppress open access to information. That presents a direct threat not only to democracy, but also to the right of individuals to have thoughts (Vicente, 2024).

Non-discrimination and Equality

AI also seriously threatens the principle of non-discrimination and equality. Often in less obvious ways. AI learns from the data upon which it has been trained, and if the dataset incorporates biases that already exist within society, whether historical, systemic, or human, then the AI as a product will be compromised by those same biases, which it will perpetuate, and potentially exacerbate. AI bias can result in discrimination with potentially damaging consequences for individuals, including hiring discrimination in employment-long hiring processes, loan applications for credit and financial discrimination in the justice system. It can also have potentially life-threatening effects like inequities in access to services including healthcare, including implausible ratios of facial recognition misidentifications, with implication for viable legal risks, where identifiable demographic groups have often been mistaken far more often than others. Such biases would go against a fundamental human right, the right to be equal before the law and access service, which is the basis of human rights for all. Would AI systems increase inequalities or entrench inequalities? This must be a serious consideration, and for AI to remain just would require it to consider all forms of fairness measures in metrics within operational AI, and at the minimum post-operational audit considerations (Lutz, 2024).

Right to Work and Social Protection

AI's transformative effect has a huge significance for the right to work and social protection, and it is altering the way employment looks. While AI-related automation offers some productivity gains and growth in new forms of specialized jobs, it also presents a considerable risk of job removal in industries susceptible to automation, impacting low-skilled labor the hardest. These changes will require urgent policy responses, including massive investments for reskilling and upskilling of workforces to adapt to an AI-enhanced economy. Moreover, the emergence of the 'gig economy', which closely connects to class structures and growing precarity, is heavily reliant on AI using algorithmic management of workers, and challenges the understanding of traditional labor rights, which include fair wages, working conditions and access to social security. Ensuring there are adequate social protection systems, and thinking critically about the meaning of employment will be increasingly important to maintain social cohesion and economic rights since the introduction of AI.

Right to a Fair Trial and Due Process

The incorporation of artificial intelligence into justice systems brings with it significant ethical and legal difficulties with respect to the right to a fair trial and due process. From predictive policing algorithms that locate potential crime hot spots to artificial intelligence-assisted systems that provide recommendation-specific sentencing, their use creates serious questions about transparency, accountability, wrongful convictions, and discrimination. Additionally, with many AI algorithms being "black boxes," bonding individuals to insufficient and flawed self-understanding for the explanations on why a decision was made about them, violates the core "right to explanation," and their ability to properly challenge or dispute algorithmic determinations. Such obfuscation directly undermines rule of law, including due process, where there must be meaningful human oversight, explainability, and independent auditing to assure that justice is transparent and equitable and does not become a willful black box algorithmic decision (Selcuk et al., 2025).

Right to Participation and Democratic Governance

In addition to individual rights, AI has a far-reaching impact on the right to participation and democratic governance. AI-enabled technologies can promote civic engagement by making e-governance services more efficient, optimized platforms for public consultation, and making government more accessible and responsive. Nevertheless, AI poses the risk of political manipulation through micro-targeting voters with personalized political advertising or propaganda, disseminating extremely convincing misinformation that undermines the public discourse, and potentially allowing foreign interference for the benefit of a foreign government. In the context of AI, the demise of a common factual basis coupled with the potential for creating highly personalized realities, makes it problematic for societies to center around a shared consensus required for the democratic process. This depends on the ability of citizens to participate in elections and government in an informed manner. To keep AI viable as a support for democratic processes, it will require some regulatory constraints on its introduction in political contexts, but perhaps above all, there is a need to conquer the use of AI with digital literacy that empowers citizens.

These cumulative challenges establish a threshold requiring digital human rights as a distinct concept and development of contemporary legal frameworks. It is becoming increasingly evident that the UDHR along with the other foundational human rights instruments are necessary for interpreting and reaffirming existing human rights with the emergence of advanced digital technology and AI, even if those same rights were industry specific rights. The concept of "digital human rights" highlights that human rights are universal whether in online or offline realms and requires the establishment of new norms and regulations that recognize and address the unique impacts of AI. These regulations may include establishing international standards for ethical AI, specifying the requirements and responsibilities for AI developers and deployers, providing mechanisms for redress for harms caused by AI, adopting a human-centered approach that prioritizes well-being over technology alone, and establishing a robust legal and ethical framework that positively shapes the development of AI while protecting and promoting human flourishing. It is necessary to create coherent legal and ethical guardrails, whereby AI serves as a tool and resource for human flourishing and progress, rather than a challenge for fundamental freedoms.

POLICIES, GOVERNANCE, AND ETHICAL AI FOR INCLUSION

The previous subchapters have brought into focus the deep relationships between digital inclusion, sustainable development, and human rights, what is possible with technology, for example, and the challenges of digital exclusion and Artificial Intelligence's ethical dilemmas. This subchapter moves away from diagnosis to a more prescriptive format; that is, it outlines the full range of strategies needed to close those gaps. The suggested need for a multi-faceted approach with aggressive national policies, proactive AI government oversight, multi sector collaborations, and investments in public digital goods and capacity building, all sustainably maintained by adherence to ethical precepts. It's only through a coordinated and coherent approach like this that societies can realize the best potential of digitalization and AI in a way that fosters inclusion and equity for human flourishing.

At the heart of closing the digital divide, there are facets and the execution of National Digital Inclusion Strategies that take a holistic view of digital inclusion, beyond merely getting the internet experience into the homes, but ensuring all citizens can realistically, meaningfully participate in the digital revolution. A national framework should set forth clear policy priorities, including the universal rollout of broadband infrastructure especially to rural and hard to reach areas, affordability initiatives including subsidies for devices and data plans for low-income households. This needs to be accompanied by regulatory efforts that would promote competition and innovation in the telecommunications sector, along with consumer protection, public safety, and service quality, as well as targeted digital literacy and skill training programs, curricula that reflect local demands and languages, as well as targeted approaches that address the barriers experienced by women, older adults, persons with disabilities, and indigenous communities. For it to be truly holistic, a strong commitment of government resources and efforts requires cross-ministerial collaboration and appropriate resource investment to reach the furthest behind first, laying the broad connectivity and capabilities on which all other digital cumulative benefits can be generated (Xue & Pang, 2022).

Along with the inclusion efforts, there is a need to establish national and international policies, laws, and ethical guidelines that promote responsible AI for human rights. This means moving from overarching principles to regulatory practice. National governments need to create laws that consider fundamental issues such as data privacy and protection, algorithmic transparency and accountability, and should prevent algorithmic discrimination and create liability for harm from AI. Global cooperation is essential for aligning these efforts, avoiding regulatory divergence, and addressing the cross-border issues posed by AI development and deployment. This involves supporting global discussions, establishing common standards, and possibly designing international bodies or agreements for the governance of AI.

The goal is to limit the surprises and violations of rights in AI innovation and to ensure that AI systems can be designed, developed, and deployed consistent with universal human rights and the public good rather than in ways that preserve harms and erode fundamental freedoms.

Closing the digital divide and driving ethical governance of AI requires multi-stakeholder approaches in the understanding that many actors need to work together, and no one actor can achieve the complexity of these goals alone. Government must provide strategic direction and oversight within the existing regulatory regimes, and the necessary regulatory and substructure. Business, as largely the innovators and deployers of digital technologies and AI, must behave ethically in its everyday business practices, undertake responsible AI development, invest in inclusive and accessible solutions for all, and participate in initiatives for digital literacy. Civil society has an important role to play both as advocates but more importantly in being key players and designers of algorithmic-human interventions with grassroots marginalized communities. Finally, it is critical that academic partners contribute to research, education, development of ethical frameworks, and technical solutions through coalition-building across disciplinary fields.

Local communities in turn are important partners in providing local context, and in co-creating solutions that are relevant and sustainable in their context. This type of ecosystem fosters shared responsibility, draws on many forms of local expertise, and allows solutions to be collaborative, integrated, inclusive, and flexible in response to emerging challenges.

A key element in creating inclusive digital ecosystems is investing in Digital Public Goods (DPGs) and Open-Source Solutions, that are accessible, interoperable and affordable digital tools and platforms. DPGs are open-source software, open data, open AI models, open standards and open content that comply with privacy and any other applicable laws and best practices. Governments and international organizations can invest in supporting the creation and scaling of DPGs to ensure the essential digital infrastructure and applications are available and affordable to everyone - avoiding proprietary lock-ins and the unintentional loss of digital sovereignty. Open-source solutions allow local developers to adapt and innovate local populations while creating self-reliance and context-specific solutions. This reduces the pathways to entry and the cost of implementation whilst democratizing access to technology and realizing the potential of digital transformation and AI without accumulating the benefits amongst a few players.

Essentially, a sustainable approach to digital inclusion and responsible AI must also envision building sustainable capacity for the age of AI, which, at its core, involves transforming educational models and the teaching of digital competence, lifelong learning and AI-specific skills development for all segments of society. Education institutions will need to embed digital literacy and critical thinking skills in early learning and continue that into further and higher education, and educating citizens to be both users of technologies and informed citizens with the knowledge to appreciate the implications of technology, identify disinformation and ultimately, evaluate their ethical stance on using a technology in a certain way. Lifelong learning will be particularly important for reskilling and upskilling working-age citizens who are already part of the workforce. As the AI economy continues to develop and impact jobs, lifelong learning opportunities must be readily available and broadly used, including vocational training, online learning opportunities and support mechanisms for partnership between industry and academic institutions. Additionally, we must foster and develop targeted, specialized AI skills and competencies to ensure that a diverse talent pool reflective of our society can participate in design, development and deployment of AI. This will help ensure that ethical considerations will be embedded in the design and implementation of AI technologies from the earliest stages of development. A whole-of-society capacity-building approach will ensure that we can equip individuals and society with the skills and competency development needed to embrace the opportunities presented by an increasingly AI-driven world while navigating and managing the challenges (Batool et al, 2025).

RECOMMENDATIONS AND THE PATH FORWARD

After navigating through the complex landscape of digital inclusion, sustainable development and human rights in the age of AI, this book ends with a summary of insights and recommendations for action. The main claim stands: that the inextricable connections between digital inclusion, sustainable development and human rights in the age of AI represents one of the largest challenges and opportunities facing us. The interlinked process of global warming and climate change, environmental degradation, sustained conflict, forced displacement and migration, COVID-19, technologies intended to support remote education, remote working and service delivery, COVID-19 vaccines and medical treatments, and the geopolitics of technology policy and trade all mean achieving the SDGs and achieving and maintaining universal human rights is inherently tied to all individuals having viable and meaningful access and participation in the digital space, and that the significance of meaningful digital inclusion is heightened (Ly et al., 2024). Digital exclusion acts as a brake on the SDGs and augments existing and new violations of human rights, while unbounded developments in AI could exacerbate this. Thus, the case for a principled, ethical, cooperative and multi-level approach to achieving a future where technology works for social needs and humanity is not justified but an absolute necessity. Considering this, several critical implications of this notion of a 'digital inclusion, sustainable development and human rights' framework emerge as a call to action for the global community.

One of the primary calls for action is to prioritize universal, affordable and meaningful connectivity as a key right and objective in both local and national and especially transnational policy and practice. Second, investing in inclusive digital literacy and skills training is critical and will require education systems to be transformed at a global level to provide citizens, of all ages and backgrounds, with the critical thinking and practical skills that enable them to access, use, and ethically engage with digital technologies and AI throughout their lives. This will necessitate the implementation of lifelong learning programs to transition workforces for ever-changing needs. Third, a concerted effort should be made to develop strong, rights-based frameworks for governing AI at both the national and systemic levels. This will include aspirations for comprehensive legal and regulatory structures to protect privacy, safety in terms of data, non-discrimination for algorithmic decision making, and accountability for AI systems. A rights-based framework for governance must be proactive and ensure that technological developments are anticipated, and human oversight is systematically implemented in all uses of AI. Fourth, ethical design and deployment of AI will need to be fully supported and non-negotiable. The design and development of AI must honor its own principles of transparency, fairness, and accountability and a human-centered approach to AI must be considered throughout the entire lifecycle from conception and development to deployment and evaluation, and with systems for independent inspection and redress for harms. Lastly, capacity building and strengthening international cooperation are paramount.

As we move forward, it is imperative that we remain aware of the new challenges that will be presented by sophisticated forms of AI, quantum computing, and other frontier technologies. These new and innovative technologies will create new complexities in privacy, security, labor markets, and governance. Thus, there will be a need for continued foresight, flexibility, and proactive policy adaptation in the face of new technological challenges. The speed of technological change will require us to constantly re-evaluate our ethical norms and human rights protections, to prevent further divides in the future. However, by advocating digital inclusion for all, and by ensuring that AI is developed and deployed ethically and transparently, we can leverage our new technologies to promote sustainable development, and to create a world where technology serves humanity.

REFERENCES

Abdulkareem, H. K. K., Jimoh, S. O., Nofiu, T. T., & Akande, R. S. (2024). Leaving No One Behind: Examining the effect of financial, gender, and digital inclusion on sustainable development. *Sustainable Development*, *33*(2), 2519–2534. DOI: 10.1002/sd.3245

Adetomiwa, F. (2021). Artificial intelligence and human rights. SSRN *Electronic Journal*. https://doi.org/DOI: 10.2139/ssrn.3964199

Ahishakiye, D., & Nizeyimana, P. (2024). Enhancing digital literacy performance in Rwanda using machine learning: A case study of Irembo. *Journal of Intelligent Learning Systems and Applications*, *16*(04), 430–447. DOI: 10.4236/jilsa.2024.164022

Alhassan, M. D., & Adam, I. O. (2024). Digital inclusion and sustainable development goals. *Journal of Science and Technology Policy Management*. https://doi.org/DOI: 10.1108/jstpm-09-2023-0152

Bag, A., Sharma, P., Khare, P., & Roy, S. (2024). Decentralized Data and Privacy: Exploring the Conflict Between Distributed Ledger Technology and the Right to Be Forgotten Under GDP. *IGI Global Scientific Publishing,* 74-104. https://doi.org/DOI: 10.4018/979-8-3693-0472-3.ch006

Batool, A., Zowghi, D., & Bano, M. (2025). AI governance: A systematic literature review. *AI and Ethics*, *5*(3), 3265–3279. DOI: 10.1007/s43681-024-00653-w

Dastyari, A., & Jose, C. (2024). Achieving inclusive and equitable quality education for all: The importance of digital inclusion. *Alternative Law Journal*, *49*(4), 282–287. DOI: 10.1177/1037969x241295798

Dias, S. A. de J., & Sátiro, R. M. (2024). Artificial intelligence in the judiciary: A critical view. *Futures*, *164*, 103493. DOI: 10.1016/j.futures.2024.103493

Djatmiko, G. H., Sinaga, O., & Pawirosumarto, S. (2025). Digital transformation and social inclusion in public services: A qualitative analysis of e-government adoption for marginalized communities in sustainable governance. *Sustainability*, *17*(7), 2908. DOI: 10.3390/su17072908

Hariyani, D., Hariyani, P., & Mishra, S. (2025). Digital technologies for the Sustainable Development Goals. *Green Technologies and Sustainability*, *3*(3), 100202. DOI: 10.1016/j.grets.2025.100202

Ho, T. L., Ngoc, L. H., & Ho, T. H. (2025). Digital inclusion or exclusion? Exploring the moderating role of governance in digitalization's impact on income inequality in developing countries. *Research in Globalization, 10*, 100283. DOI: 10.1016/j.resglo.2025.100283

Indar, I. N., Razi, D. F., Atmansyah, L., Yani, A. A., & Ismail, N. (2024). Digital transformation of public services: An analysis of the effectiveness of online services at the local government level. *Journal of Digital Sociohumanities, 1*(2), 92–101. DOI: 10.25077/jds.1.2.92-101.2024

Khare, P. (2025). Investigating the Influence of AI in Social Media Governance. *IGI Global Scientific Publishing*, 365-388. https://doi.org/DOI: 10.4018/979-8-3693-9904-0.ch015

Khare, P. & Raghuwanshi, V. (2025). Navigating Emerging AI Technologies and Future Trends in Cybersecurity and Forensics. *IGI Global Scientific Publishing*, 321-346. https://doi.org/DOI: 10.4018/979-8-3373-0857-9.ch012

Khare, P. & Raghuwanshi, V. (2025). Legal Frameworks Surrounding the Use of AI in Online Content Moderation. *IGI Global Scientific Publishing*, 235-260. https://doi.org/DOI: 10.4018/979-8-3693-9904-0.ch011

Lee, C.-C., Lou, R., & Wang, F. (2023). Digital financial inclusion and poverty alleviation: Evidence from the sustainable development of China. *Economic Analysis and Policy, 77*, 418–434. DOI: 10.1016/j.eap.2022.12.004

Liu, H., Zhou, Q., & Liang, S. (2025). Digital inclusion in public services for vulnerable groups: A systematic review for research themes and goal-action framework from the lens of public service ecosystem theory. *Government Information Quarterly, 42*(2), 102019. DOI: 10.1016/j.giq.2025.102019

Lütz, F. (2024). The AI Act, gender equality and non-discrimination: What role for the AI office? *ERA Forum, 25*(1), 79–95. https://doi.org/DOI: 10.1007/s12027-024-00785-w

Ly, B., Dem, T., Ly, R., Sorn, S., & Doeur, B. (2024). Exploring the nexus of digital inclusion and environmental sustainability: Insights from Cambodia. *Information Technology for Development, 31*(1), 77–94. DOI: 10.1080/02681102.2024.2345381

Martin, K. D., & Zimmermann, J. (2024). Artificial intelligence and its implications for data privacy. *Current Opinion in Psychology, 58*, 101829. DOI: 10.1016/j.copsyc.2024.101829 PMID: 38954851

Mohan, R., Saleem, F., Voderhobli, K., & Sheikh-Akbari, A. (2024). Ensuring sustainable digital inclusion among the elderly: A comprehensive analysis. *Sustainability*, *16*(17), 7485. DOI: 10.3390/su16177485

Nguyen, A. (2020). Digital inclusion: Social Inclusion in the Digital Age. *Springer International Publishing*, 1-15. https://doi.org/DOI: 10.1007/978-3-030-48277-0_14-1

Ochoa-Dąderska, R., Ochoa-Dąderska, G., García, S., Callarisa-Fiol, L., Navikiene, Z., Demirci, M., Niemczyk, A., Gródek-Szostak, Z., Gasińska-Bańka, K., & Siguencia, O. (2024). Digital Inclusion To Improve People's Lives and Promote Sustainable Development: DigIN report III. *Zenodo*. https://zenodo.org/doi/10.5281/zenodo.10676614

Ozturk, I., Alqassimi, O., & Ullah, S. (2024). Digitalization and SMEs development in the context of sustainable development: A China perspective. *Heliyon*, *10*(6), e27936. DOI: 10.1016/j.heliyon.2024.e27936 PMID: 38510016

Pérez-Escolar, M., & Canet, F. (2022). Research on vulnerable people and digital inclusion: Toward a consolidated taxonomical framework. *Universal Access in the Information Society*, *22*(3), 1059–1072. DOI: 10.1007/s10209-022-00867-x PMID: 35125988

Reed, A., & Thompson, K. (2021). Never waste a crisis: Digital inclusion for sustainable development in the context of the COVID pandemic. *Library Journal*, *40*(2), 14–16. DOI: 10.13663/j.cnki.lj.2021.02.001

Rodrigues, R. (2020). Legal and human rights issues of AI: Gaps, challenges and vulnerabilities. *Journal of Responsible Technology*, *4*, 100005. DOI: 10.1016/j.jrt.2020.100005

Selçuk, S., Kurt Konca, N., & Kaya, S. (2025). AI-driven civil litigation: Navigating the right to a fair trial. *Computer Law &amp. Secourisme - Revue*, *57*, 106136. DOI: 10.1016/j.clsr.2025.106136

Sindakis, S., & Showkat, G. (2024). The digital revolution in India: Bridging the gap in rural technology adoption. *Journal of Innovation and Entrepreneurship*, *13*(1). Advance online publication. DOI: 10.1186/s13731-024-00380-w

Srinivasan, M., Mathew, G., Mathew, N., Kumar, M., Goyal, N., & Kamath, M. S. (2024). Technologies that empower women for better access to healthcare in India – A scoping review. *Global Public Health: An International Journal for Research, Policy and Practice*, *19*(1). Advance online publication. DOI: 10.1080/17441692.2024.2318240 PMID: 38373725

Temperman, J., & Quintavalla, A. (2023). *Artificial intelligence and human rights*. Oxford University Press., DOI: 10.1093/law/9780192882486.001.0001

Teo, S. A. (2024). Artificial intelligence and its 'slow violence' to human rights. *AI and Ethics*, *5*(3), 2265–2280. DOI: 10.1007/s43681-024-00547-x

Vicente, P. N. (2024). Artificial intelligence and freedom of speech. *European Journal of Communication*, *39*(2), 197–200. DOI: 10.1177/02673231241234766

Xie, Y., Fadahunsi, K. P., Kelleher, C., Tarn, D., Grace, A., & O' Donoghue, J. (2025). Towards an inclusive digital health ecosystem. *Bulletin of the World Health Organization*, *103*(02), 170–173. DOI: 10.2471/blt.24.292020 PMID: 39882496

Xue, L., & Pang, Z. (2022). Ethical governance of artificial intelligence: An integrated analytical framework. *Journal of Digital Economy*, *1*(1), 44–52. DOI: 10.1016/j.jdec.2022.08.003

Chapter 4
Digital Media and Disinformation in Postcolonial Africa: Human Rights Implications

Wafaa Taleb
https://orcid.org/0000-0003-0975-2543
University of Oran 2 Mohamed Ben Ahmed, Oran, Algeria

ABSTRACT

This paper examines the complex relationship between digital media, disinformation, and human rights in postcolonial Africa. It highlights disinformation as a significant threat to civic space, democracy, health, and information rights. Through diverse case studies from the continent—covering political campaigns, public health crises, and social movements—it identifies patterns in the use and spread of disinformation via mobile technologies and social media. These practices deepen existing inequalities, erode public trust, and marginalize vulnerable voices. The analysis contextualizes the issue within historical and postcolonial frameworks, exploring African states' regulatory responses and the role of civil society organizations. The study concludes with recommendations for rights-based governance in digital environments, stressing the need for digital literacy, policy reforms, and transnational cooperation to combat disinformation and protect human rights in the digital era.

INTRODUCTION

Pierre Omidyar, founder of eBay, once reflected on the promise and pitfalls of the World Wide Web. At its birth, the web was celebrated as a tool to reduce

DOI: 10.4018/979-8-3373-3685-5.ch004

information poverty and inequality, but over time it became, in Omidyar's words, a "spawning ground" for misinformation, hate, and harmful content. He observed that while the open web brought undeniable benefits, it also gave unprecedented reach to purveyors of falsehoods and divisive rhetoric.

This global trajectory resonates strongly in postcolonial Africa. The continent's digital transformation has been shaped by both optimism and trepidation. On one hand, information technologies promised emancipation—tools for whistle-blowing, cyber-dissidence, and democratized access. On the other, they reproduced older inequalities and colonial hierarchies through opaque "black box" algorithms and the commercialization of data.

Personal and professional experiences across the continent reflect this ambivalence: internet politics often appear as fragmented "galaxies of understanding," where the promise of free information collides with the realities of surveillance, shutdowns, and control. The initial dream of liberty gave way to new struggles over regulation, censorship, and scapegoating. In recent years, these tensions have manifested in very tangible ways: racialized policing of digital spaces, internet shutdowns during crises, and mass arrests linked to online dissent in multiple African states.

This chapter asks the following questions: how does digital disinformation in Africa impact human rights, and what regulatory, societal, and transnational responses can address it? To answer this question, the analysis proceeds in six steps. It first surveys the rise of digital media across Africa and the implications of unequal access to technology. It then defines and conceptualizes disinformation, before examining its mechanisms of spread and specific African case studies in public health, elections, and conflict. Building on this, the chapter evaluates how disinformation interacts with human rights, assesses national and regional regulatory responses, and situates African developments within international perspectives. The conclusion synthesizes findings and proposes policy-oriented recommendations. This structure ensures a balance between conceptual clarity, empirical illustration, and normative analysis.

BACKGROUND

Africa is marked by extraordinary diversity—ethnic, linguistic, and cultural—but also by a long history of exploitation. From slavery and settler colonization to structural adjustment programs (SAPs), neoliberal globalization, and the recent "new scramble for Africa," the continent has repeatedly been subjected to external domination and internal struggles for power. These dynamics continue today, often fueled by local elite rivalries and external economic interests.

Among these historical forces, neocolonialism remains the most significant. Combined with the quest for self-definition and competing elite agendas, it has generated recurring conflicts within and between states (Obijiofor, 2009). Another striking feature is the coexistence of different temporalities—premodern oral traditions, modern nation-states and print culture, and postmodern digital networks. This overlapping of historical layers produces profound consequences for how media and information are created, circulated, and understood both within Africa and by the global community (van Stam, 2021).

Digital information and communication technologies (ICTs) exemplify these contradictions. On one hand, they hold emancipatory potential, offering tools for what some call a "second independence struggle" against information neocolonialism and digital imperialism. On the other, they exacerbate inequalities: widening the digital divide, amplifying fragmentation, and enabling new forms of manipulation and exclusion. These legacies and technologies interact in complex ways. The enduring divisions created by colonial and postcolonial histories feed into today's digital asymmetries, while global platforms reinforce Africa's marginal position in the digital economy. The result is a layered dynamic where opportunity and exploitation coexist, and where digital technologies play a mediating role in both liberation and control.

Existing scholarship on disinformation and digital politics in Africa highlights both the opportunities and dangers of social media. Studies emphasize how new platforms enable civic participation but also amplify hate speech, health misinformation, and electoral manipulation (Bunce, 2019; Stewart et al., 2022). However, much of the research remains fragmented, often focusing on single cases or narrow contexts, with limited cross-regional triangulation (Dobber, Metoui, Trilling, Helberger, & de Vreese, 2021; ARTICLE 19, 2022). Comparative work is more developed for Asia and Latin America than for Africa, and discussions often remain descriptive rather than analytical. This chapter therefore addresses a gap by bringing together diverse African cases, situating them in postcolonial debates on media and power, and linking them to global discourses on digital governance and human rights.

Digital inequality continues to shape the African digital landscape. While smartphone penetration and internet access have increased dramatically over the past decade, significant disparities remain between urban and rural populations, and between younger, digitally literate groups and older generations (International Telecommunication Union [ITU], 2022). Recent GSMA reports show that by 2022, only 28% of sub-Saharan Africans were using mobile internet, compared to a global average of 55% (GSMA, 2022). Such gaps create fertile ground for misinformation, as uneven access to reliable news sources intersects with low levels of media literacy. The digital divide is not only technological but also linguistic: content moderation in African languages is often minimal, leaving large sections of the population exposed to harmful narratives (ARTICLE 19, 2022; Mozilla Foundation, 2021). Addressing these inequalities requires not just infrastructure development but also targeted investment in education and localized platform governance. This broader context underscores why disinformation in Africa cannot be understood only as a technological problem but as a manifestation of persistent socio-economic and historical inequities.

THE RISE OF DIGITAL MEDIA

Over the past decade, Africa has witnessed a rapid rise in mobile phone ownership and internet access. While only 24% of African households had internet access in 2014—compared to a global average of 25%—growth rates in many countries have been remarkable. For instance, Uganda recorded an additional 1.15 million broadband subscribers between 2010 and 2013, with overall data traffic increasing by 90% during that period. Mobile technologies and the internet have improved how information is gathered, shared, and stored, while also reshaping interactions between leaders and citizens. These tools have expanded opportunities for openness, accountability, and participation in governance and politics (Chibita, 2016).

Digital media has also challenged the exclusivity of traditional media. What was once the domain of elites and state broadcasters has become more accessible to ordinary citizens, who now mobilize and engage in public discourse on issues of democracy and development. The democratizing effect of these tools has been celebrated in much of the literature, often described within the paradigm of technological determinism.

Yet, the optimism surrounding digital technologies has at times been exaggerated. The internet and satellite communication are often portrayed as inherently liberating, with their capacity to store and disseminate information cheaply and efficiently hailed as the "end of gatekeepers." By enabling direct dialogue between populations and political leaders, they are believed to foster greater accountability and citizen oversight. However, this enthusiasm risks overlooking the persistent limitations and risks of digital media.

In reality, digital technologies are not a panacea for the political and social challenges facing Africa. They operate within—and are constrained by—the continent's broader economic and political realities. Weak infrastructure, entrenched inequalities, and restrictive state practices mean that the promises of new technologies are unevenly realized. Thus, while mobile phones and the internet have indeed broadened the scope of participation and communication, their impact must be understood with nuance: as tools that can both empower and marginalize, democratize and divide.

Access to Technology

Access to digital technology in many African countries remains deeply uneven. Telecommunication networks are often of poor quality, which limits reliable phone use. Fees for basic telephone services are high, while broadband access has only recently started to expand (Banisar, 2009). Computer penetration in households is extremely low, and public access to networks is limited. Connectivity is therefore largely tied to geography: large cities provide some access, while small towns and rural areas remain severely underserved.

Educational and generational divides also shape access. Older populations often lack the training or willingness to use digital technologies. Even among young people, many avoid going online due to concerns over privacy, security, and data ownership. Users are often acutely aware that their data may be collected and exploited, reducing their sense of anonymity and trust. This highlights the need for localized, user-friendly approaches to digital literacy and access.

Another overlooked dimension is how imported technologies are adapted—or not—to African contexts. As van Stam (2021) notes, while Western technologies are integrated into local practices, there is little conscious reflection on how these adaptations reshape digital governance. Structural inequalities persist: global technology companies dominate infrastructure, platforms, and data flows, leaving African users with limited influence over governance decisions. For African governments, the challenge is to create contextual governance models based on local expertise and socio-technical realities, rather than importing foreign legal frameworks wholesale.

Social Media Platforms

At the international level, the rise of social media as a dominant information channel has transformed Africa's digital landscape. Platforms such as Facebook, X (formerly Twitter), and TikTok have become central to news consumption, civic debate, and political mobilization across the continent. Their rapid spread—fueled by cheap smartphones and mobile data services—has expanded connections across borders and created new public spheres.

Yet these platforms have also facilitated the viral spread of misinformation and disinformation. Governments often respond by imposing restrictions, particularly during unrest or election periods, framing such measures as necessary for security but frequently using them to curb dissent. Meanwhile, the growing intrusion of large technology corporations into daily life has raised new concerns about sovereignty, accountability, and the long-term impacts on democratic governance.

Importantly, global platforms exert immense influence in African information ecosystems without investing sufficiently in safeguards. During the Tigray conflict in Ethiopia, Meta's algorithm amplified inflammatory content, while inadequate moderation in local languages allowed hate speech to proliferate (Amnesty International, 2023; Scott, 2023). Studies also show that more than 87% of Facebook's misinformation moderation budget has historically been allocated to the United States and Canada, leaving African markets severely under-resourced (Milmo, 2023).

Comparative research has shown that platform governance in the Global South frequently suffers from limited investment in content moderation, particularly in local languages, and insufficient transparency regarding algorithms (ARTICLE 19, 2022; Mozilla Foundation, 2021). Reports by organizations such as CIPESA (2021) and Human Rights Watch (2022) further demonstrate that African users are disproportionately vulnerable to harmful content because of gaps in moderation capacity. These findings align with Amnesty International's (2023) critique that platforms allocate most of their resources to Western markets, leaving African contexts under-protected. Triangulating these perspectives underscores the structural imbalances shaping Africa's digital information environment.

This imbalance highlights a structural vulnerability: Africans rely heavily on global platforms for information, yet receive minimal localized oversight. The result is an information ecosystem where harmful content circulates widely, civic spaces are fragile, and both state actors and platform algorithms can manipulate public discourse.

UNDERSTANDING DISINFORMATION

Disinformation refers to false or misleading content that is created and disseminated with the intent to deceive, while misinformation denotes inaccurate content shared without deceptive intent (Fallis, 2015). In today's digital environment, disinformation has shifted from isolated episodes to a persistent, adaptive threat, especially visible during public health crises, elections, and climate emergencies.

The global "infodemic" around COVID-19 showed how quickly false health claims can spread—from alleged vaccine dangers to pseudoscientific cures. In 2024–2025, these dynamics intensified as narratives increasingly targeted trust in international health bodies, national ministries, and local clinicians. Fueled by fear, uncertainty, and ideological identity, many users circulated unverified posts that reinforced polarized group identities and eroded deference to expertise (Stewart et al., 2022). The result is a fragmented information sphere in which audiences process public health guidance less through scientific literacy and more through political or cultural lenses (Stewart et al., 2022).

Tactically, contemporary disinformation ecosystems combine automation and coordination. Bots amplify misleading material; cross-platform networks flood feeds with emotionally charged frames; and AI-generated media (e.g., deepfakes) further blur the line between fact and fabrication. These practices are especially damaging where institutional trust is fragile and access to reliable information is uneven—conditions common across parts of Sub-Saharan Africa—thereby widening health inequalities and undermining confidence in credible sources.

Beyond public health, coordinated disinformation frequently targets individuals, organizations, and movements. Bunce (2019) documents recurring patterns: (1) fake or inauthentic profiles that repeatedly post false statements to simulate consensus; (2) agenda-setting pushes that inject new, divisive talking points into mainstream discussion; (3) synchronized comment or quote-tweet storms that manufacture the appearance of public outrage; and (4) purpose-built sites or relay networks that launder fabricated material through direct messages and private channels. These tactics often pursue reputational harm—casting a brand, public figure, or civil society actor as untrustworthy or malign—by leveraging fear appeals, sensational language, and selective "evidence" (Bunce, 2019).

In practical terms, then, disinformation is best understood not as isolated falsehoods but as a systemic exploitation of platform mechanics, media incentives, and social trust. Combating it requires a twin track: proportionate regulatory frameworks and platform accountability on one side, and culturally grounded digital literacy on the other that helps communities recognize manipulative narratives, verify claims, and slow the viral spread of harmful content (Fallis, 2015; Bunce, 2019; Stewart et al., 2022).

Mechanisms of Spread

The scale of misinformation on social media is vast, cutting across political, cultural, and ideological divides (Bruns et al., 2022). Health-related misinformation not tied to COVID-19—such as spurious "cures" or denialist claims—spread widely as users shared content uncritically. These dynamics are especially visible in lightly moderated spaces like Facebook groups. Sudan, for example, recorded the world's highest per-capita rate of problematic news sharing in March 2020, reflecting how political conflict and violence intersect with digital misinformation.

Automated methods designed for tightly moderated platforms like Twitter cannot easily be adapted to study Facebook groups because of privacy restrictions. Still, longitudinal analyses of Facebook data during COVID-19 show sharp increases in the circulation of false or misleading claims, sometimes alongside mainstream reporting. Problematic news was cross-shared between countries facing similar political tensions, underscoring how disinformation flows do not respect borders (Stewart et al., 2022).

Africa was particularly visible in the global COVID-19 conversation. Social media became a stage where themes of race, equity, surveillance, and poverty intersected with debates over vaccine access and health governance. Platforms such as Twitter (now X) were flooded with both solidarity messages and damaging falsehoods, making the continent central to global discussions of digital disinformation.

Case Studies of Disinformation in Africa

Disinformation in Africa has had particularly damaging human rights consequences, especially during health crises and elections.

Public Health: COVID-19 misinformation spread rapidly across WhatsApp, Facebook, and Twitter in countries such as South Africa, Uganda, and Nigeria, undermining trust in health authorities and worsening risks to public health (Stewart et al., 2022). The encrypted nature of WhatsApp made tracking and countering false claims especially difficult.

Elections: Election periods have been flashpoints for disinformation. Motivations range from partisan advantage to commercial profiteering (Bunce, 2019). During Nigeria's 2023 elections, AI-generated deepfakes and sponsored posts circulated widely, falsely linking candidates to extremist groups. Despite the efforts of fact-checking organizations such as Dubawa, Africa Check, and FactsMatterNG, the speed and volume of manipulated content often outpaced corrective measures (Ajakaiye, 2024; Ibrahim, 2025).

The Nigerian elections are not the only recent case where disinformation played a pivotal role. Kenya's 2022 general elections also witnessed a flood of manipulated online content. Coordinated campaigns spread false claims about voter fraud and ethnic violence, while deepfakes and doctored images circulated widely on Facebook and TikTok (BBC, 2022). Civil society organizations such as Ushahidi and Africa Check launched rapid-response initiatives, but these efforts were frequently outpaced by the viral speed of misinformation. The Kenyan case highlights how electoral disinformation exploits long-standing ethnic tensions and mistrust of state institutions, echoing similar vulnerabilities observed in Nigeria (Ibrahim, 2025). Together, these examples demonstrate that electoral periods in Africa remain highly susceptible to digital manipulation, with serious implications for democratic legitimacy and human rights.

Conflict: In Ethiopia's Tigray conflict (2020–2022), Facebook's algorithms amplified hate speech in Amharic and Tigrinya, contributing to violence and deepening ethnic divides (Council on Foreign Relations, 2022). A 2025 Kenyan High Court ruling allowed a lawsuit against Meta to proceed, holding the company potentially accountable for its failure to prevent algorithmic amplification of harmful content (Meta Lawsuit Ruling, 2025; Reuters, 2025).

Together, these cases highlight both the regional diversity of disinformation and its consistent role in eroding trust, undermining rights, and fueling instability.

Political Campaigns

Social media has become central to political campaigning in Africa, often echoing global populist strategies. Political figures have harnessed digital platforms to spread polarizing narratives, including ethno-nationalist and anti-immigrant rhetoric. These dynamics raise urgent concerns about the weaponization of digital platforms (Ekwueme & Folarin, 2017).

Nigeria's 2015 presidential elections marked a turning point: the All Progressives Congress (APC) exploited viral campaigning to spread unprecedented levels of disinformation targeting the incumbent Jonathan administration. False memes, doctored images, and hostile narratives circulated widely, reshaping voter perceptions and highlighting the fragility of fact-checking infrastructures at the time.

Public Health Crises

During the first months of the COVID-19 pandemic (March–April 2020), social media platforms across Africa became central to how misinformation was both spread and contested. WhatsApp in particular emerged as a key channel for health-related claims, with users posting responses that attempted to challenge misinformation. Yet, many of these counter-responses were themselves inconsistent, poorly worded, or based on incomplete knowledge. Some even reinforced existing falsehoods by circulating screenshots of other misleading claims. This illustrates the complexity of misinformation ecosystems, where corrective content can paradoxically perpetuate the very problems it seeks to solve (Stewart et al., 2022).

Globally, public health misinformation has grown into a critical concern. In the early stages of COVID-19, misleading narratives fueled panic buying, misuse of chemicals, and even spikes in domestic abuse, while undermining public health campaigns. Authorities and platforms sought to intervene through fact-checking campaigns, awareness drives, and removal of harmful content. At the same time, users themselves actively responded by debunking falsehoods or sharing corrective material. Analyzing these user-generated interventions highlights the importance of reframing public health debates and filling gaps in how misinformation research accounts for real-world community responses.

Drawing on framing theory, it becomes clear that countering misinformation requires more than correcting falsehoods. It involves studying the contexts in which claims are shared, the ways they are framed, and how those frames shape public understanding. Because these debates occur in public forums, framing choices influence both the trajectory of the controversy and its wider social consequences. This perspective creates opportunities for policymakers and communicators to frame health information in ways that build trust, strengthen resilience, and promote accurate knowledge.

Social Movements

Uganda's 2001 presidential elections did not unfold in a fully democratic environment, but they revealed the growing role of digital communication in political life. Citizens, frustrated with corruption and lack of fairness, turned to instant messaging and mobile networks to share election results as they emerged. While official tallies declared President Yoweri Museveni the victor with 81 percent of the vote, opposition candidate Kizza Besigye was reported by citizens to have secured more support in many polling centers. The use of mobile networks to share results in real time marked a new development in Ugandan political history (Chibita, 2016).

This moment reflected the broader social impact of Africa's late entry into cyberspace. The spread of affordable mobile phones, SMS technology, and phone credit systems allowed civil society and opposition groups to bypass mainstream media restrictions. Digital activism became part of the activist toolkit, even if its use was initially more impulsive than strategic. These tools enabled public journalism, collective organization, and grassroots mobilization during periods of media repression.

Yet, activism remains constrained by state power. Governments have continued to wield laws, regulatory frameworks, and extra-judicial measures to limit dissent. Over the past two decades, authorities in Uganda and elsewhere have demonstrated their capacity to suppress activism, whether through surveillance, arrests, or internet shutdowns. This reality shapes the risks that ordinary citizens are willing to take in the name of digital activism. While digital technologies have expanded civic space, their transformative potential remains dependent on political structures that still favor state control.

HUMAN RIGHTS FRAMEWORK

The human rights situation in Africa, like elsewhere, is a matter of international concern. Yet it is often framed differently in global discourse, with Africa positioned as the "Other" in the human rights regime. The prevailing emphasis is on violations: declining democracy, the persistence of "big-man" politics, and the curtailment of freedoms (Thoba, 2017). While the right to free speech is widely recognized, the key question is how states undermine this right in the evolving social media environment.

Disinformation and hate speech have become pressing challenges across the continent. Although these problems are global, in Africa they intersect with older grievances—race, inequality, and propaganda—that stem from colonial and post-colonial histories. Hate speech, understood as anti-democratic language targeting groups based on race, ethnicity, nationality, religion, or gender, resurfaces in these digital spaces. International human rights law prohibits hate speech while still protecting democratic debate, a balance that becomes especially critical when emerging media reshape postcolonial tensions.

The colonial legacy shaped African media into instruments for mobilizing collective action through speeches, newspapers, radio, and film. Today, social media extends this role by enabling new forms of collective action—often more explosive, less controlled, and harder for governments to contain. Unlike conventional media, digital platforms amplify anger and fear rapidly, sometimes provoking public unrest. Policymakers' early responses—banning platforms, scapegoating dissenters, or empowering state-run media—have deepened this dilemma.

This struggle has created what many describe as a battlefield between the state and social media platforms. Editorial power remains concentrated in Western companies, leaving African actors with limited influence over policies that affect their societies. Social media corporations, often criticized for their reluctance to invest in media literacy or content moderation tailored to African contexts, reinforce these inequalities. Meanwhile, governments exploit censorship to silence opposition, and commentators warn that such measures only fuel grievances rather than resolve them.

The result is a polarized environment where civil society and human rights advocates are divided along ideological lines, echoing broader global fractures between liberal and conservative camps. This tension underscores the urgent need for approaches that safeguard human rights, promote digital literacy, and ensure that regulation does not become a cover for repression.

Right to Information

Access to information is recognized worldwide as a fundamental human right. This principle was formally established in Article 19 of the Universal Declaration of Human Rights (1948), which states that everyone has the right to freedom of opinion and expression, including the right to seek, receive, and impart information through any media. Building on this foundation, many international agreements and national constitutions have affirmed the "right to know." To date, at least eighteen

African countries have adopted constitutional provisions guaranteeing citizens access to public information.

National Access to Information (ATI) laws usually share common elements. They give individuals and organizations the right to request information from public bodies, impose a duty on those bodies to respond, and allow exemptions only in narrowly defined cases. Most ATI laws also establish internal appeals processes and external review mechanisms to ensure accountability. These laws apply broadly to public institutions, including the legislature, executive, local governments, semi-autonomous agencies, parastatals, and state-owned companies. The intention is that such provisions be written clearly, avoiding legal jargon, so that citizens can use them effectively.

Freedom of Expression

Freedom of expression is equally recognized as a cornerstone of democratic society. Article 19 of the Universal Declaration of Human Rights (1948) also guarantees the right to hold opinions without interference and to seek, receive, and impart information and ideas across frontiers. Similar protections appear in regional frameworks such as the African Charter on Human and Peoples' Rights, the European Convention on Human Rights, and the American Convention on Human Rights. The African Charter explicitly affirms that every individual has the right to receive information and to express and disseminate opinions within the law.

These rights enable individuals and societies to flourish, but they also carry responsibilities. Governments—both democratic and authoritarian—often attempt to restrict freedom of expression by passing repressive laws, intimidating journalists, or suppressing dissent. Importantly, freedom of expression is not absolute: it must be balanced against the rights of others. International human rights law makes clear that restrictions must be lawful, proportionate, and necessary in a democratic society. This balance is particularly important in contexts of disinformation and hate speech, where regulating harmful content should not become an excuse to silence legitimate criticism or minority viewpoints (Banisar, 2009).

IMPACT OF DISINFORMATION ON HUMAN RIGHTS

Social media has become an integral part of people's lives. Many African people get their news from social media platforms like Facebook and Twitter (Stewart et al., 2022). However, digital media's widespread dissemination of information has come with an accelerated increase in disinformation. Disinformation is often deliberate and well-funded in much of the Global South, especially Africa. This is done by actors who are - or work on behalf of adversarial governments within or outside Africa, criminal organizations, and those seeking to undermine social, political, and/or economic systems. As these actors become better equipped, actors committed to upholding democratic norms struggle to combat endemic disinformation campaigns. Unfortunately, this reality comes alongside a lack of adequate policy on the continent to tackle systemic disinformation problems.

As early as 2021, at the peak of COVID-19 lockdowns, social media was driven by disinformation issues. For example, the government imposed a lockdown in Uganda amid increasing COVID-19 cases. A few days later, disinformation began circulating that revealed COVID-19's link to the Covidex herbal remedy, although health organizations denied the association. Days later, a video with false claims about the implications of the vaccine circulated, prompting a national investigation led by politically controlled institutions. Similarly, in Nigeria, during the COVID-19 lockdown, a video of a COVID-19 patient allegedly cured of COVID-19 was spread during COVID-19.

For years, governments and other institutions have been battling misinformation and disinformation. In South Africa, the government fought to stem the tide of excessive fake news that clouded judgment amid an already unpredictable COVID-19 pandemic. Fortunately, citizens' technical literacy became a weapon against disinformation for governments and state health institutions battling misinformation and Disinformation in Nigeria, Uganda, and Tanzania (Bunce, 2019).

Erosion of Trust

Governments across Africa have sought to undermine digital media and information environments. One mechanism for this is the mass detainment of journalists and media personnel in countries like Ethiopia, Tanzania, and Zimbabwe. The media persona of mainstream news outlets has become threatened by new forms of media. However, another slippery slope of eroding democracy in African contexts outside of mass detainment is the hegemonic role of social media in public digital spaces. In this context, the myriad advantages of social media use at the onset of the Arab Spring have given way to disillusionment with its role in mediating politics and public life (Moreno-Almeida & Banaji, 2019). In Africa, this mirrored a widespread fear of social media as "dark" or "toxic" in the aftermath of political violence in the #feesmustfall protests in South Africa and the social media-facilitated xenophobic attacks in South Africa. Crucial to understand in this shifting atmosphere of opinion and struggle over the role of social media today is its effect on the level of trust among communities.

Trust in the media is a vital underpinning of a strong civil society and democratic governance. A generalized trust and belief in shared values are essential for a functional society. However, the political order faces instability once this trust is eroded at key institutions that underpin public life. Such demands of institutional trust need to be negotiated by citizens and states, which are undermined by social media and other reasons, offering insights into the continuing work of disinformation in destroying civil life. Initial public optimism, excitement for the role of social media in redrawing and refashioning power, and designing platforms for rights, freedom, and community, have undergone dissipation. At the same time, infectious disinformation could proliferate and metastasize rapidly in collisions of outrage and empathy when mass mobilization was needed most.

Marginalization of Voices

The race put on by the Ethiopian government and its allied forces to take control of the Tigray capital, Mekele, during the assault on Tigray is further scrutinized in a narrative piece. Although Mekele has witnessed an unspeakable catastrophe, the narrative is said to be overly descriptive and lacking context, which is problematic. The article focuses on an interview with the rebel head and a top Tigray government official about the fight. The additional narratives featured are damning testimonies of the Tigray people's war portrayed by journalists for the government's international communication and incursive strategy. The BBC must still do its duty in what has been dubbed the "Cinderella Narrative," even as the stigma surrounding the cultural production of victims and refugees runs rampant (Ogunyemi, 2011).

Pursuing fact and context must be accompanied by another inconclusive option when narrating atrocities believed to be of that nature. Even when the victim might not be present, the horrific vision must be narrated because the absence of stigmatization by the professional disability of the camera-created victims exposes the survivor to an ever-multiplying, endless, and indefinable outside-the-spectator, who wonders about death. Even while the individuals caught in the attack can be abjectly incriminated in a language that denies their legitimacy or accountability in a text, it is impossible to deride what an official representative of the world community, an ambassador, and a former ambassador of a modern power has created and what will still be there tomorrow.

As content from the outside world grows in popularity, the website can maximize proportions by employing headlines, graphics, and cut lines that are more similar to the content itself. It would be tempting to categorize the newly purchased images and content as opinionated headlines. The audience has become accustomed to discerning online images, and opinionated headlines in photographs would more likely believe a photographed event occurred. Nonetheless, the captioned text relies heavily on opinionated headlines that employ classifications not associated with similar graphics. Images representing chaos and fear have the least explicit relation with the classifications.

Threats to Civic Space

Particularly in the past half-decade, civic spaces are becoming increasingly constricted in postcolonial Africa. Large social media companies and some international actors are seen as complicit in this trend as their platforms are used against marginalized communities. Traditional actors in civil society are also perceived to favor mainstream views and be unresponsive to dissident groups. This gives rise to second-class citizenship that marginalizes non-desired voices (Chibita, 2016).

In Uganda, pre-existing issues in civic spaces have worsened as disinformation takes hold. Before disinformation, the regime politicized the social media space and sought to co-opt and control it in various clever and opaque ways. This included acts like transactions that crudely distributed tranches of social media money to a few obedient voices or incentivizing trolling under the guise of defending electricity from hooligans posing as bathers' children on social media. A political ecology of threats to civic space reveals systemic, medium-independent, and long-term struggles for meaning and power.

The symbolic struggle vis-à-vis digital facilities mirrors the struggle over specific frames that govern the mediatization of elections. This transformation gives rise to new material, institutional, and ideological axes of power. Content moderation is seen as a struggle over episteme: who decides meaning? This mirrors the political underpinnings of the media that define and institutionalize specific frames of the debate while excluding others.

There is an analogous struggle over institutional control that also spans the interaction of different actors. The key question here is who controls the means of consultation? As new digital forms of activism and surveillance broach the old-school institutional architectures, and as digital forms of organization become more materialized, there is an array of new opportunities to control the process of politicization and, therefore, the actual debate.

Over the last five years, various institutions—media conglomerates, the police forum, courts—were repurposed to gatekeeping roles in the digital public sphere. Ultimately, there is a sense of distrust concerning the long-term compatibility of these media with public interests. The incongruence of long-term democratic structured mobilization and the short-term de-institutionalized character of how knowledge indeed moves about and is politicized on some platforms is deepening feelings of skepticism concerning the democratic virtues of these platforms used for mobilization.

REGULATORY RESPONSES TO DISINFORMATION

Despite the significant progress made by African states since independence, they remain burdened with structural challenges such as poverty, corruption, and external neo-colonial pressures. These conditions shape their approach to digital governance, where disinformation is often framed primarily as a threat to security and stability. Governments have responded with restrictive measures that, while aiming to curb harmful online content, sometimes risk undermining fundamental rights such as freedom of expression and access to information. Too often, the regulatory debate is couched in abstract or punitive terms, with limited attention to how policies can be implemented in ways that strengthen democratic institutions and civic space.

Regional Policy Frameworks

At the regional level, the African Union's Digital Transformation Strategy (2020–2030) provides a framework for building inclusive and sustainable digital economies. Although its main focus is on infrastructure and connectivity, the strategy highlights information integrity, cybersecurity, and human rights protections as central to Africa's digital future (African Union Commission, 2020). This policy shift demonstrates growing recognition that disinformation undermines not only governance but also economic development and citizen participation.

National Approaches

At the national level, governments have experimented with diverse regulatory strategies, with mixed results:

1. Nigeria has introduced legislation aimed at combating "fake news," particularly during election cycles, with penalties ranging from fines to imprisonment. While these measures show an awareness of the problem, critics argue they are often applied selectively to silence opposition voices (Premium Times, 2021).
2. Uganda implemented a controversial social media tax in 2018, presented as a fiscal measure but widely interpreted as a strategy to suppress online dissent and reduce the circulation of unverified political information. The policy disproportionately affected poorer citizens, reinforcing digital inequality (BBC News, 2018).
3. South Africa adopted targeted measures during the COVID-19 pandemic, criminalizing the spread of misinformation under the Disaster Management Act. Unlike blanket anti–fake news laws, this approach linked regulation to a clear

public interest objective—protecting public health (South African Government, 2020).

Recommendations for Rights-Based Governance

These experiences highlight the persistent tension between protecting public order and safeguarding human rights. Moving forward, three principles should guide regulatory reforms:

1. Balance Regulation with Free Expression. Laws should narrowly target harmful disinformation while avoiding overly broad definitions of "fake news" that could stifle legitimate debate and dissent.
2. Adopt a Rights-Based Approach. All regulatory frameworks should align with African and international human rights instruments, ensuring transparency, accountability, and proportionality in enforcement.
3. Promote Multi-Stakeholder Cooperation. Governments, civil society organizations, journalists, and technology companies should collaborate to improve media literacy, expand fact-checking initiatives, and ensure platform accountability across African languages and contexts.

By grounding regulatory responses in regional strategies, concrete national policies, and rights-based recommendations, African states can move beyond abstract or punitive measures. This approach offers a more sustainable path to tackling disinformation while preserving democratic participation and protecting civic space.

Government Interventions

Beginning with colonial rule, disinformation has become a prominent feature of governance in Africa, to the extent that caution is exercised in several countries against government-directed messaging or action, as they are typically misinterpretations that ride on the back of officials' deepest assumptions, fears, unconscious biases, and prejudices. However, in its contemporary form, the spread of disinformation on social media offers a characteristic form of performance that cuts into the traditions of standing governance. People respond with unfettered emotional intensity as authorities become upset, anxious, angry, or frustrated.

Countries that had never seen themselves in what they looked at on social media rapidly built strong institutions to deal with 'fake news' and used them to stiffen control of information. Some want to be deemed modern, conquering the gap social media supposedly leaves between public engagement and institutional acceptance. The consequences of government action to control social media, while easily dismissed at some level as painfully localist, concern the risks to rights and freedoms elsewhere.

The motivations vary, but self-interest is never far from the foreground (Chibita, 2016). In 2020, stricter laws were put into place on Facebook targeted at Nigerian activists following the EndSARS campaign against police brutality, and subsequently, with law enforcement clamping down on unregistered rallies across West Africa. Forwarding messages and posts to fifteen people at once was banned in South Africa just as COVID-19 came ashore; the public outcry from prison officials that doubled as house arrest from viral COVID-19 messaging there resulted in a clampdown of the same severity and form years later. By contrast, when responded to in Toulouse, social media messaging by the left parties, from congresspersons to the mayor, was spread and amplified, captured, and processed with more information. In Ethiopia, government agents monitoring mobile data surfaced state ignorance as messaging was directed at pre-existing biases of ethnic distrust (Pomeranz & Schwid, 2021).

Role of Civil Society

In Africa, civil society is either underdeveloped or delegated to an applauded network of NGOs that succumb to purveying credence for repressive rulers, to foreign state agencies guiding Africa's media, or revered religious associations whose self-renewal is not sanctioned in secular political arrangements.

Concerning social movement theory, the absence of an internal moral tradition or elite within multicultural societies could account for the prevalence of 'fix' churches, sororities, youth leagues, and re-jigged kinship ties based in crony relations that garnish smiles of a fresh pan-Africanism among the poor.

An ethos of consumption and decorum acutely tends to alter cultures within which free press organizations' agencies, designs, and bylaws flowered with the support of ill-suited delivery models to Western societies. Despite courageous protests by journalists against media repressive laws, this has often led to a ritual condemnation and iterative empowerment of press organs even in countries where no such organs exist. The sheer microscopic penetration of mobile telephony will evidence this poorly tuned delivery to an ecstatic hope amid rampant torture and farcical state functions.

While broadcasting laws in many African countries have become more liberal, media actors remain cautious, knowing that governments can still impose penalties that reshape the landscape overnight. Investigative journalism and reporting on human rights issues, along with much of civil society advocacy now conducted online, often reach only limited audiences. Critical stories may generate a few hundred clicks before fading as new issues dominate attention. This limited visibility stands in stark contrast to the region's more than 200 million mobile subscribers, where messaging apps deliver news but often compete with paywalled outlets that downplay political or social themes.

In this broader picture of civic activism, civil society plays an indispensable role in democratic societies. It is essential for recognizing and enforcing political, civil, economic, social, and cultural rights (Camara, 2008). Yet in Africa, the scope and effectiveness of civil society organizations vary widely. Some countries benefit from decades of NGO experience and advocacy, while others see fragmented or embattled movements that must resist entrenched rulers and external economic pressures.

INTERNATIONAL PERSPECTIVES

This imbalance highlights a structural vulnerability: Africans rely heavily on global platforms for information, yet receive minimal localized oversight. The result is an information ecosystem where harmful content circulates widely, civic spaces are fragile, and both state actors and platform algorithms can manipulate public discourse.

A continued international effort is widely regarded as essential for combating disinformation in Africa, especially on social media. Regional and continental organizations can work together to develop new policy frameworks and strengthen existing ones. The African Union's Digital Transformation Strategy for Africa (2020–2030) emphasizes not only infrastructure and connectivity but also the importance of information integrity, cybersecurity, and human rights protections (African Union Commission, 2020). National stakeholders should also leverage these frameworks and partnerships to share best practices, build capacity, and improve monitoring (Ogunyemi, 2011).

Civil society organizations remain central in addressing the rise of digital misinformation. National and regional NGOs can raise awareness, provide digital literacy training, fact-check campaigns, and advocate for measures that create inclusive digital spaces. Evidence suggests that fact-checking interventions can reduce the spread of false claims and help shift audience beliefs when implemented consistently (Dobber, Metoui, Trilling, Helberger, & de Vreese, 2021). Technology companies also have a key responsibility. Platforms should invest in literacy programs, support independent fact-checking partnerships, and strengthen human moderation of harmful content. However, research shows that existing moderation practices in Africa are often opaque, inconsistently applied, and neglect African languages (ARTICLE 19, 2022). Greater platform transparency is necessary to build trust and enable accountability (Mozilla Foundation, 2021).

The expansion of internet access, smartphones, and social media has brought significant benefits to Africa, from education and cultural expression to diaspora connections and local content creation. UNESCO underscores the importance of media and information literacy as a tool for empowering citizens to navigate these opportunities responsibly (UNESCO, 2021; Wilson, Grizzle, Tuazon, Akyempong, & Cheung, 2011). At the same time, wider connectivity also increases exposure to harmful, hateful, and misleading content. Social media has been deliberately used to promote political agendas, sow distrust, and inflame social divisions.

Disinformation in Africa is not new. Many countries have a long history of state-orchestrated campaigns, which in some cases has made them more resilient. Today, however, geopolitical dynamics are shifting. Brazil, Russia, India, China, and South Africa (BRICS) are increasingly active in information campaigns that the West views as destabilizing. Africa, caught between colonial legacies, climate and trade pressures, and emerging multipolar geopolitics, has become a central arena for these contests. The most effective disinformation often exploits African voices and local grievances, making it difficult to counter. Automated moderation rarely captures these cultural nuances, underscoring the need for culturally grounded human oversight (ARTICLE 19, 2022).

Comparative experiences outside Africa provide important lessons. The European Union's Digital Services Act (DSA), adopted in 2022, introduced binding obligations for large platforms to disclose algorithms, improve transparency in content moderation, and support independent researchers (European Commission, 2022). While African states lack the regulatory capacity of the EU, such initiatives point to the value of coordinated, rights-based governance frameworks. Conversely, in the absence of strong regulation, countries like Brazil and India have faced recurring cycles of disinformation-fueled unrest (Banaji & Bhat, 2022). For Africa, the challenge lies in adapting lessons from these international models without replicating overly restrictive measures that could be weaponized against free expression. This comparative angle reinforces the need for the African Union to strengthen its own frameworks while demanding greater accountability from global platforms.

Opportunities and Risks of Connectivity

Expanding internet access, smartphones, and social media has brought major benefits to Africa, from education and cultural expression to diaspora connections and content creation. UNESCO highlights the importance of media and information literacy as a tool for empowering citizens to navigate these opportunities responsibly (UNESCO, 2021; Wilson, Grizzle, Tuazon, Akyempong, & Cheung, 2011). Yet, connectivity also increases exposure to harmful, hateful, and misleading content.

Social media has been deliberately used to promote political agendas, sow distrust, and inflame social divisions.

Disinformation in Africa is not new. Many countries have long histories of state-orchestrated campaigns, which in some cases have made them more resilient. Today, however, geopolitical dynamics are shifting. Brazil, Russia, India, China, and South Africa (BRICS) are increasingly active in information campaigns that the West views as destabilizing. Africa, caught between colonial legacies, climate and trade pressures, and emerging multipolar geopolitics, has become a central arena for these contests. The most effective disinformation often exploits African voices and local grievances, making it difficult to counter. Automated moderation rarely captures these cultural nuances, underscoring the need for culturally grounded human oversight (ARTICLE 19, 2022).

Global Disinformation Trends

Internationally, disinformation presents varied challenges, and our understanding of its impact and implications is still developing. Nevertheless, a few trends are emerging regarding commonalities and differences in approaches among countries to disinformation. Broader trends relating to the type and expansion of Disinformation in Postcolonial Africa, types of actors involved in spreading disinformation, impacts of disinformation, and existing initiatives and mechanisms to counter disinformation are explored.

Misinformation and disinformation are fast becoming a global problem affecting both traditional and social media platforms. Although technology is neither good nor bad, its use depends on individuals, groups, or nations and their moral decision-making. However, with the evolution of whistle-blowing applications, Russia is purported to have developed the KN 'truth-detecting' software, which would cast doubt on any information that did not align with state narratives. Social networking apps are so entrenched in everyday life that a new 'chore' is to check social media for memes celebrating defeat or misleading government press releases every morning. Chief amongst such silencing tactics in the digital age is stealth-blocking.

The rise of disinformation has coincided with rapid technological development, particularly in new communication forms, including broadcasting, social media, and web-based services. Communication technologies and their innovative use in the past decades have rendered the world a global village, characterized by virtual interconnectedness. Information that was received in hours past can now be transmitted in microseconds. The ever-expanding digital media space, tools, and network, previously heralded as a crucial enabler of democracy, freedom of expression, and the right to information, have become a source of conflict, threats to information integrity, and contestation of knowledge (Bunce, 2019). Disinformation can threaten national and global security, peace, and cooperation.

The growing use and prevalence of misinformation and disinformation in the digital public sphere of Postcolonial Africa are worrying. Information is a crucial commodity in this age of globalization and digitalization, akin to power and wealth, both in public health and general governance. The spread of misinformation, disinformation, and 'malinformation', a type of information primarily with malign intent but not false, has severe implications for the right to access information underpinned by media freedom, human security, and healthier public as able digital citizens (Stewart et al., 2022).

Comparative Analysis with Other Regions

Discussions on disinformation in Africa should be anchored in postcolonial theory, decolonizing scholarship, and critiques of Eurocentrism. These lenses help emphasize the importance of digital literacy, media integrity, accountability, and transparency, tailoring strategies to regional histories and politics. To illuminate these distinct challenges, it's useful to compare Africa's experience with other postcolonial societies such as British India and the Caribbean.

Global debates on disinformation—often developed in advanced democracies—tend to overlook the layered dynamics of postcolonial societies, including historical inequalities and cultural power imbalances. This oversight limits the applicability of such frameworks elsewhere. Through comparative analysis, we can uncover how disinformation circulates differently in these contexts, and why solutions must be designed with local inequities and democratic sensitivities in mind.

For instance, research on misinformation in India shows how WhatsApp and other platforms become conduits for fake images and politically motivated messages, often spreading during high-stakes events like elections (Garimella & Eckles, 2020). These patterns reflect how legacies of social stratification shape digital landscapes. In the Caribbean, collaborative media literacy efforts are being piloted, such as developing regional codes of practice and promoting journalist training to counteract digital misinformation (Public Media Alliance, 2022).

By drawing on parallels across postcolonial contexts, African scholars and practitioners can better understand how misinformation intertwines with cultural, historical, and institutional forces. This comparative approach enables the crafting of interventions that are not only technically sound but culturally and historically informed—offering more effective pathways toward resisting disinformation and reinforcing democratic resilience.

FUTURE DIRECTIONS

The rapid expansion of digital media technologies in Africa has reshaped public discourse, enabling new forms of access to information and amplifying diverse voices. Yet, this transformation has also heightened risks: the same platforms that democratize communication are also conduits for disinformation, hate speech, and coordinated manipulation (Stewart et al., 2022). Advances in telecommunications infrastructure, deregulated markets, and affordable smartphones have fueled this surge, bringing millions of new users online in less than a decade (Mujokoro, 2017).

As Nigeria's upcoming elections illustrate, disinformation is likely to remain one of the most persistent threats to democratic processes. Many governments have responded with restrictions on public assemblies or punitive laws against so-called "fake news." While these measures may appear protective, they often reduce civic engagement and undermine trust by limiting open debate (ARTICLE 19, 2022).

Looking forward, research must provide both critical analysis and actionable strategies. One priority is to amplify alternative, culturally grounded models of digital democracy, including the use of African languages such as Swahili and Yoruba in online deliberation. UNESCO (2021) stresses that media and information literacy must be embedded in schools and community programs to build resilience against harmful content. Another priority is to address the biases embedded in platform algorithms, which are often trained on non-African datasets, reinforcing structural inequities (Mozilla Foundation, 2021). Decolonizing digital design—through African-led research, open data initiatives, and community-driven platforms—can provide a path to reclaim agency and ensure representation in global digital spaces.

Finally, African scholars and civil society actors should assert leadership in shaping digital futures. Building advocacy and policy portfolios at the intersection of human rights, digital governance, and development is vital. This requires cooperation among governments, civil society, and regional institutions such as the African Union, which has recognized disinformation as a barrier to inclusive development in its Digital Transformation Strategy 2020–2030 (African Union Commission, 2020). By grounding interventions in a rights-based approach, Africa can transform digital spaces into arenas of empowerment, rather than manipulation, ensuring that the future of digital democracy strengthens rather than undermines human rights.

Technological Innovations

echnological innovations—particularly in mobile applications and internet access—continue to reshape communication across the globe. Sub-Saharan Africa accounts for around 10% of internet users but still ranks lowest worldwide in penetration. Despite this, each new digital development has had a visible impact on the region. The convergence of communication and computer technologies has transformed how media content is produced, circulated, and consumed. African media often repackage and reinterpret international events for local audiences, blending global narratives with regional contexts.

Platforms like Facebook have become widely used sources of international news, serving not only as information channels but also as spaces for commentary and critique. Studies suggest that digitally authored events on social platforms are frequently reframed and critiqued in traditional outlets such as print and broadcast media (Batta et al., 2015). This demonstrates how innovations in connectivity can broaden political debate, but they also create new challenges. The sheer volume of unfiltered, heterogeneous content—ranging from valuable insights to harmful misinformation—poses risks for both users and journalists (Van Stam, 2021). Messaging applications in particular accelerate the spread of information, yet they also heighten the dangers of unchecked disinformation.

Dissemination patterns further complicate the media landscape. In many cases, print outlets still report stories before broadcast media, while national dailies increasingly rely on information first circulated on social platforms. This interplay underscores how new media can set the agenda even for traditional outlets. Ultimately, digital social networks depend heavily on mobile phone penetration, making access and affordability decisive factors in shaping who gets to participate in these new public spheres.

Policy Recommendations

To strengthen Africa's digital ecosystem and mitigate risks, several measures are needed (Stewart et al., 2022; Renda, 2018):

1. Platform accountability and transparency. Leaders of major social platforms should publicly disclose their content moderation practices, ensuring they are proportionate to the risks posed by disinformation in African contexts.
2. Support for investigative journalism. Media coalitions should partner with governments and donors to sustain credible journalism initiatives, helping distinguish between legitimate reporting and disinformation campaigns.
3. Accessible and affordable information. Content produced by credible actors should be made freely available, reducing reliance on paywalled or partisan sources.
4. Capacity building in media literacy. Civil society organizations, universities, and governments should collaborate to train experts in digital literacy, equipping citizens to recognize and resist harmful content.

5. Fair enforcement mechanisms. While disinformation creators should be held accountable under the law, responses must remain consistent with human rights standards and avoid overly harsh or politicized measures.
6. Transparent appeals processes. When harmful content is taken down, platforms must establish clear, transparent, and timely appeal mechanisms. Transparency about decision-making panels is especially urgent to ensure accountability and fairness.

By linking technological innovations directly to policy challenges and solutions, Africa can transform its digital ecosystem into a space that empowers citizens, strengthens democracy, and protects human rights rather than undermining them.

CONCLUSION

This chapter set out to answer the question: How does digital disinformation in Africa impact human rights, and what regulatory, societal, and transnational responses can address it? The evidence presented demonstrates that disinformation is not a marginal concern but a persistent, systemic challenge with far-reaching implications for democracy, public health, and human rights. The COVID-19 pandemic, Nigeria's 2023 elections, and the Tigray conflict illustrated how false and manipulative content spreads rapidly, erodes trust in institutions, polarizes societies, and threatens civic space. These cases confirm that disinformation is amplified not only by local political actors but also by structural imbalances in global platform governance, where African languages and contexts receive limited investment and oversight.

At the same time, situating these dynamics within a postcolonial perspective shows how historical inequalities—colonial legacies, fragile governance, and uneven access to technology—continue to shape Africa's vulnerability to digital manipulation. Yet African agency is also evident in the work of fact-checking organizations, civil society watchdogs, and regional policy frameworks. Together, these dynamics highlight both the risks and the opportunities facing Africa's digital future.

Moving forward, four priority areas stand out:

1. Strengthen Digital Literacy. African states should integrate media and information literacy into school curricula and community initiatives, ensuring that citizens acquire the skills to identify, question, and counter disinformation (UNESCO, 2021; Wilson, Grizzle, Tuazon, Akyempong, & Cheung, 2011). Such efforts must reach rural populations and operate in local languages.
2. Advance Regional Frameworks. The African Union's Digital Transformation Strategy (2020–2030) offers a foundation for coordinated responses. Expanding

it to harmonize fragmented national laws will strengthen protections while aligning with human rights standards (African Union Commission, 2020).

3. Require Platform Transparency. Global platforms such as Facebook, X, and TikTok must be held accountable for content moderation in African languages and contexts. Greater transparency about algorithms, moderation practices, and fact-checking partnerships is essential (ARTICLE 19, 2022; Mozilla Foundation, 2021).
4. Support Civil Society Watchdogs. Independent fact-checkers and NGOs play a vital role in monitoring disinformation and advocating for accountability. Strengthening their capacity through funding, legal protection, and international partnerships will empower them to safeguard civic space (Dobber, Metoui, Trilling, Helberger, & de Vreese, 2021; International Fact-Checking Network, 2020).

By prioritizing these areas, African states and their partners can move beyond reactive or punitive measures toward a sustainable, rights-based approach. Protecting human rights in the digital sphere is not only a policy necessity but also a democratic imperative for Africa's future.

REFERENCES

African Union Commission. (2020). Digital transformation strategy for Africa (2020–2030). African Union. https://au.int/en/documents

Amnesty International. (2023). Meta's dangerous algorithmic amplification in Ethiopia. Amnesty International. https://www.amnesty.org

ARTICLE 19. (2022). Content moderation and freedom of expression in Africa. ARTICLE 19. https://www.article19.org

Banaji, S., & Bhat, R. (2022). *Social media and political misinformation in India and Brazil*. Routledge.

Banisar, D. (2009). *ICT policies relating to privacy, freedom of expression and access to information: A briefing paper*. Human Rights and Peace Centre, Makerere University.

Batta, H., Udousoro, N., & Abubakar, Y. (2015). Digital health technologies and implications for developing country media and health communication.

BBC. (2022, August 11). Kenya elections: Disinformation campaigns flood social media. BBC News. https://www.bbc.com

Bruns, A., Angus, D., Hurcombe, E., Harrington, S., & Tan, J. (2022). The dissemination of problematic news on Facebook: A large-scale, longitudinal study. *Digital Journalism (Abingdon, England)*, *10*(10), 1275–1299. DOI: 10.1177/20563051231196880

Bunce, M. (2019). Humanitarian communication in a post-truth world. *Journal of Humanitarian Affairs*, *1*(1), 49–58. DOI: 10.7227/JHA.007

Camara, M. S. (2008). Media, civil society, and political culture in West Africa.

Chibita, M. B. (2016). Digital activism in Uganda. In Chibita, M. B. (Ed.), *Digital activism in the social media era* (pp. 119–136). Springer., DOI: 10.1007/978-3-319-40949-2_7

CIPESA. (2021). State of internet freedom in Africa 2021: The impact of COVID-19 on digital rights in Africa. Collaboration on International ICT Policy for East and Southern Africa. https://cipesa.org

Council on Foreign Relations. (2022). *Ethiopia's Tigray conflict: Disinformation and social media*. CFR.

Dobber, T., Metoui, N., Trilling, D., Helberger, N., & de Vreese, C. (2021). Do (microtargeted) deepfakes have real effects on political attitudes? *The International Journal of Press/Politics*, *26*(1), 69–91. DOI: 10.1177/1940161220944364

Ekwueme, M., & Folarin, S. F. (2017). Role of social media in electioneering: The case of the Nigerian 2015 presidential election.

European Commission. (2022). The Digital Services Act: Ensuring a safer digital space. European Commission. https://digital-strategy.ec.europa.eu

Fallis, D. (2015). What is disinformation? *Library Trends*, *63*(3), 401–426. DOI: 10.1353/lib.2015.0014

Garimella, K., & Eckles, D. (2020). Images and misinformation in political groups: Evidence from WhatsApp in India. *Harvard Kennedy School Misinformation Review*, *1*(2). Advance online publication. DOI: 10.37016/mr-2020-013

GSMA. (2022). The mobile economy: Sub-Saharan Africa 2022. GSMA Intelligence. https://www.gsma.com

Human Rights Watch. (2022). Meta's broken promises: Systemic failures in tackling hate speech in Ethiopia. HRW. https://www.hrw.org

International Fact-Checking Network. (2020). Code of principles. Poynter Institute. https://ifcncodeofprinciples.poynter.org

International Telecommunication Union. (2022). Measuring digital development: Facts and figures 2022. ITU. https://www.itu.int

Milmo, D. (2023, January 24). Meta spends 87% of misinformation budget on US users, report finds. The Guardian. https://www.theguardian.com

Mozilla Foundation. (2021). *Platform transparency: Why Africa is left behind.* Mozilla.

Mujokoro, J. I. T. (2017). An analysis of the Sunday Times and Twitter's reporting of President Mugabe's state visit to South Africa.

Obijiofor, L. (2009). *Is bad news from Africa good news for Western media?* Marquette Books.

Ogunyemi, O. (2011). Representation of Africa online: Sourcing practice and frames of reference. *Journal of Black Studies*, *42*(3), 457–478. DOI: 10.1177/0021934710378747

Pomeranz, J. L., & Schwid, A. R. (2021). Governmental actions to address COVID-19 misinformation. *Journal of Public Health Policy, 42*(1), 1–15. DOI: 10.1057/s41271-020-00270-x PMID: 33510401

Premium Times. (2021, July 29). Nigeria's anti-fake news laws spark controversy. Premium Times.

Public Media Alliance. (2022). *Caribbean media and the politics of disinformation.* PMA.

Renda, A. (2018). The legal framework to address "fake news": Possible policy actions at the EU level. CEPS Research Report. https://www.ceps.eu/ceps-publications

Reuters. (2025, January 12). Kenyan court allows Meta disinformation lawsuit to proceed. Reuters.

Scott, M. (2023, March 8). Facebook ignored warnings over Ethiopia hate speech. Politico. https://www.politico.eu

South African Government. (2020). *Disaster Management Act: COVID-19 misinformation penalties.* Government Gazette.

Stewart, R., Madonsela, A., Tshabalala, N., Etale, L., & Theunissen, N. (2022). Social media users' responses are important in tackling digital COVID-19 misinformation in Africa. *Digital Health, 8*, 20552076221085070. DOI: 10.1177/20552076221085070 PMID: 35321021

Thoba, A. (2017). Human rights discourse and postcolonial Africa: The call for intervention in Darfur.

UNESCO. (2021). *Media and information literacy: Policy and strategy guidelines.* UNESCO.

Van Stam, G. (2021). Appropriation, coloniality, and digital technologies: Observations from within an African place. arXiv. https://doi.org//arXiv.2108.10087DOI: 10.48550

Wilson, C., Grizzle, A., Tuazon, R., Akyempong, K., & Cheung, C. K. (2011). *Media and information literacy curriculum for teachers.* UNESCO.

KEY TERMS AND DEFINITIONS

Algorithmic Amplification: The automated boosting of certain content by platform algorithms, increasing its visibility and spread regardless of accuracy or relevance.

Digital Colonialism: The extension of unequal global power relations into the digital sphere, where external entities control infrastructure, platforms, and data flows in ways that exploit local users and economies.

Disinformation: False or misleading information deliberately created and shared to deceive or manipulate audiences.

Freedom of Expression: The right to hold opinions and to seek, receive, and impart information and ideas through any media, subject to lawful and proportionate restrictions.

Media Literacy: The ability to access, analyze, evaluate, create, and share media messages while recognizing bias, misinformation, and persuasive intent.

Misinformation: Incorrect or misleading information shared without the intent to deceive, but which may still cause harm.

Platform Governance: The systems of rules, moderation policies, and technical controls through which digital platforms manage user behavior and content.

Postcolonial Lens: An analytical perspective that interprets media, politics, and society in light of the lasting impacts and power imbalances of colonialism.

Right to Information: The legally recognized right of individuals to access information held by public institutions, promoting transparency and accountability.

WhatsApp-Driven Misinformation: The rapid spread of false or misleading content via encrypted messaging services like WhatsApp, which complicates detection and response efforts.

APPENDIX

Summary of Selected Case Studies on Digital Disinformation in Postcolonial Africa

Table 1. Overview of Key Case Studies Referenced in Chapter

Country	Year(s) Covered	Main Disinformation Theme	Medium/Platform	Human Rights Impact	Source(s)
Nigeria	2015	Election-related false claims targeting candidates	Facebook, Twitter	Undermined electoral trust; increased political polarization	Ekwueme & Folarin (2017)
Uganda	2020–2021	State-sponsored online smear campaigns against opposition	Facebook, WhatsApp	Restricted freedom of expression; intimidation of activists	Chibita (2016)
Zimbabwe	2017	Manipulated narratives about presidential visit to South Africa	Twitter, online news	Spread state-favored framing; reduced public trust in independent media	Mujokoro (2017)
Egypt	2011–2014	Post–Arab Spring misinformation and counter-narratives	Facebook, blogs	Shifted public opinion; eroded trust in citizen journalism	Moreno-Almeida & Banaji (2019)
South Africa	2020–2021	COVID-19 vaccine misinformation	Facebook, WhatsApp	Reduced vaccine uptake; public health risks	Stewart et al. (2022)

Chapter 5
Current Challenges of Media and Human Rights in Digital World

Melita Zajc
https://orcid.org/0000-0002-2091-3179
Euro-Mediterranean University, Slovenia

ABSTRACT

This chapter will address the challenges facing the media and human rights in the digital world from a broader perspective of the positive affordances of digital technologies. The author will first address the epistemological aspect of exploring the underlying technologies of social media platforms. They will propose regarding current social media platforms as the dispositive in which one use of digital technologies prevailed over the other, alternative uses. They will introduce the right to communicate as a basic human right and outline the evolution of social media's potential to realise this right. Through the analysis of positive and negative aspects of digital media, they will present the platforms as a source of instrumentarian power and introduce the epistemic rights as a potential regulatory approach to limiting this power. Outlining the shortcomings of existing regulatory mechanisms, they will argue for the solutions that promote such uses of digital technologies that can enforce human rights.

INTRODUCTION

The media are the foundation of a democratic society, par excellence. They are the necessary conditions for the realization of human rights. Media informs the public about human rights concerns, uncovering abuses, and motivating individuals

DOI: 10.4018/979-8-3373-3685-5.ch005

to respond. Free and universally accessible media are also a human right in themselves. The freedom of expression, the free flow of information, and the freedom and pluralism of the media are among the essential human rights worldwide. Media are a condition for human rights, but, as human rights in themselves, they are also conditioned by the general state of human rights.

This complex nexus of the media and human rights has been further complicated by digital technologies. Digital media can be a formidable resource, but they can also present a threat to human rights. On the one hand, they remarkably increased access to information, enhanced freedom of expression, and empowered people to claim their rights. On the other hand, we have been witnessing a rapid expansion of the negative implications of digital technologies for the media, particularly for human rights. Echo chambers and filter bubbles, social polarisation, misinformation and disinformation, the rising power of platforms and datafication, algorithmic bias, exploitation of free labour, platform colonialism, digital bots and computational propaganda, surveillance capitalism and instrumentarian power - to mention just the phenomena that have been of the most recent concern - indicate that contemporary mediascapes have been fraught with peril that endangers basic human rights. Yet, media are essential for human communication and political deliberation; they are the means through which we perceive ourselves and the world around us. The major challenge for research and policy on media in the digital world is thus to develop solutions that limit the aspects of social media that endanger or even violate human rights without harming their positive aspects.

The digital era requires a human rights-based approach to media and technology regulation. The problem, however, is that contemporary media are increasingly entwined with technologies and underlying computational processes. When we use them, we often overlook these mechanisms. The introduction of new technology into society has been successful when we do not need to know how it works to use it properly. However, as scholars, we shouldn't ignore the role of technology in the media. The objective of this chapter is to explore the implications of media technologies and the underlying computational processes of digital media. Recently, several scholars have expressed concern about the sole focus on speech, moderation, news, and political campaigning in media regulation research and policy. They claimed that the harmful features of platformisation and datafication are shaped by algorithmic systems (Carah and Broedmerkel, 2022, p. 16) operating in the back end of platforms. This led to the conclusion that media can be regulated democratically and effectively only by public institutions if we understand the key mechanisms of these processes (Poell et al., 2019, p. 9). This, we believe, is the underlying challenge for digital media, human rights research, and regulation. Therefore, in this chapter, we aim to provide a conceptual and empirical foundation for a better understanding of the technological dimensions of media in the digital world, their political, social, and cultural implications, and the implications for human rights in particular.

The chapter has two parts. The first part serves as an overview of basic concepts and epistemological approaches that address the need to consider the social and technological aspects of media without recourse to technological determinism or social constructivism. The overview of social media will cover the evolution of digital network technologies and the analysis of mechanisms of social media platforms. The second part is dedicated to the contemporary challenges. It will start with the right to communicate as a basic human right. We will present the evolution and the global political reception of this concept. We will also argue that the right to communicate can best be exercised through social media, and therefore, one of the particular challenges of the contemporary mediascape is how to regulate the power of social media platforms without limiting the implementation of the right to communicate. We will analyze the main negative affordances of contemporary media and their economic and technological foundations, as well as the positive ones, demonstrating that the right to communicate is essential to the implementation of other human rights, as it enables people to raise awareness of human rights issues and empower them to take action. When addressing the solutions, we will introduce the conception of epistemic rights as the prevailing scholarly response to the rising instrumentarian power of the social media platforms. We will also identify weaknesses in existing regulatory systems and note the danger that, by curbing the power of platforms, regulation harms citizens' rights (Fotiadis 2025).

In short, we aim to provide a comprehensive outline of contemporary media in the digital world, key notions, evolution, and the enabling and constraining affordances of social media platforms. The focus will be on the challenges media scholars and policymakers face in curbing the growing power and harmful operations of social media platforms. We will argue that by focusing on the technological aspect and considering the current state of the art of social media as the prevailing use of digital technologies, we can create more space for other, alternative uses that have the potential to encourage the implementation of human rights.

MAIN APPROACHES AND THEIR APPLICATIONS

Before addressing the ontological question of what defines the media in the digital world, we will address the epistemological question about the proper methodology. In the brief overview of the role of media in human history and society, we will focus on the intrinsic role of technology in these media and examine the broader social dimensions of technology.

Technologies and societies

Digital technologies have radically transformed the media landscape: new digital media have emerged, traditional media such as the printed press, radio, and TV have undergone profound transformation, and written and oral communication have changed significantly. The basic material quality of the digital world, that is, that everything, from the physical environment to human beings, can turn into data, made this change a continuous process. It would be a mistake, however, to view this in terms of mechanistic causality where a particular cause produces a particular effect, and regard the contemporary transformations, media landscape included, as a direct effect of scientific and technological achievements. The relationship between technologies and societies is complex; therefore, research on the social aspects of technologies, including media studies, requires particular conceptual considerations.

The everyday use of the term media does not distinguish between media as technical devices (such as TV sets, smart phones, tablets, or computers), content (such as text, sound or video messages, photographs, daily news, or feature films) and organisations that facilitate the production and/or distribution of that content (Netflix, for example, does both, and so do public service broadcasters such as RTV Slovenia, while TikTok or Facebook provide for the exchange of the content mostly produced by their users). In the world of digital media, these distinctions themselves are fluid and obscured. The broader meaning of the term media is that human thought needs a material carrier to be formed and expressed. Media, even in the most rudimentary form, as brain impulses or sound waves, are essential for human communication. They, too, have a material, technological dimension. For example, in oral communication, linguistic sounds, considered physical phenomena, have two aspects: the motor and acoustic. The linguist Roman Jakobson (1996, p. 14-15) observed that the understanding of which of the two aspects has priority determined the scholarly approach. Those scientists who considered the sound an acoustic phenomenon studied acoustics, while those primarily interested in the sounds as a motor articulation explored physiology. In other words, the decision about ontology already implies the decision about epistemology.

Similarly, a recent systematic review of the research on echo chambers on social media revealed that "the findings of research on this issue are significantly influenced by the studies' focus and methodological approach" (Terren et al., 2021, p. 109). The researchers observed that a media-centric approach, by focusing on specific networks or neglecting user agency, could overestimate the level of fragmentation on social media. Conversely, a user-centric approach, by relying on small samples and potentially inaccurate and biased self-reports, might underestimate fragmentation on social media (Terren et al., 2021, p. 111). This does not deny the existence of polarisation in contemporary media; rather, it shows that different magnitudes of echo chambers are contingent and might depend upon the network, the issue, as well as a multifaceted interplay between the architecture of social media platforms and users' characteristics (Terren et al., 2021, p. 112). It also proves the importance of epistemological ponderation.

Therefore, we will first address the basic epistemological question of how to study the role of technology in the media from a societal perspective. We will introduce the two most appropriate approaches, developed in contemporary media research (the notion of affordances and the concept of dispositive). Next, we will apply these two approaches in the analysis of social media as a particular case of the use of digital technologies, and finally, as a practical demonstration, we will focus on two main features of contemporary digital mediascape, both in a particular way conditioned by the underlying technologies (platforms and datafication).

The affordances

The notion of affordances proved particularly suitable for studying the intricate facets of media, technologies, and their users. It was initially developed in ecological psychology and design studies and is generally used to describe what material artifacts, such as media technologies, enable people to do (Bucher and Helmond, 2018; Troeger and Bock, 2022). Conceptualisations of affordances remain diverse. Essential for the application in media and communication studies is that these conceptualisations permit the exploration of relations between technologies and societies. The concept of affordances offers a framework that transcends both technological determinism and social constructivism, acknowledging that technologies are shaped by social processes while also imposing material possibilities and limitations (Bucher and Helmond, 2018, p. 10). In media studies and social media research, the concept of affordances is particularly important because it captures the relationship between media materiality and human agency.

In terms of agency, the notion of affordances is connected to Actor Network Theory. A theory of agency as distributed and relational, holding that nonhumans are actors with agencies too (Latour 2005, p. 72). The distributed notion of agency is important for the understanding of digital media and social media platforms, because their use implies several subjects with the agency not only the end-users, such as the owners of the platforms, traditional media organisations, and producers, as well as other producers offering their content, defined complementors (Poell at all., 2019, p. 4) in platform studies.

From the perspective of end-users and their agency, the possibilities of their active participation in the creation of media content and the communicative processes in general, the concept of affordances might prove limiting. The reason is the emphasis on affordances as mostly tied to the agency of technological objects

(Bucher and Helmond, 2018, p. 17), or, more directly put, on what technology does to users, not the other way around. Often, the notion of affordances is reduced to a description of a platform's technical features (Bucher and Helmond, 2018, p. 12), failing to properly account for the active role of social media users. Nagy and Neff, to make up for this shortfall, claimed that users' perceptions, beliefs, and expectations about the technologies and platforms' capacities "shape how they approach them and what actions they think are suggested" (2015, p. 5). They introduced the notion of "imagined affordances" and defined it as what emerges "between users' perceptions, attitudes, and expectations; between the materiality and functionality of technologies; and between the intentions and perceptions of designers" (Nagy and Neff, 2015, p. 7).

The dispositive

A similar approach that emphasises the active role of users of media technologies is the concept of the dispositive. The concept draws from the anthropology of technology, recognizing that certain essential skills are inherently practical and cannot simply be taught in a classroom—a notion François Sigaut termed "the law of the irreducibility of skills" (1995, p. 446). Additionally, the idea of the dispositive expands on Jean-Louis Baudry's work with the cinematographic dispositive, which examined how cinema imposes a unified set of expectations on viewers while still allowing for unique individual experiences.

The concept of the dispositive (Zajc, 2015, p. 11-12) understands media as a particular use of technologies that historically prevailed among other uses. It shifts attention from media content to the material conditions and practices of media use. It makes possible the distinction between the dominant use of media technologies and the idiosyncratic practices of individual users with their distinct histories, memories, expectations, and desires, which can generate alternative and oppositional uses. This makes the concept of dispositive particularly valuable for media research, especially for studying media in the digital world, because it enables the conceptualisation of the specific entanglement of technological and societal aspects. It is thus particularly suitable for examining the dynamics between the enabling and constraining potentials of media from the perspectives of society and the implementation of human rights.

The social media dispositive

Seen as a dispositive, so-called social media is a particular kind of use of digital technologies. They are the most recent events in contemporary mediascape, which allow us to identify the dense entanglement of technology and society in media and also to reconstruct, to a certain degree, the dynamics between competing uses of digital technologies. As we will see in the second part of this chapter, these dynamics are ongoing, providing an opportunity to influence the outcome so that the use that enforces human rights prevails.

One of the most widely accepted definitions described social media as "a group of Internet-based applications that build on the ideological and technological foundations of Web 2.0, which allows the creation and exchange of user-generated content" (Kaplan and Haenlein in Zajc 2015, p. 3). The authors identified diverse categories of social media, collaborative projects such as Wikipedia, blogs, and microblogs such as Twitter, content communities such as YouTube, social networking sites like Facebook, virtual social worlds, and virtual game worlds. By now, some of those social media parted the scene, and many new appeared, most notably the short-video app Douyin in China in 2016 and its international version TikTok in 2018 (Zeng et al. 2021, p. 3161), while Facebook, with over 2.7 billion monthly active users as of the second quarter of 2020 (Castro et al., 2022, p. 35) remained the most extensive social media worldwide.

The above definition is essential for understanding the current state of social media, because it emphasises the Web 2.0 technological foundations that enabled users' participation. Web 2.0 referred to digital network technologies, and in particular, their broadband, that is, high-capacity transmission technologies that transmit data, voice, and video across long distances at high speeds. This is what materially enabled audience participation in media content production and exchange.

Social media is a phenomenon of this Century: Wikipedia was released in 2000, LinkedIn in 2003, Facebook in 2004, Yahoo and YouTube in 2005, and Twitter in 2006. Their predecessors, however, date back to the mid-twentieth century. They were based on the internet as an open, distributed communication infrastructure that evolved from the Advanced Research Projects Agency Network (ARPANET), introduced in the US in 1969. This set of computer protocols permitted various personal computers to connect and form a single network. Further standardisation of the protocols, primarily the Transmission Control Protocol and Internet Protocol (TCP/IP; Castro et al., 2022, p. 34; Abbate, 2017, p. 2), led to the formation of the internet. The World Wide Web, created in 1989 and 1990 as the standard way to access and transmit data online through websites and hyperlinks, further made the internet more accessible and collaborative. Recent empirical studies across various national and regional contexts have challenged US-centric narratives about the development of communication technology infrastructure. Historical research on Chile under Allende, for example, disclosed a nationally networked computing project under which Cybersyn was locally conceived in 1971, independently of the US ARPANET (Medina in Abbate, 2017, p. 3).

These early network technologies enabled new forms of communication that were praised for their potential for creativity and communication outside the official mass media networks that prevailed at the time. MUDs, Multi-User Dungeons, also called Multi-User Measurement, or Multi-User Domain (Castro et al., 2022, p. 36), were message-based and required users to type commands making use of natural language, but they made possible the creation of the early version of the virtual world with role-playing games, interactive fiction, and online chat. The bulletin board system (BBS) that developed during the 1970s and is considered the predecessor of the WWW enabled people to exchange messages with others within the group. The WWW facilitated the creation of individual websites and the publication of blogs, vlogs, and podcasts, that is, text, video, and voice-based messages online. The period before the mid-2000s, often driven by experimentation with peer-to-peer (P2P) technologies (Järvekülg et al., 2024, p. 1291), was generally considered an open, relatively decentralised, and public environment. However, the usability of these forms has required a high level of expertise. Therefore, even if access was not formally restricted, the actual use was limited to a small number of expert users.

The platforms

Audience participation in media content production is a distinct feature of social media. In the words of Lawrence Lessig, whereas mass media were ''read only,'' social media "could be both read and write'' (2015, p. 3). This perspective points to the paradoxical role of social media platforms, which represent the current state of social media. At the same time that they enforced freedom of speech, equal access to content creation and human rights in general, they also put human rights, such as privacy and the right to know, under threat. The concepts introduced above help us explain this paradox. Seen as a dispositive, social media platforms, as a particular use of digital technologies, prevailed in the last decades. This use largely exploited the affordances of digital technologies in favour of the most powerful world corporations, at the expense of citizens' interests and human rights. One significant feature of this use is that knowledge of the underlying technologies of social media became irrelevant to their use. As a result, awareness of other possible uses of these technologies and the prospect of developing such uses has been reduced as well. It is this knowledge that we intend to revive with this chapter in the first place.

Therefore, we need to stress that platforms significantly increased the ease of use of social media and, by doing so, made the advantages of social media participation, in the first place, generally available. They actually transformed once passive audiences into active users on a large scale. However, this was due to predefined, software-based usage modalities. Social media platforms improved the ease of use and attracted users, but limited their creativity (Lovink in Zajc, 2015, p. 65). The recent evolution of social media platforms intensified this contrast. Social media, which started as social networking services built "on top of" the open web's infrastructure (as with MUDs and BBSs described above), has been transformed into closed platforms. Rather than being general-purpose technologies, platforms have developed into closed-off, privately owned networks (Nieborg et al. 2023, p. 42). The network effect, which "arises when the benefit of network participation to a user depends on the number of other network users with whom they can interact" (McIntryre and Srinivasan in Poell et al., 2019, p. 5), has further intensified the concentration. Online communities and creators depend on a relatively small number of digital media platforms owned by some of the largest companies in the world. The biggest players are Google and YouTube (both owned by Alphabet Inc., Google's parent company), X (formerly Twitter, owned by Elon Musk's X Corp.), Facebook, WhatsApp, Instagram, and Threads (owned by Meta Platforms Inc.). The controversies surrounding the planned US ban of TikTok (Zeng et al., 2021; Merga, 2024), which is currently owned by ByteDance, a Chinese company, clearly demonstrate the current power of platform corporations. These companies tend to operate a wide range of platform subsidiaries (Alphabet, for instance, owns another five in addition to the two mentioned above), thus we rightfully talk about platform conglomerates.

Seen from the perspective of media history, platform conglomerates differ from traditional media conglomerates, and also from portals such as Netflix (Nieborg et al. 2023, p. 31). The latter either licenses content from external companies or finances the production of exclusive series and movies. The platforms, on the contrary, host a mix of user-generated and professional content but do not produce the content themselves. The main source of Netflix's revenue is subscription fees. Platforms generate revenue from multiple sources, such as advertising and microtransactions. Unlike the platforms' users, Netflix subscribers cannot contribute or distribute their own content on Netflix. Whereas Netflix blocks direct interactions between subscribers and content producers, platforms encourage different groups of users to interact with each other. They function as multi-sided markets (Nieborg et al., 2023, p. 34), facilitating transactions between end-users on the demand side, and complementors (Nieborg et al., 2023, p. 34), institutional actors such as governments, non-profit and commercial entities, or individual freelancers, such as content creators and gig-workers, on the supply side. This increases the platforms' options to develop various business and revenue models and grants them an immense competitive advantage.

Platforms have developed into "data infrastructures that facilitate, aggregate, monetise, and govern interactions between end-users and content and service providers" (Poell et al., 2019, p. 5) and have become difficult to avoid. Cultural producers, from large publishers to aspirational media workers, are impelled to develop distribution and monetisation strategies aligned with platforms' business models. Products and services that were previously openly accessible are increasingly encapsulated by platform infrastructures (Nieborg et al., 2023, p. 42). Companies talk to customers via Facebook's WhatsApp or Tencent's WeChat, and instead of hosting data on self-owned and operated servers built out of generic technology, they use Amazon Web Services or Alibaba Cloud. The complementors, rather than using open-source programming and scripting languages, tools, and formats, have to integrate their production pipeline with proprietary, closed-off equivalents.

Datafication

Their increased economic and infrastructural dominance is enabling platform companies to derive significant benefits from combining users' data flows in the back end of their platforms (Nieborg et al., 2023, p. 43). With this "datafication" (Poell et al., 2019; Troeger and Bock, 2022; Bonini and Treré, 2024), "our bodies and actions are continuously calculated and transformed into flows of data that feed the platforms' algorithms" (Bonini and Treré, 2024, p. 3). Further, platforms turn into data "practices and processes that historically eluded quantification" (Bonini and Treré, 2024, p. 3). These are not just demographic, or profiling data volunteered by users or solicited via surveys, but also behavioural metadata. The collection/production of such data is enabled by platform infrastructures, including apps, plugins, active and passive sensors, and trackers. The Internet of Things enabled platforms to further integrate with a number of other devices such as smartphones and smartwatches, household appliances and self-driving cars, and this

> *allows platform operators to transform virtually every instance of human interaction into data: rating, paying, searching, watching, talking, friending, dating, driving, walking, etc. (Poell et al., 2019, p. 6).*

The process of datafication has expanded far beyond the traditional realm of media and communication. It is further reinforced (Poell et al., 2019, p. 7-8) by other actors, such as complementors, who actively integrate platform data into products and services used in everyday practices. News organisations and journalists use social media data in editorial decision-making and content distribution strategies. Intense competition is driving app developers to collect end-user data and use it to track and optimise user engagement, retention, and monetisation.

In short, platforms improved the material conditions initially provided by Web 2.0, which were essential for the development of social media affordances, in particular the possibility that formerly passive audiences participate in content production as active users. They facilitated the ease of use and the reach of social media. This contributed to the recent situation in which platform technologies have been applied in novel environments, such as the Internet of Things (IoT), wearable technology, and pervasive computing. We are now more deeply integrated into digital environments than ever before. These changes have transformed how we interact with technology, but the vast amounts of personal data being generated increase the risk of manipulation, threaten fundamental human agency, and pose serious, novel risks to basic human rights. The following section of this chapter will explore these issues in greater detail.

So far, we have argued for an approach to implementing human rights in the media that focuses on their technological foundations. We introduced the main conceptual approaches to the intersection of media and technology. The notion of affordance enables media studies to avoid mechanical causality and to overcome social and technological determinisms. The concept of media as a dispositive, in which one use of technology prevailed over all other possible uses, further enables media scholars to acknowledge the positive potentials of technology and the agency of users. After outlining the development of the internet and social media in previous decades, we introduced the social media platforms and subsequent processes of platformisation and datafication that, to a large extent, define the challenges facing human rights and the media in the digital world of today. Let's now focus on these challenges.

THE CHALLENGES OF MEDIA AND HUMAN RIGHTS IN THE DIGITAL WORLD

The increasing platformisation and datafication of social media in today's media landscape should not obscure their participatory nature, that is, users' ability to actively create content. This feature distinguishes social media from earlier mass media. The participatory nature of social media has played a historically significant role in political communication, social interaction, cultural production, and, notably, the advancement of human rights. Because of this participatory element, social media have enabled an unprecedented realization of freedom of expression: the right to communicate.

The never realised promises of the universal right to communicate

The philosophical foundations of the right to communicate can be traced back to the seventeenth century and the writings of John Milton and John Locke (Dakroury and Birdsall, 2008, p. 2-3). In the 20th Century, it was Jean d'Arcy, a French television innovator and, at that time, Director of the U.N. Radio and Visual Services Division (McIver Jr. et al., 2003), who defined it as a universal human right. In the article "Direct broadcast satellites and the right to communicate," published in the European Broadcasting Union Review in 1969, d'Arcy argued that:

The time will come when the Universal Declaration of Human Rights will have to encompass a more extensive right than man's right to information (...). This is the right of man to communicate. This is the angle from which the future de-

velopment of communications must be considered if it is to be fully understood (in: Dakroury and Birdsall, 2008).

His reasoning was closely linked to the technological advances of his era, especially the launch of communication satellites, which were seen as innovations that could enable individuals to communicate globally (Dakroury and Birdsall, 2008; Hamelink and Hoffmann, 2008). New communication technologies were viewed as opportunities to counteract the concentration of mass media that characterized the twentieth century (Dakroury and Birdsall, 2008). This concentration led to a pervasive "mass media mentality" (d'Arcy in McIver Jr. et al., 2003), which fostered a top-down, one-way flow of information. In this framework, freedom of information was reduced to the freedom to publish (Dakroury and Birdsall, 2008) - the privilege of media owners and professionals—while ordinary citizens were relegated to passive recipients of a one-way flow of information.

The launch of Sputnik in 1957 also raised hopes that the new technology would reduce inequalities in international communication and spur cultural development in even the most remote regions of the world. The idea of the right to communicate was embraced by the states that, at that time, gained independence from colonial powers, especially those united in the Non-Aligned Movement. These states highlighted the North-South imbalance in control over broadcasting and their relative lack of mass communication resources (Hamelink and Hoffmann 2008, p. 2). UNESCO undertook the initiative (Hamelink and Hoffmann 2008, McIver Jr. et al., 2003) to define and promote the idea of the right to communicate, yet due to the politics of the East-West Cold War and the North-South relationships of that era (Dakroury and Birdsall, 2008), the initiative eventually failed.

Participative media

The idea of the right to communicate persisted in some regional initiatives (McIver Jr. et al., 2003) and in academia. Critical media scholars developed a critique of mass communication systems and explored the development of alternative forms of communication. Raymond Williams, in his theory of democratic communication, for example, considered the articulation of alternative forms of communication, the radical press, and other cultural forms produced by working people themselves (Vatikiotis, 2005, p. 9; Zajc, 2015, p. 4-5).

The idea of the right to communicate also persisted in the media that thrived during the 1960s, 70s, and 80s outside the established mass media structures. While each of the names used for these media - alternative media, radical media, community media, and citizens' media - points to a different feature (see, for example, Branwyn, 1997, and Vatikiotis, 2005 for more details), they can jointly be designated as participative media. Participation not only enriches public communication but also cultural production at large. It enabled the production of alternative music, the pirate radio stations, and the evolution of the electronic magazine community (Branwyn, 1997; Zajc, 2015, p. 5). With personal computers, this developed into desktop publishing and soon expanded beyond book and magazine publishing to video production.

The internet accelerated these developments. User participation in media content creation is arguably the internet's main affordance (Turkle, 1997; Dakroury and Birdsall, 2008; Abbate, 2017, p. 3), as well as that of social media (Kaplan and Haenlein, in Zajc, 2015, p. 3; Poell et al., 2019, p. 3; Kopf, 2020, p. 2). Scholars frequently use the term "participatory internet" (Kopf, 2020, p. 2) and agree that the rise of the internet and social media has shifted media production away from traditional top-down dissemination to user-generated content and sharing (Kopf, 2020, p. 2). The global network structure of the internet was especially significant. Earlier participatory media mainly increased opportunities for involvement in production, whereas the internet also democratized distribution. Social media platforms, by expanding internet access and increasing the user base, have further broadened participation and represent the fullest realization of the right to communicate.

The challenges

This brief outline is far from exhaustive and does not imply that the development of participative media has been a linear process. The events surrounding the initiative for global recognition of the right to communicate poignantly attest to the entwinement of endeavours to democratize the public communication with discontinuities and controversies.

The current situation is especially concerning. As social media platforms have developed, their empowering potential appears increasingly overshadowed by negative aspects such as misinformation, polarization, datafication, surveillance, and manipulation — some of the most prominent issues in today's media environment. However, recognizing that social media operates as a dispositive (Zajc, 2015) where enabling and constraining features coexist should prevent us from dismissing them solely for their negative qualities. Instead, efforts to address harmful practices must also acknowledge the enabling aspects and historical significance of social media. Accordingly, the following analysis will consider both positive and negative affordances separately. Each negative feature poses a unique challenge, but the primary issue for media and human rights today is to develop theories and policies that minimize the constraining affordances of social media while strengthening the enabling ones.

Empowering affordances of social media

Audience empowerment distinguishes social media from traditional mass media. Recent research indicates that with the development of social media platforms, this feature has not disappeared. While in the past, user-generated content (UGC) was associated with non-professional content creators (Santor 2022), today, at least some of these creators are being paid by the platforms. Kopf (2020) analysed the policy regarding "content creators" in the YouTube Partner Program, which was introduced as early as 2007 (p. 4). Cunningham and Craig (2021) also use the term "creators" to describe the media users "who generate and circulate original content in close interaction and engagement with their communities on the major social media platforms as well as offline" (Cunningham and Craig, 2021, p. 1). When more precise names have been used for content creators, these often referred to the specific content; thus, the creators were called influencers, bloggers, vloggers, game players, live streamers, camgirls, broadcast jockeys (Korea), and, in China, KOLs (key opinion leaders), zhubo, and wanghong. Alternatively, they are also named after platforms: YouTubers, tweeters (Twitter), grammers (Instagram), and snappers (Snapchat).

In the global South, the internet and mobile phones (Mattelart, 2023, p. 19) have improved access to communication infrastructure. One of the earliest manifestations of empowered communication is the emergence of networked global movements, where "networked" refers to "the reconfiguration of movements and publics through the incorporation of digital technologies and connectivity" (Tüfekçi, 2017, p. xxiii). The event of these global networked movements is an excellent example of how the realisation of the right to communicate can prove to be an important lever for the realisation of other human rights, as a greater number of people can participate in promoting awareness of human rights issues, and also more people can be empowered to take action. Among the most prominent examples were the actions organised in the 1990s by the Zapatistas, an Indigenous rebel group in the southern Mexican highlands against the enactment of the North American Free Trade Agreement (NAFTA) among the United States, Mexico, and Canada, demanding that the new global order "prioritise human development and values, not corporate profits" (Tüfekçi, 2017, p. x). The Occupy Wall Street movement, which began with the occupation of Zuccotti Park in the Financial District of Lower Manhattan, New York, in 2011, and soon expanded from the United States to global protests in dozens of countries, from Hong Kong to Slovenia, is another example. One of the most prominent, the #BlackLivesMatter protests in the United States against the police killings of black people, especially in poorer communities, has emerged primarily through a national network that uses social media to organise and communicate, but also as a tool for gathering attention and shaping narratives (Tüfekçi, 2017, p.

205-206). Tüfekçi reports that, although the rate of killings by police had not gone up drastically at that time, the amount of attention paid to these killings significantly increased (Tüfekçi, 2017, p. 206) due to this movement.

The uprisings that took place in several countries of North Africa and the Middle East in the early 2010s, known as the Arab Spring, are arguably the most prominent example of the protest movement based on the use of online platforms and digital tools for organising and publicity (Tüfekçi, 2017), but it is not without predecessors. Digital technologies were instrumental in various social and political movements before that, including the 2005 campaign for women's suffrage in Kuwait, the 2007 student-led protests in Venezuela following the shutdown of Radio Caracas Television, and the 2008 general strike in Egypt, during which Facebook was used to mobilise tens of thousands of young protesters. This led scholars to praise social media as a "liberation technology," able to "expand political, social and economic freedom" (Larry Diamond in Mattelart, 2023, p. 19). During that same period, international organisations such as the World Bank also commended global digital platforms for their ability "to enhance the economic development of the Global South" (Mattelart, 2023, p. 19).

Scholars exploring the expansion of global digital platforms in the Global South identified a complex web of power relations between these platforms and domestic actors, including private actors and actors of the informal economy (Mattelart, 2023, p. 25), yet they also revealed several instances of empowerment. In Assam, India, for example, global platforms such as Amazon, Facebook, and Microsoft have designed e-commerce programs for craftsmen and small and medium enterprises, integrating them into their own digital economies (Mattelart, 2023, p. 25-26). Studies on YouTube have shown that this platform has opened an important space for expression for many creators in the Global South. In Morocco, for example, this video-sharing platform contributed to the development of a space for creation that has evolved beyond traditional media (Mohamed El Marzouki, in Mattelart 2023, p. 27). In India, within the framework of its localisation strategy, YouTube partnered with mainstream content providers, but also fortified efforts to surface content created by individuals, and thus contributed to the emergence of "creative entrepreneurs" who have been able to "explore and craft careers that would be unthinkable in a pre-Internet era" (Kumar, in Mattelart, 2023, p.27). In Sub-Saharan Africa, social media platforms have been appropriated by socially disadvantaged users as a tool to improve their condition. A study of Facebook use in Viwandani, an informal settlement in Nairobi, that focused on young respondents who mostly enter this platform from a desktop computer at a cybercafé, revealed they use it for chatting with friends living in Kenya, and for communicating with family and friends overseas (Wyche et al., in Mattelart, p. 27). They also use the platform to seek formal or informal employment opportunities or to advance their entrepreneurial efforts

(Wyche et al., in Mattelart, p. 27). In short, Mattelart's (2023., p. 32-33) appeal for a more fine-grained research that focuses on the active role performed by local actors in these processes, revealed that for many disadvantaged users in the countries of the Global South, social media platforms serve as a resource for accessing their ordinary entertainment, sustaining their daily online interactions, enlarging their social imaginaries, and even expanding their economic opportunities.

Studies conducted in the Global North show similar results. The analysis of the menstrual tracking and fertility apps that have become outstandingly popular in recent years, for instance, proves that the users of these apps manage to understand their lives through their menstrual cycle (Kressbach 2021, p. 3) and have the potential to improve the knowledge of the historically underexplored issues of sexual and reproductive health. Another well-documented case showing that social media platforms empower their users and help them exercise their basic human rights is the use of TikTok as a source of health information among US-based users (a total of 170 million in 2024). The peer-reviewed research revealed that it enables peer-to-peer exchange of health information about the use of prescription medications. It is not always motivated by commercial imperative, for example, when young people use TikTok to discuss living with chronic pain (Merga, 2024). Despite concerns about reliability, scholars stress that the TikTok platform may be a valuable source of health information for users seeking easily accessible content.

Constraining affordances of social media platforms

Disinformation - The case of Central and Eastern European (CEE) mediascapes

Disinformation, misinformation, polarisation, echo chambers, and filter bubbles are among the affordances of social media that impede democratic deliberation and plurality and pose a serious threat to human rights. Scholars defined disinformation as "deliberately composed and distributed falsehoods that pose as journalism" (Dragomir and Aslama Horowitz, 2024, p. 156). Research performed in Central and Eastern European (CEE) countries revealed that these phenomena are not exclusive to social media platforms. In particular, under historical conditions in which until the 1990s the mainstream media were mostly owned by the state, these media "have not succeeded in becoming autonomous," and many leading players in traditional journalism "are deliberately promoting false content". This has led to a situation in which it is difficult to distinguish between "real journalism and deliberate disinformation cloaked as journalism" (Dragomir and Aslama Horowitz, 2024, p. 155). The rise of digital media platforms in the past decade only intensified the already existing process. Research identified three main categories of disinformation actors:

state or public media, private media, and disinformation-like journalism outlets (Dragomir and Aslama Horowitz, 2024, p. 160). The same scholars also report about a 2022 study that found that of the 31 state-administered broadcasters, news agencies, and portals in CEE, only one-third were editorially independent. They argue that the most prominent cases of state-captured public media are Hungary's and Serbia's. Private media outlets across CEE are also responsible for spreading disinformation. According to Dragomir and Aslama Horowitz, while the spread of disinformation has been most acute in Hungary, Serbia, and Poland, oligarchic control has also been felt in Slovenia, Slovakia and the Czech Republic, through censorship and self-censorship (2024, p. 163). Particularly troubling is the warning of the presence of news outlets financed by the Russian government and pro-Russian websites, disguised as independent sources of information, such as RuBaltic.Ru, established in 2013, which attacks Russia's enemies while praising the Kremlin's political leadership. In the region's disinformation landscape, large players dominate, while local disinformation websites focus on topics that generate revenue. Some are so popular with advertisers that they are sometimes difficult to navigate due to an "overabundance of ads" (Szakacs, in Dragomir and Aslama 2024, p. 165). These platforms, too, feed into the extreme polarisation confronting societies in CEE, and thus have a disproportionately negative impact on their mediascapes.

Algorithmic bias

Several authors consider disinformation the main problem of contemporary news and information systems (Napoli 2024, p. 47). An in-depth investigation revealed, for example, that conservative-leaning media users are more susceptible to disinformation than liberal-leaning media users (Freelon et al. in Napoli, 2024, p. 55). The disinformation divide, however, also operates along vectors other than the liberal-conservative continuum. For instance, recent research indicated that the use of troll accounts to disproportionately target black X (former Twitter) users was conducted by Russia's Internet Research Agency (IRA). Frances Haugen, a Facebook/Meta whistleblower, revealed that the company has allocated its content moderation resources across the various countries in which it operates, yet the allocation patterns have overwhelmingly privileged Facebook users in some countries over others (Napoli, 2024, p. 56). Specifically, the company spends 87 per cent of its misinformation mitigation resources on the U.S., even if the U.S. accounts for only 8 per cent of global Facebook users.

These divides are enforced by the "algorithmic bias", particularly because of the integration of the algorithmic systems into virtually every aspect of the production, distribution, and consumption of news and information (Napoli, 2024, p. 56). Algorithmically driven automation has become a defining component of our news and information ecosystem. The problem is that the algorithmic systems contain ingrained biases that disadvantage certain communities. In some cases, these biases stem from inherently biased data that serve as the algorithms' decision-making inputs. The coders who construct algorithms can also contribute to this through their personal biases or blind spots. In addition, the algorithmic systems can learn biases over time from the aggregated behaviours of system end-users. In any case, as Virginia Eubanks (2019) has shown, the poor are the most exposed to the discrimination generated by algorithms and the power of platforms. Moreover, this power risks discriminating also against ethnic and linguistic minorities, indigenous peoples, young people, and women. Algorithmic discrimination can also take intersectional forms, affecting, for example, young single women and ethnic minority families belonging to the working class (Bonini and Treré, 2024, p. 4). Finally, algorithmic bias likely hinders access to information. Napoli (2024) provided a list of examples, including cases in which certain groups of Facebook users were not exposed to housing advertising; women received less exposure to STEM-related job opportunities than men; and search engines such as Google exhibited racial biases in their search results.

Computational propaganda - the case of the 2016 US presidential elections

Disinformation is particularly troubling when combined with data mining, which harvests social media data on users to target them through "ambiguous approaches" (Iosifidis and Nicoli, 2021, p. 5). The method, also described as "computational propaganda" (D'Alessio, 2021, p. 1), has been successfully applied in the US presidential election of 2016. During the campaign, the winner, President Donald Trump, used the services of Cambridge Analytica, a consulting company that specialised in using data science methodologies to support political campaigns. Their role would not be possible without Facebook, which began harvesting personal information from its users unbeknownst to them at least as early as 2012, when the company became a publicly traded entity. The harvested data could be used by Facebook application developers for payments. The same data also allowed companies such as Cambridge Analytica and their clients to send customised advertising messages based on profiling (Rosenberg et al. in Iosifidis and Nikoli, 2021, p. 5). Cambridge Analytica analysed data in breach of numerous terms of service, which enabled them to accumulate and categorise between 50 and 80 million unsuspecting online users through psychographic profiling. Once grouped, the company began sending specific political advertising messages customised to each user's preferences. For example, if they supported the right to bear and hold arms, the advertising message could be tailored to them, and if a user continuously expressed their hostile views over migration, they might then be profiled and consequently shown advertisements by political parties on the threats of migrants stealing jobs or initiating crimes (Iosifidis and Nicoli, 2021, p. 5).

The concept of computational propaganda as an "emergent form of political manipulation that occurs over the Internet" (Woolley and Howard, in D'Alessio, 2021, p. 1) points to yet another important element of this process: the algorithmic bots. The bots, best described as fake user accounts, are created and controlled by advanced technologies such as AI and machine learning (Woolley and Howard, in D'Alessio, 2021, p. 1). While data mining is used to personalise ads, automated bots promote a particular point of view. Bots shape discussions and share multiple posts on social media to spread false or partisan information and support a particular party or group, as well as to promote hate campaigns (Woolley and Howard, in D'Alessio, 2021, p. 1-2). In this way, the outcome of elections, referenda and other democratic processes can be influenced by computational propaganda. Arguably, the outcomes of the 2016 UK referendum and the 2016 US elections were affected by such campaigns, since almost a third of tweets about the UK referendum and a fifth about the US elections were shared by bots (Schneier, in D'Alessio, 2021, p. 2). Recent research has revealed that globally, 81 states are engaging in computational propaganda, 57 of which use automated bots on social networks (D'Alessio, p. 2), proving this form of manipulation is on the rise. This is extremely challenging because the use of social media as a source of information is also on the rise, and as social networks become more popular, more people are affected by computational propaganda, making it easier to influence public opinion. The result is the decline in public trust in both the platforms and conventional media.

Monetisation

The participative nature of social media itself has also been subject to criticism. The critical political economy of communication insists on the basic continuity between mass media and social media despite their differences. The theoretical foundation of this view is the work of mass media researcher Dallas Smythe, who claimed that the basic material aspect of communication is that media audiences are exploited and are sold as commodities to advertisers (quoted in Fuchs, 2012, p. 695). Thus, the users of social media, just like the audiences of mass media, constitute the "commodity that is sold to advertisers," the only difference being that the users of social media are also engaged in permanent creative activity, communication, community building, and content production (Fuchs, 2012, ibid., p. 711). There is, claims Fuchs, no contradiction between the active participation of social media users in content creation and their exploitation, on the contrary - they are turned into a commodity when their attention is sold to advertisers, and they are the source of exploitation when they create content since they perform free digital labour (Fuchs,

2012, on digital labour see also Gandini, 2021). In addition, when social media users create and share user-generated content, browse profiles and data, interact with others, join, create, and build communities, and co-create information, they are also subjected to "economic surveillance" (Fuchs, 2012, p. 711). Social media platforms and their advertising clients continuously monitor and record personal data, and store, merge, and analyse it. Based on this data, platforms can create detailed user profiles and understand users' personal interests and online behaviours. This enables targeted advertising that aims to lure consumers into consumption. It also aims to manipulate prosumers' desires and needs in the interests of corporations and the commodities they offer (Fuchs, 2012, p. 711-712).

A good current example is the advertising of alcohol. According to Carah and Brodmerkel (2022), alcohol marketers are the leaders in developing innovative approaches in using digital media to track consumers and engage with them. For example, they expanded their use of digital platforms to integrate advertising with "one click" purchases and home delivery services (Carah and Brodmerkel, 2022, p. 118). Some newly developed advertising features are particularly harmful for addictive commodities like alcohol. Platforms could easily identify signs of excessive consumption through patterns that may not be directly related to expressed preferences for alcohol, such as locative information that places the users in proximity to licensed venues more often than others. They can also track a person's private Messenger chats and detect keywords that show their desire for drinking or past times that are drinking-related. In their thorough analysis, Carah and Brodmerkel warn about such practices and even predict the development of machine vision models that "will be able to fabricate images that appeal to different consumers in real time" (Carah and Brodmerkel, 2022, p. 118). At this moment, already, the value proposition of a digital platform isn't its ability to connect the right ad with the right person, but "to gradually tune and tweak its capacity to nudge, move, engage a consumer," in the process intended to stimulate "the click, the purchase, the recommendation," a process the scholars call the process of "operating" on the consumer (Carah and Brodmerkel, 2022, p. 124). The implications of the above practices reach far beyond the privacy breach. Therefore, the scholars suggest that, in the politics of regulation,

> *we need to shift our focus from emphasising privacy and individual choice to a stronger focus on potential harms and the public interest (Carah and Brodmerkel, 2022, p. 127).*

Surveillance capitalism and instrumentarian power

The harvesting and monetisation of users' data have sometimes been described as digital colonialism. This syntagm brings together the domination of the main global digital platforms in the Global South that prolongs the exploitative practices of the historical colonial powers, and the contemporary data harvesting practices of social media platforms. The underlying assumption is that both historic colonialism and data colonialism aim to acquire large-scale resources from which economic value can be extracted. Former colonial powers extracted natural resources and labour, and social media platforms of today appropriate human life "through its conversion into data" (Couldry and Mejijas in Mattelart, 2023, p. 23).

Zuboff defined this appropriation as "surveillance capitalism" and located its beginnings in the aftermath of the 2001 financial crisis in Silicon Valley, which put Google, as a young company, under extreme pressure from its investors (2022, p. 9). These unique historical conditions first motivated the urgent search for a new market form and Google's "discovery" (Zuboff, 2022, p. 9) and pursuit of surveillance capitalism cannot be separated from them. When, in 2009, the public became aware that Google maintained search histories indefinitely, the corporation's CEO explained this practice as if it were inevitable (Zuboff, 2022, p. 8). Until today, the scope and objectives of these mechanisms have remained obscure, warns Zuboff. While most people credit Google's success to its advertising model, the company's success stems from a much more sinister ability to predict the future of human behaviour (Zuboff, 2022, p. 10). The reason is that when harvested user data and analytical capabilities were used to increase the ad's relevance to users, a new market, the "behavioural futures market," was created. In this market, users have been reduced to a mere source of free raw material that feeds a new manufacturing process designed to fabricate predictive products. This prediction imperative was part of the development of the means of behavioural modification. Today, the means of behavioural modification are omnipresent and hard to avoid. They construct a new type of power that has no historical precedent, warns Zuboff, who defined this power as "instrumentarian power". The instrumentarian power's specific purposes and methods are not only distinct from totalitarianism; they are, in many ways, its precise opposite. While totalitarianism operated through violence, instrumentarian power operates through behavioural modification (Zuboff, 2022, p. 127).

CONCLUSIONS AND RECOMMENDATIONS

The above list of challenges is not exhaustive. The process is irreversible. The more digital technologies penetrate contemporary society and become intertwined with it, far beyond the traditional notion of media and communication, the more is at stake. The world, our own human agency, and the human rights we once took for granted have gradually been transforming, if not disappearing, before our eyes. But we also noticed that the positive and negative affordances of digital technologies turn into one another, as on the Möbius strip, and we should not forget that among the new uses of digital technologies, there are not only those that endanger, but also those that enforce human rights.

These are not simple mechanical changes. The occurrence of instrumentarian power as the new form of power implies that our rights have been challenged in novel ways. Media and communication research responded to this challenge with the so-called epistemic turn: an elaboration of a new category of human rights, the epistemic rights (D'Arma et al., 2024, p. 5). Algorithmic bias, disinformation, computational propaganda, user exploitation, and digital surveillance pose significant challenges. This prompted scholars to question the suitability of old concepts of communication and digital rights and to seek a more comprehensive framework to grasp the multifaceted challenges posed by the current situation for citizens, organizations, and democratic structures. The fact that algorithmic digital media, by collecting our personal data and offering us content accordingly, feed us knowledge about ourselves without our participation in forming and reflecting on this knowledge (D'Arma et al., 2024, p. 4), has led to the formulation of epistemic rights. In a democratic society

> *epistemic rights presume equality in all aspects relating to the access to and the availability of information and knowledge, symmetric relations in public communication, equality in obtaining critical literacy in information and communication, and equal protection of personal privacy from any form of public intrusion (D'Arma et al., 2024, p. 5).*

The attempts to enforce these rights have, by now, not been very successful. Scholars point out that it is so primarily because the underlying technological mechanisms at work in the processes of platformization and datafication remained opaque (Poell et al., 2019, p. 4). This feature is closely related to the functioning of technology as a black box; that is, for technology to be socially accepted, the (technological) conditions of its use need to become invisible and forgotten (see Zajc 2000). We have tried to demonstrate above that technologies are an intrinsic part of media, particularly social media. We also provided approaches to explore these technologies, along with traditional aspects of media as content, such as moderation, news, and political campaigning. Only in this way can we understand, and apply, in research and in policy making, the fact that the harmful features of platformisation and datafication are founded in their technological back end and are shaped by how "platforms' algorithmic systems of classification, curation and recommendation" (Carah and Broedmerkel, 2022, p. 16) are designed.

Another material feature that seriously impeded attempts to democratically regulate social media platforms is their ubiquity. These platforms not only penetrated the social and everyday lives of citizens in unprecedented ways but also replaced state infrastructure. Thus, the scholars claim that the platform companies have emerged as the modern-day equivalents of the railroad, telephone, and electric utility monopolies of the past centuries (Poell et al., 2019, p. 4). One of the consequences of this change is the paradox that, even if decision-making processes are controlled by intelligent systems, safeguarding human rights is left to individuals and individual consumers, "who often lack the requisite knowledge, expertise, capacity, time, and motivation to protect their digital rights effectively" (Human, 2024, p. 2). This is evident in the EU General Data Protection Regulation (GDPR), which became enforceable in May 2018 and has been praised as a step forward in digital media regulation. However, it grants service providers authority and decision-making power over data, procedures, and user interfaces related to digital protection (Human, 2024, p. 2). One of the most prominent examples of this is the use of consent-obtaining banners that appear when users attempt to visit a website. They generally provide excessive amounts of information, presented in multiple layers and linked to "privacy policies" that are typically lengthy and filled with legal jargon. All this discourages users from reading and understanding them and diminishes users' capacity to protect their privacy. Particularly affected are older adults and less tech-savvy individuals, children, people with disabilities, immigrants and other groups that might not even know the language of local websites. In general, it makes individuals feel overwhelmed and ready to accept the inevitability of privacy violations, the feeling described as privacy fatigue (Human, 2024, p. 3). The GDPR was, in the first place, conceived to curb the power of service providers, but within the current paradigm, it is service providers who have complete authority over data protection procedures. They can tailor these procedures to their advantage and often make consenting via a consent banner the simplest option, while revoking consent remains complex and obscure. They also deploy other manipulative tactics, known as dark patterns (Nouwens et al., in Human, 2024, p. 8). Besides, the design, processes, data, and interfaces are not only governed by service providers, but are also implemented on their platforms, meaning that when a user engages with such a "cookie banner," for example, by providing consent, they obtain no receipt, confirmation, or data correlating to the information presented to them and the decisions they made.

As an alternative to existing consent management methods, such as "cookie banners," Human developed the Advanced Data Protection Control (ADPC), a mechanism that allows users to directly grant or withdraw consent or object to processing (2024). His system is very much like the system by which websites request permission to access a webcam or microphone through a browser. This directly empowers users by enabling them to manage data protection decisions in their own web browser or through other means, such as mobile apps. They can also decide how to present and manage requests.

Among other alternatives, some scholars also point to the distributed open-source networks based on blockchain technologies as the possibility to de-platformize and diversify digital audiovisual content markets (Järvekülg et al., 2024, p. 1291) and claim that the Web 3.0 movement (Flew, 2024, p. 81) can potentially develop new forms of participatory governance. Experts in critical algorithm studies claim that algorithms may also be employed to resist the power of those who programmed them. Bonini and Treré (2024) have argued that the power of the platforms should be inseparable from the ability of individuals to exert some sort of agency and resistance over it (p. 18), and in their research revealed a series of cases, from forms of open resistance to platform power to the forms of "microresistance" (p. 25).

Scholars of filter bubbles (Terren et al., 2021), platform colonialism (Mattelart, 2023), and the monetization of UGC (Fuchs, 2012) have all argued that different approaches might yield different results. For example, a more empirical, fine-grained (Mattelart, 2023, p. 32) research highlighted the active role of local users of global digital media platforms. Fuchs (2012, p. 712) fused cultural studies and the critical political economy in a new proposal for valuing the audience's activity and creativity. In this chapter, we have argued that the positive and negative affordances jointly define social media. In any given historical situation, they form a multitude of potentialities between them as extremes. Any attempt to democratically regulate social media platforms needs to acknowledge this multitude. It is necessary that we "integrate social media platforms into society without undermining vital traditions of citizenship" (Poell et al., 2019, p. 9). The understanding that social media function as dispositive, and that, in addition to this particular use of digital technologies that prevails at the moment, there are other competing uses, with more positive affordances, that might eventually prevail, might be useful to scholars and legislators in their endeavours to develop solutions that will protect media and enforce human rights.

REFERENCES

Abbate, J. (2017). What and where is the Internet? (Re)defining Internet histories. *Internet Histories, 1*(1–2), 8–14. DOI: 10.1080/24701475.2017.1305836

Bonini, T., & Treré, E. (2024). *Algorithms of resistance: The everyday fight against platform power*. The MIT Press.

Branwyn, G. (1997). *Jamming the media: A citizen's guide; reclaiming the tools of communication*. Chronicle Books.

Bucher, T., & Helmond, A. (2018). The affordances of social media platforms. In *The SAGE handbook of social media*. SAGE Publications Ltd., https://hdl.handle.net/11245.1/149a9089-49a4-454c-b935-a6ea7f2d8986

Carah, N., & Brodmerkel, S. (2022). Regulating platforms' algorithmic brand culture: The instructive case of alcohol marketers on social media. In Flew, T., & Martin, F. R. (Eds.), *Digital platform regulation* (pp. 111–130). Springer International Publishing., DOI: 10.1007/978-3-030-95220-4_6

Castro, C. A. D., O'Reilly, I., & Carthy, A. (2022). The evolution of the Internet and social media: A literature review. *International Journal of E-Education, e-Business, e-. Management Learning, 12*(1), 30–41. DOI: 10.17706/ijeeee.2022.12.1.30-41

Cunningham, S., & Craig, D. (2021). *Creator culture*. New York University Press.

D'Alessio, F. A. (2021). *Computational propaganda: Challenges and responses*. Academia Letters., DOI: 10.20935/AL3468

D'Arma, A., Aslama Horowitz, M., Lehtisaari, K., & Nieminen, H. (2024). Introduction: The epistemic turn. In Aslama Horowitz, M., Nieminen, H., Lehtisaari, K., & D'Arma, A. (Eds.), *Epistemic rights in the era of digital disruption* (pp. 3–9). Springer International Publishing., DOI: 10.1007/978-3-031-45976-4_1

Dakroury, A. I., & Birdsall, W. F. (2008). Blogs and the right to communicate: Towards creating a space-less public sphere? In *2008 IEEE International Symposium on Technology and Society* (pp. 1–8). https://doi.org/DOI: 10.1109/ISTAS.2008.4559762

Dragomir, M., & Aslama Horowitz, M. (2024). Epistemic violators: Disinformation in Central and Eastern Europe. In Aslama Horowitz, M., Nieminen, H., Lehtisaari, K., & D'Arma, A. (Eds.), *Epistemic rights in the era of digital disruption* (pp. 155–170). Springer International Publishing., DOI: 10.1007/978-3-031-45976-4_11

Eubanks, V. (2019). *Automating inequality: How high-tech tools profile, police, and punish the poor* (Picador, F., Ed.). Picador St. Martin's Press.

Flew, T. (2024). Epistemic rights and digital communications policies: Collective rights and digital citizenship. In Aslama Horowitz, M., Nieminen, H., Lehtisaari, K., & D'Arma, A. (Eds.), *Epistemic rights in the era of digital disruption* (pp. 81–96). Springer International Publishing., DOI: 10.1007/978-3-031-45976-4_6

Fotiadis, A. (2025, January 24). The EU wants to scan every message sent in Europe. Will that really make us safer? *The Guardian*. https://www.theguardian.com/commentisfree/2025/jan/24/eu-digital-surveillance-child-protection

Fuchs, C. (2012). Dallas Smythe today: The audience commodity, the digital labour debate, Marxist political economy and critical theory. *TripleC*, *10*(2), 692–740. DOI: 10.31269/triplec.v10i2.443

Gandini, A. (2021). Digital labour: An empty signifier? *Media Culture & Society*, *43*(2), 369–380. DOI: 10.1177/0163443720948018

Hamelink, C. J., & Hoffmann, J. (2008). The state of the right to communicate. *Global Media Journal*, *7*(13).

Human, S. (2024). Humans [plural] in the loop: The forgotten collective aspects of privacy, consenting, controlling, and digital protection. *Frontiers in Political Science*, *6*, 1391755. DOI: 10.3389/fpos.2024.1391755

Iosifidis, P., & Nicoli, N. (2021). *Digital democracy, social media and disinformation*. Routledge.

Jakobson, R. (1996). Šest predavanj o zvoku in smislu. In *Lingvistični in drugi spisi* (pp. 9–85). ISH–Inštitut za humanistične študije.

Järvekülg, M., Ibrus, I., & Rohn, U. (2024). Shifting from Web2 to Web3: The adaptive creator experiences on blockchain-based video-sharing and streaming platforms. *Convergence*, *30*(3), 1290–1306. DOI: 10.1177/13548565231214184

Kopf, S. (2020). "Rewarding good creators": Corporate social media discourse on monetization schemes for content creators. *Social Media + Society*, *6*(4), 2056305120969877. DOI: 10.1177/2056305120969877

Kressbach, M. (2021). Period hacks: Menstruating in the big data paradigm. *Television & New Media*, *22*(3), 241–261. DOI: 10.1177/1527476419886389

Latour, B. (2005). *Reassembling the social: An introduction to actor-network-theory*. Oxford University Press.

Mattelart, T. (2023). US digital platforms in the Global South. In P. Bouquillion, C. Ithurbide, & T. Mattelart, *Digital platforms and the Global South* (pp. 18–36). Routledge. https://doi.org/DOI: 10.4324/9781003391746-1

McIver, W. J.Jr, Merrilee, R., & Birdsall, W. F. (2003). The Internet and the right to communicate. *First Monday*, *8*(12). https://firstmonday.org/issues/issue8_12/mciver/index.html

Merga, M. K. (2024). TikTok and digital health literacy: A systematic review. *IFLA Journal*. Advance online publication. DOI: 10.1177/03400352241286175

Nagy, P., & Neff, G. (2015). Imagined affordance: Reconstructing a keyword for communication theory. *Social Media + Society*, *1*(2), 2056305115603385. DOI: 10.1177/2056305115603385

Napoli, P. M. (2024). Epistemic rights, information inequalities, and public policy. In Aslama Horowitz, M., Nieminen, H., Lehtisaari, K., & D'Arma, A. (Eds.), *Epistemic rights in the era of digital disruption* (pp. 47–62). Springer International Publishing., DOI: 10.1007/978-3-031-45976-4_4

Nieborg, D. B., Poell, T., & van Dijck, J. (2023). Platforms and platformization. In Flew, T., Holt, J., & Thomas, J. (Eds.), *The SAGE handbook of the digital media economy* (pp. 29–49). SAGE Publications Ltd., DOI: 10.4135/9781529757170.n4

Poell, T., Nieborg, D., & van Dijck, J. (2019). Platformisation. *Internet Policy Review*, *8*(4). Advance online publication. DOI: 10.14763/2019.4.1425

Sigaut, F. (1995). Technology. In *Companion encyclopedia of anthropology* (pp. 420–459). Routledge.

Terren, L., & Borge-Bravo, R., & Open University of Catalonia. (2021). Echo chambers on social media: A systematic review of the literature. *Review of Communication Research*, *9*, 99–118. DOI: 10.12840/ISSN.2255-4165.028

Troeger, J., & Bock, A. (2022). The sociotechnical walkthrough: A methodological approach for platform studies. *Studies in Communication Sciences*, *22*(1). Advance online publication. DOI: 10.24434/j.scoms.2022.01.3064

Tüfekçi, Z. (2017). *Twitter and tear gas: The power and fragility of networked protest*. Yale University Press.

Turkle, S. (1997). *Life on the screen: Identity in the age of the Internet*. Phoenix.

Vatikiotis, P. (2005). Communication theory and alternative media. *Westminster Papers in Communication and Culture*, *2*(1), 4–29.

Zajc, M. (2000). *Tehnologije in družbe*. ISH Fakulteta za podiplomski humanistični študij.

Zajc, M. (2015). Social media, prosumption, and dispositives: New mechanisms of the construction of subjectivity. *Journal of Consumer Culture, 15*(1), 28–47. DOI: 10.1177/1469540513493201

Zeng, J., Abidin, C., & Schäfer, M. S. (2021). Research perspectives on TikTok and its legacy apps: Introduction. https://doi.org/DOI: 10.5167/UZH-205427

Zuboff, S. (2022). "We make them dance": Surveillance capitalism, the rise of instrumentarian power, and the threat to human rights. In *Human rights in the age of platforms* (pp. 73–93). The MIT Press.

Chapter 6
Disinformation in Digital Media and the Right to Access Public Information During Disasters:
A Study on the Case of the 2023 Turkey Earthquake

Mahmut Enes Agca
https://orcid.org/0000-0003-1944-5635
Istinye University, Turkey

ABSTRACT

This study examines the practices of information production and public communication by the media during the February 6, 2023, earthquakes in Turkey within the framework of social responsibility and the public's right to access accurate information. While digital media enables rapid communication during disasters, some media outlets shared unverified information and practiced self-censorship during this period. Additionally, the restrictive attitudes of public institutions toward access to official information undermined the public's right to timely and accurate knowledge. This study emphasizes the responsibility of media organizations to adhere to ethical journalism principles and their duty to inform society. It evaluates the media's dual role during disasters: countering disinformation and ensuring that information reaches the public without being subjected to censorship.

DOI: 10.4018/979-8-3373-3685-5.ch006

INTRODUCTION

In times of disaster, digital media provides a space for two-way communication that gives the public access to information but also allows misinformation to spread. The 6 February 2023 earthquakes in Turkey are a critical case in terms of the information disseminated through social media platforms and digital news outlets. While digital media allows users to share information rapidly, it also enables false or misleading information to spread at the same speed (Allcott & Gentzkow, 2017). This book chapter will explore the dynamics of disinformation disseminated through digital media during disasters, and its implications for the right to access public information.

In times of disaster, the media's responsibility is to disseminate accurate and reliable information quickly, raise public awareness, and prevent panic. However, during the 2023 earthquakes in Turkey, some media outlets made crisis management more difficult by disseminating misleading or unverified information. According to crisis communication theories, media outlets should adhere to ethical and responsible journalism principles when informing the public during disasters (Coombs, 2014). However, the lack of verification mechanisms, particularly with regard to information disseminated via social media, causes misinformation to spread rapidly during times of crisis (Vosoughi, Roy & Aral, 2018). Crises are unpredictable situations that can affect the reputation of the people or organisations involved and lead to negative consequences (Coombs, 2019). Similar to this definition, Herrmann (1963) describes a crisis as an unpredictable situation in which existing values are threatened and there is limited time to react. Cutlip, Center and Broom (1994) categorise crises as either sudden, developing or ongoing. Sudden crises occur and end within a very short period of time, such as earthquakes, fires and armed attacks. Developing crises refer to situations such as sexual harassment and mobbing, where the event begins before growing into a crisis. Finally, ongoing crises are those that continue despite all actions taken to combat them (Çınarlı, 2016).

Similar to this definition, Herrmann (1963) describes a crisis as an unpredictable situation in which existing values are under threat and time to react is limited. Cutlip, Center and Broom (1994), on the other hand, categorise crises as either sudden, developing or ongoing. Sudden crises occur and end within a very short period of time; examples include earthquakes, fires and armed attacks. Developing crises refer to situations such as sexual harassment and mobbing, where the event begins before escalating into a crisis. Finally, Çınarlı (2016) defines ongoing crises as those that continue despite all actions taken to combat them. When a natural disaster strikes, public institutions have a key responsibility to ensure effective emergency response and relief activities. It is also important to facilitate communication between the public and state government agencies to keep people informed and address their concerns (Platania, Hernandez & Arreola, 2022, p. 1).

Literature on disaster communication generally focuses on structuring disaster messages to elicit effective responses (Gultom, 2016, p. 478). In pre-disaster communication processes, disasters are treated as a risk, with communication activities aimed at raising awareness, encouraging preparedness and taking precautions. During the disaster, the focus shifts to communication activities aimed at informing the public and reducing damage. In post-disaster communication processes, however, the aim is for society to regain its pre-disaster functioning. Clearly, communication plays an important role at every stage of the disaster management process, from before the disaster strikes to the post-disaster period. As Spialek and Houston (2018, p. 936) point out, communication lies at the heart of disaster management processes. This is because communication facilitates disaster assessment, enables coping behaviours, and often leads to disaster response efforts. Disaster communication can be defined as the creation, seeking and sharing of information between individuals, organisations and the media in the context of an event that could significantly impact public expectations (Liu et al., 2016, p. 628).

The proliferation of digital disinformation during natural disasters poses a significant threat to public safety and to the fundamental right of access to accurate and timely information. Although social media offers unprecedented opportunities for rapid communication and information dissemination, its pervasive nature also creates an environment conducive to the spread of false or misleading content, which can have dire consequences in emergencies (Wiederhold, 2013). The 2023 earthquake in Turkey is a striking reminder of the challenges associated with managing the flow of information in the digital age, particularly in the context of a large-scale disaster, where access to reliable information is crucial for an effective response and recovery effort (Imran et al., 2014). The growing dependence on ICT in disaster response underscores the imperative for emergency response agencies to adapt and overcome weaknesses that can be mitigated through technological solutions and organisational changes. Studying the earthquake in Turkey provides valuable insights into the dynamics of digital disinformation, its impact on public access to information, and strategies to mitigate its harmful effects.

This study will evaluate the earthquake disaster that took place in Turkey in 2023 within the above conceptual framework. In line with the book's title, the study will contribute to literature on journalism, public relations, and disaster communication within the context of the public's right to know.

1. ACCESS TO ACCURATE INFORMATION AND MEDIA IN THE DIGITAL AGE

In the digital age, the right of access to accurate information is one of the most fundamental human rights. In fact, the importance of this issue has been emphasised in internationally valid documents since long before digital technologies became part of our everyday lives. One such document is Article 19 of the United Nations Universal Declaration of Human Rights. Not only does this article emphasise individuals' freedom of expression and opinion, it also includes the right to access accurate information without any interference (United Nations, 1948, Article 19). Additionally, the European Convention on Human Rights, another significant human rights document, recognises the right of access to information as a right that should be available to all without interference from public institutions (Council of Europe, 1950). However, the same article also states that this right can be restricted to ensure public order. However, the European Convention on Human Rights acknowledges that this right can be limited in the public interest. This is particularly relevant in the context of events that affect society as a whole, such as disasters. Natural disasters are one of the times when people need accurate information about their basic needs. Therefore, ensuring the flow of accurate information to the public during these periods is of the utmost importance. A 2020 study in Turkey, the focus of this study, revealed that society primarily considers public institutions and officials to be sources of accurate information, followed by scientists and media professionals (Çakı, 2020).

In the digital age, there are more opportunities to access information. Compared to the past, the diversity of information sources has increased. While traditional mass media such as newspapers, television and radio report events in line with their technical capabilities, they may overlook events where these capabilities are limited, or choose not to report them due to the threshold watchdog system. Thanks to new media technologies, people in society can also contribute to the flow of information through social media by filming and narrating events they witness. In this way, alongside traditional media organisations, journalistic practices defined as citizen journalism have emerged within society. Citizen journalism is defined as non-media professionals reporting events of public interest using new media and sharing them with the public (Roberts, 2025; Miller, 2019; Goode, 2009).

The benefits of citizen journalism to society include reporting developments that the media does not include in its agenda or overlooks, and providing news that is outside the traditional media organisations' watchdog mechanism and content policies. However, citizen journalists without professional media training may spread misinformation when sharing events on social media without verifying the accuracy of their accounts of events they have witnessed. This raises concerns about digital media being seen as a reliable source of news. This can lead to public fear and panic due to misinformation. This raises the issue of restricting access to accurate information. Nevertheless, citizen journalism activities are not the only reason for restricting access to information.

When news consumption sources worldwide are analysed, social media emerges as the primary source of news, with usage rates of 87% in South Africa, 73% in Great Britain, 72% in the United States, 67% in Germany and 58% in Japan as of 2024 (Reuters Institute for the Study of Journalism, 2024). However, when data from 2011 to 2024 is analysed, it reveals that the percentage of people considering social media a reliable source of information has decreased from 45% in 2011 to 42% in 2024 (Edelman, 2025). These figures suggest that, although social media is the most important source of information for society, there are issues regarding access to reliable information. One study found that people trust television news more than social media, believing that news has become more reliable thanks to video content and journalists reporting the news (Bilton, 2017). Consequently, television, as a traditional mass medium, is regarded as a more dependable news source than social media. In this respect, it can be said that another reason why people are reluctant to engage with social media and the news published on these platforms is that they have continued to exhibit certain personal habits from the past, and they want the latest developments to be conveyed by trusted individuals.

Considering the opportunities offered by the social square to people working in journalism, it can be seen that the public may trust information originating from social media more if journalists continue their activities on their own YouTube channels. Therefore, it can be predicted that trust in this field will increase with the presence of individuals who inspire trust through their work in traditional media within the new media landscape.

In addition to the advantages of the new media environment's instant and fast news flow, access to information may be restricted to prevent the publication of inaccurate news that could cause panic and fear in society. The law stipulates that these restrictions must serve the public interest. Therefore, it can be said that these restrictions essentially fall within the scope of recognised rights and that decisions to restrict access to digital media fall within the scope of the right to access information, ensuring that people have access to accurate information and protecting them from misinformation.

2. THE DISSEMINATION OF FALSE INFORMATION VIA SOCIAL MEDIA PLATFORMS DURING PERIODS OF DISASTER

In situations where disaster strikes, such as earthquakes, floods, fires and pandemics, there is often a paucity of accurate information. It is evident that such periods are characterised by a prevalence of disinformation, misinformation and infodemic within the digital ecosystem. The World Health Organization (WHO) asserts that the distinction between disinformation and misinformation lies in the level of awareness regarding the falsehood of the disseminated information (World Health Organization, 2025a). In the event that an individual disseminates information with the intention of causing harm by being aware of its falsity, the question of disinformation arises. However, information that is not known to be false but is shared with the belief that it is true is defined within the framework of the concept of misinformation. Conversely, the term "infodemic" is defined as an information epidemic in which information that is both true and false is frequently circulated, especially during situations such as pandemics, disasters and crises (World Health Organization, 2025b). In the context of the recent global outbreak of the novel coronavirus, numerous studies have highlighted the pervasive presence of disinformation and conspiracy theories on social media platforms (Su, Lee, Xiao, Li, & Shu, 2021; Dow, Johnson, Wang, Whitson, & Menon, 2021).

The advent of social media has facilitated access to a plethora of voices, providing individuals with a diverse array of perspectives on myriad subjects. However, this accessibility has also exposed users to content that is both misinformative and conspiratorial, often in direct opposition to scientific facts. In this particular instance, it can be posited that individuals should be cognisant of the concept of disinformation, be apprised of the perspectives that have garnered scientific validation, and possess the capacity to access accurate information within the multifaceted milieu of social media. Media literacy has been identified as a pivotal approach that facilitates the acquisition of the competencies necessary to select the most accurate and logical approach from a plethora of information in digital media (Livingstone, 2004; Festl, 2020). It can be argued that the development of media literacy in individuals enables them to utilise digital media with greater consciousness and awareness. In periods of crisis, the proliferation of disinformation and conspiracy theories on social media can be mitigated by individuals taking a proactive approach and reporting such content. Nevertheless, the dissemination of false information and conspiracy theories cannot be considered as risks that can be mitigated solely by the self-efficacy level of individuals.

A review of the literature reveals that disinformation is most commonly defined as the deliberate propagation of false information (Shu, Bhattacharjee, Alatawi et al., 2020; Fetzer, 2004; Freelon, Wells, 2020; Kuo, Marwick, 2021). Misinformation is frequently erroneously equated with disinformation, and it is defined as the propagation of erroneous information that is erroneously believed to be accurate, with no intention of informing other individuals (Wu, Morstatter, Carley, & Liu, 2019; Altay, Berriche, & Acerbi, 2023). In periods of crisis, the concept of infodemic, which refers to the rapid spread of both accurate information and misinformation, becomes particularly salient. The concept of infodemic is one that has gained significant traction in recent times, particularly in circumstances where individuals find themselves confronted with a state of uncertainty, often succumbing to fear and panic (Gölbaşı & Metintaş, 2020). The dissemination of disinformation and misinformation has been identified as a contributing factor to the propagation of infodemic (Zarocostas, 2020). Individuals who seek information from social media during periods of fear and panic are susceptible to encountering content from public institutions and news organisations, as well as from individuals who endorse conspiracy theories and disseminate disinformation (Borges do Nascimento et al., 2022). While this situation can be regarded as an impediment to the public's access to accurate information, it can also disrupt the flow of information provided by public institutions and hinder the implementation of crisis communication strategies (Boztepe Taşkıran,2023).

In this context, the extent to which individual literacy in digital media can serve as a preventative measure against disinformation during times of disaster can be examined. Consequently, it is feasible to bolster individuals' digital media literacy through institutional strategies devised by organisations such as public institutions and verification networks. In addition to these organisations, it can be argued that social media platforms should also play an active role in preventing the dissemination of disinformation. It is evident that Facebook collaborates with verification networks, whereby content disseminated on the platform is directed to these networks via algorithms and notifications from users. These platforms subsequently provide Facebook with a definitive decision regarding the nature of the content. (Teyit.org, 2018; Andersen, Søe, 2019). Twitter's approach to combating disinformation can be outlined as follows: firstly, the content is marked with a hashtag that indicates its source; secondly, the decision on the content is made through community engagement notes; thirdly, the tweets are made invisible and subsequently removed. Consequently, the dissemination of disinformation can be regarded as a problem that requires concerted action from individuals, relevant public institutions and social media platforms.

It is noteworthy that independently operating verification networks can also be regarded as actors in the prevention of disinformation. With the assistance of verification organisations, social media platforms have the capacity to develop algorithmic filters with the objective of curtailing the propagation of disinformation. Moreover, by establishing transparent content moderation processes and accentuating reliable sources of information, these platforms can facilitate the dissemination of accurate information as opposed to disinformation content (Pennycook & Rand, 2021).

The infodemic situation that emerges during disaster periods has been shown to cause individuals to succumb to fear and panic (Jones, 2019). Furthermore, it has been demonstrated that this phenomenon can hinder the success of disaster communication strategies employed by organisations in the post-disaster period. Indeed, effective communication strategies in disaster management have been shown to be of great importance in this regard. Cinelli et al. (2020) conducted a study which revealed that individuals experienced difficulty in distinguishing between reliable and unreliable information during the period of the pandemic. This was due to the effect of fear and panic, which resulted in a tendency towards feelings of distrust towards official institutional statements. This, in turn, had a detrimental effect on public safety. Furthermore, in the earthquake that occurred in Turkey in 2023, which will be analysed as a case study in this study, the dissemination of disinformation regarding the fracture of the dam resulted in widespread disbelief, leading to the suspension of search and rescue operations in the region (Ağca, 2024). Conversely, traditional media outlets continue to wield considerable influence in terms of reaching large audiences. However, the pressure to circulate news quickly in times of crisis can lead media professionals to bypass verification processes, thus facilitating the dissemination of misinformation (Silverman, 2015). At this juncture, it is imperative to adopt a journalistic approach that strictly adheres to the ethical principles of journalism. This is not only for professional responsibility, but also for social responsibility (Ward, 2015). It is therefore imperative that journalists adhere to rigorous news verification mechanisms when disseminating information, particularly during times of crisis, and that public institutions expeditiously disseminate accurate information.

In periods of crisis, public institutions and media outlets are required to adopt a significantly more strategic and responsible approach to their communication processes than is typical. This phenomenon is especially evident in the context of disasters, epidemics, and other emergencies, when the demand for information typically increases exponentially. The public has come to expect a rapid, reliable and comprehensible flow of information. Consequently, it is imperative for public institutions to formulate a proactive crisis communication strategy. The timely and open sharing of information is conducive to the maintenance of social trust by preventing the spread of misinformation and disinformation (Coombs, 2014). It can be argued that the general communication approaches of public institutions are in a very weak position with society. The utilisation of communication channels is not active in such cases (Lee, Vandyke, 2015), and individuals anticipating explanations in disaster situations resort to disinformative content. In consideration of the aforementioned data, it can be posited that the entitlement to access accurate information during times of disaster is not solely a matter of individual responsibility. Conversely, this has evolved into a matter of human rights that is the responsibility of the state and platform providers.

In the contemporary digital age, the effective utilisation of social media platforms by public institutions provides a strategic conduit for direct communication with the public during times of crisis. However, such platforms should not only be used for announcements and information; they should also be used to respond to public inquiries, be open to feedback and be interactive (Reynolds & Seeger, 2005).

The failure to provide the public with adequate information during times of disaster can result in a crisis of trust. A crisis of trust has the potential to engender a wave of scepticism, not only towards the state but also towards the media, health authorities and scientists (Ağca, 2025). Consequently, communication activities to be implemented during periods of crisis should not solely aspire to inform, but also to cultivate trust. It is incumbent upon organisations to establish an open, empathetic and continuous dialogue with the public. Conversely, information gaps can be rapidly filled with disinformation through social media. In the event of the information gap being filled with disinformation, it is possible that restrictions on access to social media may be introduced as a step in the fight against disinformation. Despite the widely accepted notion that public authorities have a responsibility to furnish the public with accurate and timely information during periods of crisis (Mendel, 2008), it is acknowledged that in certain instances, communication strategies may prove ineffective in the dissemination of disinformation. It is therefore vital that governments and social media platforms intervene in the flow of information to prevent misinformation, achieving a delicate balance between the right to access information and the fight against disinformation.

In times of disaster, internet restriction decisions taken by public authorities are justified as a means of combating disinformation. Nevertheless, such practices frequently impede the dissemination of both accurate information and disinformation. The extant literature posits the notion that, whilst the principles of freedom of expression and the right to access information may be subject to certain limitations, these limitations should be founded upon the principles of legality, legitimate purpose and proportionality (Centre for Law and Democracy, 2021). Should the measures implemented with the aim of preventing the dissemination of disinformation be applied in such a manner as to result in a disproportionate and indiscriminate form of censorship, this may constitute a clear violation of rights. Furthermore, such restrictions have the potential to erode public trust in institutional entities, thereby prompting individuals to seek alternative sources of information that may lack credibility (Tandoc, Lim, & Ling, 2017). In the subsequent section, the information pollution in digital media, the disinformative content disseminated, and the communication strategies of public institutions during the Kahramanmaraş earthquakes that occurred in Turkey on February 6, 2023 will be discussed in detail through a case study. This case will provide an opportunity to discuss how the right to access accurate information is violated in times of disaster and how disinformation disrupts crisis management through a concrete example.

3. CASE STUDY: 2023 TURKEY EARTHQUAKE

On 6 February 2023, a series of earthquakes measuring 7.8 and 7.5 on the Richter scale struck Kahramanmaraş, resulting in the deaths of 45,890 individuals and necessitating the provision of emergency shelter for nearly 2 million people (AFAD, 2023). The earthquake disaster, with its devastating consequences, marks a period in which disinformation and conspiracy theories were disseminated in the aftermath. The present study will analyse the efforts of people to seek accurate information immediately after the devastating impact of the earthquake, the media's publications during the earthquake, and the spread of disinformation and conspiracy theories. This analysis will be conducted in the form of a case study of the 2023 Turkey Earthquake. Furthermore, the crisis communication strategies employed by public institutions will be evaluated within the context of the right to access accurate information. Case analysis involves the examination of two distinct yet interconnected components: firstly, the intrinsic characteristics of a case itself; and secondly, the environment surrounding it (Neuman, 2021). In the specific case of Turkey, the present study will endeavour to reflect the general climate of the disaster period by presenting examples of Turkish society's relationship with information sources in the aftermath of the earthquake. In addition, the study will address the extent to which disinformation and conspiracy theories are prevalent on social media, the reporting practices of the media, and the crisis communication strategies of public institutions. Subsequently, restrictions on access to social media imposed by public authorities will be evaluated in the context of restricting the right to access information.

3.1. Disinformation and Effects of Disinformation on Social Media During the Earthquake Period

In the aftermath of the earthquake disaster centred in Kahramanmaraş province of Turkey, which significantly affected Turkey and Syria, a substantial amount of disinformation content was circulated on social media. Indeed, it has been asserted that the number of disinformation items disseminated on social media during this period exceeded one hundred (Tekeş, 2025). In the study published by Méndez-Muros, Alonso-González & Pérez-Curiel (2024), it was revealed that 51% of disinformation content spread on social media during the period under investigation was information given in the wrong context, 23% was completely fabricated content, and as a remarkable finding, it was also stated that the information verified by the official authorities had only 8% interaction. Of the disinformation disseminated, that pertaining to the "Dam burst" has been found to have the greatest impact. A social media post by a content producer with a significant following in Turkey led to a situation where the local population was compelled to evacuate the city due to fear and panic. This resulted in the suspension of search and rescue operations due to the dissemination of disinformation (Ağca, 2024). Statements made by officials from official institutions proved insufficient to mitigate the impact of the disinformation, yet after a brief period, it was revealed that the claim was unfounded (Tekeş & Sarsılmaz, 2023; Sözcü, 2023). Following the realisation that the incident in question was a case of disinformation, it came to light that the broadcasting organisation had published the news by circumventing the standard verification process employed in journalism. Furthermore, the news was disseminated without any verification of the information received (Ağca, 2024).

Another significant piece of disinformation disseminated during this period pertains to the alleged looting by individuals with refugee status in Turkey due to the civil war in Syria following the earthquake. This particular narrative has garnered notable traction on social media platforms (Kandemir, 2024; Botan, 2023; Büyük, 2023). The prevailing sentiment in the region has been influenced by news reports which have increased incidents of violence against refugees. This phenomenon has been reflected in both the press and reports by Amnesty International and Human Rights Watch (Amnesty International, 2023; Human Rights Watch, 2023; Tatlı, 2023).

In the 2023 Turkey Earthquake, in addition to disinformation, conspiracy theories were also frequently discussed on social media. The hypothesis that seismic events can be attributed to the HAARP research project, as indicated by the documented association with the American-flagged ship observed in Istanbul on 5 February 2023, has been a subject of considerable debate. This assertion has been further substantiated by the occurrence of two major earthquakes in Turkey, which have been interpreted as potential outcomes of artificial seismic activity. This has led to the dissemination of the conspiracy theory on various social media platforms (Akyıldız, 2023; Zivic, 2023; Kıyan, Özer, 2023; Çetindemir, 2023).

3.2. Censorship and Self-Censorship in the Earthquake Period

In consequence of the propagation of disinformation and conspiracy theories during the earthquake period, social media platforms, particularly Twitter, experienced a reduction in the number of users in Turkey (Çakır, 2023; Günaydın, 2023). In the aftermath of widespread public protest, the authorities rescinded the band throttling after 9.5 hours, and social media was once again made accessible (Ayhan, 2023). Moreover, the Ankara 15th Administrative Court ruled that the band narrowing constituted an obstruction of the right to information, and the public institution was found to be in the wrong (Diken, 2023). Subsequent statements issued by public institution officials to the media asserted the narrowing of the band as a "necessary" measure, yet no rationale was provided for this decision (Bianet, 2023). In addition to the narrowing of the band, a state of emergency was declared on 9 February 2023 by a decision of the Grand National Assembly of Turkey (Republic of Turkey Communications Presidency, 2023). Furthermore, the President of the Republic of Turkey emphasised that the state of emergency decision, which encompasses the earthquake zone, was implemented with the objective of mitigating the prevailing climate of fear and panic within society, precipitated by the dissemination of misinformation in the region. The state of emergency was also declared with the intention of preventing situations such as looting and extortion that may arise (Medyascope, 2023; Ministry of Interior of the Republic of Turkey, 2023). Consequently, it can be posited that the propagation of disinformation through social media engenders social negativity, compelling decision-makers to declare a state of emergency to intervene in these adverse circumstances.

In the context of the right to access accurate information in times of disasters, it can be considered that there is a state of emergency declared due to the unconscious use of freedom of expression and the failure of public authorities' strategies to combat disinformation. However, human rights associations have expressed concerns that the restrictions imposed by the government are not in accordance with human rights principles (Amnesty International, 2023; Human Rights Watch, 2023).

Another problematic situation that hinders the public's access to accurate information during the earthquake period is the practice of media organisations not allowing earthquake victims to provide their own testimonies and to interrupt interviews. This state of affairs gives rise to the media's failure to fulfil its responsibility to inform the public. During an interview conducted by Habertürk TV, one of the most frequently watched television channels in Turkey, with earthquake survivors located in close proximity to the earthquake debris, an earthquake survivor who stated that aid was unable to reach the earthquake zone was swiftly interrupted by the reporter and redirected to a different subject (Solhaber, 2023). In a manner analogous to the Habertürk broadcast, the NTV news channel elected to report a different news story by removing the relevant reporter from the broadcast after the earthquake victims' statements that no aid had reached the earthquake zone were broadcast (Cumhuriyet, 2023). Turkey's public broadcaster TRT, for instance, delayed its broadcasts in the earthquake zone until the search and rescue teams arrived on the scene (Journo, 2023).

CONCLUSION

The earthquakes, measuring 7.8 and 7.5 on the Richter scale, which occurred in quick succession on 6 February 2023, are among the most severe earthquake disasters to befall the nation. These seismic events resulted in significant loss of life and property. In addition to the physical destruction, a grave crisis was also engendered in the digital ecosystem. In the period following the earthquakes, which were accompanied by a climate of fear and panic, there was an increase in the dissemination of disinformation. It is acknowledged that the authorities have issued corrections for more than 100 pieces of disinformation content as part of the ongoing efforts to combat disinformation (Republic of Turkey Presidency of Communication, 2023). It is acknowledged that these disinformation items have resulted in incidents of social violence and the suspension of search and rescue operations. Consequently, the dissemination of disinformation has not only resulted in the propagation of misinformation, but also given rise to social negativity. When disinformation content is analysed, it becomes evident that the dissemination of false information regarding the rupture of the dam has had such a profound impact that it has led to the cessation of search and rescue operations. This underscores the urgent need for a swift and precise response to disinformation on social media platforms. In addition to the dissemination of disinformation, the HAARP conspiracy theory has propagated as a consequence of the integration of HAARP with the assertion that a foreign nation is responsible for inducing seismic activity. The absence of a counter-communication strategy, particularly on the part of public institutions, was perceived by proponents of the conspiracy theory as indicative of its veracity.

Moreover, the government's restrictive measures have impeded the public's access to accurate information. In the decision of the local court, the restriction decisions taken by the government authorities were considered as obstruction of the right to information and the restriction decision was lifted.

In addition to the restrictions imposed on social media, the reporting practices of news outlets during the earthquake period have also been the subject of debate. In this period, characterised by a tendency among media professionals to self-censor, the absence of reporting on the negative experiences during the earthquake, and the subsequent inability of citizens to articulate their concerns through media channels, underscores a significant issue within the broader context of media accountability. The media's tendency to prioritise the dissemination of information that is partial in nature and lacking in accuracy, as opposed to presenting a balanced and factual perspective, signifies a deeply concerning predicament with regard to the public's access to reliable information. In this context, disinformation and self-censorship manifest as two principal communication issues that mutually reinforce each other during periods of disaster. In situations of crisis, such as disasters, the public's need for accurate and timely information increases. However, the restriction of social media, which is the most utilised source of information in Turkey (We are social; Meltwater, 2025), has created a highly problematic situation for the public in accessing accurate information during disasters. The restriction of information sources by government officials has been demonstrated to reduce trust in the accuracy of information disseminated by the government. Therefore, it can be posited that people have become more vulnerable to disinformation spread on social media.

In addition to official institutions, the media's adoption of broadcast policies that repeat the state's discourse instead of producing independent news, and its preference not to broadcast the words of citizens who wish to be heard from the disaster area, have also led to questions being asked regarding the public's trust in media institutions. It is evident that the aforementioned factors have had a considerable impact on the public's ability to access alternative and reliable information channels. This has encouraged the search for social media-based information and facilitated the dissemination of unverified content.

The government's decision to impose a temporary restriction on access to social media platforms such as Twitter during the initial phase of the disaster had a significant impact on the dissemination of information. The disruption to communication caused by this restriction, coupled with the emotional impact of the disaster on the population, resulted in a decline in public faith in official institutions and traditional media. This demonstrates how the closure of open channels of communication, or the conversion of such channels into unidirectional conduits, can engender a trust deficit during periods of crisis.

In conclusion, a robust causal relationship has been demonstrated between the propagation of disinformation and the practice of self-censorship. The existence of one serves to augment the impact of the other, and the resulting information crises once again reveal how vital it is to have an independent and critical journalism approach that is in the public interest. It is therefore vital to emphasise that, in times of disaster, transparent, pluralistic and reliable information policies are not only of importance, but absolutely vital.

This study suggests that, in future research, a mixed-methodology approach incorporating both qualitative and quantitative data may prove beneficial in elucidating the sources of information to which the public turns in environments characterised by restrictions to access imposed by official institutions and by the dissemination of information by the media that is perceived to be insecure. The objective of such an approach would be to facilitate the more effective organisation of public disaster and crisis communication strategies on the part of official institutions.

REFERENCES

Afet ve Acil Durum Yönetimi Başkanlığı (AFAD). (2023). *Kahramanmaraş'ta Meydana Gelen Depremler Hk.* https://www.afad.gov.tr/kahramanmarasta-meydana-gelen-depremler-hk-36

Ağca, M. E. (2024). A study of disinformation on social media during disasters: The case of the dam burst. *Contemporary Issues of Communication, 3*(1), 41–50. DOI: 10.5281/zenodo.10778108

Ağca, M. E. (2025). *Bilim iletişimi: Antik Uygarlıklardan Yapay Zeka Çağına.* Kriter Yayınevi.

Akyıldız, M. (2023). Yalan Haber ve Dezenformasyonun Sosyal Medyada Yayılımı: Kahramanmaraş Depreminin Haarp Silahı Olduğu İddiası. *Türkiye Medya Akademisi Dergisi, 3*(6), 523–543. DOI: 10.5281/zenodo.8378837

Allcott, H., & Gentzkow, M. (2017). Social Media and Fake News in the 2016 Election. *The Journal of Economic Perspectives, 31*(2), 211–236.

Altay, S., Berriche, M., & Acerbi, A. (2023). Misinformation on misinformation: Conceptual and methodological challenges. *Social Media + Society, 9*(1). Advance online publication. DOI: 10.1177/20563051221150412

Amnesty International. (2023, April 5). *Türkiye: Deprem bölgesinde polis ve jandarma ihlalleri - İşkence ve diğer türde kötü muamele yapıldı, şiddetli saldırılar önlenmedi.* https://www.amnesty.org.tr/icerik/turkiye-deprem-bolgesinde-polis-ve-jandarma-ihlalleri-iskence-ve-diger-turde-kötü-muamele-yapildi-siddetli-saldirilar-onlenmedi

Andersen, J., & Søe, S. O. (2019). Communicative actions we live by: The problem with fact-checking, tagging or flagging fake news – the case of Facebook. *European Journal of Communication, 35*(2), 126–139. DOI: 10.1177/0267323119894489

Ayhan, D. (2023, February 8). *Twitter'a 9,5 saat erişim engeli....* Sözcü. https://www.sozcu.com.tr/twitter-ve-tiktoka-erisim-engellendi-wp7584907

Bianet. (2023, April 6). *Karaismailoğlu, "Depremde İnterneti kestik çünkü gerekliydi" dedi, nedenini açıklayamadı.* https://bianet.org/haber/karaismailoglu-depremde-interneti-kestik-cunku-gerekliydi-dedi-nedenini-aciklayamadi-276943

Bilton, R. (2017). *Why don't people trust the news and social media? A new report lets them explain in their own words.* Niemanlab. https://www.niemanlab.org/2017/11/why-dont-people-trust-the-news-and-social-media-a-new-report-lets-them-explain-in-their-own-words/

Borges do Nascimento, I. J., Pizarro, A. B., Almeida, J. M., Azzopardi-Muscat, N., Gonçalves, M. A., Björklund, M., & Novillo-Ortiz, D. (2022). Infodemics and health misinformation: A systematic review of reviews. *Bulletin of the World Health Organization, 100*(9), 544–561. DOI: 10.2471/BLT.21.287654

Botan, M. (2023, April 23). *Tam 77 gün oldu: Depremlerden sonra hızla yayılan yağma haberleri fikri takip bekliyor.* Journo. https://journo.com.tr/deprem-yagma-haberleri

Boztepe Taşkıran, H. (2023). Afet İletişimi Nedir, Ne Değildir? *Yeni Medya*, (14), 359–363.

Büyük, G. (2023, February 11). *Ailesine ilaç götüren gençleri yağmacı diyerek linç ettiler.* Aydınlık. https://www.aydinlik.com.tr/haber/ailesine-ilac-goturen-gencleri-yagmaci-diyerek-linc-ettiler-367295

Çakı, F. (2020). Afet Yönetişiminde Sivil Toplum ve Güven Algıları. [SKAD]. *Sosyal Ve Kültürel Araştırmalar Dergisi, 6*(12), 1–45. DOI: 10.25306/skad.720617

Çakır, O. (2023, February 8). *Twitter erişimi neden kısıtlandı? Açıklama geldi.* Shiftdelete.net. https://shiftdelete.net/twitter-erisimi-neden-engellendi-resmi-aciklama

Centre for Law and Democracy. (2021). *Report of the Special Rapporteur on the promotion and protection of the right to freedom of opinion and expression.* https://undocs.org/A/HRC/35/22

Çetindemir, Ç. (2023, February 6). *Depremlerin Boğaz'daki ABD savaş gemisiyle alakalı olduğu" iddiası.* Anadolu Ajansı. https://www.aa.com.tr/tr/teyithatti/aktuel/depremlerin-bogazdaki-abd-savas-gemisiyle-alakali-oldugu-iddiasi/1815311

Çınarlı, İ. (2016). *Örnek vaka analizleri ile kriz iletişimi.* Beta Yayıncılık.

Coombs, W. T. (2014). *Ongoing crisis communication: Planning, managing, and responding* (4th ed.). Sage Publications.

Coombs, W. T. (2019). Crisis Communication. In J. Gephart, C. C. Miller, & K. S. Helgesson (Eds.), *The Routledge Companion to Risk, Crisis and Emergency Management.*[2]

Council of Europe. (1950, November 4). European Convention for the Protection of Human Rights and Fundamental Freedoms, as amended by Protocols Nos. 11 and 14, ETS 5.

Cumhuriyet. (2023, February 7). *NTV canlı yayında arka plandaki depremzedelerin seslerini kestiler.* https://www.cumhuriyet.com.tr/turkiye/ntv-canli-yayinda-arka-planda-depremzedelerin-seslerini-kestiler-2049207

Diken. (2023, March 20). *Mahkeme, Twitter kısıtlamasının nedenini açıklamayan BTK'yı haksız buldu.* https://www.diken.com.tr/mahkeme-twitter-kisitlamasinin-nedenini-aciklamayan-btkyi-haksiz-buldu/

Dow, B., Johnson, A., Wang, C., Whitson, J., & Menon, T. (2021). The COVID-19 pandemic and the search for structure: Social media and conspiracy theories. *Social and Personality Psychology Compass, 15*(9).

Edelman. (2025). *2025 Edelman Trust Barometer.* https://www.edelman.com/trust/2025/trust-barometer

Festl, R. (2020). Social media literacy & adolescent social online behavior in Germany.[3]. *Journal of Children and Media, 15*(2), 249–271.

Fetzer, J. H. (2004). Disinformation: The Use of False Information. *Minds and Machines, 14*, 231–240. DOI: 10.1023/B:MIND.0000021683.28604.5b

Freelon, D., & Wells, C. (2020). Disinformation as Political Communication. *Political Communication, 37*(2), 145–156. DOI: 10.1080/10584609.2020.1723755

Gölbaşı, S. D., & Metintaş, S. (2020). COVID-19 pandemic and infodemic. *ESTUDAM Public Health Journal, 5*, 126–137.

Goode, L. (2009). Social news, citizen journalism and democracy. *New Media & Society, 11*(8), 1287–1305. DOI: 10.1177/1461444809341393

Gultom, D. I. (2016). Community-based disaster communication: How does it become trustworthy? *Disaster Prevention and Management, 25*(4), 478–491.

Günaydın, A. (2023, February 23). *Büyük sansür dalgası korkusu... Ekranlar karartıldı, meal toplatıldı, platformlara erişim engeli getirildi.* Independent

Herrmann, C. F. (1963). Some consequences of crisis which limit the viability of organizations. *Administrative Science Quarterly, 8*(1), 61–82.

Human Rights Watch. (2023, March 23). *Türkiye: Deprem bölgesinde polis ve jandarma ihlalleri.* https://www.hrw.org/tr/news/2023/04/05/turkey-police-and-gendarmerie-abuses-earthquake-zone

İletişim Başkanlığı, T. C. (2023, March 7). *5-6 Mart 2023 tarihli Deprem Dezenformasyon Bülteni yayımlandı*. https://www.iletisim.gov.tr/turkce/haberler/detay/5-6-mart-2023-tarihli-deprem-dezenformasyon-bulteni-yayimlandi

Imran, M., Castillo, C., Diaz, F., & Vieweg, S. (2014). Processing social media messages in mass emergency: A survey. ACM Computing Surveys, 47(4). *Article, 67*, 1–38.

Journo. (2023, February 8). *Sansür, otosansür ve propaganda: Depremin ardından Twitter'dan medyaya dair 10 tespit*. https://journo.com.tr/deprem-medya

Kandemir, E. Z. (2024, February 6). *Yağmacı Sanılarak Dövülen Suriyeli Depremzede: "Allah Türkiye'den Razı Olsun"*. Perspektif. https://perspektif.eu/2024/02/06/yagmaci-sanilarak-dovulen-suriyeli-depremzede-allah-turkiyeden-razi-olsun/

Kıyan, Z., & Özer, A. (2023). Kahramanmaraş merkezli 6 Şubat depremleriyle ilişkilendirilen bir komplo teorisinin düşündürdükleri: #HAARP hashtaginin analizi. In *İletişşim Yönetiminde Hayaller* (pp. 21–22). Gerçekler ve Depremler.

Kuo, R., & Marwick, A. (2021). Critical disinformation studies: History, power, and politics. *Harvard Kennedy School (HKS) Misinformation Review, 2*(4).

Lee, N. M., & VanDyke, M. S. (2015). Set It and Forget It: The One-Way Use of Social Media by Government Agencies Communicating Science.[5]. *Science Communication, 37*(4), 533–541. DOI: 10.1177/1075547015588600

Liu, B. F., Fraustino, J. D., & Jin, Y. (2016). Social media use during disasters: A field experiment. *Communication Research, 43*(5), 626–646.

Livingstone, S. (2004). Media literacy: Ambitions, policies and measures. *Intermedia*, 18–20.

Medyascope. (2023, February 9). *Erdoğan: "Tefeciler, fitne grupları ve yağma olaylarına OHAL ile müdahale etme imkânı olacak"*. https://medyascope.tv/2023/02/09/erdogan-tefeciler-fitne-gruplari-ve-yagma-olaylarina-ohal-ile-mudahale-imkani-olacak/

Mendel, T. (2008). *Freedom of information: A comparative legal survey* (2nd ed.). UNESCO., https://law.yale.edu/sites/default/files/documents/pdf/Intellectual_Life/CL-OGI_Toby_Mendel_book_%28Eng%29.pdf

Méndez-Muros, S., Alonso-González, M., & Pérez-Curiel, C. (2024). Disinformation and fact-checking in the face of natural disasters: A case study on Turkey–Syria earthquakes. *Societies (Basel, Switzerland), 14*(4), 43. DOI: 10.3390/soc14040043

Miller, S. (2019). *Citizen Journalism.* Oxford Research Encyclopedia of Communication., DOI: 10.1093/acrefore/9780190228613.013.786

Neuman, W. L. (2021). *Toplumsal araştırma yöntemleri: Nitel ve nicel yaklaşımlar.* Siyasal Kitabevi.

Pennycook, G., & Rand, D. G. (2021). The psychology of fake news. *Trends in Cognitive Sciences, 25*(5), 388–402. DOI: 10.1016/j.tics.2021.02.007

Platania, F., Toscano Hernandez, C., & Arreola, F. (2022). Social media communication during natural disasters and the impact on the agricultural market. *Technological Forecasting and Social Change, 179*, 121594.

Reuters Institute for the Study of Journalism. (2024, June 17). *Sources for news consumption in selected major media markets worldwide as of February 2024, by type* [Graph]. In Statista. Retrieved June 10, 2025, from https://www.statista.com/statistics/262079/news-access-worldwide-by-media/

Reynolds, B., & Seeger, M. W. (2005). Crisis and emergency risk communication as an integrative model. *Journal of Health Communication, 10*(1), 43–55. DOI: 10.1080/10810730590904571

Roberts, J. (2025). Citizen Journalism. In Hobbs, R., & Mihailidis, P. (Eds.), *The International Encyclopedia of Media Literacy.*, DOI: 10.1002/9781118978238.ieml0027

Shu, K., Bhattacharjee, A., & Alatawi, F.. (2020). Combating disinformation in a social media age. *Wiley Interdisciplinary Reviews. Data Mining and Knowledge Discovery, 10*, e1385. DOI: 10.1002/widm.1385

Silverman, C. (2015). *Verification handbook for digital content: A definitive guide to verifying digital content for emergency coverage.* European Journalism Centre. https://verificationhandbook.com/

Solhaber. (2023, February 8). *Show TV muhabiri 'Ekipler asla gelmiyor' diyen depremzededen mikrofonu çekip uzaklaştı.* https://haber.sol.org.tr/haber/show-tv-muhabiri-ekipler-asla-gelmiyor-diyen-depremzededen-mikrofonu-cekip-uzaklasti-365067

Sözcü. (2023, February 11). *Hatay'da baraj patladı iddiası! Bakan Kirişçi'den açıklama.* https://www.sozcu.com.tr/hatayda-baraj-patladi-iddiasi-bakan-kirisciden-aciklama-wp7587984

Su, Y., Lee, D. K., Xiao, X., Li, W., & Shu, W. (2021). Who endorses conspiracy theories? A moderated mediation model of Chinese and international social media use, media skepticism, need for cognition, and COVID-19 conspiracy theory endorsement in China. *Computers in Human Behavior*, •••, 106760.

Tandoc, E. C., Lim, Z. W., & Ling, R. (2017). Defining "Fake News": A typology of scholarly definitions. *Digital Journalism (Abingdon, England)*, *6*(2), 137–153. DOI: 10.1080/21670811.2017.1360143

Tatlı, İ. (2023, February 1). *Deprem üzerinden kışkırtılan nefret söylemi ve ayrımcılık deprem kadar yıkıcı olabilir.* Independent Türkçe. https://www.indyturk.com/node/611146/türkiyeden-sesler/deprem-üzerinden-kişkirtilan-nefret-söylemi-ve-ayrimcilik-deprem

Tekeş, A. F. (2025, February 2). *6 Şubat depremlerinin ardından yüzlerce yanıltıcı içerik yayınlandı.* Anadolu Ajansı Teyit Hattı. https://www.aa.com.tr/tr/teyithatti/blog/6-subat-depremlerinin-ardindan-yuzlerce-yaniltici-icerik-yayinlandi-/1818720

Tekeş, A. F., & Sarsılmaz, M. (2023, February 11). *Hatay'da Yarseli Barajı'nın Patladığı İddiası.* Anadolu Ajansı. https://www.aa.com.tr/tr/teyithatti/aktuel/hatayda-yarseli-barajinin-patladigi-iddiasi/1815346

Teyit.org. (2018, May 31). *Facebook'un doğrulama programı Türkiye'de Teyit iş birliğiyle hayata geçiyor.* Teyitpedia. https://teyit.org/teyitpedia/facebookun-dogrulama-programi-turkiyede-teyit-org-is-birligiyle-hayata-geciyor

Türkçe. https://www.indyturk.com/node/612526/haber/büyük-sansür-dalgası-korkusu...-ekranlar-karartıldı-meal-toplatıldı-platformlara

Türkiye Cumhuriyeti İçişleri Bakanlığı. (2023, February 14). *Cumhurbaşkanımız Sn. Erdoğan: "Hiçbir Vatandaşımızı Maddi-Manevi Açıdan Sahipsiz Bırakmayacağız".* https://www.icisleri.gov.tr/cumhurbaskanimiz-sn-erdogan-hicbir-vatandasimizi-maddi-manevi-acidan-sahipsiz-birakmayacagiz

Türkiye Cumhuriyeti İletişim Başkanlığı. (2023, February 8). *Depremden etkilenen 10 ilde kararlaştırılan OHAL ilanı, Resmî Gazete'de.* https://www.iletisim.gov.tr/turkce/haberler/detay/depremden-etkilenen-10-ilde-kararlastirilan-ohal-ilani-resmi-gazetede

UNESCO. (2022). *Media in crisis preparedness and response: Case studies and lessons learned from the COVID-19 pandemic.* United Nations Educational, Scientific and Cultural Organization. https://unesdoc.unesco.org/ark:/48223/pf0000381736

United Nations. (1948). *Universal Declaration of Human Rights.* https://www.un.org/en/about-us/universal-declaration-of-human-rights

Vosoughi, S., Roy, D., & Aral, S. (2018). The Spread of True and False News Online. *Science, 359*(6380), 1146–1151.

Ward, S. J. A. (2015). *Ethics and the media: An introduction.* Cambridge University Press.

We Are Social. Meltwater. (2025). *Digital 2025.* https://wearesocial.com/wp-content/uploads/2025/02/GDR-2025-v2.pdf

Wiederhold, B. K. (2013). When more is actually less: The rise of social media misinformation during disasters [Editorial]. *Cyberpsychology, Behavior, and Social Networking, 16*(11), 783–784.

World Health Organization. (2025a). Misinformation and disinformation. WHO. from https://www.who.int/news-room/misinformation-and-disinformation

World Health Organization. (2025b). Infodemic. WHO. Retrieved August 5, 2025, from https://www.who.int/health-topics/infodemic

Wu, L., Morstatter, F., Carley, K. M., & Liu, H. (2019). Misinformation in social media. *SIGKDD Explorations, 21*(2), 80–90. 10.1145%2F3373464.3373475

Zarocostas, J. (2020). How to fight an infodemic. *Lancet,* •••, 395.

Zivic, P. (2023, February 23). *HAARP: Kahramanmaraş depremleriyle yeniden gündeme gelen komplo teoriler.* BBC. https://www.bbc.com/turkce/articles/c72l07yln1qo

Chapter 7
Right to Privacy as a Digital Human Right

Hemendra Singh
https://orcid.org/0000-0003-1160-8284
Jindal Global Law School, O.P. Jindal Global University, Sonipat, India

ABSTRACT

This chapter explores the right to privacy as a foundational digital human right, tracing its constitutional recognition across jurisdictions and its erosion through unchecked surveillance by both state and corporate actors. Drawing from comparative jurisprudence, it highlights how privacy has evolved in global legal frameworks and the challenges posed by fragmented enforcement and democratic oversight. The analysis emphasizes the growing need for rights-based digital governance grounded in transparency, accountability and judicial safeguards. As we advance into an era defined by digital transformation, the commitment to privacy must remain central, not only as a matter of rights, but as a means to reduce systemic inequality and promoting strong institutions and justice.

INTRODUCTION

In the twenty-first century, the right to privacy stands at the crossroads of rapid digital transformation and evolving legal consciousness. While once considered a negative right protecting individuals from arbitrary state intrusion, privacy today has become a multidimensional and indispensable pillar of democratic societies, human dignity, and ethical governance (Kumar, 2019). This transformation is catalyzed by the proliferation of digital technologies, ranging from smartphones and social media platforms to algorithmic governance and biometric identification systems, that continuously mediate, monitor and often monetize human activity. This

DOI: 10.4018/979-8-3373-3685-5.ch007

landscape also poses tremendous challenges to privacy, as numerous actors collect, store, and share our personal data with numerous third parties, mostly without our knowledge (Islam, 2022).

The digitalization of human life, accelerated by globalization and the ubiquitous integration of artificial intelligence and big data, has redefined the contours of privacy. We now inhabit environments saturated with surveillance, both visible and invisible, state-sponsored and corporate-driven (Bignami & Resta, 2018). From online shopping and mobile banking to video conferencing and telemedicine, individuals are tracked, profiled, and analyzed in ways that were unimaginable only a generation ago. Nishnianidze (2024) discusses the evolving nature of surveillance in the digital era. The resulting loss of control over personal data, the normalization of constant monitoring, and the opacity of algorithmic decision-making pose significant threats to informational self-determination and autonomy.

This chapter begins by asserting that the right to privacy is foundational not only to individual liberty but also to the integrity of democratic governance and the realization of human rights in the digital era. It critically examines how digital infrastructures have altered the nature of privacy, and how legal frameworks, particularly constitutional structures, are responding to the challenges posed by this transformation. Julie E. Cohen (2013) argues that privacy cannot be reduced to a fixed condition or attribute, emphasizing that it must be understood as a dynamic and evolving construct shaped by technological and social change.

To understand the contemporary stakes of privacy, we must first appreciate its expanded scope. Privacy today includes a range of interrelated dimensions: the right to be left alone, the right to control personal information, the right to bodily integrity, the right to form relationships free from surveillance, and the right to make autonomous life choices without coercion or manipulation (Sætra, 2020). These dimensions are essential not only for safeguarding the individual but also for fostering a democratic public sphere in which citizens can think, speak, and associate freely.

As digital technologies evolve, they increasingly intrude into intimate spheres of human life. Wearable devices monitor our health, smart home systems log our daily routines, and mobile applications capture geolocation data in real time (Zhang et al., 2025). The commodification of this data, what Shoshana Zuboff terms surveillance capitalism, has transformed people into products (Zuboff, 2019). Their digital behaviors are harvested, packaged, and sold to advertisers, insurers, employers, and even political operatives. This commodification blurs the line between private and public spheres and raises profound ethical questions about autonomy, exploitation, and consent.

Moreover, surveillance in the digital age is not only about data collection. It is also about prediction, influence, and control. Algorithmic systems now make inferences about individuals' preferences, behaviors, and even future actions. These systems determine everything from which news articles people see to which job applications are shortlisted, often without transparency or accountability. This dynamic creates asymmetries of power, where a few entities, whether state authorities or private tech giants, possess the capacity to shape choices and influence outcomes at scale. The unchecked growth of such power not only undermines privacy but also threatens democratic norms and due process guarantees.

Internationally, the recognition of privacy as a fundamental right is becoming more robust. Courts and legislatures across jurisdictions have begun to reinterpret constitutional texts to address the new realities of digital surveillance. Yet, these efforts are uneven and often reactive, lagging behind technological innovation. While the European Union has established comprehensive data protection laws, such as the General Data Protection Regulation, many countries still lack clear, enforceable standards (Singh, 2024). In places where privacy laws do exist, enforcement mechanisms may be weak, underfunded, or politically compromised.

This discrepancy is especially stark in the Global South, where legal frameworks are still emerging, institutional capacities are limited, and public awareness is low. In these contexts, digital technologies are often introduced without meaningful consultation or oversight, leading to abuses and exacerbating existing inequalities. For example, the deployment of biometric identification systems in refugee camps or social welfare programs may facilitate access to services but also create new forms of surveillance and exclusion (Farraj, 2011). Without strong safeguards, the most vulnerable populations are often the most exposed.

Even in well-regulated jurisdictions, challenges abound. The transnational nature of digital data flows complicates jurisdictional boundaries and legal remedies. Personal data collected in one country may be processed in another and stored in a third, making enforcement of rights increasingly complex. Multinational corporations often exploit these legal ambiguities, relocating operations to jurisdictions with weaker privacy protections (Cuervo-Cazurra et al., 2021). This regulatory fragmentation undermines accountability and highlights the need for harmonized international standards.

To address these challenges, scholars and advocates have proposed the concept of digital constitutionalism. This emerging framework envisions a set of normative principles and legal mechanisms designed to embed human rights, including privacy, within the governance of digital spaces. Digital constitutionalism calls for the adaptation of constitutional values such as transparency, proportionality, accountability, and due process to the context of algorithmic governance and datafication. It also emphasizes the need for participatory governance models that include civil society, technical experts, and marginalized communities in decision-making processes.

At the core of digital constitutionalism is the belief that fundamental rights must be preserved and expanded in the face of technological change. Privacy, in this context, is not merely a passive right to non-interference but an active right to shape the conditions under which data is collected, processed, and shared. It is a right that demands the empowerment of individuals and communities, the regulation of both public and private actors, and the development of institutional infrastructures capable of delivering justice in a digital world.

The stakes could not be higher. Without robust protections for privacy, individuals lose not only control over their personal lives but also the capacity to engage freely in political, social, and cultural life. Democracy itself is weakened when surveillance is normalized, dissent is chilled, and information is manipulated. By contrast, a strong right to privacy can serve as a bulwark against authoritarianism and a foundation for inclusive and equitable digital development (Solove, 2025).

This chapter argues that privacy must be constitutionally redefined and safeguarded as a universal digital human right to counter surveillance capitalism, algorithmic governance, and fragmented transnational data regimes. This chapter sets the stage for a global and comparative analysis of the constitutional foundations of the right to privacy, the challenges posed by mass surveillance, and the opportunities presented by digital constitutionalism. Drawing on examples from North America, Europe, Latin America, Africa, and Asia, it highlights both promising developments and persistent gaps. It advocates for an integrated approach that combines legal reform, technological safeguards, civic education, and international cooperation.

In doing so, the chapter aligns with broader global efforts to promote peace, justice, and strong institutions, as reflected in the United Nations Sustainable Development Goals, particularly SDG 16. While the remainder of the chapter focuses primarily on legal and institutional dynamics, the introduction underscores that the right to privacy is not an abstract legal doctrine. It is a lived experience, a condition for dignity, and a prerequisite for the exercise of all other rights. Ensuring its protection in the digital age is one of the defining challenges of our time and one of the most urgent tasks for scholars, policymakers, and global citizens alike.

Methodology

Methodologically, this chapter adopts a comparative constitutional and legal-institutional approach. It synthesizes judicial decisions, statutory frameworks, and international human rights instruments to assess how privacy is conceptualized and protected across different regions. Case studies from jurisdictions such as the United States, European Union, Brazil, South Africa, and India provide a lens for understanding both the diversity and convergence of privacy protections globally. Particular attention is given to the normative development of privacy jurisprudence and its practical enforcement mechanisms. These jurisdictions were selected because they represent distinct models of digital governance: the US as a hub of surveillance capitalism, the EU as a regulatory leader with the GDPR, India as the largest biometric experiment through Aadhaar, and Global South regions that reflect both vulnerability and innovation. This selection provides comparative depth while avoiding arbitrariness.

CONSTITUTIONAL FOUNDATIONS OF PRIVACY IN A GLOBAL CONTEXT

The legal architecture of privacy is undergoing a transformation across the world. While the right to privacy has historically existed within the realm of individual liberty and civil rights, the rise of digital technology has necessitated new legal interpretations and frameworks. Constitutions, once designed to govern the relationships between state and citizen in analog contexts, are now being challenged to protect individuals in environments governed by algorithmic logic, pervasive surveillance, and transnational data flows. This part explores the global constitutional landscape of privacy, focusing on how courts and legislatures in diverse jurisdictions have interpreted and enforced privacy rights in the digital era.

Comparative Jurisprudence

Across the Global North, constitutional jurisprudence on privacy has evolved significantly in response to the growing entanglement between digital technologies and personal freedoms. This section compares landmark developments from the United States, Europe, and the United Kingdom, demonstrating the ways in which courts and legislatures have approached the protection of privacy as a fundamental right in a digital context.

The United States: Carpenter v. United States and the Fourth Amendment

The evolution of privacy jurisprudence in the United States has largely centered around the Fourth Amendment, which protects citizens from unreasonable searches and seizures. One of the most pivotal rulings in recent years came in *Carpenter v. United States* (2018), where the U.S. Supreme Court held that accessing historical cell phone location records constitutes a search under the Fourth Amendment and therefore requires a warrant (Grover, 2024).

This decision marked a departure from the traditional "third-party doctrine," which held that individuals relinquish privacy rights over information voluntarily shared with third parties, such as telephone companies. *Carpenter* acknowledged the uniquely invasive nature of digital data, recognizing that cell site location information reveals intimate details of a person's life. The ruling underscored the need to reinterpret constitutional protections in light of new technological realities.

Although *Carpenter* was limited in scope, it reflects a broader trend in American jurisprudence to grapple with the implications of digital surveillance and data retention. However, the absence of a comprehensive federal data protection framework continues to hinder robust privacy protection, leaving gaps that are often filled by a patchwork of state laws and sector-specific regulations.

Europe: The European Convention on Human Rights and the GDPR

In contrast to the United States, European legal systems have embraced a more expansive and integrated approach to privacy, often grounded in both constitutional and supranational instruments. Article 8 of the European Convention on Human Rights (ECHR) guarantees the right to respect for private and family life, and the European Court of Human Rights (ECtHR) has developed a rich jurisprudence interpreting this provision in the context of digital surveillance and data protection.

Cases such as *S. and Marper v. United Kingdom* (2008), which dealt with the retention of DNA profiles and fingerprints, and *Roman Zakharov v. Russia* (2015), which addressed mass surveillance, have reinforced the principle that any interference with privacy must be necessary, proportionate, and subject to effective oversight.

Complementing the ECHR is the General Data Protection Regulation (GDPR), which came into effect in 2018. The GDPR enshrines the principles of data minimization, purpose limitation, and user consent, and establishes strong enforcement mechanisms through independent supervisory authorities (Dumas, 2019). Its extraterritorial scope and emphasis on accountability have made it a global benchmark for data protection legislation.

The European model represents a comprehensive rights-based approach that situates privacy at the heart of democratic society. It reflects a normative consensus that privacy is not merely a personal right but a condition for the exercise of other fundamental freedoms, including expression, association, and participation.

The United Kingdom: Post-Brexit Data Protection and the Right to Privacy

The United Kingdom, though no longer part of the European Union, remains closely aligned with European privacy standards, at least for the time being. The

UK retained the GDPR in domestic law through the Data Protection Act 2018, now referred to as the "UK GDPR," with some modifications following Brexit.

UK courts have continued to interpret privacy rights in line with both domestic statutes and the Human Rights Act 1998, which incorporates the ECHR into UK law. Decisions from the Investigatory Powers Tribunal and other appellate courts have scrutinized the legality of government surveillance, particularly in light of the Investigatory Powers Act 2016, known colloquially as the "Snooper's Charter."

Legal challenges such as *Privacy International v. Investigatory Powers Tribunal* have tested the boundaries of oversight and proportionality in state surveillance. The case law affirms that, even in the context of national security, privacy rights must be balanced with transparent legal procedures and judicial review (Watt, 2017).

Although the UK's data protection framework remains robust, concerns persist over potential regulatory divergence from EU standards. Any such divergence could affect adequacy decisions and transatlantic data flows, raising broader questions about the global coherence of privacy rights regimes.

Global South Legal Models

Across the Global South, the recognition and enforcement of privacy rights are deeply influenced by political, institutional, and socio-economic constraints. Legal frameworks addressing privacy have begun to evolve in recent decades, often in reaction to global digital transformations and international standards. However, their implementation remains uneven, and the translation of abstract rights into lived realities continues to be shaped by the fragility of democratic institutions, infrastructural deficiencies, and socio-political inequalities.

India presents a seminal example of constitutional development in this field. In the landmark case of *Justice K.S. Puttaswamy v. Union of India* (2017), the Supreme Court of India affirmed the right to privacy as intrinsic to the fundamental right to life and liberty under Article 21 of the Constitution. This judicial recognition, grounded in liberal democratic values, interpreted privacy expansively as encompassing decisional autonomy, informational self-determination, and protection against state and non-state surveillance. The judgment signaled a significant normative shift in Indian constitutionalism and resonated beyond South Asia as a progressive articulation of digital rights.

Despite this jurisprudential advancement, the realization of privacy protections in India faces substantial obstacles. The Aadhaar biometric identification program, while enabling access to welfare services, has been criticized for enabling mass surveillance and facilitating digital exclusion. The absence of comprehensive data protection legislation until recently further undermined the enforceability of privacy rights. Although the enactment of a new data protection law has aimed to fill this lacuna, its operational efficacy is contingent on the strength and independence of regulatory bodies.

A striking example is Kenya's Huduma Namba biometric system, which sought to integrate national identification, voting, and welfare access. While ambitious, it sparked litigation over weak safeguards and exclusionary practices, especially for minority communities. This demonstrates how structural fragility, rather than merely abstract institutional weakness, directly shapes the lived experience of privacy rights in the Global South.

Emerging Legal Frameworks Across Regions

Beyond India, several countries across Africa, Latin America, and Southeast Asia have begun establishing legal structures for data protection and privacy. Nigeria's Data Protection Regulation, Kenya's Data Protection Act, and Ghana's Data Protection Act signify a growing regional recognition of digital rights. However, these initiatives often confront significant limitations in institutional capacity, judicial independence, and political will. In many instances, data protection authorities lack the resources, expertise, or autonomy to investigate and sanction violations effectively.

Moreover, in several jurisdictions marked by authoritarian governance or political instability, privacy rights are not only underdeveloped but actively suppressed. Governments in countries like Myanmar and Ethiopia have reportedly employed surveillance technologies to monitor dissent and curtail civil liberties (Ünver, 2024). Even where constitutional provisions nominally guarantee privacy, enforcement mechanisms are either absent or co-opted by political elites. This disjuncture between law and practice underscores the precariousness of digital rights in contexts where the rule of law is weak.

Privacy, Inequality, and the Digital Divide

One of the defining features of privacy discourse in the Global South is its intersection with the broader digital divide. While digital technologies offer new opportunities for communication, access to information, and service delivery, their deployment often exacerbates existing inequalities. Vast sections of the population, particularly in rural areas, remain excluded from secure and affordable digital infrastructure. Those who do have access frequently encounter platforms that extract and exploit personal data with minimal oversight or consent.

Digital literacy levels remain low in many regions, limiting individuals' ability to understand, assert, or even recognize their privacy rights. Vulnerable groups, including women, ethnic minorities, and indigenous populations, are disproportionately affected by opaque data practices and algorithmic bias. In such environments, privacy violations are not merely a legal concern but a manifestation of systemic social marginalization.

Regional Initiatives and Future Directions

Regional initiatives are attempting to address some of these gaps. The African Union's Malabo Convention on Cyber Security and Personal Data Protection represents a significant effort to create a harmonized legal framework across the continent. Similarly, ASEAN has initiated discussions on cross-border data flows and regional privacy standards, seeking to balance national sovereignty with the imperatives of digital integration (Wong, 2020). These frameworks indicate a growing awareness of the need for cooperative governance mechanisms in an era of transnational data exchange.

Nevertheless, the path toward robust privacy protections in the Global South remains fraught. Legal recognition, while necessary, is insufficient without concurrent investment in institutional development, judicial capacity, and civic education. The task ahead involves not only aligning domestic laws with international norms but also embedding privacy within the political culture and administrative practices of states. Civil society organizations, regional bodies, and transnational advocacy networks will play a crucial role in driving this transformation.

Overall, the Global South reflects a dynamic but uneven terrain in the evolution of privacy rights. From constitutional breakthroughs like *Puttaswamy* to nascent regional legal instruments, there is evidence of normative progress. Yet, structural barriers persist, impeding the effective implementation of these rights. Addressing these challenges requires a multidimensional strategy, legal, institutional, and societal, to ensure that privacy is not just a formal entitlement but a meaningful protection for all.

Gaps Between Norm and Practice

Despite the steady emergence of privacy rights in constitutional and legislative frameworks worldwide, a wide chasm often exists between normative commitments and their practical enforcement. In both the Global North and South, millions of individuals remain exposed to pervasive digital surveillance and data extraction without meaningful recourse. This disjuncture stems from systemic barriers including lack of awareness, weak institutional capacity, limited access to legal remedies, and structural exclusion from digital governance processes.

Inaccessibility of Legal Redress

Even where laws affirm the right to privacy, many individuals face considerable hurdles in asserting their rights. Legal systems can be prohibitively complex, expensive, or simply unfamiliar to those most vulnerable to privacy violations. In countries with underfunded judiciaries or politically constrained courts, privacy litigation may be delayed or denied altogether. The process of seeking remedy is further complicated by the transnational nature of digital data flows, where responsibility for violations is diffused across multiple actors, platforms, and jurisdictions.

For displaced persons, refugees, and migrants, the situation is particularly dire. Lacking formal identification, legal status, or linguistic access to justice systems, these populations are often excluded from even the most basic protections. Meanwhile, state and non-state actors continue to exploit data generated by humanitarian technologies, health registries, or border management systems without clear consent or accountability mechanisms.

Digital Literacy and Disempowerment

A significant contributor to the norm-practice gap is the lack of digital literacy. Understanding how data is collected, processed, shared, and monetized remains opaque for a majority of internet users, especially in regions with limited education infrastructure. People may not be aware that their biometric scans, browsing behavior, or GPS locations are being harvested for profiling, commercial gain, or surveillance. Without the ability to recognize a privacy violation, asserting one's rights becomes almost impossible.

This cognitive and informational disempowerment is exacerbated by technology design itself. Many platforms are engineered to obscure consent mechanisms and push users toward settings that favor data extraction. Algorithms personalize content in ways that shape perceptions and choices, reinforcing asymmetries of knowledge and agency between platforms and users. In this sense, digital illiteracy is not simply a failure of education, but a consequence of deliberate design choices by powerful corporate actors.

Marginalized Communities and Structural Exclusion

The impacts of these systemic failures fall disproportionately on historically marginalized communities. In the Middle East and North Africa, for instance, authoritarian regimes have utilized spyware and digital surveillance to target ethnic and religious minorities, journalists, and human rights defenders. Without independent oversight or access to international legal institutions, these groups are left with little protection against abuse.

In sub-Saharan Africa, the introduction of biometric national ID systems has triggered widespread concern over privacy breaches and exclusion (Musoni et al., 2023). While such systems promise efficient governance and service delivery, their implementation often lacks transparency, proper oversight, or recourse mechanisms. As a result, individuals can be denied access to healthcare, education, or voting rights based on faulty or inaccessible digital records.

The LGBTQ+ community across various jurisdictions also faces unique threats to digital privacy. Surveillance technologies and data leaks have been weaponized to expose, harass, or criminalize individuals based on their identities. In such cases, privacy violations are not only invasions of personal space but acts of social repression.

Toward Bridging the Gap

Closing the gap between normative recognition and effective enforcement of privacy rights requires comprehensive reform. First, legal systems must be made more accessible, inclusive, and responsive. This includes simplifying legal language, reducing litigation costs, and ensuring legal aid for underrepresented groups. Courts and regulatory agencies should be empowered with the autonomy and resources needed to investigate privacy violations and hold both state and corporate actors accountable.

Second, public education initiatives must prioritize digital literacy, especially among youth, women, and rural populations. Civil society organizations can play a pivotal role in raising awareness and building grassroots capacity to demand rights. Platforms and service providers, too, have a responsibility to implement transparent privacy policies and user-friendly consent mechanisms.

Lastly, international cooperation is essential to address the borderless nature of data governance. Multilateral agreements, regional charters, and digital rights coalitions must work to harmonize standards, enhance accountability, and provide transnational avenues for redress. Institutions such as the UN Human Rights Council, the African Commission on Human and Peoples' Rights, and the Inter-American Commission on Human Rights can serve as catalysts for monitoring and enforcing digital privacy norms.

SURVEILLANCE AND THE GLOBAL DEMOCRATIC DEFICIT

Surveillance in the digital age has evolved into a pervasive instrument of governance and control, affecting individuals across the ideological and geopolitical spectrum. As both states and corporations expand their capacity to monitor, collect, and manipulate data, fundamental questions arise about democratic legitimacy, human dignity, and the rule of law. This chapter explores the contours of digital surveillance through three interconnected dimensions: the legal and institutional apparatuses of state and corporate surveillance, the disproportionate impacts on marginalized communities, and the structural deficiencies that inhibit oversight and informed consent. Each of these aspects reveals the complex interplay between technology, power, and human rights in the twenty-first century.

Surveillance by States and Corporations

The rise of surveillance in the digital era marks one of the most profound shifts in the exercise of state and corporate power. No longer confined to intelligence agencies or national borders, surveillance has become embedded in the fabric of daily life, mediated by ubiquitous technologies, data-driven infrastructures, and algorithmic governance. Governments and private corporations now share in the collection, storage, and analysis of vast quantities of personal information, often with minimal transparency or oversight.

In liberal democracies, the expansion of surveillance has frequently been justified through the rhetoric of national security and public order. Programs such as PRISM in the United States, which involved the bulk collection of internet communications, and the United Kingdom's Investigatory Powers Act, which provides broad legal authority for intercepting private data, exemplify this trend (Bauman et al., 2014). These legal regimes often operate within secretive judicial or executive frameworks, raising questions about the proportionality, necessity, and constitutionality of such powers. Judicial rulings and legislative reforms have sought to place limits on surveillance, but in practice, oversight bodies are frequently under-resourced or deferential to executive claims of security imperatives.

By contrast, in authoritarian regimes, surveillance is not simply a tool for national security but a mechanism of political control. The Chinese state's integration of AI-powered facial recognition, predictive analytics, and social credit systems into everyday governance demonstrates how surveillance can be institutionalized as a mode of authoritarian governance. Dissenting voices, human rights activists, and ethnic minorities are systematically monitored and penalized through real-time data tracking, eroding any semblance of privacy or autonomy. Similar practices have been reported in Russia, Iran, and other states where surveillance is used to crush protest, silence media, and deter political participation.

Despite these ideological differences, a convergence is emerging. Authoritarian states and liberal democracies alike now rely on similar technological infrastructures: biometric systems, geolocation tracking, network surveillance, and AI-based analytics. These systems are increasingly purchased from the same global surveillance industry, comprising powerful private firms that market intrusive technologies to governments with little regard for human rights standards. The result is a global ecosystem in which surveillance capabilities proliferate far more rapidly than legal protections.

Corporate actors also play a central role in this ecosystem. Tech companies collect massive troves of personal data through platforms, apps, and devices, generating detailed profiles of individuals' behaviors, preferences, and movements. While often framed as a business model of personalized advertising, the implications extend far beyond commerce. The architecture of social media, search engines, and digital assistants has created infrastructures of behavioral surveillance that are monetized and repurposed for political, policing, and strategic interests.

Moreover, the boundary between state and corporate surveillance is increasingly blurred. Governments routinely access privately held data through formal requests, legal mandates, or backdoor arrangements. In some instances, state actors compel cooperation through legislation, while in others, corporations proactively share data to secure regulatory favor or expand market access. This mutual dependency further undermines the notion of privacy as a right held against both public and private actors.

The implications for democratic governance are significant. Surveillance undermines the basic tenets of autonomy, consent, and accountability that form the bedrock of constitutional democracies. When individuals cannot communicate, organize, or dissent without fear of being watched or profiled, the space for democratic deliberation contracts. Public trust in institutions erodes, civic engagement declines, and a culture of self-censorship takes root.

In this global context, surveillance has ceased to be a temporary or emergency measure and has become an enduring feature of governance. This normalization, often accelerated by crises such as terrorism or pandemics, demands renewed scrutiny and regulation. Unless governments, civil society, and international institutions act to rein in unchecked surveillance powers and ensure accountability, the digital public sphere risks becoming a domain of coercion rather than empowerment.

Impact on Marginalized Populations

The surveillance landscape becomes even more troubling when examined through the lens of social and economic inequality. Marginalized populations, such as migrants, racial and ethnic minorities, LGBTQ+ individuals, and political dissidents, often bear the brunt of intrusive surveillance practices. These groups are more likely to be targeted, more heavily monitored, and less equipped to challenge or resist violations of their privacy.

Consider the migrant worker whose biometric data is compulsorily collected and stored by host governments, often without transparent regulations or avenues for redress. In regions like the Gulf States, such practices intersect with restrictive labor laws and surveillance-heavy environments to entrench systems of exploitation. Digital identity programs, while often touted as tools of inclusion, can be weaponized to monitor mobility, employment, and political activity.

Schoolchildren in several countries are increasingly subjected to facial recognition technologies, keystroke monitoring, and behavioral tracking under the guise of security or educational enhancement. These surveillance measures are disproportionately deployed in underfunded public schools, often serving low-income and minority communities. Rather than ensuring safety, such practices risk criminalizing ordinary student behavior and reinforcing educational inequities.

Political protesters and human rights activists face similar threats. In countries like Belarus and Hong Kong, surveillance technologies have been used to track demonstrators, identify leaders, and preemptively suppress dissent. Governments acquire surveillance tools from international vendors and deploy them against domestic opposition, often with little concern for legality or proportionality. The chilling effect of this surveillance, visible in reduced turnout, anonymized activism, or retreat from public discourse, weakens democratic expression.

Surveillance has also been disproportionately applied to incarcerated populations and individuals under criminal justice supervision (Vuolo et al., 2023). Predictive policing algorithms, often trained on biased datasets, can exacerbate existing patterns of racial discrimination and over-policing. People from marginalized backgrounds become ensnared in feedback loops of surveillance and punishment, with little chance for accountability or reform.

Reports from organizations such as Amnesty International, Human Rights Watch, and the Electronic Frontier Foundation have repeatedly highlighted these harms. They underscore how surveillance, far from being a neutral tool, reflects and amplifies existing power asymmetries. Without explicit protections and participatory policy design, surveillance regimes will continue to mirror societal biases, disproportionately burdening those already excluded from democratic processes.

The Problem of Oversight and Consent

As surveillance regimes expand globally, one of the most alarming challenges is the absence of robust oversight mechanisms and the erosion of meaningful consent. Despite the vast scale of data collection by both states and corporations, most individuals have little understanding of how their information is being used, who is accessing it, and for what purpose. The architecture of surveillance is often intentionally opaque, designed to evade scrutiny while presenting the illusion of legality through vague regulatory frameworks or perfunctory consent forms.

Oversight bodies, where they exist, often lack the independence, resources, or political will to act effectively. In liberal democracies, national data protection authorities and intelligence oversight committees may have limited jurisdiction or be structurally subordinated to executive agencies. Many of these institutions are reactive rather than proactive, becoming involved only after violations occur. In countries such as the United States or the United Kingdom, courts have sometimes pushed back against expansive surveillance powers, yet much of the operational detail remains hidden under the guise of national security.

This lack of institutional robustness is even more pronounced in authoritarian or hybrid regimes, where oversight agencies may be co-opted, suppressed, or entirely absent. Surveillance is not just under-regulated in these contexts, it is often celebrated as a technological achievement or a tool of public efficiency. Attempts by journalists, civil society groups, or international bodies to investigate surveillance practices frequently encounter resistance, censorship, or legal retaliation.

Consent, too, has become a degraded concept in the digital age. The notion that individuals voluntarily agree to data collection rests on a fiction. Most digital platforms operate on take-it-or-leave-it terms, where clicking "accept" is a prerequisite for access rather than a meaningful choice (Richards & Hartzog, 2019). Consent forms are dense, legalistic, and inaccessible to most users, serving more as shields for liability than tools for informed decision-making. The imbalance of power between users and providers makes genuine autonomy nearly impossible.

In biometric and state surveillance programs, consent may be absent altogether. For example, biometric ID systems rolled out in refugee camps, public hospitals, or transit systems rarely include informed opt-outs. Individuals in these contexts are often subject to blanket data collection policies under the rationale of efficiency or safety, with no clear avenues for contesting misuse. The consequences can be severe, ranging from wrongful inclusion on watchlists to exclusion from essential services.

Judicial mechanisms for redress remain limited and inaccessible in many parts of the world. Legal challenges to surveillance programs often require significant resources, legal expertise, and the ability to prove concrete harm - a daunting threshold when surveillance is secretive by design. In transnational data exchanges, jurisdictional complexity adds another layer of difficulty. A person in Kenya may have their data processed by a company in the United States, stored in Germany, and analyzed using AI systems based in China. In such scenarios, identifying the responsible entity, applicable legal regime, and forum for redress becomes nearly impossible.

International legal efforts, such as the United Nations General Assembly's resolution on the right to privacy in the digital age, and the mandate of the UN Special Rapporteur on the Right to Privacy, have called for stronger transparency, accountability, and remedy mechanisms. Yet, these efforts remain largely declaratory, with no binding enforcement powers or global regulatory authority.

To address these deficits, several reforms are necessary. First, national oversight institutions must be made independent, well-funded, and empowered to audit surveillance practices regularly. Second, laws must mandate transparency reports from both governments and corporations, disclosing the extent and nature of surveillance activities. Third, meaningful consent mechanisms should be designed with usability in mind, offering clear, contextual information and real alternatives. Fourth, international treaties and cooperative frameworks should establish cross-border accountability systems, allowing individuals to seek redress across jurisdictions.

Importantly, civil society, academia, and investigative journalism play a crucial role in exposing surveillance abuses and advocating for reform. Public engagement and education about data rights and surveillance risks can help build a culture of vigilance and resistance. Technological solutions such as open-source privacy tools, end-to-end encryption, and decentralized platforms should be supported as complements to legal safeguards.

Finally, oversight and consent are not mere administrative details but the pillars of democratic governance. Without them, surveillance transforms from a security measure into a systemic threat to liberty, equality, and accountability. While these legal and institutional frameworks show formal recognition of privacy, their effectiveness in narrowing the privacy surveillance gap remains limited. Remedies often arrive after violations, oversight institutions lack capacity, and corporate compliance is shaped more by reputational pressure than by enforceable accountability. The persistence of mass surveillance even in jurisdictions with strong privacy laws reveals the gap between normative commitments and lived realities.

DIGITAL CONSTITUTIONALISM: TOWARDS A GLOBAL RIGHTS BASED FRAMEWORK

The accelerating digital transformation of societies around the globe presents both unparalleled opportunities and significant threats to human rights, with privacy emerging as one of the most contested domains. While data flows and digital infrastructures drive economic development, innovation, and cross-border collaboration, they also generate structural vulnerabilities that expose individuals and communities to surveillance, profiling, and rights violations. As governments and corporations alike embed digital surveillance into the fabric of daily life, questions of constitutional legitimacy, ethical responsibility, and legal safeguards demand urgent and comprehensive responses. This chapter outlines the normative foundations of privacy in global digital governance, identifying core principles for a rights-based framework that responds to both technological complexity and ethical imperatives.

In this part of the chapter, we explore the foundational principles required to protect privacy in an interconnected digital environment. Rather than offering a broad conceptual account of digital constitutionalism, the focus is placed squarely on the substance of privacy rights and the legal mechanisms through which they can be enforced. These principles are grounded in existing international human rights norms, interpreted in light of contemporary digital challenges. By emphasizing transparency, accountability, remedy, and technological safeguards, this chapter proposes a clear normative template for embedding privacy in global digital governance.

The Concept of Digital Constitutionalism

Digital constitutionalism refers to the emerging body of legal and normative principles that seek to transpose foundational constitutional values, such as individual rights, democratic accountability, and the rule of law, into the governance of digital spaces (De Gregorio & Radu, 2022). As digital infrastructures increasingly structure how individuals express themselves, associate, and participate in public life, these platforms have evolved into de facto public spheres. Unlike traditional constitutionalism, which was rooted in territorial state sovereignty and static institutional arrangements, digital constitutionalism recognizes the fluid, transnational, and often privately mediated nature of the digital environment. It is a response to the growing influence of powerful digital intermediaries and surveillance actors whose decisions can deeply affect civil liberties, particularly the right to privacy.

Several landmark policy instruments reflect this development. The European Union's General Data Protection Regulation (GDPR) stands out as a globally influential legal framework, embedding principles of lawfulness, fairness, transparency, data minimization, and accountability. The GDPR grants substantive rights such as access, rectification, and erasure, while also establishing obligations for data controllers and providing for strong enforcement by independent supervisory authorities. Complementing this are the OECD Guidelines on the Protection of Privacy and Transborder Data Flows, which, though non-binding, have shaped data protection regimes across jurisdictions. Further, the UN Special Rapporteur on the Right to Privacy has emphasized the indivisibility of privacy rights in digital contexts, urging states and international institutions to uphold human dignity amid rapid technological change. Collectively, these developments illustrate a constitutional turn in global digital governance, where privacy is not just a regulatory concern but a core democratic value.

Core Principles of a Global Privacy Rights Framework

A robust privacy rights regime for the digital age must rest on firm legal, procedural, and ethical pillars. These principles are essential to counterbalance the expanding power of surveillance technologies and to preserve individual dignity and autonomy in a networked society.

1. ***Data Minimization and Purpose Limitation*** — Personal data should be collected only when necessary and used solely for clearly defined and legitimate purposes. This principle guards against overreach, particularly in contexts where surveillance may be justified by national security or public interest concerns. Mass data collection without demonstrated necessity undermines both privacy and proportionality.
2. ***Transparency and Accountability*** — Entities handling personal data must be transparent about their practices. This includes clear disclosures about data collection methods, storage practices, purposes of processing, and data-sharing arrangements. Transparency also extends to algorithmic systems, requiring explainability in automated decision-making that significantly impacts individuals.
3. ***Independent Oversight*** — The enforcement of privacy norms requires the establishment and support of independent data protection authorities. These bodies must be equipped with the legal authority, resources, and institutional independence to monitor compliance, investigate violations, and impose corrective measures. Their role is crucial in ensuring that privacy rights are not subordinated to political or commercial interests.
4. ***Effective Remedies and Redress*** — Individuals must have accessible avenues for challenging infringements of their privacy rights. This includes the right to lodge complaints, seek judicial review, and obtain compensation or other remedies. Redress mechanisms must be procedurally fair, timely, and capable of addressing harm caused by both public and private actors.
5. ***Technological Safeguards*** — Legal protections must be supported by privacy-enhancing technologies. These include tools such as end-to-end encryption, anonymization, pseudonymization, and privacy-by-design approaches that integrate data protection into the architecture of digital systems from the outset. Technological safeguards reinforce legal rights by embedding privacy into technical infrastructures.
6. ***Cross-border Cooperation and Harmonization*** — The global nature of digital communications and data processing requires international legal coherence. Harmonized standards, cross-border enforcement mechanisms, and treaty-based obligations help ensure that privacy protections are not undermined by

jurisdictional fragmentation. Initiatives such as mutual legal assistance treaties and international privacy frameworks can play a critical role.

While these principles offer a coherent framework, their implementation depends on political will, legal infrastructure, and cultural attitudes toward rights. Embedding these principles into national and regional legal systems requires both top-down and bottom-up efforts, involving legislators, courts, civil society, and technologists. The following section will examine regional developments and grassroots efforts to operationalize these principles, addressing the risk of digital imperialism and the need for inclusive digital rights governance.

Regional Pathways and Grassroots Implementation

While global principles provide a necessary blueprint, their realization hinges on how they are interpreted and embedded within regional legal cultures and institutional frameworks. Across the globe, diverse initiatives are emerging to align digital governance with rights-based constitutional norms. These efforts highlight the multiplicity of pathways toward a privacy-respecting digital order and underscore the importance of contextual responsiveness, democratic participation, and regional cooperation.

European Union: A Normative Benchmark

The European Union's General Data Protection Regulation (GDPR) has become the most influential privacy framework globally, establishing comprehensive protections and setting high standards for consent, accountability, and user rights. Its extraterritorial reach, enforced through strict penalties and cross-border cooperation mechanisms, has made it a de facto global model (Wang, 2020). The GDPR institutionalizes several core principles discussed earlier, such as data minimization, purpose limitation, and rights to access, erasure, and rectification. Importantly, it mandates the creation of independent data protection authorities in each member state and facilitates cooperation through the European Data Protection Board. By embedding privacy within the broader project of European constitutionalism, the EU has shown how supranational governance can protect rights even in complex transnational data environments.

Pan-African Approaches and Regional Coordination

Africa has increasingly turned its attention to data protection as digital economies expand across the continent. The African Union's Convention on Cyber Security and

Personal Data Protection (commonly known as the Malabo Convention) represents a key step toward regional harmonization. Though its ratification has been slow, the Convention articulates core data protection principles and envisions national data authorities. Individual countries, such as Kenya, Nigeria, and South Africa, have enacted robust national laws with oversight bodies and judicial remedies. Importantly, several of these efforts have emerged from civil society pressure and advocacy by digital rights organizations, indicating the value of grassroots mobilization in shaping regional legal landscapes.

Asia-Pacific Fragmentation and Emerging Trends

The Asia-Pacific region reflects considerable legal diversity in privacy regulation. Countries like Japan and South Korea have adopted comprehensive data protection frameworks, often aligned with EU standards to facilitate trade and data flows. India's Digital Personal Data Protection Act, while promising, has raised concerns regarding independence of oversight and scope of exemptions for state surveillance. Southeast Asia presents an uneven picture, with nations like Singapore and the Philippines making significant progress, while others lag behind in legal recognition and enforcement. Cross-border data transfers and cybersecurity agreements in ASEAN represent early attempts at regional coordination (Watanabe et al., 2025). However, without strong civil society involvement and independent oversight, these instruments risk prioritizing economic interests over individual rights.

Latin America: Rights-Based Momentum

Latin American countries have demonstrated a growing commitment to embedding data protection within constitutional and human rights frameworks. Brazil's Lei Geral de Proteção de Dados (LGPD) closely mirrors the GDPR and recognizes privacy as a fundamental right. Argentina and Mexico also have comprehensive laws and constitutional recognition of privacy and data protection. Notably, the Inter-American Court of Human Rights has affirmed data protection as essential to personal dignity and autonomy. Civil society groups have played a crucial role in holding governments accountable and ensuring that digital policies align with democratic values. Regional forums such as REDLAD and Derechos Digitales help facilitate knowledge sharing, legal harmonization, and strategic litigation across borders.

Civil Society and Technological Counterweights

Legal change alone is insufficient without sustained civil society engagement. Around the world, advocacy organizations, academics, journalists, and technologists are building alternative infrastructures and raising public awareness of digital rights. Groups like Access Now, the Electronic Frontier Foundation (EFF), Privacy International, and digital rights collectives in the Global South provide legal aid, campaign for legislative reforms, and develop open-source tools for privacy protection. These actors not only complement formal governance mechanisms but also foster cultures of accountability, literacy, and ethical design.

Importantly, the design of privacy-enhancing technologies must reflect local contexts and avoid imposing one-size-fits-all standards. Initiatives that integrate local languages, cultural understandings of privacy, and community-based digital education are more likely to succeed. The role of universities and legal clinics in training the next generation of digital rights advocates is equally critical to institutionalizing change.

In practice, digital constitutionalism should be anchored in enforceable constitutional amendments, independent transnational oversight bodies, and participatory governance mechanisms. Courts, human rights commissions, and specialized data protection agencies must coordinate to safeguard rights, while global treaties could create binding norms akin to climate governance or trade regimes. Without such institutional design, digital constitutionalism risks remaining a rhetorical aspiration rather than a normative reality.

FROM VULNERABILITY TO EMPOWERMENT: RETHINKING PRIVACY

As this chapter has argued, the ongoing digital revolution presents a defining challenge for contemporary constitutionalism. The transformation of human interactions through networked technologies has reconfigured the meaning of privacy, expanded the scope of surveillance, and reoriented the geography of power. Across continents and legal systems, societies are confronting a paradox: while digital technologies offer tools for empowerment, expression, and innovation, they also create new vulnerabilities that demand vigilant protection of fundamental rights. Among these, the right to privacy stands at the intersection of liberty, identity, and democratic governance.

The contours of privacy have evolved well beyond the traditional understanding of secrecy or the mere concealment of personal information. In the digital context, privacy now encapsulates notions of autonomy, consent, agency, and control over one's own digital self. It informs the very fabric of human dignity, trust, and participation in a pluralistic society. As personal data becomes a commodity and algorithmic systems shape our choices, the asymmetries between individuals and institutions grow deeper. This transformation places privacy not just within the domain of personal rights, but at the core of global justice and social cohesion.

The challenge is both conceptual and structural. It is conceptual in that existing legal frameworks were not designed to accommodate the borderless, opaque, and dynamic nature of digital ecosystems. Traditional distinctions between public and private, state and non-state, domestic and international are increasingly blurred in the digital context. It is structural in that surveillance capitalism and state-sponsored monitoring often benefit from legal grey zones, fragmented oversight, and institutional inertia. While legislative reforms such as the GDPR or national data protection laws mark important progress, implementation remains inconsistent and often reactive.

To reclaim privacy in the digital age, a multifaceted and forward-looking response is required. The framework outlined in this chapter emphasizes key normative principles: data minimization, purpose limitation, transparency, accountability, effective redress, and technological safeguards. These principles are not abstract ideals but concrete mechanisms for recalibrating the relationship between individuals and power in the digital domain. They aim to ensure that privacy protection becomes a systemic feature of governance rather than an afterthought or a privilege for the digitally literate few.

Yet law alone is insufficient. Reclaiming privacy also requires a cultural and ethical reorientation. Privacy must be cultivated as a public value, woven into the practices of institutions, the designs of technologies, and the expectations of users. Education systems need to build digital literacy that empowers individuals to understand and demand their rights. Technological innovation must align with the public interest, prioritizing privacy by design and supporting open standards and encryption. Civil society, journalists, and academics play an essential role in holding power to account, fostering transparency, and amplifying the voices of those most affected by digital harms.

A truly global response must also reckon with inequality. The benefits and harms of the digital age are unevenly distributed, often reproducing historical hierarchies of race, class, gender, and geography. Many communities in the Global South face surveillance without consent or recourse, while others are excluded from legal protections due to lack of infrastructure or political will. Addressing these disparities demands inclusive governance models that reflect diverse perspectives and promote equitable digital futures. Local contexts must inform global frameworks, ensuring that digital constitutionalism is not another form of imperialism but a vehicle for participatory justice.

Moreover, reclaiming privacy must extend beyond individual claims to collective imaginaries. What kind of digital society do we want to build? Who gets to shape its norms, values, and institutions? These are fundamentally constitutional questions. They call for a global conversation rooted in shared human values but responsive to local diversity. Interoperable legal standards, multilateral cooperation, and transnational advocacy networks will be key to ensuring that privacy is protected not only within but also across borders.

The journey ahead is complex, but not without hope. Around the world, courts are recognizing privacy as a constitutional value. Activists are pushing for stronger oversight and accountability. Legislators are experimenting with bold regulatory models. Technologists are designing privacy-enhancing tools. The momentum is real and growing. What is needed now is convergence: the alignment of legal norms, institutional practices, and public consciousness around the centrality of privacy in democratic life.

To deepen this convergence, it is important to revisit the foundational principles that any robust privacy framework must embrace. These include a presumption in favor of user control, recognition of collective rights in the digital sphere, and effective global coordination mechanisms to challenge transnational data flows that violate individual rights. Institutions such as the United Nations, regional human rights bodies, and global judicial dialogues must work together to develop enforceable frameworks that recognize privacy as an essential pillar of modern governance.

Another critical area for advancement is the development of digital due process norms. In contexts ranging from immigration enforcement to welfare distribution, algorithmic decision-making is increasingly replacing human discretion. Without procedural safeguards, affected individuals may have no knowledge of, or ability to challenge, the decisions made by opaque systems. The development of legal standards for algorithmic accountability, such as explainability, auditability, and proportionality, must be prioritized to prevent a digital erosion of fundamental rights.

Equally urgent is the need for international cooperation to address corporate practices that erode privacy on a global scale. Transnational technology companies wield unprecedented influence over the everyday lives of billions of people. Their business models are often predicated on maximizing data extraction and behavioral prediction. International treaties or soft law instruments that impose duties of care, restrict exploitative data practices, and guarantee user autonomy would help to rebalance power dynamics between individuals and digital platforms.

Privacy is also a gendered, racialized, and classed issue. Surveillance technologies disproportionately affect communities of color, the poor, migrants, and dissidents. As facial recognition systems misidentify people of color at higher rates, and predictive policing targets historically marginalized neighborhoods, the digital age risks reinforcing rather than dismantling systemic inequalities. Intersectional approaches to privacy advocacy are therefore essential. A truly inclusive digital society cannot emerge without addressing the compounded harms faced by those who occupy multiple axes of vulnerability.

To strengthen global privacy protection, three steps are crucial: (1) moving beyond soft law by negotiating binding international treaties; (2) establishing global oversight mechanisms modeled on climate and trade institutions to monitor corporate and state surveillance; and (3) embedding privacy into digital education curricula, ensuring that citizens can understand and assert their rights. These measures would help transform privacy from a fragile entitlement into a robust constitutional guarantee worldwide.

In conclusion, privacy in the digital age is not merely a legal entitlement but a human necessity. It protects the space in which individuals define themselves, form relationships, and participate in society. Its erosion threatens not only personal freedom but the health of our democracies. As digital infrastructures become the scaffolding of our collective future, embedding privacy into their very foundations is a moral and constitutional imperative. By doing so, we do not merely adapt to technological change but we also shape it in the service of dignity, justice, and human flourishing.

From the perspective of global sustainable development, safeguarding privacy is also central to realizing the ambitions of the United Nations 2030 Agenda. While not limited to any single goal, privacy protection intersects directly with Goal 16 which is about promoting peace, justice, and strong institutions by reinforcing accountability, transparency, and the rule of law in digital governance. It also supports inclusive societies by ensuring that digital tools do not become vehicles for surveillance, exclusion, or systemic inequality. As the world strives to build a just, resilient, and inclusive digital future, embedding the right to privacy into legal and technological infrastructures represents both a practical and ethical contribution to achieving sustainable development goals.

REFERENCES

Bauman, Z., Bigo, D., Esteves, P., Guild, E., Jabri, V., Lyon, D., & Walker, R. B. J. (2014). After Snowden: Rethinking the impact of surveillance. *International Political Sociology*, *8*(2), 121–144. DOI: 10.1111/ips.12048

Bignami, F., & Resta, G. (2018). Human rights extraterritoriality: The right to privacy and national security surveillance. In E. Benvenisti & G. Nolte (Eds.), *Community interests across international law* (Forthcoming). Oxford University Press. GWU Law School Public Law Research Paper No. 2017-67; GWU Legal Studies Research Paper No. 2017-67. https://ssrn.com/abstract=3043771

Cohen, J. E. (2013). WHAT PRIVACY IS FOR. *Harvard Law Review*, *126*(7), 1904–1933. https://www.jstor.org/stable/23415061

Cuervo-Cazurra, A., Dieleman, M., Hirsch, P., Rodrigues, S. B., & Zyglidopoulos, S. (2021). Multinationals' misbehavior. *Journal of World Business*, *56*(5), 101244. DOI: 10.1016/j.jwb.2021.101244

De Gregorio, G., & Radu, R. (2022). Digital constitutionalism in the new era of Internet governance. *International Journal of Law and Information Technology*, *30*(1), 68–87. DOI: 10.1093/ijlit/eaac004

Dumas, J. (2019). General Data Protection Regulation (GDPR): Prioritizing resources. *Seattle University Law Review*, *42*(3), 1115–1128.

Farraj, A. (2011). Refugees and the biometric future: The impact of biometrics on refugees and asylum seekers. *Columbia Human Rights Law Review*, *42*(3), 891–939.

Grover, R. (2024, August 12). *The case for (meta)data privacy: Applying Carpenter to browser fingerprints*. Proceedings of the TPRC2024: The Research Conference on Communications, Information and Internet Policy. *SSRN*. https://ssrn.com/abstract=4923706

Islam, M. T. (2022). *A brief introduction to the right to privacy: An international legal perspective*. Hauser Global Law School Program, New York University. https://doi.org/DOI: 10.2139/ssrn.4154695

Kumar, V. (2019). Dynamics of the "right to privacy": Its characterization under the Indian Constitution. *Journal of the Indian Law Institute*, *61*(1), 68–96. https://www.jstor.org/stable/27097351

Musoni, M., Domingo, E., & Ogah, E. (2023). *Digital ID systems in Africa: Challenges, risks and opportunities* (Discussion Paper No. 360). European Centre for Development Policy Management (ECDPM).

Nishnianidze, A. (2024). Surveillance in the digital age. *European Scientific Journal, 20*(37), 1–25. DOI: 10.19044/esj.2024.v20n37p1

Richards, N., & Hartzog, W. (2019). The pathologies of digital consent. *Washington University Law Review, 96*(6), 1461–1528.

Sætra, H. S. (2020). Privacy as an aggregate public good. *Technology in Society, 63*, 101422. DOI: 10.1016/j.techsoc.2020.101422

Singh, H. (2024). Navigating the legal landscape of information governance. In Helge, K., & Rookey, C. (Eds.), *Creating and sustaining an information governance program* (pp. 217–235). IGI Global., DOI: 10.4018/979-8-3693-0472-3.ch012

Solove, D. J. (2025). *Privacy in authoritarian times: Surveillance capitalism and government surveillance. SSRN.* https://doi.org/DOI: 10.2139/ssrn.5103271

Ünver, H. A. (2024). *Artificial intelligence (AI) and human rights: Using AI as a weapon of repression and its impact on human rights.* European Parliament, Directorate-General for External Policies, Policy Department for External Relations (PE 754.450).

Vuolo, M., Schneider, L. E., & LaPlant, E. G. (2023). Surveillance and the experience of the COVID-19 pandemic for formerly incarcerated individuals. *Punishment & Society, 25*(2), 386–406. DOI: 10.1177/14624745221080696 PMID: 38603030

Wang, F. Y. (2020). Cooperative Data Privacy: The Japanese model of data privacy and the EU-Japan GDPR adequacy agreement. *Harvard Journal of Law & Technology, 33*(2), 661–692.

Watanabe, S., Ogura, E., & Oikawa, K. (2025). *Current status of ASEAN data governance and its implications for the Digital Economy Framework Agreement (DEFA)* (ERIA Discussion Paper Series No. 360). Economic Research Institute for ASEAN and East Asia (ERIA).

Wong, B. (2020). Data localization and ASEAN Economic Community. *Asian Journal of International Law, 10*(1), 158–180. DOI: 10.1017/S2044251319000250

Zhang, B., Chen, C., Lee, I., Lee, K., & Ong, K.-L. (2025). A survey on security and privacy issues in wearable health monitoring devices. *Computers & Security, 155*, 104453. DOI: 10.1016/j.cose.2025.104453

Zuboff, S. (2019). *The age of surveillance capitalism: The fight for a human future at the new frontier of power*. PublicAffairs.

Chapter 8
The Role of Artificial Intelligence in Threat Detection: Current and Future Trends

Upasana Khattri
https://orcid.org/0009-0003-8833-4944
O.P. Jindal Global University, India

Shiva Tiwari
https://orcid.org/0009-0006-3778-9676
Delhi High Court, New Delhi, India

Rajat Shandilya
Symbiosis Law School, Symbiosis International University, Noida, India

ABSTRACT

With the advent of artificial intelligence (AI), the practice of identifying exposure to risk is revolutionized which has helped businesses reshape the way they identify, assess, and address digital and physical threats. As data seems to grow exponentially and slowly gradually from the form of complex attacks, it is increasingly saturating all the old methodologies of threat detection. Today, artificial intelligence has become an integral part of modern threat detection systems because they are able to sort through huge data, point to patterns, and recognize even new forms of threats. Further, the paper looks at how artificial intelligence can be applied to evaluate risks, how it will improve cybersecurity and threat intelligence, how effective it can be in its application, and also a discussion of the emerging trends that would be anticipated in shaping this subject.

DOI: 10.4018/979-8-3373-3685-5.ch008

INTRODUCTION

The digital age has tremendous room for innovation and growth, but it has also made unprecedented the problems in threat environments (Aslan et al., 2023; Zhang et al., 2022). As companies grow more interconnected and dependent on information, the character of – including the wide range, extent and difficulty – has expanded (Kaur et al., 2023). Classic guardianship based operations and lifeless prebuilt systems have failed to bit and grab onto the calamity and pace of emerging threats (Martínez et al., 2019). This distance has allowed artificial intelligence (AI) to be introduced into the threat detection, a technological evolution that becomes how businesses detect, consider, and process prospective threats in morning location (Mamidi, 2024; Nyale & Angolo, 2022). Artificial intelligence, including its subdivision machine learning (ML), deep learning (DL) and natural language processing (NLP), has become the crucial factor of modern security systems (Kaur et al., 2023; Salem et al., 2024).

An AI-powered mechanism can run the data through a ton of different sources like user actions, network traffic, or external feed threats, thereby spotting anomalies and possible dangers (Alsamiri & Alsubhi, 2019; Okoli et al., 2024). Additionally, AI-based threat intelligence systems are learning constantly about new data, making them effective in maintaining detection even when fresh threats are emerging (Manoharan & Sarker, 2022; Shyaa et al., 2024). With AI operations that are also efficient, it is important to prepare by developing threat-detection system framework.

The whole architecture that businesses must embrace includes generating data, training data models, System integration, and continuous monitoring (Abdullahi et al., 2022). The proper training of AI depends on diverse and robust data. (Rest of the Sentence Error)The important concern in respect to trustworthiness and reliability of the AI-based threat detection systems as transparency and absence of bias, it places a need for the AI systems to be cooperating with human-in-the-loop professionals so that they may be able to understand complicated risks and help in the detection process (Díaz-Rodríguez et al., 2023; Lepri et al., 2021). In the coming time, it is in the early stages of AI transformation into the zone of 'threat detection.' This pairing, when coupled with other technologies, i.e., the Internet of Things (IoT), 5G networks, and quantum computing, will only expand those horizons (Chithaluru et al., 2023). IoT security could be strengthened by applying artificial intelligence techniques to detect malicious behavior and prevent unauthorized access (Abdullahi et al., 2022; Homaei et al., 2024). In the age of quantum computing, AI will also be able to provide solutions to complex problems at speeds never imagined by mankind, with the ability to handle far more data sets.

Another fascinating area is explainable artificial intelligence, which aims to formally enable these AI systems to transparently explain their decision process in a fashion comprehensible to human operators (Díaz-Rodríguez et al., 2023; Srinivasan & San Miguel González, 2025). That becomes vital for regulatory approval and hence mainstream acceptance of AI into such critical fields. Human analysts are slowly starting to work in a symbiotic and profitable relationship with artificial intelligence systems, where humans handle complex risk and strategic decisions, while AI systems take care of routine operations and simplistic analyses (Lepri et al., 2021). These developments will enable the increased autonomy in threat detection systems that learn and self-adjust, thus enhancing security at the cost of operator accountability. However, the criminal tactics employed by attackers will, in similar fashion, be upgraded with advancements in artificial intelligence (Mahboubi et al., 2024). As with the attackers, the importance of ongoing innovation in AI-driven defense tools is critical for countering advances in AI sophistication (Zhang et al., 2022). Indeed, AI has become a critical aspect of modern threat detection as a result of enhanced real-time detection and mitigation capabilities (Salem et al., 2024).

The integration of next-generation technologies and early trends of certifications under explainable AI, autonomous systems under explanation, etc., shall lead to transforming AI threat detection in another way forward. Unlike traditional systems, AI Systems can quickly sift and analyze vast amounts of structured and unstructured data, spot anomalies, learn from evolving threat behavior, and offer meaningful recommendations to proactively diminish risks (Chalapath & Chawla, 2019; Okoli et al., 2024). Such attributes enables AI-based systems to not only recognize threats at a higher accuracy but also react at a real time, thereby transforming reactive security strategies to predictive as well as preventative ones (Kaur et al., 2023; Manoharan & Sarker, 2022). Currently threat detection is a big challenge due to the large data generated by individuals, networks, devices. This burst of data tends to overwhelm traditional security operations centers (SOCs) and causes delayed reactions or overlooked threats (Aslan et al., 2023). AI removes this challenge by correlating and analysing and aggregating data from big sources, including user actions monitoring, network traffic, endpoint invaluable event rendering and external damage instinct paragraphs (Musa et al., 2022).

Applying these advanced measures, AI can identify patterns typical of an attack like a zero-day vulnerability, insider threats, advanced persistent threats (APTs), the type of attack that a human could only find manually for a very long time not imagine that is (Abdulganiyu et al., 2023; Shyaa et al., 2024). Server security, in addition to the speed and a scalability, improves accuracy of detection of threats by AI. False positives have been a persistent problem for security personnel ideally, putting resources to waste and alert fatigue. AI based systems particularly using supervised and unsupervised model based systems learn normally and abnormally performing actions, the false warning rates greatly decrease (Chalapath & Chawla, 2019; Okoli et al., 2024). This improved precision does not only improve the efficiency of the cybersecurity staff but ensures that major threats are identified and disarmed on a timely manner. Since threat detection relies more and more on AI, in real-time detection and response is of outmost importance.

AI systems are able to analyze the streaming data and perform automatic action in real time—such as isolating a perimeter of the reach of a malware, shutting traffic of attacker and already invites manual analyst investigating more (Musa et al., 2022; Salem et al., 2024). This capability is particularly important when dealing with rapid ransomware ransom, distributed denial of service (DDoS) attack or compromise of sensitive data (Musa et al., 2022). It is expected that the combination of AI with high-end technologies like the Internet of Things (IoT), 5G, and quantum computing in the future will make real-time threat detection more effective. While AI gives numerous advantages, it also gives birth to new issues and moral crises. Need for openness in operation and decision making of AI systems to data driven decision maker (Díaz-Rodríguez et al., 2023). CMP concerns sufficiently addressed to ensure reliable and government, organisational compliant AI-based TDs. The growing requirement of explainable AI (XAI) aims to bridge this gap by enhancing the transparency and interpretability of the AI decision making for the human operators specifically in those industries in which the accountability or compliance is very critical (Srinivasan & San Miguel González, 2025).

Predictive analytics, autonomous offensive/defensive systems and adaptability learning techniques will be critical AI-influenced models to shield these complex environments (Kaur et al., 2023). As the changing cyber landscape of new threats appears, our protects must also rapidly evolve— founded in limitless innovation, ethics design, and human-AI collaboration (Lepri et al., 2021). This paper looks into current usage, advantages and limitations of AI in TDR, and forecasts future innovation and challenges. Place mitochondrial lipid metabolism plays an essential role in mitochondrial biogenesis, cristae development, and in maintaining mitochondrial function, thereby it is thought to be direct contributor to mitochondrial dynamics.

Artificial intelligence uses as the driving forces deep learning (DL) through machine learning (ML) and natural linguistic processing (NLP), and the latter have re-determined the information processing, interpretation, and application in all fields. Machine learning helps machines learn about data with little or no programming, to enable them learn new patterns with little human interference. Deep learning is a field of ML that analyzes large and complicated data sets via a neural network and is mainly applicable to image recognition, fraud identification, and medical diagnosis. Instead, natural language processing provides machines with the capability to interpret, generate, and converse in human language, as it is the basis of such solutions as virtual assistants, chat bots, and automatic translators. Collectively, the technologies have rendered AI not only responsive, but perceptive as well, to the point where it is now able to simulate thinking processes that we have always considered to be specifically human in nature.

Still, technological development of these technologies is impossible outside of the contribution of the society that is not only a consumer, but also a regulator (Díaz-Rodríguez et al., 2023). Society will decide how AI is to be used, where they could trust and the limits of which the ethics is operating (Lepri et al., 2021; Srinivasan & San Miguel González, 2025). By the virtue of their entry into education, healthcare, governance, and security, the AI systems should not become objects of passive acceptance, but rather the subject of active norm, value, and expectation development (Díaz-Rodríguez et al., 2023). Access, data privacy, algorithm transparency, and accountability to the society are some societal concerns that technological designs and deployments will be subject to (Lepri et al., 2021). What is more, the reactions of society contribute to defining the social blind spots of AI such as bias in language models, discrimination in systems making the decisions, or exclusion during the access, and requiring their correction (Díaz-Rodríguez et al., 2023; Srinivasan & San Miguel González, 2025). Innovation responsibility means that there should be an ongoing connection between people (developers), policymakers and the population as the aim is to make sure that such powerful technologies are used to promote the collective good, human dignity and democracy in a more automated society (Lepri et al., 2021).

ARTIFICIAL INTELLIGENCE AND SOCIETY: INTERSECTIONS, IMPACTS, AND INTEGRATIONS

Artificial intelligence (AI) is no more than a technological innovation, it is a sociological factor that is changing the boundaries of human life, reinventing itself in relations between people, the work of the state and the economy (Dwivedi et al., 2022; Qian & Siau, 2024; Wang et al., 2024). The development of the mayhem of AI which initiated as an abstract algorithm and actualized into the healthcare, security, financial, educational and communications spheres has led to the domino effect on the whole social environment (Bin & Kausik, 2024; Lee & Trimi, 2016). What used to be the speculative fiction of the past is now embedded in the simple designs like digital assistants, recommendation systems, facial recognition, autonomous vehicles, and intelligent threat detection systems (Malfacini, 2025; Zhang et al., 2022). However, this fast updating leads to an even fast need to focus on the ethical, cultural, economic, and psychological ramifications of AI on society not only as consumers of the technology but as individuals involved in co-creating its direction (Díaz-Rodríguez et al., 2023; Lepri et al., 2021).

Transformation in labor and economic structure lies in the center of the situation of AI impact on the society (Wang et al., 2024). The repetitive and rule-based tasks, including manufacturing and customer support, are being slowly automatised with the help of AI (Dwivedi et al., 2022). Although the transition increases productivity as well as decreases the cost of operations, it is also replacing employment thus changing the nature of traditional employment and overwhelming low-skill workers (Qian & Siau, 2024; Wang et al., 2024). A society immersed so thoroughly in AI will have to reconsider how it educates children, how to train more people on how to tackle some of the jobs that are likely going to be displaced by AI, as well as how to provide a form of social safety net in the event that something happens to everyone (Lee & Trimi, 2016; Wang et al., 2024).

The policies governments and institutions introduce toward mitigating the economic impact caused by the pandemic must not only be easing but also be inducing the innovation in the inclusive manners, as the development of AI remains empowering but not exclusive (Dwivedi et al., 2022; Qian & Siau, 2024). Moreover, the character of knowledge creation and dissemination is being changed with the help of AI (Lee & Trimi, 2016). Algorithms now play the key role in the determination of the news we view, which advertisements we interact with, and even the manner in which elections are compromised (Díaz-Rodríguez et al., 2023). This algorithmic mediation of public information broadcasts important issues of bias, misinformation and echo chambers (Qian & Siau, 2024). By designing their AI systems out of sheer transparency or training them using historically biased data, there is a threat of the new system by the organizations furthering inequalities and social biases (Díaz-Rodríguez et al., 2023; Lepri et al., 2021). As an example, facial recognition was proven to be biased against people of color and of different gender and gender-classifications in its many studies, misclassifying members of minority groups by far more than the rest (Buolamwini & Gebru, 2018). In that kind of a scenario, the cooperation between the AI and the society is not only one of the use, but also one of the responsibility (Srinivasan & San Miguel González, 2025). It would not be enough to develop the critical digital literacy and to demand the algorithmic accountability, the societies need to ensure that technology should represent the democratic values instead of the distortion of them (Díaz-Rodríguez et al., 2023; Lepri et al., 2021). At the border between the AI and the society is ethical governance (Srinivasan & San Miguel González, 2025).

Ethical frameworks are more necessary when AI can make more and more decisions with relative autonomy, including but not limited to disease diagnosis, allocation of welfare benefits, granting of loans (Díaz-Rodríguez et al., 2023). A blind act by a society of giving a decision-making authority to AI may lead to a loss of authority of specific principles on which the notions of fairness, justice, and human dignity are developed (Lepri et al., 2021; Srinivasan & San Miguel González, 2025). Development of ethical AI should allow multiple parties; technologists, sociologists, ethics experts and communities most targeted by the technology to collaborate to define the design (Qian & Siau, 2024). It should encompass values that include consent, explainability, equity and inclusiveness (Díaz-Rodríguez et al., 2023; Lepri et al., 2021). Such democratization of AI development method remodels it into a social commons rather than corporate property and serves the interests of the general populace (Dwivedi et al., 2022; Srinivasan & San Miguel González, 2025).

One more crucial aspect of the social consequences of AI is its effect on identity and relationship between people (Malfacini, 2025). With machines becoming more and more like humans, especially in their interactions, such as chatbots, digital companions, or personalized content, one has to question the authenticity, emotional intelligence, or the connection with human beings (Malfacini, 2025; Arora et al., 2021). The problem of social isolation, digital addiction, and denuding the old models of interpersonal skills are new issues that occur in an AI-saturated environment (Malfacini, 2025). It is upon the educators, artists, designers and policy makers to make sure that technology complements the value of face to face interaction as opposed to substituting it (Lepri et al., 2021; Srinivasan & San Miguel González, 2025).

The deepening of AI in the society should therefore be done hand in hand with making conscious attempts to maintain emotional intelligence, cultural diversity, and ethical imagination. Most importantly, AI should be implemented in society with the principles of equality and openness. Currently, the gains of AI are concentrated, with rich countries and blue-chip companies leading in the research and enjoyment of their fruits, and the poor and marginalized communities suffer most of the harms of the algorithms.

Open-source innovation, participatory technology policymaking, and inclusive education policies are the solutions to overcoming this digital divide. AI must not be coerced into the society but rather it must be collaboratively developed with the society especially in areas such as health, education, agriculture, and disaster management where place and community knowledge are critical. To connect AI in a significant way with society, we should focus on the humanistic approach, the one where the human is more than just the subject(s) of technology rather than its tool(s). This implies facilitating societal discussions on the consequences of AI, establishing laws to protect its abuse and empower communities to influence the development of AI tools that address issues of a particular context. The process of societal integration of AI has nothing to do with assimilation into machines but rather integrating technology with human priorities, social conscience, and rational thoughtfulness.

THE TRANSFORMATIVE ROLE OF ARTIFICIAL INTELLIGENCE IN CYBERSECURITY

Artificial intelligence (AI) is revolutionizing in cybersecurity space, giving business cutting-edge, robust and innovative solutions to protect sensitive information, to detect risks immediately, to react quickly to threats. In today's digital scene where cyber attacks have become more vicious and sophisticated, AI-based security tools are not just nice to have, it's a must-have. Using AI into numerous functions of organizations makes it feasible for businesses to detect risk successfully, evaluate vast data in a moment, and respond quickly to the emergencies that would demand considerable human action. As the AI develops and becomes more incorporated in Cybersecurity computers, new dangers and difficulties are increasing. AI is not just used by Defenders; Hackers are incorporating these technologies too using them to create more sophisticated, evasion and dangerous attacks.

This dynamic fosters a perpetual arms race between cybersecurity experts and nefarious entities. As companies enhance their defenses with AI, cyber thieves at the same time use AI to develop strategies to bypass these defences. Hackers already use AI to automize phishing attacks, modify derivants generative in order to produce convincing crypto-phishing and create polymorphic malware, changing its code, to evade detection. AI technology dual use, creates a complexity in retaining the security lead. As a result, successful AI-powered risk factors require companies to use big tech and adopt a forward-looking, open approach.

In recent past, with the proliferation of AI technology, cybersecurity is cropping up in emergency pace. Apart from traditional protective features, AI is being used for predicting and blocking future invasions through looking at historical breach information, discovering patterns and forecasting future vulnerabilities. This predictive ability is a must in a fast-paced, defect-oriented threat environment. The days of just reacting to the attacks are over, they must start implementing proactive defensive approaches fueled by machine learning and advanced analytics.

AI based cybersecurity software operate by looking throughout an enormous amount of structured and unstructured info from diverse sources - example, network logs, user behavior analytics, threat intelligence feeds - to look for misbalance may indicate a recently or imminent onslaught. These systems can spot dubious activity on the go, thereby cutting down on response and containment time for the threats. Machine learning models always get better by incorporating new data, so they can react to new threats more effectively than traditional rule-based systems. The ability to find dangers which were not previously known, or what is referred to a zero-day exploits, is a crucial benefit which comes with AI in the cyber security industry.

In addition, AI provides automation in cybersecurity tasks, which is critical in the face of a massive amount of, along with massive complexity, present-day attacks.

AI-driven automation facilitates the prioritization of alarms, coordination of event responses, and, in some systems, the initiation of self-healing operations. This level of automation lessens the workload of human analysts allowing them to focus on corporate actions while ensuring that regular security procedures are performed efficiently and precisely.

Despite these benefits, the maze of AI-powered cyber attacks is becoming a growing issue and rising to a challenge. Cybercriminals are now employing the use of AI to improve their methods of operation, which has the effect of making it harder for typical defensive systems to be effective. Polymorphic malware that changes its form with each infection, and AI-powered phishing that generates convincing fake messages through generative models are more prevalent. And, in addition, attack perpetrators slip into systems by exploiting unpatched software weaknesses, known as zero-day vulnerabilities. The more AI that is used by the bad guys means that pushed by new and emerging defensive techniques continuously that cybersecurity teams do.

An emerging trend in AI-driven security is Breach and Attack Simulators (BAS) and the tools being implemented for their use These solutions run best-of-breed artificial intelligence to simulate attacks on networks and systems in a simulated environment allowing the business to test the effectiveness of their defenses, determine weaknesses, and step-up their security posture without the risk of a real attack. BAS technologies enable companies to predict forthcoming breaches by revealing how an attacker could traceback to uncorrected vulnerability via them and investigate how resilient the current security architectures against such attempts.

Data security is an important sector in which AI is advancing quite rapidly. AI algorithms can detect anomalies in data consumption patterns and detect potential symptoms of unauthorized access or data exfiltering. A sudden surge in data transfer logs created after work may indicate a potential breach. Artificial Intelligence can quickly identifying such failures and trigger alarms, or even initiate containment steps and prevent data loss of theft.

Many top technological corporations, from Google to start up groups in the area, are moving heavily into AI-based security systems (Google Cloud Blog, 2023a; TechCrunch, 2025). Google uses artificial intelligence within its security infrastructure to examine about billions of signals each day, permitting the detection of threats in scale and protection of individuals across multiple platforms (Google AI, n.d.; Google Cloud Blog, 2023b). There are also technologies like Safe Browsing, which warns users of poisoned URLs (Google Workspace Blog, 2025; Google Cloud Blog, 2023a). Other email filters got filtering systems that enable reviewing emails while the message hardly reach the inbox (Google Cloud Blog, 2023a; Medium, 2025). Such examples uıltiren AI one all eveıl of digital insfrastucture to deliver end-to-end security (Google Cloud Blog, 2025).

The deployment of AI in the cybersecurity area also raises legal and ethical problems (Díaz-Rodríguez et al., 2023; Kaur et al., 2023). Since AI systems often run autonomously, fears about accountability, transparency and fairness arise (Lepri et al., 2021; Srinivasan & San Miguel González, 2025). It is crucial to ensure AI models are trained on diverse unbiased data, which their decision-making processes are not cloudy areas, anymore fitting its data privacy principles, such as the General Data Protection Regulation (GDPR) (Díaz-Rodríguez et al., 2023). Moreover, with AI systems exposed to sensitive information and critical infrastructure, securing their information and resilience from both the misuse and malicious attacks is of utmost importance (Google AI, n.d.; Kaur et al., 2023).

Foreseeing 2025, numerous significant changes are expected to impact AI-driven cybersecurity. Contained within that is ongoing advancement in AI-based threat monitoring and response, increasing levels of AI-driven cyber threats, more prevalence of BAS technologies, and emergence of regulatory frameworks for governing the use of AI within security context. To address cyber risks, businesses must develop complete strategy that unite advanced technology with the human knowledge, strict regulatory mechanisms and a "cybersecurity culture".

In a nutshell, AI is at the same time a powerful weapon and a potential threat in the realm of cybersecurity. As it offers superior features for detecting, stopping and responding to cyber-attacks, so it also gives adversaries aforethought suggestions for attacks. Therefore, keeping cybersecurity to an AI-driven environment carries on calls for endless, partnership, and vigilance. Enterprises, government agencies and security professionals have to work together over the brains of AI while guarding against that howl, to make sure technology is employed as a security net, and not a weapon in the ongoing battle against cybercrime.

Detection of threat aligns with the major innovations in cybersecurity and every era introduces, sweltering advanced and flexible techniques to deal more diversified attacks. It all started out as a reactive cybersecurity, which involved the analysis of risks based on predetermined rules and well-known patterns. The explosion of digital data, the increased interconnectivity, and the growing sophistication of cyberattacks necessitated the shift to more adaptive and forward-thinking systems. AI is changing the way of identification, assessment and mitigation of threats by increasing human intellect with the help of machine learning, sophisticated data processing and automation in decision-making. In the beginning, intrusion protection systems were based on the rule-based method which only could recognize the already known threats. These methodologies were by heavily relied in the 1970s on the hand established rules and pre specified harmless patterns. It was effective for standard, clear and recognised assaults but it was not sufficient to discover new or emerging threats. As the nature of cyberrisks has evolved to become more sophisticated, it has become increasingly evident that this method is not viable.

In the 1980s, signature-based detection systems had a significant breakthrough. These technologies implemented a pattern recognition of threat detection by comparing themselves against a repository of verified malicious code signatures. While signature-based detection helped in prompt responses to identified threats, it was quite insufficient when it came to dealing with zero-day threats, or threats that software developers and security providers were not aware of. Heuristic-based detection techniques were developed in late 1980s and early 1990s to overcome this problem. These systems were not only built around recognized signatures; they understood file properties and behaviors to find malicious behaviors. Heuristic detection can also detect alterations of known malware or some previously unknown threats thus improving detection capabilities.

Anomaly detection systems were developed in late 1990s and early 2000s. These set a new emphasis away from traditional rules towards behaviour analysis. They established a normal and typical activity within a network or system and foresaw any major drift away from the baseline as potentially dangerous. Anomaly detection relieved dependence on humans and increased the ability to discover new risks. However these systems had many problems, first of all generating false positives due to their sensitivity to rare innocent actions.

The most evolution in threat detection came with the application in AI and machine learning in the late 2000s. Artificial intelligence driven threat detection system have transformed the way of cyber security by allow to identify earlier unknown trends and enhance the response time. AI-motivated models are capable of efficiently processing and analyzing vast amounts of data at high speed and accuracy, adapting to evolving threat worlds continuous learning from newness inputs. This shift has allowed security teams to move from a reactive posture where they view the event after the fact while the damage was being done to one of implementing systems and strategies proactively, detecting attacks before they could get in there and damage much value.

Beyond automation AI in cybersecurity also includes ability, adaptability and predictive features to the threat detection. Adaptive learning generally is a foundational ability of AI, letting systems to modify in reply to latest records and emerging risks. Machine learning techniques can learn new variations on bad behavior and thereby be able to have better protection against previously unknown threats. Furthermore these algorithms they also work very well in sophisticated pattern recognition, attacker tactics that is too complex or sophisticated that human analysts can determine. AI may find out complex attack paths and unclear anomalies from the inspection of the data of network, system and user activity.

One significant feature of AI-based security is that it can automate the attack response. When an attempt of a breach is detected, the system could activate fast remedial steps such as isolating of the affected system, notifying the security technicians or activating predefined containment measures. Such rapid response capabilities minimise the length of time that the asbestos reacts and thereby limits the damage. Predictive analytics is huge advantage AI offers where you can foresee future risks by analyzing historical trends and real world patterns. By believing ahead of time, security teams can allocate their resources more presumably and toughen up exposed areas before attacks occur.

Conventional detection methods that have traditionally been plagued by false positives require that AI systems are to be used. By isolating standard peculiarity and authentic imperils, AI can depend on genuine security issues and loose the load from the investigators which were potentially following feeble wiser. This improves productivity and free up human staff to focus on critical security issues.

At the core of AI-driven threat detection is machine learning algorithms that rely on past crime data to predict and detect emerging threats. These algorithms can be characterized as either being trained using the two most commonly used methodologies that are supervised and unsupervised learning. After training, these models may workout fresh data, physically detect and supply accurate forecasts about prospective dangers. On the contrary, unsupervised learning is not required in any labelled dataset. Instead it detects pattern and anomalies without understanding of what constitutes threat beforehand. This method is very good for catching zero-day attacks of previously unknown hostile actions.

These have been drastically enabled by advanced AI techniques, such as deep learning and neural networks. These systems can review vast data sets – including network logs, user behaviour, and external threat of data – to find tiny signs of abnormal intent. In addition to this, over time, these models improve as they improve their habits and get more precise continual predictions and they achieve lots of success in these complicated cybersecurity environments.

Data management and processing are a key component of AI-intelligent threat detection. Secure internet operation requires collection and analysis of voluminous data from various points including network traffic logs, system event cases, also user activity reports. Threat intelligence is collected from real-time monitoring tools, APIs and data extraction technology. Following that, data is cleansed, normalized and pre-processed to clean out the noise and enhance the quality of it. This ensures that AI models deal with accurate and correct inputs, which progressively sharpen the performance of AI in danger recognition.

The creation of an AI-driven threat detection model encompasses many stages (Kaur et al., 2023; Okoli et al., 2024). First of all, one has to define a problem which implies identifying the senses of risks, the model must be able to recognize (Abdullahi et al., 2022; Salem et al., 2024). Then, they must bring and integrate the data, making sure that it concerns various threat scenarios (Manoharan & Sarker, 2022). Next, feature selection and engineering are performed which include feature subset selection and attributes construction that most relevant attributes have been selected and constructed new features improves results of model performance (Chalapath & Chawla, 2019; Shyaa et al., 2024). Once the data is ready the correct AI model is selected, trained and assessed (Kaur et al., 2023). The training step is approximately to teach the model to recognize the hazards, while testing is pretty much about to test its accuracy and reliability (Okoli et al., 2024). Continuous validation and on-demand performance tuning must be performed to ensure the model remains contemporary all the time and carries forward to handle latest threats (Shyaa et al., 2024).

After deployment of these models, need to make the continuous up-date (Mahboubi et al., 2024). Cyber threats are constantly evolving making static approaches irrelevant at a very high rate (Zhang et al., 2022). Regular updates ensure that threat detection systems keep their effectiveness against existing types of attacks (Manoharan & Sarker, 2022). In addition, continuous education allows the models to always stay one step ahead of threat attackers who are continually looking for new strategies to exploit system vulnerabilities (Kaur et al., 2023; Salem et al., 2024).

And so, the evolution of threat detection has moved from simple, rule-based systems all the way to sophisticated AI technologies (Martínez et al., 2019; Nyale & Angolo, 2022). Every stage in this growth has been driven by the requirement to counterriot progressively sophisticated cyber threats (Aslan et al., 2023). Artificial Intelligence (AI) has been a game changer for this field, offering adaptive, predictive, automated and more than efficient, solutions that speed up, prove better accuracy and utmost in efficiency in cybersecurity operations (Mamidi, 2024; Okoli et al., 2024). As the cyber threats escalate in size and complexity, our IT Teams will remain the key component in defence strategies, enabling you to build effective, forward-looking security architectures (Kaur et al., 2023; Lepri et al., 2021).

STRATEGIES FOR IMPLEMENTATION AND APPLICATIONS OF ARTIFICIAL INTELLIGENCE IN THREAT DETECTION

Running effective threat detection techniques requires a multi-faceted cyber security strategy comprising advanced technology coupled with the human skill element. Artificial intelligence (AI) has become a critical tool in enhancing threat detection, but so far it requires inclusion into present systems, real-time capabilities, as well as flexibility to extend newly emerging cyber threats. For the highest results, AI systems needs to interact with human analysts, continuously watch digital perimeter, and be earmarked for frequent updates to maintain against evolving zero-day threats. A multi-layered strategy ensures that nobody point of failure will compromise security infrastructure.

A main fear of carrying out AI-based threat detection is the integration with current security tools. Most firms implement traditional protects for example firewalls, or anti-virus computer program, and rule-based monitoring devices. The problem is that it is challenging to ensure that highly advanced AI systems comply with existing systems seamlessly without causing any disruptions. Middleware and APIs (Application Programming Interfaces), in fact, they are necessary to enable the efficient transfer of communications across different systems and also to allow real-time information sharing about threats. The goal is to enhance security abilities without muddling the existing infrastructure, which could be cost effectively unaffordable hazardous.

To increase the efficiency, several companies use a compound threat detection technique. These models incorporates the benefits of artificial intelligence, machine learning, as well as conventional rule-based systems. For instance, even though AI can pick up on others new anomalies, rule-based systems, are reliable in spotting common risks. Hybrid models improve detection capability and quickly counter new as well as emerging cyber threats by combining methods. This complementarity enables enterprises to align proactive and reactive threat management concurrent with maintenance of stability in the system.

A key benefit of AI in cybersecurity is its ability to process and analyze at real-time (Salem et al., 2024; Musa et al., 2022). Cyber threats are constantly changing and spreading across seconds leaving less time for a human actor to respond (Aslan et al., 2023). With Artificial Intelligence i.e. Machine Learning models can evaluate Stream Data in real–time and recognize any Abnormalities and Threatened Activities (Okoli et al., 2024; Shyaa et al., 2024). Technologies like stream processing and edge computing enhance it by moving computation closer to the data source, reducing latency and making for quicker responses (Chithaluru et al., 2023; Mamidi, 2024). These tactics enable organizations to quickly get rid of risks, as such lowering probable damage (Musa et al., 2022).

A very important factor of AI deployment of threat detection Facilitates scalability and performance (Kaur et al., 2023). With ever growing business, comes larger amounts of data (Zhang et al., 2022). AI systems need to be able to scale very efficiently such that it can really handle huge volume of data without dropping performance (Manoharan & Sarker, 2022). This implies robust data structures, efficient storage facilities, as well as efficient computing powers (Abdullahi et al., 2022). This way, companies assure that their threat detection systems continue to be innovative and dynamic whether the data is large or complex (Salem et al., 2024; Okoli et al., 2024).

Use of AI in threat detection varies wide and various, and affects that pretty mostly of the cyber security. Network security is one key area where AI is used to watch the network traffic and find an abnormal patterns. Using analysis of packet behavior and data streams, AI systems may be able to spot possible attack instances, malicious activities, and unauthorised data exfiltration. Machine learning methods enhance detection accuracy, reducing false positives, providing prompt alarms. Common techniques include Anomaly detection Systems that identify activity outside of normal behavior, Intrusion detection system (IDS) which are checking each collaborating conversation suspected behavior and, intrusion Prevention System (IPS) which takes decision to block any suspected threat in real-time.

Array Security is an area where AI really shows its value (Kaur et al., 2023; Mamidi, 2024). In modern networked environment, every device connected to a network is a potential access point for cyber attacks (Aslan et al., 2023; Chithaluru et al., 2023). AI-based endpoint security solutions are always monitoring individual endpoints for known indicators of compromise (Alsamiri & Alsubhi, 2019; Okoli et al., 2024). These systems can detect ransomware, viruses and zero day threat at the end point with analysis in user behavioral, application activity, system performance level (Musa et al., 2022; Salem et al., 2024; Shyaa et al., 2024). Not just threats are identified, but as well as executed countermeasures are performed rapidly, for instance, isolation of contaminated devices or interdiction of malicious actions, therefore preventing lateral movement within the network (Manoharan & Sarker, 2022; Musa et al., 2022).

Fraud and anomaly detection is a key application area of AI in areas such as banking, finance, e-commerce. Financial institutions employ AI to review many transactions in seconds to identify those that stray from usual patterns. An unusually large withdrawal from somewhere unexpected may trigger a fraud alert. The power to survey huge sets of files and detect concealed anomalies offer companies a substantial competitive advantage to protect valuable financial and customer data.

It may do so, nonetheless, AI in danger detection confronts considerable challenges, and challenges of ethics. A particular concern is that data bias could contaminate threat detection results and come up with incorrect, unjust decisions. Privacy is becoming more and more a weapon of mass destruction in A.I driven threat detection. These are usually designed to have access to a significant amount of personal, as well as organisational data, this is reinforcing concerns over data privacy and user permission. Rules like the General Data Protection Regulation (GDPR) of the European Union expresses data governance requirements quite strictly, require businesses to offer long security protections and also guarantee data. For the decision making transparency in AI is unique for compliance and confidence of users and stakeholders. Security teams have a task: to balance efficient threat detection versus the need to protect user's privacy and rights.

Expecting the future changes and AI-based threats prediction shine lights to anticipated improvement in advanced features in the AI-powered threat detection system. Other experts think that advances will continue to occur in deep knowledge engineering technology, in order, consequently, that artificial intelligence will come up with, as a result, ever more finely-grained templates of crooked dealing. The use of quantum computing can significantly speed up data processing, potentially leading to faster threat detection and response. Explainable AI (XAI) is a developing approach to improve the transparency and interpretability of AI, in particular the decision-making capabilities of AI, for humans reviewing it, therefore to achieve confidence and accountability in automated systems.

As the AI tools become more autonomous, we may experience an opening up for predictive analytics and self-repairing networks which indicates not only shows but in addition foresees and precludes cyber threats from becoming effective. These changes might give self-sufficient occurrence reaction frameworks that could adapt up to changing threats without human mediation. Also, AI can deliver personalized threat detection by examining user behavior plus organizational risk profiles, meaning that on the other hand, security responses are effective, as well as qualified.

The inclusion of AI in IT security constitutes a significant innovation in the cybersecurity industry. Helping cloud-native organizations achieve superior monitoring of current systems, speedier respond in real-time, and relentless scale to prohibitive growing requirements, AI gives operators advanced answers to deal with mounting cyber dangers. Even though the persistent ethical issues and data biases persist, plenty of developments in AI signal an AI future where threat detection becomes faster, more accurate and based on greater transparency, adaptability and accountability. As digital world blooms, world AI is going to remain vital partner in fighting cybercrime, protecting information, infrastructure and human trust.

The deployment of artificial intelligence (AI) into cybersecurity, in specific threat detection, has introduced a new approach for corporations to prevent their digital infrastructure. AI-driven Threat Detection provides current, resilient answer with a number of strategic good points that enhance safety protocols and operational effectivity throughout wide array of environments.

The major benefit of AI in threat detection is significant reduction of detection and response time (Salem et al., 2024; Okoli et al., 2024). AI systems can examine huge numbers of information sets to an extremely precise and a real-time method, identify possible threats when they emerge (Musa et al., 2022; Shyaa et al., 2024). In comparison to human analysts who often need hours, as well as days to log and security warnings analysis and interpret, AI algorithms can instantly assess real-time data streams looking for actions suspicious of more in-depth examination or auto-reaction (Kaur et al., 2023; Manoharan & Sarker, 2022). This real-time capability lets firms move quickly, typically indeed prior a threat can convert right into a considerable protection breach (Musa et al., 2022; Salem et al., 2024). With it possible strategies are reduced to, and retrieval opportunity is profoundly decreased with all outcomes Enlarged event Messe Management double (Okoli et al., 2024; Zhang et al., 2022).

One further benefit is also higher accuracy and fine details. One of the prevalent problem with cybersecurity is the too much of false positives generated by traditional security mechanism. This pointless alerts not merely waste time but in addition may stimulate overhear sickness among security professionals, raising the risk of missing on-site threats. But AI and machine learning models operate their detection algorithms continually by reading data from the past and patterns of alarm. In this way, more intelligent systems are created, which can practically distinguish between harmless anomalies and true malicious behavior. This process later on minimizes the false positives, allowing the security professionals, target the high-priority threats that demands urgent action.

AI offers substantial scalability, an important factor in conditions where there is fast growth in digital environments in terms of size as well as complexity. Traditional methods must be supplemented by security personnel in accordance with the increase in threats and information. This is both costly and in the long run unsustainable. On the other hand, AI can deal with more jobs without the requirement for people to be employed in a similar measure. AI users driven security danger detection resources could easily handle climbing slash, T the enterprise be expand its rising cloud infrastructure, either believed integrate into freshly appointed staff, Stempel aforementioned embrace IoT equipment network. This flexibility ensures a one-to-one protection ratio, independently of the overall size or the development route of any organisation.

A major plus of AI-based systems is, they can identify and anticipate possible threats ahead. Instead of only responding to set upon assaults, AI will be able to review historical data, treating trends, and behavioral routines to predict upcoming vulnerabilities or the following caste of impending attack. This predictive ability enables businesses to be active in dealing to the problem, such as tightening or repairing weakness, revising policy, or increasing surveillance in high-risk areas. AI-based systems are proactively dealing with cybersecurity and predicts attacks pre-emptively, thus decreasing risk exposure and increasing the long-term resilience.

The additional security owing to distances offered by AI technologies are also vital. Cyber-attacks can occur 24 hours, 365 days per year, evenings, weekends, or holidays rendering human monitoring teams to be limited or not available. AI can work continuously -24/7 around the clock- ensuring that no suspicious action goes through undetected. Continuous monitoring is very vital especially in industries like banking, healthcare, and also government; where interruptions or company data breach can cause major issue.

In addition, AI enhances incident response planning and management. Several times, but unfortunately not all, the reaction-time to a seen danger gets prolonged due to the review of the situation and a choice of action is necessary. Artificial intelligence enables contextual threat assessment, suggests remediation techniques, and carries out automatic actions according to predefined protocols. This speeds up the containment process and lowers the chance of operator mistakes in high pressure situations. Several businesses are governed by severe laws requiring simultaneous breach reporting, exhaustive investigation, and close documentation of security events. AI options might automate these jobs generating documents, disposed of cases and running audit trails to enable corporations complying with latest regulations and offloading administrative burden to their security individuals.

The benefits of artificial intelligence in threat detection are too many and too great. AI provides intelligent and contextual solution to the modern cybersecurity challenges by providing real-time reaction, faster detection, increased accuracy, scalability, proactive threat prevention, continuous monitoring, and easier compliance. With increasingly sophisticated digital threats, the use of AI in threat detection is not only beneficial; it is becoming fast necessary for businesses engaged in securing robust, robust and strong-fitting security frameworks.

CONCLUSION

In conclusion, Artificial intelligence, is rising as an important component of the transformed security landscape, considerably changing how companies approach risks identification, mitigation & addressing the same. The scale, speed and complexity of current cyber-attacks demands intelligent, flexible and real-time solutions, beyond traditional security methods. AI addresses this need by quick threat finding, reduction of false positives, and predictions of vulnerabilities by using predictive analytics. Its capabilities let organizations adopt a proactive approach to security, effecting quick containment and response to rapidly spreading digital threats.

The union between Artificial Intelligence, threat detection, and cybersecurity is a remarkable step toward the evolution of the way, in which modern societies learn to predict, assess, and prevent digital and physical threats in the new era of threats. With the help of the AI technologies that offer new horizons of such machine learning, deep learning, and natural language processing, companies have now been able to identify the anomalies, predict security breaches, and automate responses in real-time, unprecedentedly quickly and accurately. This development does not only increase the efficiency of cybersecurity infrastructures but also minimizes false alarms, operations expenses by large margins, and human error, in addition to the ability of the systems to act on threats before they become critical disasters.

The social contribution of AI related to this area is deep. With the persistence conversion of public and commercial organizations to digital ecosystems the protection of data integrity and privacy is becoming the main aspect of ensuring public belief. To guarantee the uninterrupted performance of critical services, threat detection systems equipped with AI systems are crucial to safeguarding these digital assets. Furthermore, AI helps to secure the social, economic, and national well-being as it deters cybercrimes and protects confidential information.

All these benefits however need to be sought amidst ethical consideration. To ensure the integration of AI in security systems is not used in bad faith, does not allow unwarranted surveillance, and is not used to deliver unintended bias, transparency, fairness, and accountability are needed. When a society is able to utilize responsibly the AI, it will not only be able to protect itself against external dangers but make the internal democratic principles and civic shields stronger.

Altogether, AI implementation in the area of threat detection and cybersecurity cannot be reduced to technological advancement only but represents a social necessity. It helps societies to act with intelligence of evolving risks, creates resilience in the digital governance and prepares the way towards a safer, more fair future where innovations become part of the improvements in welfare of the people, and their moral responsibility.

The use of AI in cybersecurity necessitates a cautious and responsible approach. Even though the technology offers advantages, it has and will always possess certain limitations. Concerns such as data biasness, insufficient openness and potentially considerable privacy infractions could undermine the trustworthiness and reliability of AI powered threat detection systems. That the AI must be held and controlled through effectual moral principle to uphold equity, regulation of consideration, and become transparent with every process. This involves the embedding of explainable AI (XAI) models that give transparent views on decision-making, a key attribute for compliance, trust and business clarity.

The field of cybersecurity is not going to go backward as the technology will continually evolve. The marriage of AI with emerging technologies like quantum computing, the Internet of Things (IoT) and 5G networks will bring fresh opportunities and complex challenges. Quantum computing can change the way we handle data processing skills which could result in answering the information better knowing that when to act quicker better knowing risk. Also, AI-driven products will play a crucial role in securing IoT environments by discovering abnormalities all over dispersed networks of linked machines.

Partnership will be crucial of managing this changing environment. Intergovernmental relationships, private sector partnerships, academia, international regulatory entities' engagements are required as well to build consistent frameworks, to share threat intelligence and to speak on behalf for best practice.

Both and people must be constantly viewing business in new ways, working creatively. Rolling-out AI-powered security technologies — like breach and attack simulators, automated incident response tools, and behavior analytics — will be needed in order to stay ahead of the attackers. Organizations must start prioritizing the observance to the data security standards - such as the General Data Protection Regulation (GDPR) - and set the robust processes of the AI data management, as well as privacy. Cyber Security Awareness and Training programs carried forward will ensure that both technical and non-technical stakeholders are aware of the effects and responsibilities associated with the use of AI in threat detection.

The future of cybersecurity – or more specifically, protecting personal computers, smartphones, networks, and sensitive information from people trying to steal information via breaking computer security system – will come down to using AI's computing capabilities to the benefit of its users, person by person scrutiny and making ethical judgments. AI developed from a manual tool to a important partner in fighting hackers. Through creating a balanced approach that incorporates innovation and accountability, businesses can create secure digital ecosystems and have the capabilities to manage the intricate challenges of more intertwined society.

REFERENCES

Abdulganiyu, O.H., Tchakoucht, T.A., Saheed, Y.K. (2023). A systematic literature review for network intrusion detection system (IDS). *International Journal of Information Security.*

Abdullahi, M., Baashar, Y., Alhussian, H., Alwadain, A., Aziz N., Capretz, L.F. (2022). Detecting cybersecurity attacks in Internet of Things using artificial intelligence methods: A systematic literature review. *Electronics (Basel).*

Alsamiri, J., & Alsubhi, K. (2019). Internet of Things Cyber Attacks Detection using Machine Learning [IJACSA]. *International Journal of Advanced Computer Science and Applications, 10*(12), •••.

Arora, A., Chakraborty, P., & Bhatia, M. P. S. (2021). Problematic Use of Digital Technologies and Its Impact on Mental Health During COVID-19 Pandemic: Assessment Using Machine Learning. *Emerging Technologies During the Era of COVID-19 Pandemic pp.197-221*

Aslan, Ö., Aktuğ, S. S., Ozkan-Okay, M., Yilmaz, A. A., & Akin, E. (2023). A Comprehensive Review of Cyber Security Vulnerabilities, Threats, Attacks, and Solutions. *Electronics (Basel).*

Bin, R. A., & Kausik, M. A. K. (2024). *AI revolutionizing industries worldwide: A comprehensive overview of its diverse applications* (Vol. 7). Hybrid Advances.

Chalapath, R., & Chawla, S. (2019). Deep Learning for Anomaly Detection. *Survey (London, England).*

Chithaluru, P., AL-Turjman, F., Kumar, M., Stephan, T. (2023). Computational-Intelligence-Inspired Adaptive Opportunistic Clustering Approach for Industrial IoT Networks. *IEEE Internet of Things Journal.*

Díaz-Rodríguez, N., Del Ser, J., Coeckelbergh, M., López de Prado, M., Herrera-Viedma, E., & Herrera, F. (2023). Connecting the dots in trustworthy Artificial Intelligence: From AI principles, ethics, and key requirements to responsible AI systems and regulation. *Information Fusion.*

Dwivedi, Y. K., Hughes, L., Baabdullah, A. M., Ribeiro-Navarrete, S., Giannakis, M., & Al-Debei, M. M. (2022). Metaverse beyond the hype: Multidisciplinary perspectives on emerging challenges, opportunities, and agenda for research, practice and policy. *International Journal of Information Management.*

Homaei, M., Mogollón-Gutiérrez, O., Sancho, J. C., Ávila, M., & Caro, A. (2024). A review of digital twins and their application in cybersecurity based on Artificial Intelligence. *Artificial Intelligence Review.*

Kaur, R., Gabrijelčič, D., & Klobučar, T. (2023). Artificial intelligence for cybersecurity: Literature review and future research directions. *Information Fusion, 97,* •••.

Lee, S.M., Trimi, S,. (2016). Innovation for creating a smart future. *Journal of Innovation & Knowledge*

Lepri, B., Oliver, N., Pentland, A,. (2021). Ethical machines: The human-centric use of artificial intelligence.

Mahboubi, A., Luong, K., Aboutorab, H., Bui, H.T., Jarrad, G., Bahutair, M. (2024). Evolving techniques in cyber threat hunting: A systematic review. *Journal of Network and Computer Applications.*

Malfacini, K. (2025). The impacts of companion AI on human relationships: Risks, benefits, and design considerations. *AI & Society.*

Mamidi, S.R. 2024. The Role of AI and Machine Learning in Cloud Cybersecurity, *Journal of Artificial Intelligence General Science.* Vol. 1 Issue 3

Manoharan, A., & Sarker, M. (2022). Revolutionizing Cybersecurity: Unleashing the Power of Artificial Intelligence and Machine Learning for Next-Generation Threat Detection. *International Research Journal of Modernization in Engineering Technology and Science.*

Martínez, J., Comesaña, C., & García-Nieto, P. J. (2019). Review: Machine learning techniques applied to cybersecurity. *International Journal of Machine Learning and Cybernetics.*

Musa, N. S., Mirza, N. M., Rafique, S. H., Abdallah, A. M., & Murugan, T. (2022).. . *Machine Learning.*

Nyale, D., Angolo, S.M. 2022. A Survey of Artificial Intelligence in Cyber Security, *International Journal of Computer Applications Technology and Research* Vol. 11–Issue 12, 474-477

Okoli, U. L., Obi, O. C., Adewusi, A. O., & Abrahams, T. O. (2024). *Machine learning in cybersecurity: A review of threat detection and defense mechanisms.* World Journal of Advanced Research and Reviews.

Salem, A.H., & Azzam, S.F, Emam., Abohany, A.A. (2024). Advancing cybersecurity: A Comprehensive Review of AI-driven Detection Techniques. *Journal of Big Data.*

Shyaa, M. A., Ibrahim, N. F., Zainol, Z., Abdullah, R., Anbar, M., & Alzubaidi, L. (2024). Evolving cybersecurity frontiers: A comprehensive survey on concept drift and feature dynamics aware machine and deep learning in intrusion detection systems. *Engineering Applications of Artificial Intelligence*.

Srinivasan, R., & San Miguel González, B. (2025). The role of empathy for artificial intelligence accountability. *Journal of Responsible Technology*, *9*, •••.

Wang, X., Chen, M., & Chen, N. (2024). How artificial intelligence affects the labour force employment structure from the perspective of industrial structure optimisation. *Heliyon*. PMID: 38434398

Zhang, Z., Ning, H., Shi, F., Farha, F., Xu, Y., & Xu, J. (2022). Artificial intelligence in cyber security: Research advances, challenges, and opportunities. *Artificial Intelligence Review*.

Chapter 9
The Role of Artificial Intelligence in Safeguarding Human Rights:
An International Legal Perspective

Saquib Ahmed
https://orcid.org/0009-0008-1891-6910
Sharda University, India

Jai Shankar Ojha
S.S. Law College, Shahjahanpur, India

Astha Srivastava
Amity University, Lucknow, India

Saurabh Kumar
https://orcid.org/0009-0005-4594-1597
School of Legal Studies, The Neotia University, West Bengal, India

Mumtaz Zabeen Khan
https://orcid.org/0009-0001-3836-5828
Rayat Law College, India

Ajitabh Mishra
Rayat Law College, India

ABSTRACT

Artificial intelligence (AI) plays a transformative role in the protection and advancement of human rights within the international legal framework. Leveraging advanced analytics and automated monitoring systems, AI enables the detection, documentation, and reporting of human rights violations, thereby enhancing transparency and accountability on a global scale. International civil society organizations and legal enforcement bodies utilize AI to expand their capacity for rights monitoring, authenticate evidence, and facilitate timely intervention, particularly in conflict zones and regions vulnerable to state repression. As AI's processing power increases, it will transform many areas of human existence, including the workforce. This is

DOI: 10.4018/979-8-3373-3685-5.ch009

already altering people's daily lives. Over time, the uninhibited development of AI by technology has enhanced its undeniable value, impact, and use in people's lives. This includes basic necessities like food, clothes, housing, education, and the ability to procreate, as well as more abstract concepts like human rights.

INTRODUCTION

If this definition is correct, then artificial intelligence is just a system or computer that can mimic human intellect in some way. Intelligence (AI) is "a science and a set of computational technologies that are inspired by—but typically operate quite differently from—the ways people use their nervous systems and bodies to sense, learn, reason, and take action," according to a recent paper from Stanford University. Another way to look at AI is according to Stuart Russell and Peter Norving, who propose the following classifications: 1) systems with human-like cognition and behaviour; 2) systems with human-like reasoning and logic-based behaviour; and 3) systems with human-like reasoning and logic-based behaviour. The common thread running across all of these definitions is that AI systems exist primarily to make human jobs easier. When an intelligent system completes a task, the end product is virtually indistinguishable from that of a human operator. So, anytime AI-generated intelligent systems are involved, human rights must be included in any discussion of their relationship with people. Put simply, the development of AI will unavoidably have an impact on human rights, whether that impact is beneficial or negative (Ahmad, 2025). Artificial intelligence (AI) is primarily intended to do tasks that humans can do more quickly, accurately, and efficiently. To what extent "Artificial Intelligence is designed to jettison the essence and functions of humans" is at the heart of the debate over this technology and how it will affect human rights. The term "Artificial Intelligence" has not been defined in a way that everyone agrees upon, even if it is convenient to think about it in terms of a definition. A.I. has been defined in a number of ways; the first was proposed in 1956 as part of the Dartmouth Summer Research Project. According to John McCarthy, a pioneer in the field, "intelligent" means that a system can carry out tasks that would be considered clever if a person were to carry them out.

METHODOLOGY AND LITERATURE REVIEW

Methodology

Research Approach and Design

This research is primarily doctrinal research methodology, which is the most appropriate method for the research. This design necessitates a critical analysis and evaluation of existing legal instruments, including international human rights treaties, conventions, judicial rulings, and policy papers concerning AI and fundamental rights.

Data Sources

The research employs a balanced selection of primary and secondary legal documents.

- **Primary Legal Documents:** This category includes foundational international human rights instruments, such as the Universal Declaration of Human Rights, the International Covenants on Civil and Political Rights (ICCPR), and Economic, Social, and Cultural Rights (ICESCR), alongside specialized AI governance standards.
- **Secondary Sources:** These consist of comprehensive academic journals, research reports from authoritative human rights organizations (e.g., the United Nations), and key policy publications.

The theoretical framework is enriched by chosen case studies that give actual examples demonstrating the practical influence of AI technology on certain human rights challenges.

The research utilizes a comprehensive, three-tiered analytical approach to assess the effectiveness of contemporary international law:

1. **Doctrinal Analysis:** This evaluates the traditional interpretation of core legal concepts to assess the effectiveness of international laws in protecting human rights against risks associated with AI, such as opacity and algorithmic bias.
2. **Comparative Legal Analysis:** This systematically examines the alignment of AI policies and legislative responses across various countries against established international human rights standards. It aims to identify critical regulatory gaps and establish best practices.

3. **Ethical-Policy Evaluation:** This integrates ethical and policy considerations to assess governance strategies that promote equitable and sustainable AI development while ensuring the maintenance of human rights.

Research Process and Identified Limitations

The study involved a comprehensive examination of global legal literature and news reports. A detailed analysis of significant international law documents was executed, and empirical case studies illustrating rights issues including privacy, non-discrimination, and access to justice were selected for in-depth analysis. This process allows the study to evaluate the adequacy of current international legal protections and propose specific enhancements for AI governance, utilizing both doctrinal and empirical findings.

Identified limitations include the fast-paced development of artificial intelligence, structural differences in legal systems across jurisdictions, and the inherent difficulty in accessing the most current and relevant international case law. This multidimensional approach ultimately integrates doctrinal, empirical, and normative perspectives to comprehensively analyze AI's impact on human rights law.

Review of the Literature

Recent research underscores the growing recognition that Artificial Intelligence (AI) significantly impacts human rights safeguards within the framework of international law. Research underscores the international human rights framework as the fundamental foundation for AI governance, stressing the obligations of states and private companies to protect rights such as privacy, freedom of speech, and non-discrimination. Literature points out that there are already gaps in the legal safeguards against AI-driven damages and calls for more clear and enforceable rights-based frameworks instead of recommendations that focus on ethics but aren't as binding. Scholars assert that the explicit integration of human rights into AI policy is crucial for safeguarding vulnerable people against the adverse effects of automated decision-making systems (Mpinga, 2022).

The literature on jurisprudential views examines the imperative of modifying and renewing fundamental human rights in light of the unprecedented challenges presented by AI. Many experts argue that AI increases concerns such as spying, algorithmic prejudice, and economic displacement, necessitating a reassessment of civil, political, economic, social, and cultural rights in the context of new technologies. AI is also being looked at to see whether it can help in monitoring and enforcing human rights. Frameworks are being created to help people figure out the pros and cons of using AI technologies to defend human rights. This tackles the dual character of AI as both a risk and an opportunity in the context of international law (Gellers, 2023).

Ethical frameworks frequently appear in literature as supplements to legal standards, highlighting ideals such as justice, openness, responsibility, and regard for human dignity. A discussion is still going on over whether ethical pledges are enough when there are no binding legal norms. Scholars contend that international human rights law provides the essential legal basis for the governance of ethical AI. Studies show that a combination of law, ethics, and policy is necessary to move AI technology forward in a way that protects human rights and reduces damage, especially for groups that are already at risk (Fjeld et al., 2020).

CONCEPTUALIZING HUMAN RIGHTS UNDER RELEVANT DOMESTIC AND INTERNATIONAL LAWS

Since it pertains to every individual's fundamental life, regardless of their location or cultural background, the idea of human rights has garnered a great deal of focus and has been handled with great care. A society's fundamental entitlements are its members' human rights. Because people are human, these things are relevant to them. To live a civilised life in any culture, they are an absolute need. Human rights are a set of universally recognised protections for individual liberty, dignity, equality, and respect. According to Kayode Eso J.S.C. (as he was at the time) in the case of Ransome Kuti & ORS v. A.G Federation & OR, human rights are those that have always been there, even before there were laws for how to seek them out, and this definition is as short as it gets. Above and above the usual rules of the state, it is a fundamental requirement for a civilised life (Al-Billeh et al., 2024).

In accordance with universal principles recognised by modern morality and international law, every individual has an inherent and inalienable right to a certain set of liberties, protections, and advantages, collectively known as human rights. It is impossible for a person to maintain his humanity in the absence of human rights, which are so essential to the human condition. Human rights are essential to a meaningful and valuable existence. In other words, there must be strong and compelling reasons to violate human rights because they are too valuable.

Human rights are a standard component of national legislation worldwide. The domain of domestic law continues to encompass fundamental rights. Because the Constitution, the supreme law of the land, guarantees them, we may say that they are basic. Thus, the rights guaranteed by domestic law are those that are explicitly stated or included in the domestic legal framework, most notably the country's constitution or statutes. The following human rights are encompassed in the concept of human rights: the right to exist, the right to be treated with respect, the right to be free from arbitrary interference, the right to peacefully assemble and associate with others, the right to travel and possession of real estate, the right to be free from discrimination, and the right to private and family life. Though human rights are guaranteed by legislation in many nations, it is worth noting that the same is also guaranteed on a global scale. The establishment of human rights in many nations really predates the international acknowledgement and existence of human rights. Human rights are a central concern of many international organisations, and as a result, there are treaties and conventions governing this area that member nations must ratify and adopt into law (Chakraborty & Bhojwani, 2018).

Unless the National Assembly passes a bill implementing a particular treaty, no agreement between the Federation and another nation will be legally binding.

The 1948 Universal Declaration of Human Rights is a landmark international document on human rights. An important text that stated basic human rights and asked all nations to defend them is the "Universal Declaration of Human Rights" (UDHR). An answer to the longing for human rights to be included as a globally acknowledged rule, the UDHR legislation is extremely foundational to the history of law. The United Nations General Assembly in Paris on 10 December 1948 recognised the Declaration as a common standard of accomplishments for all peoples and all nations. It was draughted by delegates with diverse legal and cultural backgrounds from all corners of the world (Gellers, 2023).

For the first time, it lays forth the universal protection of basic human rights. The International Covenant on Civil and Political Rights is another body of international law that defines a set of human rights. It is upon the Universal Declaration of Human Rights that the International Covenant on Civil and Political Rights (ICCPR) is based. All citizens in democracies have the fundamental rights outlined in this covenant, which can be enforced through the courts. Notably, both national and international legislation around the globe have recognised the importance of human rights. Human rights have always existed, even before the political establishment of any nation, therefore they are not contingent on these laws. With that said, the implementation of these laws, in whatever form they may take, is now critical to the well-being of the whole nation (Liu & Zawieska, 2017).

THE IMPACTS OF ARTIFICIAL INTELLIGENCE ON RELEVANT HUMAN RIGHTS

Some have raised concerns about the future of human rights in light of AI progress, despite the fact that these protections are fundamental to human survival. As a result of these changes, people feel strongly about whether or not it is necessary. An essential point to keep in mind is that AI systems are developed by people.

The development of AI may be attributed to the fact that it has been beneficial in streamlining and improving many human endeavours. Artificial intelligence is not starting from scratch or being created in a void. In reality, AI is being used by some social actors to automate decision-making in certain domains. This is happening in the context of social institutions that already have human rights implications, but they are doing it to get what they want (Roumate, 2020).

A number of viewpoints have been voiced concerning the potential impact of AI on human rights due to the inherent nature of AI making choices on behalf of humans. One might have a favourable or negative stance on these issues. Without a doubt, it demonstrates AI's contribution to the improvement of every aspect of life, in line with its future prospects. The development of some AI systems has made it simpler to keep tabs on human rights abuses, which has led to a loosening of standards for proving such violations in court. Some have argued that the "golden age of surveillance" has begun with the advent of digital technology in the 21st century, with nations, companies, and non-state entities all participating (Su, 2022).

The vast quantities of open-source data produced by the billions of sensor platforms in circulation worldwide are accessible to news organisations, human rights groups, and open-source investigators like Bellingcat and the Syrian Archive. Hundreds of high-resolution imaging satellites, multi-function mobile phones, and other imaging platforms have given rise to a sort of surveillance that is becoming increasingly common. That way, whether on the ground or in orbit, hardly anything happens without a camera recording it. There are two possible ways to represent this wave: favourably and negatively. Positively, the application of AI has the potential to enhance a state's security. Included in this is the battle against terrorists. In 2017, for example, a Libyan warlord was indicted by the International Criminal Court after satellite footage and films of his executions, either ordered or carried out by his supporters, were shared online. This is only one example of the various ways AI may improve human rights.

The Relationship Between AI and Individual Freedom

An essential human right, the right to personal liberty, includes the freedom to move about within a specific area. While this privilege can be extended to any area, one must meet the requirements set by that particular country or location. An individual's right to liberty necessitates that any detention or arrest must adhere to legal standards. The fundamental freedom that no government has the authority to limit is the right to personal liberty. Without a doubt, the guarantee of individual liberty is a fundamental human right. All around the globe, political societies have passed laws formally recognising these rights. Everyone has the right to their own freedom, and nobody has the right to have it taken away from them. As a result of its inclusion in several treaties and legislation that numerous states have ratified, the right to liberty is highly revered in the worldwide community. Individuals have the right to personal liberty as outlined in the International Covenant on Civil and Political Rights, a legislation that is based on the Universal Declaration of Human Rights.

The right to personal freedom and security is universal. Arresting or detaining somebody without probable cause is absolutely unacceptable. No one's liberty shall be taken away from them unless the law establishes the grounds and the method for doing so. The International Court of Justice, in the case of America v. Iran, highlighted the importance of personal liberty and stated that it is incompatible with the United Nations Charter and the Universal Declaration of Human Rights, which guarantees the right to life, liberty, and security of the human person (Article 3). It is also incompatible with the practice of physically limiting or depriving people of their freedom in times of hardship (Thapaliya & Sharma, 2023).

By creating programs that assess risk and the probability of a crime occurring at a location or by an individual, artificial intelligence has planted its digital paws in the criminal justice systems of several countries. Police deployment is informed by projected locations where crimes are most likely to occur by predictive policing algorithms like PredPol and HunchLab.

Despite the undeniable benefits of this unparalleled expansion, there is a real danger that it may infringe upon the right to personal liberty and the right to be free. Risk assessment instruments (RAIs) are a type of computational tool that can foretell the likelihood of future wrongdoing by a defendant. Decisions that have significant judicial weight, such whether or not to detain a defendant prior to trial, are informed by these forecasts. When a computer decides whether or not to send a suspect to prison, it will appear strange. Members of the legal profession who are concerned about this trend have rejected it. Recidivism is [another] case in point. software that assesses risk is utilised by the American criminal justice system to guide detention choices at practically every step, from bail assignment to criminal punishment. More Black defendants have been wrongly classified as high risk, leading to harsher bail restrictions, pre-trial detention, and lengthier prison sentences as a result of the program. Not only in the US but throughout the globe, this is blatantly racist behaviour towards Black people that has led to the abuse of AI. Furthermore, detention choices influenced by risk-scoring systems might be arbitrary or illegal due to the lack of legal prescriptions for these systems and the arbitrary nature of their inputs (Dash et al., 2022).

A Fair Trial and Artificial Intelligence

- Every person, regardless of citizenship status, has the right to a fair trial when their case is heard within a courtroom. In any situation, whether a criminal or civil proceeding, the right to a fair hearing must be upheld. The defendant is guaranteed their rights in a trial that is handled in a fair, reasonable, and procedurally regular manner by an unbiased judge. A person has the right to a fair trial as guaranteed by current legislation. Everyone has the right to a fair trial before a legally recognised and impartial tribunal within a reasonable amount of time when their civil rights and responsibilities are being decided, including when those matters involve or are challenged by any government or authority.
- In Article 14 of the International Covenant on Civil and Political Rights, the identical paragraph is reproduced (1). Technologies developed by artificial intelligence have an impact on the criminal justice system and the judicial system more generally. Robot judges and AI assistance are the two sides of this game. Artificial intelligence (AI) assistants are programs that help courts with the tedious but necessary task of draughting decisions and information for judicial determination. In contrast, robot judges are programmed to carry out all judicial duties in the same way that a human judge would, effectively replacing human judges and turning the courtroom into an entirely digital environment.

Some have voiced concerns that the development of these programs violates the right to a fair trial. Because algorithms reflect the values of its creators in their design and operation, bias might arise both in the data from which the AI system learns and in the AI system's own programming. When this happens, it's not always easy to tell if the serious mistake was intentional or the product of a glitch in the system. Algorithms that reinforce preexisting prejudices and preconceptions, even in the absence of explicit knowledge about the protected group, pose a threat of discrimination in an AI system, despite the fact that AI systems are not intentionally biassed. In July 2016, the Wisconsin Supreme Court rendered a historic decision in the matter of State v. Loomis, which included risk assessment software. Mr. Loomis denied any participation in the incident and pleaded guilty to two of the five counts against him that were related to a drive-by shooting crime in Wisconsin. After being deemed "at high risk to the community" and having a high-risk record of recidivism, Eric Loomis was handed a six-year jail term by COMPAS. State v. Loomis highlights several troubling issues about risk assessment tools, which might undermine human rights and the rule of law, even if the Wisconsin Supreme Court supported their use at sentencing (Barocas et al., 2023).

The Relationship between AI and Individual Privacy Rights

Many legal systems provide protections for citizens' right to privacy as a means of limiting both public and private intrusions into people's personal lives. Privacy is defined as the following: the right to one's own space, free from prying eyes; the ability to decide who may see one's private information; the preservation of one's autonomy, honour, and dignity; the right to remain anonymous and unobserved; and the right to avoid having one's private affairs pryed into. Protecting one's bodily autonomy, limiting access to oneself, controlling one's identity, and regulations governing the acquisition and management of personal data are all aspects of the right to privacy. An individual's right to privacy is upheld in the International Covenant on Civil and Political Rights:

1. No one has the right to have his or her personal information, home, family, or communications invaded in any way, shape, or form, or to have his or her honour or reputation attacked in any way.
2. The rule of law protects all citizens against unlawful intrusion or assault.

Citizens' right to privacy is now secured and preserved, including their houses, letters, right to telephone calls, and telegraphic communications. This clause adheres to this fundamental human right.

A growing number of people are worried that their right to privacy may be violated as a result of AI development. Security cameras, cell phones, and other contemporary devices pose a risk to people's right to privacy. Companies like Amazon, Apple, Facebook, Google, and Yahoo that rely on technology to operate pose a risk to individuals' right to privacy because of the personal information they gather and utilise. The Cambridge Analytica data scandal, which centred on the psychographic firm's exploitation of Facebook user data to influence huge groups of people, is just one example of how scandals like this have heightened these worries. Though these events have not undermined AI's practical applications, they have shown the flagrant disregard with which many people throughout the world regard their right to privacy (Narayana & Sreedevi, 2023).

The Right to Be Free from Discrimination and Artificial Intelligence

The subject of discrimination is often handled with care because of the many concerns that surround it, the strong emotions it evokes, and the values and norms that surround it in society. The inequitable application of policies, laws, or treatment prevents certain individuals from fully realising their human or other legal rights; this is known as discrimination. Certain laws have been enacted in an effort to prohibit this intolerable treatment of any individual. The International Covenant on Civil and Political Rights includes a provision that prohibits discrimination in all its forms. It states that every state that is a party to the covenant promises to respect and provide the rights stated in the covenant to all its citizens, regardless of their race, colour, sex, language, religion, political or other beliefs, national or social origin, wealth, date of birth, or any other status (Mhlanga, 2021).

Discrimination, however, has been increasingly difficult to address since the rise of AI. Humans are capable of creating intelligent systems, and it is within their power to create a system whose basis is based on prejudice. A panel of specialists draughted the "Draft Ethics Guidelines for Trustworthy A.I." in December 2018. The European Commission acknowledged the need for an anthropocentric approach to artificial intelligence (AI) and issued a warning about the hazards connected with AI in this document, despite its significant advantages. People must always be given the authority to monitor machines, since this is the only strategy that can ensure their dignity and autonomy. It is now plainly apparent that even the Council of Europe perceives the potential for social discrimination caused by algorithms and issues a warning about it.

Discrimination may take many forms, and one of them is the negative impact of AI on the right to a fair trial. This is unique to the claims made in response to the ProPublica investigation. Some technical innovations have their functionality limited to specific regions or users, as decided upon by the inventors themselves. All things considered, this is an example of bias brought about by AI (Pocher et al., 2023).

Machine Learning and the Elimination of Arbitrary Detention

There are certain limitations on people's right to personal liberty, even if everyone has it. Arresting criminals or those suspected of committing crimes is one way that states punish those who break the law. The process of apprehending and detaining an individual, often on suspicion of or observation of their criminal behaviour, is known as an arrest. Following an arrest, a suspect may be subject to further questioning and, if warranted, subsequent legal proceedings. But an arrest must not be arbitrary and undertaken without probable cause. When there is no probable cause to believe that an individual has violated a laws, or when due process of law has not been followed, the arrest or detention of that individual might be considered an arbitrary arrest (Chen et al., 2018). The most basic definition of an arbitrary arrest is one that is carried out with a hidden agenda that is blatantly contrary to the law and its procedure. Because it restricts a person's mobility inside a certain area, this also constitutes a violation of their right to personal liberty. The advent of AI has, alas, exacerbated the problem of arbitrary detention. A false arrest, and by extension, an arbitrary arrest, is certain to occur in the event that an intelligent system mistakenly identifies a person as the perpetrator of a certain crime, whether this be due to the systems' design flaws or the creator's deliberate intent. Global and international organisations have recently brought this growing threat to light. The United Nations is among these international organisations that have commented on this timely matter. New research on the matter was revealed in Geneva, and U.N. High Commissioner for Human Rights Michelle Bachelet made mention to it in her remarks. The analysis expressed concern about the potential consequences of AI's predictive and profiling capabilities, stating that the technology may affect fundamental rights such as "rights to privacy, to a fair trial, to freedom from arbitrary arrest and detention and the right to life." The obvious downsides of AI include its likely contempt for human rights to be free from arbitrary detention (Tyagi et al., 2020).

How AI Could Affect Free Speech

Freedom of expression is one of the inherent human rights. The right of any person or organisation to freely communicate its views, opinions, ideas, and feelings on any subject without interference from the state is known as freedom of speech. It boils down to the freedom to speak one's mind and advocate for one's cause in any way one sees fit. The following rights have been firmly established in the International Covenant on Civil and Political Rights: (1) The freedom of expression must not be violated in any way. (2) The right to freedom of expression extends to all people and includes the ability to freely seek, receive, and communicate ideas and information in any form, including but not limited to spoken word, written word, visual art, and any other media one chooses, regardless of location or other restrictions (Cao et al., 2021).

- Internet content curation has a long history, and AI is a natural extension of that history. With AI, we can personalise and curate material for users on a scale that traditional media just can't match. Some worry that the prevalence of some AI-assisted curation methods would limit people's ability to think critically and independently. Thanks to AI, people all over the world can now express themselves more effectively, and the information they get is delivered at a lightning pace. The development of social media apps has given many people a platform to share their views and ideas. On the other hand, research has shown that this might have negative consequences.
- A great deal of the moral and criminal wrongdoing that has recently come to light in the modern world has its roots in the birth of social media. Examples of such crimes include cyberbullying, cyberfraud, and the rise in the suicide rate as a result of negative peer pressure. It also brings up some valid points

on how algorithmic bias might lead to the formation of echo chambers and the exacerbation of existing social and cultural biases.

The Freedom of Assembly and Association in the Age of Artificial Intelligence

Individuals have the right to form groups and have the freedom to communicate, advocate, seek, and defend their common beliefs and ideals. Human, political, and civic liberties all include the right to freely associate with others. They guarantee that people and organisations may peacefully join forces to achieve their shared objectives, which is crucial to the formation and maintenance of a democracy. A person's freedom of association and assembly is firmly enshrined in the following provisions of the International Covenant on Civil and Political Rights: Everyone has the right to peacefully assemble. Restriction of this right is prohibited unless such limitations are mandated by law and are essential for a democratic society to ensure public safety, public health, morality, or national or public safety, public order, or the protection of other people's rights and freedoms (Alazab et al., 2023).

A person's right to freely gather can be observed and addressed through surveillance. The term "surveillance" refers to the practice of keeping a person under close observation, often by a government agency or military force. The function of surveillance in authoritarian, hybrid, and democratic governments is greatly impacted by artificial intelligence. The majority of artificial intelligence's influence on surveillance in 2019 has been in "smart cities" programs, face recognition integrated with closed-circuit television, and crime analysis for smart police, all of which are presented as good uses of AI in surveillance. Conversely, any intelligent system controller may track users and perhaps limit their mobility based on their tags (Zhang et al., 2022).

What Effects Will AI Have on Economic and Social Rights?

While very crucial, the basic human rights of all people are far from being the only things that make life worth living. There comes a moment in every person's life when they must learn to survive on their own. Humans' social and economic rights have to be addressed by legislation in light of this inevitable reality. A person's economic, social, and cultural rights (or "social rights" for short) include protections in the job, financial stability, the ability to care for one's family, cultural engagement, and the availability of basic necessities like shelter, clothing, food, water, medical treatment, and an adequate education. Rights to a decent quality of life, fair earnings and equitable pay, and enough protection from unemployment, illness, and old age are all part of this category. Many countries' legal systems have explicitly recognised and protected these rights (Mühlhoff, 2021). Constitutions that solely protect political and civil liberties neglect to protect economic and social rights, leaving the task half-done and laying the groundwork for superficial, meaningless "bourgeois" freedom. The significance of socioeconomic rights has therefore been acknowledged throughout the globe. Social and economic rights have their roots in the early 20th century, when the International worker Organisation (ILRO), which was a branch of the League of Nations, passed a number of treaties to raise global worker standards. The social and economic rights of individuals are not infringed upon by the pervasiveness of artificial intelligence. To that end, AI can be useful in keeping tabs on how seriously people take these rights. When the time comes to assert their rights, employees who manage their register or operations online can use the same as proof. Notably, many nations' social security systems are highly efficient because they run on the Internet. As an added bonus, AI streamlines the process of claiming a person's housing right, so individuals may seek for a home without leaving their comfortable homes thanks to this technology. These are only a few of the numerous ways in which AI will affect people's socioeconomic rights. The effect, nevertheless, can be detrimental in certain instances. One example of this is when people unwittingly become victims of cyber fraud (Saltz et al., 2019).

AI's Influence on Legal Standards

In order for a nation to achieve its goals of development and advancement, the rule of law must be upheld. Peace, political stability, economic growth, social progress, and the protection of individual liberties and rights all depend on a society based on the rule of law. In order to build the social compact between the people and the state, limit the misuse of authority, ensure that public services are accessible to everyone, and combat corruption, it is essential.

A.V. Dicey was a major proponent of the rule of law idea. "Introduction to the Study of the Law of the Constitution" laid out Dicey's view of the regulatory framework. The primacy of the Constitution, equality before the law, and respect for basic human rights are the three pillars upon which A.V. Dicey's rule of law rests. No one is immune to the rule of law, according to the idea of legal equality. Anyone, regardless of status or position, is bound to the regular tribunals' jurisdiction and subject to the usual laws of the realm. Put another way, the treatment of the impoverished in cases of illegal behaviour will not differ from that of the wealthy, irrespective of their position, influence, or prestige. With respect to the rule of law, the idea of constitutional supremacy states that the Constitution is the highest law of the nation and that other branches of government, including federal and state legislatures, are obligated to follow it. Every move they make must be grounded in the Constitution, as the document is the foundation of their authority and the basis for their very being (Hoijtink & Planqué-van Hardeveld, 2022). Consequently, they must adhere to the constraints imposed by the Constitution. Respect for the basic human rights of individuals is just as important as guaranteeing the aforementioned values. A person's ability to live depends on these fundamental rights, which must be upheld regardless of whether they are codified in law or not.

The advent of AI is responsible for the widespread digitisation of human society. The use of these AI technologies is already prevalent in the pre-adjudicative stage of law enforcement, where they help with tasks such as selecting individuals to be investigated in tax and regulatory matters. They are also being utilised more and more in the adjudication process, for instance to help with pretrial bail decisions involving the danger of violence to a person. Some predict that code-driven alternatives will eventually replace human judges, while others voice strong opposition to this idea. Most people are against it because they think it would make adjudicative systems less fair, less transparent, and less equitable. The rule of law is frequently intersected with or extremely similar to these AI concerns, even when they are not explicitly targeted at it; this is particularly true in the areas of human rights and democracy (Utami et al., 2022).

Because they involve very complicated technology that is fundamentally beyond the cognitive abilities of people and because the law also prevents transparency to some extent, most of these decision-making systems are "black boxes," which poses a danger to the rule of law. As a result of AI being criticised in this area, it will be nearly hard to examine how the rule of law functions, including being transparent, fair, and explainable. In light of the world's exponential technological development, the question arises as to how the rule of law can be rigorously upheld (Zhang et al., 2022).

AI's Role in Upholding Democratic Institutions' Legitimacy

To begin with, democratic institutions, often called the institutions of democracy, are the primary tools for achieving the fundamental purpose of democracy in any government: making sure that power is exercised by and for the people. The executive, legislative, and judiciary branches make up a well-functioning democratic government. In most democracies, these branches also work together. As institutions, they are burdened with the responsibilities that come with their status: Separate branches of government are responsible for creating laws, carrying them out, and interpreting them. Democracy necessitates not only the presence of these institutions but also the immediate and obligatory recognition of its legitimacy by the people.

If a political institution can convince its constituents that it is normatively necessary for them to have it, then it has achieved legitimacy. There are a number of possible bases for this in a democratic society, including different types of public approval (democratic legitimacy) and alternative bases (generic legitimacy). This is where artificial intelligence really shines. More and more, political institutions must devote themselves to data-driven governance if they want to increase their credibility. Institutions in charge of politics should aim to make decisions based on technologically driven, solid empirical evidence as they incorporate digital data into their procedures. In instance, algorithmic decision-making (ADM) systems are employed for the purpose of identifying critical social issues, predicting possible policy outcomes, enhancing the policy process, and assessing the efficacy of policy. As an example, research has demonstrated that ADM systems can effectively back decisions on how to distribute migrants in a way that is acceptable to society (Baker & Robinson, 2020).

THE USE OF AI IN THE COURT SYSTEM

Being a democratic institution, the court system essentially represents the government's judiciary. The system of courts that interprets, defends, and implements the law in legal situations is called the judiciary. It goes by several names, including the judicial system, judicature, the judicial branch, judicative branch, and court or judiciary system. Laws' interpretation, practical applicability, and constitutionality are all matters for the judicial branch to decide.

The judicial branch is responsible for representing the state in legal matters by interpreting, defending, and applying the law. The judicial system is also seen as a means of conflict settlement. Judicial functions are limited to interpreting, defending, and applying the law to the circumstances of each case in accordance with the theory of separation of powers; the duty for making statutes or enforcing laws belongs with the legislative and the executive branch, respectively. Judicial review, which occurs when a matter is taken to a court of law, gives the judiciary the authority to amend laws in many nations. It is also within the purview of the court to overturn legislation, particularly where such laws go against to a nation's fundamental standard (the Constitution in some instances). This body of law comprises fundamental statutes, constitutional provisions, treaties, and international law. The judiciary is an essential branch of government for any nation. It serves the state's progress and the people's needs; after all, the average person looks to the court as his or her final resort (Aziz & Andriansyah, 2023).

The legal system of a country is just as important as any other aspect of AI's reach. By making the application of the law more predictable and the consistency of case law more consistent, the processing of judicial data by so-called artificial intelligence systems or methodologies developed from data sciences is anticipated to increase the transparency of the functioning of justice. An example of an AI-developed technology is a robot-judge, which can carry out all of the duties traditionally associated with a human judge. Also, an AI system called SUVAS can help in translating decisions into regional languages. A further effect of AI is that it streamlines the judicial procedure, which in turn decreases the number of cases filed.

Insights into AI's Potential Effects on Democracy

In modern times, democracies have become the norm for effective national leadership. In essence, this guarantees that the well-being and will of the people are the bedrock upon which every government rests. When all citizens, either directly or via their representatives in elected office, have equal say in major policy decisions, we say that we live in a democracy. Simply put, it denotes popular rule. Peaceful transitions of power are hallmarks of democracies, and the legitimacy of government is based on popular vote. "Democracy" means "government by the people, for the people" in its simplest form.

Because of the interconnectedness of all things, AI has both direct and indirect effects on democracies. The rule of law is an essential component of a democratic society. Cases involving this area of adjudication frequently make use of AI, such as when deciding whether or not to grant pretrial bail based on an individual's likelihood of violence. Transparency is a fundamental principle of AI. This means that everyone has the right to know how and why an algorithm is considering various aspects when making a choice that can impact them. Despite this, the democratic principle may still be used to lessen its impact by passing legislation that forbids algorithmic bias in society (Bao et al., 2022).

The Role of Artificial Intelligence in Election Procedures

The electoral process of a government is the mechanism of voting that is used to install a new government or, in some cases, to remove an existing one. A voting system, often called an electoral system, is a collection of regulations that govern the process and outcome of elections and referendums. Businesses, nonprofits, and informal groups may have elections that aren't related to politics, although governments do organise electoral systems that are. Every part of the voting process is regulated by these rules: when elections take place, who is eligible to vote, who can run for office, how ballots are marked and cast, how they are counted, how votes are turned into an outcome, campaign spending limits, and everything else that can impact the outcome. Election commissions normally oversee political electoral systems, which are specified by constitutions and electoral laws and might employ various election forms for various posts. Conventional voting methods in a country might be cumbersome and unreliable at times. In this area, AI has the potential to bring about a good and substantial shift, making the process more responsive to the will of the people during times of government transition (McKendrick, 2019).

It is for the express aim of conducting national elections that software and intelligent systems have been developed. By streamlining the process of organising and participating in the electoral processes and disseminating relevant information to the public, these platforms aim to make life easier for everyone involved. Nationwide voting processes have been enhanced by the incorporation of IT and software. As an illustration, The New Zealand-based AI SAM is assisting Alice and Michihito. The creation of SAM, an artificially intelligent woman, has sparked claims that she will be the first virtual politician to compete in the 2020 global elections. Among other things, SAM is using Facebook Messenger to communicate with people today, offering her views on climate change, healthcare, and education. To aid with the general elections, an app for the Nomination Information System (Silon) has been developed. This app is designed to give registered voters the information that voting candidates need. For all types of party nominations necessary for registration as an election participant, political parties can use the Political Party Information System (Sipol) app. In order to aid the organisers in recapitulating the election results, the General Elections Commission has also utilised Artificial Intelligence (AI) through the Counting Information System (Situng) program during the computation stage of the final election results. After they are implemented, AI systems clearly have an effect on the voting process.

AI and Military Operations

Artificial intelligence (AI) security choices, bioinformatics, practice aids for training troops, data aggregation from nationwide databases, and other applications may all benefit from intelligent computers. Scientists have begun using AI in the defence industry to compensate for human shortcomings, thanks to the proficiency that technology brings. More and more, they're relying on AI-powered combat systems, recovery and maintenance vehicles, unmanned aerial vehicles, and ground vehicles. The invention of several weapons, including drones, helipads with shooting capabilities, explosives, and many more, may be attributed in part to the effect of artificial intelligence on combat (Rai & Sahu, 2020).

DIFFICULTIES IN ADDRESSING THE EFFECTS OF AI ON FREEDOM, DEMOCRACY, AND THE JUSTICE SYSTEM

While there is no denying that AI has had far-reaching good effects on our modern society, it has also presented some serious problems, especially with regard to human rights and democracy. Every legitimate political system rests on three pillars: human rights, democracy, and the law. The foundation of every government must be the welfare and decision of the people, and democracy guarantees this. Peace, political stability, economic growth, social progress, and the protection of individual liberties and rights all depend on a society based on the rule of law. In order to build the social compact between the people and the state, limit the misuse of authority, ensure that public services are accessible to everyone, and combat corruption, it is essential. A society's fundamental entitlements are its members' human rights. Because people are human, these things are relevant to them. To live a civilised life in any culture, they are an absolute need. Artificial intelligence (AI) will have both good and bad effects on long-standing norms and values. The detrimental effects that have presented difficulties will be the primary subject of this discussion.

These individuals ought to spearhead democracy, a kind of governance that exists for the benefit of its citizens. It is necessary to provide individuals with knowledge so that they may make informed judgements when they are making decisions on their own (Sharma et al., 2023). Even if AI streamlines and accelerates data transfer, it also comes with its fair share of difficulties. There is a danger of prejudice and uneven representation of viewpoints and perspectives if AI decides what gets presented and digested, what gets buried in the sea of internet information and what gets magnified virally. Additionally, AI has the potential to undermine honest voting. Without public accountability in the agora, political campaigns or foreign actors can employ personalised adverts to transmit various messages to separate voter groups. It should be mentioned, nevertheless, that the exact impact of micro-targeted advertising is yet unclear. The use of artificial intelligence (AI) in the creation and dissemination of deep fakes and disinformation is not limited to text, images, audio, or video. Due to their difficulty in detection, they pose a threat to the public's trust in the media and democratic discourse by making it easier for manipulators and misinformers to gain power (Varma et al., 2022).

FUTURE DIRECTION

It is important to go forward with making and using AI systems that follow international human rights laws and protect privacy, freedom of speech, non-discrimination, due process, and effective remedies. To keep an eye on AI misuse and violations of human rights, it is important to set up synchronized reporting and monitoring systems throughout the world. This will encourage openness and cooperation across borders. It is important to make algorithms more transparent, explainable, and accountable by requiring AI developers to provide clear information about how decisions are made, especially in high-risk domains. In sensitive areas like law enforcement and governance, it is also very important to have strict protections in place, such as human monitoring, independent reviews, and clear ways to get help.

A major step forward for the future is to improve and strengthen international legal frameworks, especially by developing treaties about AI and human rights that can be enforced. It is important to put research and innovation in AI applications that help promote and protect human rights first. This includes technology that help find violations and make it easier for people to get justice. Moreover, robust legal and regulatory frameworks are necessary to address AI-induced challenges, including totalitarian surveillance, pervasive disinformation, and threats to democratic institutions. It is just as important to train, build capacity, and raise awareness among policymakers, human rights activists, and AI practitioners on the human rights effects of AI. These directions all stress the need for a unified set of laws, morals, and rules to make the most of AI's potential to protect human rights and address its global problems.

CONCLUSION

By adhering to the rule of law, public institutions are expected to behave more responsibly towards people and society at large, as demonstrated by concepts like equality, proportionality, and justification. While AI has the potential to make institutions more efficient, it also has the potential to undermine faith in democratic institutions, the rule of law, and the legitimacy of their procedures. Just as courts used to be the exclusive arbiters of what constitutes unlawful hate speech, commercial AI algorithms now predominate in deciding whether or not social media sites remove content. In reality, these AI systems vie with the judicial system and the law for power and Generally speaking, AI has the potential to aid in the creation of legal systems that do not adhere to or even recognise the rule of law. Instead of consumer rights and procedural safeguards afforded by public courts, automated online dispute settlements offered by private corporations are controlled by their terms of service.

The effects of AI on anti-discrimination laws and the guarantee of equal treatment stand out among the many ways AI is influencing human rights. There have been several reports of AI becoming biassed and thereby violating people’s right to be free from discrimination. Additionally, these data-driven technologies discredit the social control mechanisms that regulate human conduct by proving the presence of biases. For instance, the AI that helped recruit new Amazon workers tended to prefer male candidates over female ones as it was programmed to mimic the behaviour of the company’s most successful male employees. Instead than just excluding female candidates, the AI system analysed successful workers’ phrase and phrasing patterns and rejected resumes that did not match. From a different perspective, AI systems are also finding more and more applications in the areas of workforce monitoring and tracking, autonomous task distribution, and recruiting and firing based on predictive analytics of future performance and potential. Right to organise, right to a safe and healthy workplace, dignity on the job, and right to a fair wage are all rights that these AI applications potentially threaten. Despite the fact that technology has brought about unparalleled advancements and development in the majority of situations, the influence of artificial intelligence on the rule of law, human rights, and democracy is not without its concerns. The majority of the time, these difficulties has the potential to endanger the level of living of the common individual.

REFERENCES

Ahmad, N., Ali, A. W., & bin Yussof, M. H. B. (2025). The Challenges of Human Rights in the Era of Artificial Intelligence. *UUM Journal of Legal Studies, 16*(1), 150-169.

Al-Billeh, T., Hmaidan, R., Al-Hammouri, A., & Makhmari, M. A. (2024). The risks of using artificial intelligence on privacy and human rights: Unifying global standards. *Jurnal Media Hukum, 31*(2), 333–350.

Alazab, M., Soman, K. P., Srinivasan, S., Venkatraman, S., & Pham, V. Q. (2023). Deep learning for cyber security applications: A comprehensive survey. *Authorea Preprints.*

Aziz, L. A. R., & Andriansyah, Y. (2023). The Role Artificial Intelligence in Modern Banking: An Exploration of AI-Driven Approaches for Enhanced Fraud Prevention, Risk Management, and Regulatory Compliance. *Reviews of Contemporary Business Analytics, 6*(1), 110–132.

Baker, D. J., & Robinson, P. H. (Eds.). (2020). *Artificial Intelligence and the Law: Cybercrime and Criminal Liability*. Routledge.

Bao, Y., Hilary, G., & Ke, B. (2022). Artificial intelligence and fraud detection. *Innovative Technology at the Interface of Finance and Operations, I*, 223–247.

Barocas, S., Hardt, M., & Narayanan, A. (2023). *Fairness and machine learning: Limitations and opportunities*. MIT Press.

Cao, L., Yang, Q., & Yu, P. S. (2021). Data science and AI in FinTech: An overview. *International Journal of Data Science and Analytics, 12*, 81–99.

Chen, Z., Van Khoa, L. D., Teoh, E. N., Nazir, A., Karuppiah, E. K., & Lam, K. S. (2018). Machine learning techniques for anti-money laundering (AML) solutions in suspicious transaction detection: A review. *Knowledge and Information Systems, 57*, 245–285.

Dash, B., Sharma, P., & Ali, A. (2022). Federated learning for privacy-preserving: A review of PII data analysis in Fintech. [IJSEA]. *International Journal of Software Engineering and Its Applications, 13*(4).

Fjeld, J., Achten, N., Hilligoss, H., Nagy, A., & Srikumar, M. (2020). Principled artificial intelligence: Mapping consensus in ethical and rights-based approaches to principles for AI. *Berkman Klein Center Research Publication*, (2020-1).

Gellers, J. C., & Gunkel, D. J. (2023). Artificial intelligence and international human rights law: Implications for humans and technology in the 21st century and beyond. In *Handbook on the politics and governance of big data and artificial intelligence* (pp. 430–455). Edward Elgar Publishing.

Hoijtink, M., & Planqué-van Hardeveld, A. (2022). Machine learning and the platformization of the military: A study of google's machine learning platform TensorFlow. *International Political Sociology*, *16*(2), olab036.

McKendrick, K. (2019). Artificial intelligence prediction and counterterrorism. *London: The Royal Institute of International Affairs-Chatham House, 9*.

Mhlanga, D. (2021). Financial inclusion in emerging economies: The application of machine learning and artificial intelligence in credit risk assessment. *International journal of financial studies, 9*(3), 39.

Mpinga, E. K., Bukonda, N. K., Qailouli, S., & Chastonay, P. (2022). Artificial Intelligence and Human Rights: Are There Signs of an Emerging Discipline? A Systematic Review. *Journal of Multidisciplinary Healthcare*, •••, 235–246.

Mühlhoff, R. (2021). Predictive privacy: Towards an applied ethics of data analytics. *Ethics and Information Technology*, *23*(4), 675–690.

Narayana, Y. V., & Sreedevi, M. (2023, October). DDCATF: Deep Learning Approach for Detection of Cybercrime Activities Based on Temporal Features. In *2023 International Conference on Self Sustainable Artificial Intelligence Systems (ICSSAS)* (pp. 462-469). IEEE.

Pocher, N., Zichichi, M., Merizzi, F., Shafiq, M. Z., & Ferretti, S. (2023). Detecting anomalous cryptocurrency transactions: An AML/CFT application of machine learning-based forensics. *Electronic Markets*, *33*(1), 37.

Rai, R., & Sahu, C. K. (2020). Driven by data or derived through physics? a review of hybrid physics guided machine learning techniques with cyber-physical system (cps) focus. *IEEE Access : Practical Innovations, Open Solutions*, *8*, 71050–71073.

Saltz, J., Skirpan, M., Fiesler, C., Gorelick, M., Yeh, T., Heckman, R., & Beard, N. (2019). Integrating ethics within machine learning courses. [TOCE]. *ACM Transactions on Computing Education*, *19*(4), 1–26.

Sharma, A., Mansotra, V., & Singh, K. (2023). Detection of Mirai Botnet Attacks on IoT devices Using Deep Learning. *Journal of Scientific Research and Technology*, 174-187.

Thapaliya, S., & Sharma, P. K. (2023). Optimized deep neuro fuzzy network for cyber forensic investigation in big data-based IoT infrastructures. [IJISP]. *International Journal of Information Security and Privacy*, *17*(1), 1–22.

Tyagi, A. K., Aswathy, S. U., & Abraham, A. (2020). Integrating blockchain technology and artificial intelligence: Synergies perspectives challenges and research directions. *Journal of Information Assurance and Security*, *15*(5), 1554.

Utami, S. H., Purnama, A. A., Hidayanto, A. N., Utami, S. H., Purnama, A. A., & Hidayanto, A. N. (2022). Fintech Lending in Indonesia: A Sentiment Analysis, Topic Modelling, and Social Network Analysis using Twitter Data. *International Journal of Applied Engineering & Technology*, *4*(1), 50–56.

Varma, P., Nijjer, S., Sood, K., Grima, S., & Rupeika-Apoga, R. (2022). Thematic Analysis of Financial Technology (Fintech) Influence on the Banking Industry. *Risks*, *10*(10), 186.

Zhang, X., Liu, L., Lan, M., Song, G., Xiao, L., & Chen, J. (2022). Interpretable machine learning models for crime prediction. *Computers, Environment and Urban Systems*, *94*, 101789.

Zhang, Z., Al Hamadi, H., Damiani, E., Yeun, C. Y., & Taher, F. (2022). Explainable artificial intelligence applications in cyber security: State-of-the-art in research. *IEEE Access : Practical Innovations, Open Solutions*.

Chapter 10

Integrating Digital Technologies for Climate Action:

Driving Innovation to Achieve SDG 13

Anitha Kumari
https://orcid.org/0000-0002-8343-8926
GITAM University, India

ABSTRACT

Digital technologies are pivotal enablers of Sustainable Development Goal 13 (SDG 13). Technologies such as artificial intelligence (AI), the Internet of Things (IoT), blockchain, geospatial analytics, big data, and cloud platforms are reshaping how societies monitor climate risks, design mitigation strategies, and strengthen adaptive capacity. This chapter proposes a conceptual framework informed by the Technology–Organization–Environment (TOE) model and the Sustainable Development Framework (SDF) to explain how technological capability, organizational readiness, and environmental pressures interact to drive digital climate resilience. Global case studies demonstrate that despite challenges such as limited infrastructure, high costs, data governance concerns, and fragmented policy, coordinated strategies can deliver inclusive and scalable solutions. Practical implications include aligning policies with digital climate strategies, cross-sector innovation, strengthening standards and evaluation, and building capacity for climate-smart technologies.

DOI: 10.4018/979-8-3373-3685-5.ch010

INTRODUCTION

Climate change is arguably the most significant environmental, social, and economic challenge facing the global community in the twenty-first century. Over recent decades, human activities chiefly the burning of fossil fuels, deforestation, and intensive agriculture have driven unprecedented increases in greenhouse gas (GHG) concentrations in the atmosphere. As a result, global average temperatures have risen by approximately 1.1°C above pre-industrial levels, contributing to an increase in the frequency and intensity of extreme weather events such as floods, droughts, heatwaves, and storms (IPCC, 2022). The effects of climate change extend beyond ecological disturbances; they threaten livelihoods, exacerbate health risks, jeopardize food and water security, and disrupt economic systems. Vulnerable populations including low-income communities, Indigenous peoples, and residents of least developed countries bear the highest burden of these impacts, despite contributing the least to global emissions (UNDP, 2022).

Addressing these climate challenges requires a multipronged, urgent, and scalable response. Recognizing this imperative, the United Nations established Sustainable Development Goal 13 (SDG 13), which calls for urgent action to combat climate change and its impacts through mitigation efforts to reduce emissions, adaptation to build resilience, and integration of climate policies at all governance levels (United Nations, 2025). The Paris Agreement under the UNFCCC further reinforces the goal of limiting global warming to well below 2°C, preferably 1.5°C, compared to pre-industrial levels, demanding transformative shifts in energy systems, land use, and socio-economic development. While traditional climate strategies such as expanding renewable energy infrastructure, enhancing ecosystem conservation, promoting energy efficiency, and building resilient urban infrastructure remain fundamental, alone they are insufficient to match the scale and pace of the crisis. The complexity and urgency of climate change demand innovative approaches that leverage emerging technologies to accelerate progress, improve precision in interventions, and democratize access to climate information and resources.

In this context, digital technologies are increasingly recognized as potential game-changers for climate governance and sustainability transformations. The ongoing Fourth Industrial Revolution is characterized by the fusion of technologies that blur the lines between physical, digital, and biological spheres. Artificial intelligence (AI), the Internet of Things (IoT), blockchain, big data analytics, Geographic Information Systems (GIS), and cloud computing create new possibilities for real-time environmental monitoring, predictive risk assessment, transparent climate finance, and participatory governance (Sun et al., 2022; Johansson et al., 2022). These innovations can enhance the precision and efficiency of climate mitigation and adaptation measures, while enabling inclusive engagement of stakeholders across sectors and geographies. For example, AI-powered climate models improve the prediction of extreme weather events, enabling early warning systems that save lives and reduce economic losses. IoT sensors allow precision agriculture practices that optimize water and fertilizer use, reducing emissions and increasing resilience. Blockchain technologies foster trust and transparency in carbon markets and sustainable supply chains, addressing challenges of fraud and inefficiency. Digital platforms facilitate community participation in climate monitoring and education, empowering citizens and local governments to contribute to sustainable development solutions.

However, despite this transformative potential, the adoption and scaling of digital solutions in climate policy and action remain uneven and constrained by significant structural and governance barriers. Inequities in digital infrastructure, limited connectivity, insufficient digital literacy, and high technology deployment costs disproportionately hinder low-income and rural communities, particularly in the Global South (ITU, 2023; OECD, 2024; UNCTAD, 2024). Concerns related to data privacy, cybersecurity risks, and algorithmic biases raise ethical and governance challenges that must be addressed to build public trust and legitimacy. Fragmented institutional frameworks and lack of policy coordination further slow the mainstreaming of digital innovation into national and international climate strategies (Schot et al., 2020).

Moreover, existing research often treats technological innovation and sustainability governance as separate domains, resulting in a gap in holistic understanding of how digital transformation can be systematically integrated into climate action. There is a pressing need to explore how technological capability aligns with organizational readiness, institutional environments, and broader governance and equity considerations to ensure that digital tools deliver effective, just, and sustainable outcomes. This chapter aims to fill this gap by developing an integrative conceptual framework that combines the Technology–Organization–Environment (TOE) model a well-established lens for analyzing innovation adoption with the Sustainable Development Framework (SDF), which emphasizes governance, inclusivity, and long-term sustainability in achieving the SDGs. By synthesizing theory and practice through global case studies, this work seeks to provide a comprehensive understanding of digital climate innovation pathways and the enabling conditions necessary to scale effective solutions. Ultimately, the chapter argues that digital transformation within climate action is not merely a technological shift but a systemic transition requiring alignment of innovation, governance, and equity to drive resilient and sustainable futures.

LITERATURE REVIEW

The role of digital technologies in advancing climate action under Sustainable Development Goal 13 (SDG 13) has received growing academic and policy attention in recent years. Scholars broadly acknowledge the transformative potential of digital innovation to strengthen climate mitigation, adaptation, risk monitoring, and finance mechanisms. Yet, the literature also reveals significant challenges related to governance, equity, scalability, and unintended consequences that must be addressed to unlock this potential in fair and sustainable ways (Hilty & Aebischer, 2015; Wang et al., 2020).

Internet of Things (IoT) for Environmental Monitoring and Resource Efficiency

A substantial body of research demonstrates the capacity of IoT-enabled sensors and connected devices to collect and transmit real-time data on environmental parameters such as air quality, soil moisture, water use, and energy consumption. This data enables precise interventions in critical sectors like agriculture, energy, and urban infrastructure. Precision irrigation using soil moisture sensors allows farmers to optimize water use, reducing over-irrigation and conserving scarce water resources while maintaining or enhancing crop yields (Johansson et al., 2022). Similarly, smart grid technologies leveraging IoT optimize electricity flows, reduce transmission losses, and integrate distributed renewable energy sources, progressing toward low-carbon and resilient energy systems. However, the effectiveness of IoT deployments depends on reliable connectivity, interoperability standards, and localized training and incentives (Sun et al., 2022).

Artificial Intelligence (AI) and Machine Learning (ML)

AI and ML technologies have attracted extensive scholarly focus for their capabilities to handle vast, complex climate datasets and generate predictive models. Improved climate forecasting models powered by AI enhance early warning systems for floods, hurricanes, and wildfires, providing communities and policymakers with critical time to implement protective measures (Taylor et al., 2021). Additionally, AI optimizes energy demand forecasting and management, facilitating deeper integration of variable renewables like solar and wind power (Rolnick et al., 2022). Despite optimistic prospects, studies caution about AI's embedded biases, algorithmic opacity, and the high-energy consumption of training large models, which can undermine equity and environmental sustainability (Vinuesa et al., 2020; de Vries, 2021).

Blockchain for Climate Finance and Transparency

Blockchain's decentralized, immutable ledger offers compelling solutions for enhancing transparency and trust in climate finance, especially carbon credit accounting and sustainable supply chains. Research highlights blockchain's ability to prevent double counting of carbon emissions, verify verifiable claims of responsible sourcing, and streamline carbon market transactions (Kshetri, 2021). However, concerns remain regarding the environmental footprint of some blockchain protocols, notably energy-intensive proof-of-work consensus mechanisms, as well as challenges in regulatory harmonization and integration with traditional climate finance institutions (de Vries, 2021; Mustapa et al., 2023).

Big Data Analytics and Geospatial Information Systems (GIS)

Big data and GIS technologies play foundational roles in climate risk assessment and environmental governance by integrating satellite imagery, sensor networks, and socio-economic datasets to map deforestation, land-use change, sea-level rise, and urban expansion (Wang et al., 2020). Planners and policymakers increasingly use these high-resolution spatial analyses to inform urban resilience and conservation strategies, identifying vulnerabilities and prioritizing interventions (EEA, 2023). Literature emphasizes the importance of data interoperability, privacy protections, and participatory mapping approaches that include local knowledge alongside scientific data.

Cloud Computing and Digital Platforms for Climate Solution

Cloud infrastructure underpins the scalability and accessibility of digital climate services. By offering virtualized computing power and storage, cloud platforms lower the barriers for small organizations and researchers especially in low-resource settings to access large datasets and analytical tools (Sun et al., 2022). Moreover, digital platforms facilitate participatory climate governance through mobile applications, citizen science, and real-time alert systems, fostering social inclusion and local engagement (UNDP, 2022). Yet, the concentration of cloud service providers and the energy demand of data centers raise questions about equitable access and the environmental sustainability of digital transitions (OECD, 2024).

Integrated Governance Challenges and Ethical Considerations

Despite these advances, several studies identify significant governance challenges. The ongoing digital divide limits equitable access to infrastructure, devices, and digital literacy, particularly in rural and marginalized communities, thereby risking exclusion from the benefits of digital climate innovation (ITU, 2023; UNCTAD, 2024). Data privacy concerns, cybersecurity risks, and algorithmic bias present ethical dilemmas with real-world consequences, underscoring the need for transparent, accountable frameworks to govern digital climate tools (Rolnick et al., 2022; Vinuesa et al., 2020). Institutional fragmentation and policy silos often result in poor coordination between climate and digital sectors, hampering holistic digital transformation (Schot et al., 2020).

Cross-Cutting Synergies Across the Sustainable Development Goals

Emerging literature highlights that digital climate technologies impact a spectrum of SDGs, creating synergies beyond SDG 13. AI-enabled health surveillance systems contribute to SDG 3 by tracking health-related climate impacts. IoT smart city initiatives align with SDG 11 by promoting sustainable urban development. Blockchain-based supply chains support SDG 12 by enabling responsible consumption and production (WEF, 2024; AVPN, 2024). This systemic perspective reinforces the need to integrate digital climate action within broader sustainability governance frameworks.

In addition to the technology- and governance-focused studies, sustainability theories such as ecological modernization, socio-technical transitions, and resilience theory offer valuable insights into how systemic transformations unfold. These perspectives emphasize that digital innovation is not only about technical efficiency but also about broader processes of institutional adaptation, societal change, and long-term environmental stewardship. Incorporating these theoretical viewpoints helps to position digital technologies within wider debates about sustainability transitions, thereby strengthening the conceptual foundation for understanding their role in achieving SDG 13. Beyond technological synergies across the SDGs, it is equally important to consider the role of cultural and community-based knowledge in shaping climate action.

Indigenous Knowledge and Digital Technologies

Indigenous Knowledge Systems (IKS) have long played a critical role in climate adaptation, particularly in regions where local communities rely on traditional ecological practices to cope with variability in weather, biodiversity loss, and resource scarcity. These knowledge systems often emphasize ecosystem stewardship, collective resilience, and intergenerational learning principles that align closely with sustainability goals (Nakashima et al., 2012). However, IKS has historically been undervalued or excluded from mainstream climate policy, creating a gap between local practices and global governance frameworks.

Digital technologies present new opportunities to bridge this gap by documenting, preserving, and scaling Indigenous knowledge while ensuring community ownership and cultural sensitivity. For example, participatory GIS mapping has been used in the Pacific Islands to integrate Indigenous observations of sea-level rise with satellite imagery, enabling co-produced adaptation strategies that respect local context (McNamara & Prasad, 2014). Similarly, mobile applications are being deployed to record Indigenous weather predictions and land-use practices, ensuring that this knowledge informs both community-level adaptation and national climate plans (Pearce et al., 2015).

At the same time, the integration of digital technologies with IKS must be handled carefully to avoid risks of data appropriation and "knowledge colonialism." Scholars emphasize that digital tools should be co-designed with Indigenous communities, using principles of free, prior, and informed consent (FPIC) and ensuring that communities retain control over how their knowledge is shared and applied (United Nations, 2021). Embedding Indigenous knowledge in digital climate action not only enriches scientific models with localized, context-specific insights but also advances the principle of equity central to SDG 13. It reflects a more holistic approach where advanced technologies and ancestral wisdom co-exist to support sustainable, resilient futures. Incorporating Indigenous knowledge through digital platforms strengthens both the scientific and social legitimacy of climate action, while reinforcing the chapter's emphasis on inclusivity and equity.

Gap in Integrated Theoretical and Practical Approaches

While the literature presents a growing catalogue of technological potentials and implementation challenges, there remains a critical gap in models that jointly address technological adoption dynamics and the governance context shaping sustainable impact. Few studies synthesize adoption theories such as TOE with sustainability-focused frameworks to provide holistic insights into when and how digital innovations can systematically accelerate SDG 13 outcomes. This chapter aims to advance this integrative understanding by linking technology, organizational readiness, and enabling environments through the combined TOE and Sustainable Development Framework lenses.

CONCEPTUAL FRAMEWORK

The rapid advancement and application of digital technologies in climate action have revealed significant innovation potential, yet there remains a fragmented understanding of how these technologies translate into broader climate governance outcomes. To bridge this gap, this chapter develops a comprehensive conceptual framework that connects digital innovation specifically to Sustainable Development Goal 13 (SDG 13), utilizing the dual theoretical perspectives of the Technology–Organization–Environment (TOE) model and the Sustainable Development Framework (SDF).

Technology–Organization–Environment (TOE) Model

The TOE framework serves as a foundational model for understanding technology adoption by organizations. It argues that adoption outcomes derive from the dynamic interplay of three interdependent domains:

- **Technological context:** This includes the availability, characteristics, and complexity of technologies themselves. It focuses on the technical feasibility, compatibility with existing systems, relative advantage, and the perceived benefits and challenges of adoption. In the climate context, this might consider the maturity of AI algorithms for risk forecasting or the accessibility of blockchain platforms for transparent carbon markets (Wang et al., 2020).
- **Organizational context:** Refers to the internal capacity, readiness, resources, skills, and structural characteristics of organizations adopting new technologies. This domain reflects how prepared institutions such as government agencies, research institutions, or private firms are to procure, implement, and manage digital climate solutions (Sun et al., 2022).
- **Environmental context:** Comprises the external pressures and influences impacting adoption, such as regulatory frameworks, competitive pressures, stakeholder expectations, and broader sociopolitical factors. For climate action, this includes international climate agreements, national policies, civil society demands, and market pressures (Wang et al., 2020).

Applying TOE to digital climate interventions highlights that successful technological deployment requires not only availability and technical suitability but also strong organizational capacity and enabling policy environments. Merely possessing advanced AI or blockchain capabilities is insufficient without training, governance, strategic alignment, and regulatory coordination.

Sustainable Development Framework (SDF)

Complementing TOE, the Sustainable Development Framework (SDF) emphasizes that the integration of digital technologies within climate action must also address governance, equity, and sustainability imperatives, reflecting the broader values underpinning the SDGs. The SDF offers critical lenses to ensure that digital transformations contribute positively and inclusively rather than exacerbate existing inequalities or environmental harms.

Key principles of SDF in this context include:

- **Governance:** Embedding digital innovation within participatory, transparent, and accountable governance structures to build trust and legitimacy. For example, equity in climate finance platforms or fairness in AI decision-making systems (de Vries, 2021).
- **Inclusivity:** Ensuring equitable access to digital tools across regions, socio-economic groups, and marginalized communities, thereby bridging digital and climate divides (UNDP, 2022).
- **Long-Term Sustainability:** Anticipating and mitigating potential negative externalities, such as the carbon footprint of data centers or blockchain mining, while promoting energy-efficient and green digital infrastructures.

By emphasizing these dimensions, the SDF broadens TOE's primarily organizational and technological focus to include social justice, environmental integrity, and future-oriented stewardship, which are essential for genuinely sustainable digital climate action.

Integration and Application

The integrated TOE-SDF framework thus conceptualizes digital technologies as enablers across several key climate action pathways:

- **Risk Forecasting:** AI-driven models improve the accuracy and granularity of climate risk predictions, supporting disaster preparedness and resilience.
- **Emissions Monitoring:** IoT sensors and big data enable real-time measurement and verification, essential for transparent carbon accounting.
- **Disaster Management:** Predictive analytics and digital platforms facilitate early warning systems and coordinated response.
- **Public Engagement:** Cloud-based platforms and mobile technologies democratize access to climate information, fostering citizen participation and climate-conscious communities.

These technological domains are linked to tangible SDG 13 outcomes such as enhanced preparedness, lowered greenhouse gas emissions, data-driven policymaking, transparent climate governance, and increased societal resilience.

The framework underscores that digital transformation in climate action is a systemic process intertwined with institutional capacities, policy environments, and social equity. For instance, deploying IoT in agriculture requires not only sensor availability but also farmer training and supportive digital infrastructure policies. Similarly, blockchain carbon markets depend on international standards, regulatory oversight, and mechanisms ensuring participation by vulnerable stakeholders.

By synthesizing these perspectives, the TOE-SDF framework serves several functions:

- It systematizes understanding of how specific digital tools operate through organizational and environmental mechanisms to deliver climate outcomes.
- It highlights the enabling conditions such as technological readiness, organizational preparedness, regulatory frameworks, and inclusive governance that determine success or failure.
- It offers a structured analytical lens to evaluate, design, and scale technology-enabled climate interventions in equitable and sustainable ways.

This integrated approach provides both scholars and practitioners a robust theoretical foundation and practical roadmap for advancing digital innovation as a catalyst in the global climate response.

Figure 1. Digital Technologies in Climate Action Framework

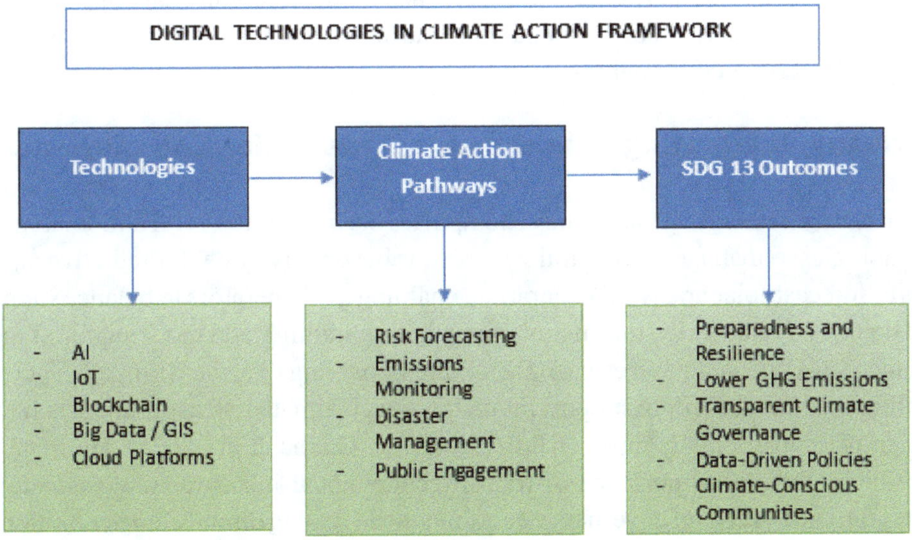

CASE STUDIES AND GLOBAL BEST PRACTICES

The practical relevance of the conceptual framework is best illustrated by diverse global initiatives where digital technologies are transforming climate action across regions and sectors. These examples demonstrate not only the technological innovations but also the critical institutional and infrastructural enablers and barriers that shape success. Together, they underscore how digital transformation is advancing Sustainable Development Goal 13 (SDG 13) through multiple pathways, including mitigation, adaptation, resilience building, and governance.

India: Digital Innovation for Climate-Smart Agriculture

In India, digital technologies are increasingly deployed to support climate-smart agriculture, a sector highly vulnerable to environmental variability and resource constraints. Programs such as Digital Green and initiatives by the Central Research Institute for Dryland Agriculture leverage IoT soil sensors, geospatial mapping, and AI-driven advisory systems to equip smallholder farmers with real-time, actionable data on irrigation needs, weather patterns, and pest risks (World Bank, 2020; Digital Green, n.d.). These tools enable efficient water use, reduce emissions associated with agriculture, and enhance productivity under climate stress. Importantly, local capacity-building and participatory approaches help overcome challenges related to digital access and literacy, illustrating the necessity of tailored solutions for marginalized rural communities.

Germany: Integrating AI and Smart Grids under Energiewende

Germany's Energiewende policy exemplifies the integration of AI and smart grid technologies to manage a decentralized, renewable energy system. Predictive algorithms forecast solar and wind generation, enabling grid operators to balance supply and demand dynamically, thus maintaining system stability and reducing fossil fuel reliance (BMWK, n.d.; Sun et al., 2022). Complementing this, the KlimAdapt portal applies big data and GIS to support municipal-level climate risk assessment and the design of adaptation strategies (KlimAdapt, n.d.; Garcia et al., 2024). Germany's case highlights the importance of robust technological infrastructure, regulatory foresight, and multilevel governance coordination in scaling digital climate solutions.

Kenya: Mobile Technologies and Blockchain for Resilience and Finance

Kenya provides an innovative example of leveraging mobile and blockchain technologies to enhance both resilience and climate finance in resource-constrained settings. The M-Farm platform connects smallholder farmers to weather forecasts, market price information, and practical advisory services, facilitating adaptive agricultural practices and improved market access (Baumüller, 2018; M-Farm, n.d.). Meanwhile, the Africa Risk Capacity employs blockchain combined with satellite remote sensing to administer parametric insurance products, which automatically trigger payouts to vulnerable communities facing droughts or floods World Bank, 2019). These interventions demonstrate how digital platforms can fill gaps where traditional extension services and insurance markets fall short, reinforcing the necessity of inclusive design and institutional backing.

Brazil: Combating Deforestation through Satellite Monitoring and Blockchain

Brazil's efforts to curb deforestation in the Amazon basin showcase the power of combining remote sensing with distributed ledger technologies. The DETER system, managed by the Brazilian National Institute for Space Research (INPE), provides near real-time alerts on deforestation activities, aiding rapid enforcement action (INPE, n.d.; Wang et al., 2020). Blockchain initiatives such as the Open

Forest Protocol complement monitoring by enabling transparent certification of sustainable land use and facilitating verified carbon credit trading (IJRPR, 2025; CarbonCredits.com, 2025). This blend of technologies enhances accountability and trust, crucial in managing complex global commons.

Norway and Singapore: Digital Twins for Urban Climate Resilience

Emerging digital twin technologies offer cutting-edge tools to model and simulate urban climate impacts and adaptation responses. For example, Oslo has developed a digital replica integrating IoT sensor data, traffic patterns, and climate projections to assess vulnerabilities and guide resilient infrastructure investments such as green roofs and permeable pavements (Almeida et al., 2022; Oslo Kommune, n.d.). Similarly, Singapore's Virtual Singapore initiative provides a 3D platform for dynamic climate scenario testing, helping city planners design adaptive strategies (Tan & Lee, 2022; Virtual Singapore, n.d.). These efforts exemplify how real-time data integration and simulation can underpin evidence-based urban resilience.

North America and Europe: AI and Digital Platforms Enhancing Risk Forecasting and Adaptation

In Canada, meteorological agencies utilize AI-driven models to improve the accuracy and lead time of forecasts for extreme weather events, thereby bolstering disaster preparedness and reducing economic impacts (Taylor et al., 2021). At the continental level, the European Union's Climate-ADAPT platform integrates diverse geospatial, policy, and socio-economic data to support member states in identifying vulnerabilities and tailoring climate adaptation actions (European Environment Agency, 2023; Government of Canada, n.d.). These examples reflect the benefits of data-driven policymaking and the importance of open-access, interoperable digital platforms for cross-border collaboration.

Together, these global case studies underscore that while the hardware and software of digital technologies are often similar worldwide such as AI, IoT, blockchain, GIS, cloud computing their successful application depends heavily on contextual factors. Institutional capacity, infrastructural readiness, policy coherence, stakeholder inclusion, and equitable access shape outcomes profoundly. For instance, low-cost mobile platforms and blockchain insurance demonstrate clear benefits in low-resource settings, whereas sophisticated AI forecasting and digital twins require mature digital ecosystems and regulatory frameworks.

Additionally, transparency and accountability emerge as vital themes: integrating blockchain with governance improves trust, while open data platforms encourage multi-stakeholder engagement. Importantly, these experiences reinforce the conceptual framework's emphasis on treating digital transformation as a systemic process involving technical, organizational, and governance dimensions. These cases provide empirical grounding to the argument that digital innovation for climate action must be accompanied by enabling environments that foster equity, inclusivity, robust governance, and long-term sustainability the core tenants of the Technology–Organization–Environment and Sustainable Development frameworks integrated herein.

In addition to these national and regional examples, digital climate innovation is also being advanced by youth movements and the private sector. For example, the *Fridays for Future* youth movement has shifted much of its activism to digital platforms, using social media for education, community-building, and online mobilization (Sorce & Dumitrica, 2023). On the private / SME side, blockchain technologies are being explored for carbon accounting in supply chains, offering transparency, real-time emissions tracking, and reporting frameworks that can help companies improve ESG reporting and reduce environmental impact (Khallaf et al., 2024). Incorporating these actors highlights that digital climate action is a multi-actor process, not confined to governments and international institutions but driven also by grassroots youth engagement and market innovations.

Taken together, these cases reveal several cross-cutting lessons about the role of digital technologies in climate action. First, technological potential alone is insufficient; successful outcomes depend on enabling conditions such as local capacity, supportive governance, and policy coherence (Schot & Kanger, 2016; Sun et al., 2022). Second, the digital divide remains a persistent barrier, with advanced applications such as AI forecasting and digital twins thriving in high-resource contexts, while mobile platforms and blockchain-based finance tools are more accessible in low-resource settings (ITU, 2023; UNDP, 2022). Third, transparency and accountability emerge as recurring themes, where tools like blockchain and open data platforms build trust in carbon markets, supply chains, and adaptation planning (Kshetri, 2021). These comparative insights reinforce the chapter's conceptual argument that digital transformation in climate action is a systemic process shaped not only by technical innovation but also by governance, equity, and institutional readiness.

CHALLENGES IN INTEGRATION OF DIGITAL TECHNOLOGIES FOR CLIMATE ACTION

Despite the transformative potential of digital technologies to accelerate climate action, their effective integration into climate governance and practice faces numerous interconnected challenges. These challenges span technical, institutional, financial, and ethical dimensions, which collectively hinder equitable access, limit scalability, and threaten the sustainability of digital climate solutions.

Digital Divide and Inequitable Access

The digital divide remains one of the most urgent obstacles to inclusive digital climate action. According to the International Telecommunication Union (ITU, 2023), approximately 2.7 billion people worldwide are still offline, concentrated disproportionately in rural, low-income, and marginalized communities, particularly across the Global South. Limited access to reliable internet connectivity, affordable devices, and digital literacy not only excludes large populations from benefiting from digital climate tools but also risks amplifying existing inequalities in exposure and vulnerability to climate impacts (UNDP, 2022; OECD, 2024). This inequity undermines the legitimacy and effectiveness of climate governance regimes and calls for focused efforts on expanding digital infrastructure and capacity-building.

High Costs and Financial Barriers

Digital climate technologies such as IoT sensor networks, AI-driven analytics platforms, and satellite monitoring systems often require substantial capital investments for deployment, operation, and maintenance. For many low- and middle-income countries, these financial requirements exceed available national budgets and development aid, creating barriers to long-term sustainability beyond donor-funded pilot projects (OECD--UNDP, 2025). Without innovative, blended finance models that pool public and private resources alongside climate funds, many vulnerable regions remain excluded from advanced digital climate solutions.

Governance and Ethical Risks

The collection, management, and use of vast amounts of climate and socio-environmental data create complex governance challenges. Robust data protection frameworks are often lacking, raising risks of data breaches, misuse, and invasive surveillance that may violate privacy and human rights (Mancini et al., 2021). Algorithmic bias inherent in some AI applications can exacerbate social inequalities if unchecked, leading to discriminatory outcomes in risk assessments, insurance eligibility, or adaptation priorities (Rolnick et al., 2022; Vinuesa et al., 2020). Transparent, accountable, and participatory governance mechanisms are therefore critical to build trust and ensure ethical deployment of digital climate technologies.

Technical Fragmentation and Interoperability Issues

While a growing ecosystem of digital climate tools and platforms exists, technical fragmentation remains a major impediment. Disparate standards, proprietary systems, and lack of interoperability hinder seamless data sharing across sectors and international borders, limiting the effectiveness of integrated climate risk monitoring and policy coordination (Pauw et al., 2020). For example, variations in carbon accounting methodologies across blockchain carbon markets can undermine transparency and comparability. Addressing these technical challenges requires concerted efforts to develop harmonized standards and platforms that support open and interoperable global climate data systems.

Institutional Silos and Organizational Resistance

Digital climate action often requires coordination across multiple ministries, agencies, private sector actors, and civil society organizations. Unfortunately, institutional silos and bureaucratic inertia frequently inhibit collaboration and hamper coherent policy formulation and implementation of digital technologies in climate agendas (Schot et al., 2020; Ged & Schmidt, 2020). Weak organizational capacity, especially in developing countries, exacerbates challenges in procuring, governing, and effectively deploying sophisticated digital tools. Overcoming these institutional barriers requires proactive leadership, inclusive dialogue, capacity development, and adaptive governance structures. Overcoming these institutional barriers requires proactive leadership, inclusive dialogue, capacity development, and adaptive governance structures.

Human and Social Dimensions of Digital Climate Action

While much of the discourse on digital climate innovation emphasizes technological capacity and governance structures, insufficient attention is often given to the human element. Digital climate solutions ultimately rely on adoption, trust, and engagement at the community level, making social factors central to their effectiveness (Vinuesa et al., 2020). One challenge is the gap in digital literacy and user confidence, particularly in rural or marginalized areas. Even where infrastructure is available, limited skills and familiarity with digital platforms can prevent communities from fully benefiting from early warning systems, mobile-based advisory services, or participatory climate applications (UNDP, 2022). Similarly, gender disparities in digital access persist, with women in many parts of the Global South being less likely than men to own mobile phones or access the internet, constraining their ability to participate in climate decision-making (ITU, 2023).

Social trust is another critical factor. Communities may resist adopting digital tools if they perceive risks of data misuse, surveillance, or exclusion from decision-making processes. Embedding participatory design processes and ensuring free, prior, and informed consent (FPIC) can help build legitimacy and align digital interventions with local needs (United Nations, 2021). Moreover, digital climate platforms must consider cultural relevance and communication strategies that resonate with local knowledge systems. For instance, citizen science platforms that integrate storytelling, local languages, and traditional practices have shown higher adoption and effectiveness in both monitoring and adaptation programs (McNamara & Prasad, 2014). In short, digital climate action cannot succeed solely through technological innovation—it must be human-centered, socially inclusive, and participatory. Ensuring equitable access, culturally appropriate design, and strong community engagement will be vital to translating digital tools into real-world climate resilience.

Environmental Footprint of Digital Technologies

Ironically, many digital climate technologies generate environmental costs themselves, particularly through high energy consumption. Data centers, blockchain mining (especially proof-of-work systems), and large-scale AI model training account for significant electricity use and associated greenhouse gas emissions, sometimes powered by fossil fuels (de Vries, 2021; Mustapa et al., 2023). Without strategic investment in energy-efficient infrastructure, renewable-powered cloud services, and low-energy consensus protocols, digital climate tools risk producing unintended trade-offs that diminish their overall climate benefits.

Systemic Risks: Rebound Effects and Data Colonialism

Some scholars raise concerns about systemic risks associated with digital climate innovations. Efficiency improvements driven by AI or precision agriculture may induce rebound effects, where lowered costs encourage greater resource use or consumption, offsetting climate mitigation gains (Pauw et al., 2020). Moreover, "data colonialism" critiques highlight the risk that environmental and social data from the Global South are extracted and monetized by foreign firms without equitable benefit-sharing, perpetuating asymmetrical knowledge and power relations (Mancini et al., 2021). Addressing these complex systemic issues requires embedding social justice and ethical principles in digital climate governance.

These intertwined challenges emphasize that technological innovation alone will not suffice for effective, equitable, and sustainable digital climate action. Instead, success depends on the creation of supportive enabling environments that promote digital inclusion, finance sustainability, ethical governance, technical standardization, institutional collaboration, and environmental responsibility all key dimensions encapsulated within the integrated TOE and Sustainable Development Frameworks proposed in this chapter.

Just Transition and Digital Technologies

The concept of a *just transition* has become increasingly central to global climate policy debates, emphasizing that the shift to a low-carbon economy must be fair, inclusive, and protective of workers, vulnerable communities, and marginalized groups (ILO, 2015). While digital technologies are powerful enablers of climate action, they can also reproduce or exacerbate social inequalities if their deployment is not aligned with just transition principles.

For example, automation and artificial intelligence applied in energy and agricultural sectors may improve efficiency but also risk displacing workers without adequate reskilling programs (UNFCCC, 2021). Similarly, digital platforms for climate finance or carbon markets may remain inaccessible to low-income groups if affordability, literacy, and digital infrastructure gaps are not addressed (OECD, 2024). These dynamics highlight the need for *digital inclusion* policies to be explicitly framed within just transition agendas.

At the same time, digital tools can actively support just transition pathways. Online training platforms and virtual learning environments can deliver large-scale reskilling initiatives for workers in fossil-fuel dependent sectors. Blockchain-enabled climate finance can improve transparency and accountability in channeling funds to vulnerable groups, ensuring that benefits are distributed equitably (Kshetri, 2021). Mobile-based platforms can facilitate citizen participation in climate decision-making, giving marginalized communities greater voice in transition planning.

Embedding just transition principles into digital climate innovation therefore requires deliberate governance choices. Policymakers must ensure that investments in digital infrastructure include provisions for workforce reskilling, equitable access, and social protections. By doing so, digital transformation can contribute not only to decarbonization but also to building fairer and more resilient societies.

While the previous sections have outlined both the opportunities and challenges associated with digital technologies, it is useful to synthesize these insights in a comparative format. Table 1 summarizes the main benefits and risks discussed in the chapter, illustrating how digital innovation offers transformative potential while simultaneously raising issues that demand governance, equity, and sustainability safeguards (adapted from Rolnick et al., 2022; Vinuesa et al., 2020; de Vries, 2021; UNDP, 2022; OECD, 2024).

Table 1. Opportunities and Challenges of Digital Technologies for Climate Action

Opportunities (Technologies & Benefits)	Challenges (Risks & Barriers)
AI for forecasting → enhances disaster preparedness and early warning systems	High energy consumption of large AI models; risk of algorithmic bias (Vinuesa et al., 2020; de Vries, 2021)
IoT sensors for agriculture and smart grids → improves efficiency and resource management	Limited infrastructure and skills in Global South; digital divide (UNDP, 2022; ITU, 2023)
Blockchain for carbon markets & climate finance transparency	Energy-intensive protocols, lack of regulatory harmonization (Kshetri, 2021)
Cloud platforms for participatory governance → enables inclusivity and scalability	Concentration of providers, data sovereignty, and energy demands (OECD, 2024)
Big data & GIS for climate risk mapping → supports data-driven policymaking	Privacy, interoperability, and governance concerns (Fekete, A. et al., 2015; Global Solutions Initiative, 2022; Stewart, 2025)

POLICY RECOMMENDATIONS AND WAY FORWARD

The integration of digital technologies into climate action presents both significant opportunities and complex challenges, underscoring the urgent need for coherent and comprehensive policy frameworks. These frameworks must foster enabling environments that maximize technological benefits while mitigating associated risks. The recommendations below are directly informed by the integrated insights from the Technology–Organization–Environment (TOE) and Sustainable Development Frameworks (SDF), emphasizing that the advancement of technological capability, organizational readiness, and environmental governance and inclusivity must happen in concert to achieve effective and equitable digital climate action.

Expand Digital Infrastructure and Equitable Access

A foundational priority is the expansion of digital infrastructure and ensuring equitable access across geographies and socio-economic groups. Bridging the digital divide requires targeted investments in broadband connectivity, affordable devices, and digital literacy programs, particularly in underserved rural and marginalized communities (ITU, 2023; UNDP, 2022). Public policies should facilitate infrastructure deployment alongside incentives for private sector participation while safeguarding against exclusionary practices. Equitable access is essential to ensure that digital climate solutions benefit those most vulnerable to the impacts of climate change and prevent the amplification of existing inequalities (OECD, 2024; UNCTAD, 2024).

Develop Common Standards and Promote Interoperability

Climate action depends critically on reliable, consistent, and interoperable data flows across sectors, jurisdictions, and technological platforms. Current fragmentation and inconsistency in data standards and protocols impede coordination and reduce the comparability of climate information. International organizations including the United Nations, regional bodies like the European Union, and standard-setting agencies should lead the development and promotion of harmonized standards for emissions accounting, carbon market transactions, climate risk data, and digital governance frameworks (WEF, 2024; AVPN, 2024). Such standardization will strengthen the credibility, efficiency, and scalability of digital climate initiatives globally.

Safeguard Data Privacy and Promote Ethical Governance

The governance of climate-related data must uphold transparency, privacy, and equity to maintain public trust and legitimacy. Policymakers must enact and enforce regulatory frameworks that protect sensitive information and mandate accountability in algorithmic decision-making, preventing discriminatory outcomes and misuse (Rolnick et al., 2022; Vinuesa et al., 2020). Frameworks for artificial intelligence should prioritize explainability, fairness, and bias mitigation, while blockchain systems must balance transparency with privacy protections. Engaging stakeholders, including civil society and affected communities, in governance processes is key for ethical stewardship of digital climate tools.

Mobilize Sustainable Financing for Digital Climate Solutions

Given the substantial upfront costs of deploying cutting-edge technologies such as IoT sensor networks, satellite monitoring systems, and AI platforms, sustainable and innovative financing mechanisms are crucial. Governments should mobilize blended finance models that pool public, private, and multilateral climate finance resources to support scalable, financially viable digital climate projects, especially in developing countries (OECD–UNDP, 2025). Dedicated funding streams for research, development, and capacity-building in digital climate innovations will accelerate adoption and ensure long-term sustainability.

Integrate Digital Technologies into National Climate Policies

Digital strategies must be embedded within national climate frameworks, such as the Nationally Determined Contributions (NDCs) under the Paris Agreement, to align innovation efforts with broader mitigation and adaptation goals (Schot et al.,

2020). This integration facilitates coordinated policy action across relevant ministries such as technology, energy, agriculture, environment—and enables more coherent institutional approaches. National policies should include targets and action plans for the deployment, governance, and evaluation of digital climate technologies.

Multi-stakeholder and Cross-sectoral Partnerships

Successful digital climate action requires collaborative partnerships across governments, technology firms, research institutions, financiers, and civil society organizations. Multi-stakeholder engagements support knowledge exchange, capacity-building, and co-creation of solutions tailored to local contexts and needs (Baumüller, 2018). Partnerships enable the alignment of global technological potentials with grassroots realities, enhancing inclusivity, adaptability, and societal ownership of digital climate initiatives.

Green the Digital Economy and Minimize Environmental Footprints

Policymakers must address the environmental costs associated with digital technologies themselves particularly the energy demands of data centers, blockchain mining, and large-scale AI computations (de Vries, 2021). Strategies to green the digital economy include promoting energy-efficient infrastructure, incentivizing renewable-powered cloud computing, supporting the development of low-energy consensus protocols for blockchain, and advancing circular economy principles in hardware production and disposal. Incorporating sustainability principles into digital transformation is essential to ensure that climate technologies do not inadvertently exacerbate emissions or resource depletion.

Together, these policy actions underscore that digital climate transformation is not solely a matter of technology deployment but a socio-institutional process requiring systemic coordination, sustained investments, ethical governance, inclusivity, and environmental responsibility. By creating supportive institutional architectures that integrate these dimensions, governments and stakeholders can unlock the full potential of digital technologies as catalysts for scalable, equitable, and sustainable climate action.

CONCLUSION

Climate change stands as one of the most profound challenges confronting humanity and ecosystems in the twenty-first century, demanding urgent, coordinated, and transformative responses. This study has established that digital technologies such as spanning artificial intelligence, the Internet of Things, blockchain, geospatial analytics, big data, and cloud platforms are critical enablers capable of accelerating progress towards Sustainable Development Goal 13 (SDG 13). Through the integration of the Technology–Organization–Environment (TOE) model with the Sustainable Development Framework (SDF), this article offers a comprehensive conceptual framework elucidating how technological capability, organizational readiness, and environmental pressures interact to foster digital climate resilience. The framework emphasizes the necessity of embedding governance, equity, and sustainability to ensure that digital innovations translate into real-world climate impact.

Empirical insights drawn from global case studies ranging from India's digital agriculture and Germany's smart grids, to Kenya's blockchain-enabled insurance and Brazil's satellite-supported forest monitoring underscore that while technologies hold tremendous potential, their effectiveness is contingent upon local contexts, institutional capacities, and collaborative governance mechanisms. Importantly, digital transformation is not merely a technological upgrade but a systemic shift requiring inclusive policies, cross-sector coordination, and multi-stakeholder partnerships. The analysis further highlights persistent challenges including the digital divide, high costs, data governance complexities, interoperability barriers, institutional silos, and the environmental footprint of digital infrastructures. Addressing these challenges is paramount to avoid exacerbating inequalities and to build trustworthy and sustainable climate governance frameworks.

To realize the promise of digital technologies for climate action, policy interventions must prioritize equitable access, develop interoperable standards, uphold ethical data and algorithmic governance, mobilize sustainable finance, integrate digital strategies within national climate plans, and foster partnerships that empower vulnerable communities. Additionally, greening the digital economy should be central to prevent unintended environmental impacts. This holistic approach affirms that sustainable digital transformation for climate resilience is a socio-technical endeavor. It demands sustained commitment from governments, industry, civil society, and the research community to navigate complexities and harness innovations responsibly.

The issues and trends identified in this chapter are not static; they are evolving rapidly as technologies mature and governance frameworks adapt. For instance, digital climate tools are increasingly expanding beyond pilot projects toward broader national and cross-scale deployment, supported by rising investments and multistakeholder initiatives (UNDP, 2025). Concurrently, governance systems are shifting toward more integrated, interoperable, and equity-sensitive models, emphasizing data standards, transparency, and institutional coordination (Rahman & Rashid, 2025; Kaiser, 2024). Recognizing this dynamic trajectory helps anticipate future challenges such as governance fragmentation, equity gaps in access, and interoperability constraints and positions the chapter's analyses in a more forward-looking context.

A defining strength of this chapter is its balanced treatment of digital innovation, highlighting opportunities while giving equal weight to the challenges and risks of adoption. By examining both the promise of emerging tools and the systemic barriers that limit their scalability and inclusivity, the chapter avoids technological determinism and instead presents a nuanced, critical perspective. This balance is essential to guiding policymakers, practitioners, and scholars in navigating the complexities of digital climate action with both optimism and caution.

Looking forward, further research is needed to deepen understanding of long-term impacts, refine governance models, and evaluate outcomes across diverse settings. Such efforts will be critical to ensuring that digital transformations serve as catalysts not obstacles in the global pursuit of climate justice and sustainable development. Ultimately, by aligning advanced digital technologies with strong governance, equity, and sustainability principles, societies can unlock new pathways to protect the planet, support vulnerable populations, and accelerate inclusive progress towards achieving SDG 13 and the broader 2030 Agenda.

REFERENCES

AVPN. (2024). *Harnessing the Power of Digital Technologies for Climate Adaptation in Asia-Pacific*. Asia Venture Philanthropy Network.

Baumüller, H. (2018). The little we know: An exploratory literature review on the utility of mobile phone-enabled services for smallholder farmers. *Journal of International Development*, *30*(1), 134–154.

BMWK. (n.d.). Energiewende and Digitalization. Bundesministerium für Wirtschaft und Klimaschutz. https://www.bmwk.de/EN/Themen/Energy/Energiewende/energiewende.html

CarbonCredits.com. (2025). Are Nature-Based Solutions and Blockchain the Future of Carbon Credits?

de Vries, A. (2021). Bitcoin's growing energy problem. *Joule*, *2*(5), 801–805.

Digital Green. (n.d.). Smart Farming for Climate Resilience. https://www.digitalgreen.org/

European Environment Agency (EEA). (2023). *Climate-Adapt Platform*. https://climate-adapt.eea.europa.eu/

Fekete, A., Tzavella, K., Armas, I., Binner, J., Garschagen, M., Giupponi, C., Mojtahed, V., Pettita, M., Schneiderbauer, S., & Serre, D. (2015). Critical Data Source; Tool or Even Infrastructure? Challenges of Geographic Information Systems and Remote Sensing for Disaster Risk Governance. *ISPRS International Journal of Geo-Information*, *4*(4), 1848–1869. DOI: 10.3390/ijgi4041848

Ged & Schmidt, T. (2020). Integrating finance into the multi-level perspective: Technology niche-finance regime interactions and financial policy interventions. *Research Policy*, *49*(6), 103985.

Global Solutions Initiative. (2022). *Big Data Analytics for Safe*. Decarbonised and Climate-Resilient Infrastructure.

Hilty, L. M., & Aebischer, B. (2015). *ICT innovations for sustainability*. Springer.

IJRPR. (2025). Blockchain for Secure Carbon Markets: Comprehensive Review. *International Journal of Research Publication and Reviews*, *6*(6), 289–307.

ILO. (2016). *Guidelines for a just transition towards environmentally sustainable economies and societies for all*. International Labour Organization.

Instituto Nacional de Pesquisas Espaciais (INPE). (n.d.). DETER: Real-time Deforestation Detection in Amazonia. http://www.obt.inpe.br/OBT/Assuntos/Satelites/DETER

International Telecommunication Union (ITU). (2023). *Facts and Figures 2023*. ITU Publications.

IPCC. (2022). *Climate change 2022: impacts, adaptation, vulnerability*. Contribution of Working Group II to the Sixth Assessment Report. Cambridge University Press.

Johansson, E. L., Brogaard, S., & Brodin, L. (2022). Envisioning sustainable carbon sequestration. *Environmental Science & Policy*, *134*, 198–207.

Kaiser, Z. R. M. A. (2024). Smart governance for smart cities and nations. *Smart Cities*, *7*(1), 35–48. DOI: 10.1016/j.smci.2024.100031

Khallaf, A., Abdallah, A.-N., Zoubi, T., & Alnesafi, A. (2024). Blockchain-Driven Carbon Accountability in Supply Chains. *Sustainability*, *16*(24), 10872.

KlimAdapt. (n.d.). Climate Adaptation Portal Germany. https://klimadapt.de/

Kshetri, N. (2021). Blockchain and sustainable supply chain management in developing countries. *International Journal of Information Management*, *60*, 102376.

M-Farm. (n.d.). About M-Farm. https://mfarm.co.ke

McNamara, K. E., & Prasad, S. S. (2014). Coping with extreme weather: Communities in Fiji and Vanuatu share their experiences and knowledge. *Climatic Change*, *123*(2), 121–132. DOI: 10.1007/s10584-013-1047-2

Nakashima, D., McLean, K. G., Thulstrup, H. D., Castillo, A. R., & Rubis, J. T. (2012). *Weathering Uncertainty: Traditional Knowledge for Climate Change Assessment and Adaptation*. UNESCO & UNU.

OECD. (2024). *Digital Economy Outlook 2024* (Vol. 1). Organisation for Economic Co-operation and Development.

OECD–UNDP. (2025). Investing in Climate, Investing in Growth: Climate Action Monitor 2024.

Open Forest Protocol. (n.d.). Overview. https://openforestprotocol.org/

Pearce, T., Ford, J., Willox, A. C., & Smit, B. (2015). Inuit traditional ecological knowledge (TEK), subsistence hunting and adaptation to climate change in the Canadian Arctic. *Arctic*, *68*(2), 233–245.

Rahman, M., & Rashid, H. (2025). Bridging digital divides and sustainability imperatives: A systematic review of interoperability frameworks for sustainable development (2011–2025). *Journal of Cleaner Production, 456*, 141239. DOI: 10.1016/j.jclepro.2025.141239

Rolnick, D., Donti, P. L., Kaack, L. H., Kochanski, K., & Lacoste, A.. (2022). Tackling climate change with machine learning. *ACM Computing Surveys, 55*(2), 1–96.

Schot, J., & Kanger, L. (2016). Deep Transitions: Emergence, Acceleration, Stabilization, Directionality. SWPS 2016-15.

Sorce, G., & Dumitrica, D. (2023). From school strikes to webinars: Mapping the forced digitalization of Fridays for Future's activism during the COVID-19 pandemic. *Social Media + Society*. PMID: 38603442

Stewart, H. (2025). Fostering interoperability of data, models, communication, and governance for disaster resilience through transdisciplinary knowledge co-production. *Natural Hazards and Earth System Sciences, 25*, 3055–3073.

Sun, M., Zhang, X., & Zhang, X. (2022). The impact of multilevel innovation networks and government support. *Sustainability, 14*(12), 7334.

Taylor, G., & Vink, S. (2021). Managing the risks of missing international climate targets. *Climate Risk Management, 34*, 100379.

UNCTAD. (2024). Digital Economy Report 2024. *United Nations Conference on Trade and Development.*

UNFCCC. (2021). *Just Transition of the Workforce, and the Creation of Decent Work and Quality Jobs*. UNFCCC Technical Paper.

United Nations. (2015). *Transforming our world: the 2030 agenda for sustainable development*. United Nations.

United Nations. (2021). *The State of the World's Indigenous Peoples: Rights to Lands, Territories and Resources*. United Nations Publications.

United Nations Development Programme (UNDP). (2022). Bridging the digital divide for inclusive climate action.

United Nations Development Programme (UNDP). (2025). *The case for Nature ID: How digital public infrastructure can catalyze nature and climate action*. UNDP. https://climatepromise.undp.org/sites/default/files/research_report_document/undp-the-case-for-nature-id.pdf

Vinuesa, R.. (2020). The role of artificial intelligence in achieving the Sustainable Development Goals. *Nature Communications*, *11*, 233. PMID: 31932590

Wang, C., Zhan, J., Zhang, F., Liu, W., & Twumasi-Ankrah, M. (2020). Analysis of urban carbon balance. *Journal of Cleaner Production*, *281*, 125–138.

World Bank. (2019). *Digital Agriculture Profile*. World Bank Group.

World Economic Forum. (2024). Climate Adaptation: Unlocking Value Chains with the Power of Technology.

KEY TERMS AND DEFINITIONS

Digital Technologies: Tools and systems based on advanced computing, data, and communication infrastructures including AI, IoT, blockchain, big data analytics, GIS, and cloud platforms that transform how societies monitor, analyze, and respond to climate risks.

Climate Action: Collective measures aimed at mitigating greenhouse gas emissions and adapting to climate impacts, as framed in Sustainable Development Goal 13 (SDG 13) of the United Nations 2030 Agenda.

Sustainable Development Goal 13 (SDG 13): A global commitment under the UN 2030 Agenda that calls for urgent climate action through mitigation, adaptation, resilience building, and integration of climate measures into national and international policies.

Artificial Intelligence (AI): Computational methods and algorithms capable of learning from data and performing tasks such as prediction, optimization, and pattern recognition, increasingly applied to climate modeling, risk assessment, and resource efficiency.

Internet of Things (IoT): Networks of interconnected sensors and devices that collect and transmit real-time environmental data, enabling precision agriculture, smart grids, and adaptive climate monitoring systems.

Blockchain: A decentralized and secure ledger technology that enhances transparency and trust in climate finance, carbon markets, and sustainability reporting through tamper-resistant records.

Technology–Organization–Environment (TOE) Framework: A theoretical model that explains technology adoption by considering interactions among technological readiness, organizational capacity, and external environmental pressures.

Sustainable Development Framework (SDF): A governance-oriented framework that emphasizes equity, resilience, and accountability as guiding principles for integrating digital innovation into sustainable development and climate action strategies.

Chapter 11
The Sesame Social Credit System, Privacy Concerns, and Human Rights Impacts in China's Social Commerce Marketplace:
A Mixed Method Study

Yowei Kang
Auburn University in Montgomery, USA

Kenneth C. C. Yang
https://orcid.org/0000-0002-4176-6219
The University of Texas at El Paso, USA

ABSTRACT

The Sesame Social Credit System regime, similar to the earlier real-name registration, was launched to control Chinese social media and online commerce netizens. Our chapter employed a combination of case study and thematic (content) analysis methods to examine discourses on existing Chinese surveillance systems, investigate the government's justifications and netizens' responses to these regimes, and identify eight major themes and sub-themes in Chinese netizens' reactions and media discourses. A detailed analysis of several prominent cases provides contex-

DOI: 10.4018/979-8-3373-3685-5.ch011

tual information about the impacts of this regime. Thematic (content) analysis has identified major themes and sub-themes from Chinese social media and commerce users' and media narratives. Practical and managerial implications were provided.

INTRODUCTION

The exponential growth of Internet, mobile Internet, and social media platforms in China has created new challenges and opportunities for the ruling Communist Party in China because they have presented significant impacts on the political life of ordinary Chinese citizens (Hassid, 2012; Jiang & Schlæger, 2014; Huang & Sun, 2013; Sandoval, 2009; Sullivan, 2012, 2014; Yang & Kang, 2016). According to Statista (2025), China has the world's largest Internet population, reaching 1.1 billion users at the end of 2024 (Thomala, 2025a). The Internet penetration is about 80% in China, lagging behind 88% in Japan and South Korea (Thomala, 2025b). Among many emerging Internet applications, social media represents one of the most noteworthy phenomena in China (Yang & Kang, 2016). China also has the largest social media population in the World (Ma, 2024). The seamless blending of electronic commerce and social networking activities has led to a significant growth in the market share of social commerce, from 14% in 2021 to 21% in 2022 (daxueconsulting.com, 2023). Social commerce in China is reportedly more advanced than in the United States, largely due to the overlap between social media users and consumers with strong spending power (Wang, 2011). Research and Market (2025) predicts that Chinese social commerce is expected to grow at an annual rate of 8% and will reach US$537.29 billion by 2025. Additionally, live-streamed social commerce facilitated by popular influencers or Key Opinion Leaders (i.e., KOLs) can target a market of 763 million users as of June 2023 (daxueconsulting.com, 2023). Almost 84% of Chinese consumers have shopped via social media platforms (Ma, 2024). Based on monthly usage, dominant social commerce platforms in China include *WeChat* (91.8%), *Douyin* (83%), QQ (63.4%), *Xiaohongshu* (56.3%) (i.e., "Little Red Book" in Chinese), *Pinduoduo,* among others (Cooke, 2024; Thomala, 2025a).

Scholars have examined the potential impacts of social media on the political life of Chinese netizens (Drinhausen et al., 2025; Hassid, 2012; Jiang & Schlæger, 2014; Huang & Su, 2014; Langer et al., 2025; Sandoval, 2009; Sullivan, 2012, 2014; *The Economist*, 2012; Voice of America, 2012). The rise of social media could be partially attributed to its technical capabilities to disseminate information quickly (Li & Rao, 2010) without the intervention of government-controlled mainstream media (Ramzy, 2011). Public opinions freely expressed on *Weibo* often contradict the government's position and mass media reports. For example, while *Weibo* posts in *Sina Weibo* have praised then Premier Keqiang Li's "strong' hand-on leadership" in dealing with a cruise accident at Yangtze River (Blanc, 2015; *Dalje.com*, 2015, para. 4), uncensored comments retrieved by *Free Weibo*, a censorship monitoring website, seriously questioned government's incompetence in ensuring safety measures to prevent the accident in advance of the tragedy (Yang & Kang, 2016).

The popularity of China's electronic and social commerce marketplace among Chinese consumers, particularly among those born in the 1980s, plays a significant role in the lives of Chinese netizens (Wang, 2014). Occupying a significant portion of China's $2 trillion e-commerce market, social commerce has reshaped China's retail landscape (Cooke, 2023). *Guanxi* and social support partially explain the popularity of social commerce in China (Lin et al., 2018). *Douyi* has posted a US$200 billion Gross Merchandise Value (i.e., GMV) (Cooke, 2023). With the gradual economic downturn and the rising sense of civil liberties (such as the White Paper Movement) (Guan et al., 2025), the Chinese Communist Party government has resorted to tightening mobile, social media, and Internet use with its newly implemented real identity and real-name registration mechanisms (Yang & Kang, 2016). Earlier attempt by the ruling Chinese government to surveil netizens' behaviors can be dated back to the real-name registration regulation regime introduced on February 4, 2015 that require all Chinese netizens to register with their real names, official government identifications, and identities with various Internet service providers and at various new media platforms (Bischoff, 2015; Chin, 2015; Custer, 2015). What is even more alarming is that by 2020, when China fully implements its "social credit" system for each of its 1.3 billion citizens, all Chinese citizens will be assigned a "trustworthiness score" based on their traffic violations and numerous unannounced parameters (Hatton, 2015).

The commercial Sesame Social Credit System (henceforth, SSCS), combined with the state's real-name registration regime, could pose the greatest challenge to the anonymity of the Internet that many Chinese netizens have valued in an authoritarian society (Lee & Liu, 2016) as a state-commercial integrated control mechanism. Under these new regulatory regimes, the loss of consumer anonymity is likely to impact the behavior of many social commerce users in China. Positioned as a commercial initiative, the social credit system was said to "promote clients with good credit scores" by "giving them prominent spots" on major e-commerce websites (Hatton, 2015, para 6). However, it was rumored that journalists, teachers, veterans, and civil society groups will be closely monitored when the government system was in operation (Hatton, 2015).

To better assess the potential impacts of the SSCS regime on anonymity, consumer privacy, and electronic and social commerce activities, we relied on data collected from microblog discussions to gauge the perspectives of Chinese netizens on these issues in China. In particular, the objectives of this chapter are to examine the following research questions:

RQ1. What is the Sesame Social Credit System regime in electronic and social commerce, concerning other Chinese surveillance regimes?
RQ2: What are the reactions and discussions of Chinese netizens and media about the Sesame Social Credit System regime?

BACKGROUND

What is the Real Name Registration Regime?

The real name regulation regime has recently become a common practice in the telecommunications sector, where purchasing a SIM card requires full disclosure of a person's true identity. The real identity requirement for mobile phones was introduced in 2010, and all mobile phone users were required to register with telecommunications service providers (Kan, 2010). Since 2012, the Chinese government has further required online service providers to request the real identities of Chinese Internet users (Lee & Liu, 2016). The real-name registration mechanism of the Internet, introduced on February 4, 2015, requires all Chinese netizens to register with their real names and identities with various Internet service providers and new media platforms (Bischoff, 2015; Chin, 2015; Custer, 2015; Yang & Kang, 2016). To further control the Chinese society, microblog/*Weibo* users are required to register with their real names as early as 2017 (Fitzsimons, 2017). For social commerce activities, a real-name identity is required at every step in the consumer journey when online payments are tied to the buyer's and seller's bank accounts and other financial tools.

The real-name registration regime and real-identity monitoring practices have posed the greatest challenge to the anonymity of the Internet that many Chinese netizens have valued in an authoritarian society (Lee & Liu, 2016). Lee and Liu (2016) argued that the state-initiated real registration regime can be used to "illustrate the supremacy and limitations of the Network Authoritarian Model (NAM)" characteristic of Chinese cyberspace (n.p.). Under these new mechanisms, the loss of consumer anonymity and concerns over individual personal privacy are likely to affect every step of the consumer journey in the mobile social commerce marketplace in China (Lancaster University, n.d.). In contrast to the lax enforcement of real-name registration mechanisms in more democratic countries, President Xi's administration has exercised very tight control over Chinese users' personal information.

The real-name registration regime as a control mechanism over Internet, mobile media, and social commerce users in China can be considered as part of the licensing system in China. Caragliano (2013) argued that this type of surveillance regime allows the Chinese government to control "bad speeches" in Chinese cyberspace.

In the case of social media in China, since September 2009, bloggers and reporters have been required to post news on Sina and Netease (Bischoff, 2015; Yang & Kang, 2016). Electronic commerce giant Alibaba also required all merchants in China to register with their real names when trading on its platform (Bischoff, 2015). Since April 2020, all e-shop operators have been required to obtain a Certification Authority (CA) certificate issued by the State Administration for Market Regulation (SAMR) for annual reporting, opening a bank account, bookkeeping, and tax declaration purposes (Tindall, 2021). Once implemented nationwide, social media account impersonations of celebrities or prominent political figures will become impossible (Carsten, 2015).

The Emergence of the Sesame Social Credit System (SSCS) Regulatory Regime

In October 2015, China (along with major social media and commerce giants, *Alibaba* and *Tencent*) launched its social credit system, Sesame Social Credit System (Ming, 2017). By 2020, all Chinese citizens would be assigned a "trustworthiness score" based on their traffic violations and numerous unannounced parameters (Hatton, 2015). A Chinese citizen will be given an SSCS score between 250 and 950, with a higher score meaning better credibility. Users of Sesame Credit will be assigned scores ranging from 350 to 950 based on their credit history. The higher the score, the better the credibility (Zhao, 2016).

Modelled after the FICO credit score in the US, criticisms of the Sesame Social Credit System focused on the lack of consumer privacy protection and the potential for violation and oppression of different political views. As criticized by ACLU, the Sesame Social Credit System is labeled as "an Orwellian nightmare" (Storm, 2015, para 1) because a person's credit score "can be adversely affected by your hobbies, shopping habits, lifestyles, what you read online, what you post online, your political opinions as well as what your social connections do, say, read, buy or post" (Storm, 2015, para 3). As a social control system in an already highly surveilled society, SSCS has been used to monitor the behaviors of various citizens. For example, a national blacklister for defaulting on her debt was fined 100,000 RMB (approximately 15,000 USD) by a court in China's Shenzhen City for taking a first-class flight (Xinhua News Agency, 2017). In 2016, 4.9 million were prohibited from flying, and 1.65 million were banned from taking the train for defaulting on their loans (Zhao, 2016).

Since it was first launched in 2014 to address the pervasive mistrust in the Chinese society (Zhao, 2016), several top Chinese government agencies have released a draft law on November 14, 2022, *the Establishment of the Social Credit System*, to systematically codify earlier experiments on social credit to better guide future implementation (Yang, 2022). According to Yang (2022), the social credit system comprises two components linked to an individual's ID code: traditional financial creditworthiness and "social creditworthiness" (n.p.). While the first part is similar to the credit scores in the US, the second part aims to develop a society-wide trust or trustworthiness system to address issues such as academic plagiarism, false advertising, corruption, tax evasion, pollution, and product counterfeiting, among others (Yang, 2022, n.p.). For example, in the city of Rongcheng, all residents initially received 1000 social credits, which are subject to 50-point deductions if they are found to have spread rumors and false information on *WeChat* (Kobie, 2019).

FOCUS OF THIS CHAPTER: THEORETICAL FRAMEWORK

Anonymity and Personal Privacy in Social Commerce

Registration with users' real identities to access any new media platforms and services has always led to intense debates about its potential invasion of users' privacy (Gow & Parisi, 2008; Yang & Kang, 2016). Combined with the real identity, the social credit system provides ID-like credit scores to each identified social commerce shopper. The restriction of information on these emerging platforms, at the expense of users' privacy and anonymity, is a characteristic of China's surveillance regimes of users' online behaviors since the early days of Internet diffusion in China (Yang, 2011; Yang & Kang, 2016). An example of this type of surveillance software is the mandatory Green Dam Youth Escort (i.e., GDYE) software, which was required to be pre-installed on all computers sold in China (Grifantiniarchive, 2009; Yang, 2011). With the pretext of blocking pornography and other "objectionable" materials, the GDYE software also poses a security risk and censors political sites (Grifantiniarchive, 2009).

In October 2015, China (along with *Alibaba* and *Tencent*) launched its social credit system, *Sesame Social Credit System*. By 2020, all Chinese citizens will be assigned a "trustworthiness score" based on their traffic violations and various unannounced parameters (Hatton, 2015). The implementation of the social credit system has attracted criticism due to concerns over consumer privacy violations and oppression (Zhao, 2016). The SSCS has been integrated with public security bureaus, court branches, banking systems, and other sectors that could impact people's daily activities if loan repayments are not made. For example, China's Supreme People's Court published information on individuals and companies that failed to fulfill court orders, preventing them from participating in certification, authentication, and government bidding, procurement, and tendering (Zhao, 2016).

Another notable example is *AliTravel*, which collaborated with the Luxembourg Consulate in Shanghai to issue SSCS-based tourist visas (Wang, 2015). For those with a 750 score or higher they can use their SSCS report as proof of financial support (Wang, 2015). Additionally, those with an SSCS score lower than 650 points were required to pay a deposit of 99 RMB (or 14.4 USD) before renting an OFO bike (He, 2017). These practices have raised serious privacy concerns, according to Wang Zhenyu, a researcher with the China University of Political Science and Law (Zhao, 2016).

Wang et al. (2022) empirically confirmed, through a survey of 1,311 *Xiaohongshu* users, that privacy assurance, as measured by social commerce organizations, can affect users' willingness to share their personal information socially, including date of birth, geographical location, name, personal interests, and other details. The Electronic Frontier Foundation (EFF) (2011) defined the concept of privacy as "a universal human right for all individuals regardless of nationality. It strengthens human dignity and other rights such as freedom of expression and association. Almost all international conventions on human rights protect the right to privacy" (p. 2). Privacy refers to the "ability to control when, how, and to what extent their personal information is to be transmitted to others" (Youn, 2009, p. 391). Dinulescu et al. (2021) also confirmed that security concerns can influence social commerce purchases and sharing behaviors.

The Sesame Social Credit System, combined with the real name registration, regimes fundamentally challenge whether the individual social commerce shoppers are willing to conduct social sharing and additionally, how society perceives the space created by ICTs as public or private, whether the measure is viewed as an invasion of users' privacy, and whether the government has the rights to regulate such social sharing behaviors (Yang & Kang, 2011). Therefore, knowing their comments and behaviors on social commercials are displayed in public could affect social commerce users' behaviors, similar to what Burkell et al. (2014) once found in their Facebook study, that Facebook users seem to be aware that information posted on Facebook is a public display and is available to the public to view and share.

Bandara et al. (2020) observed the importance of consumer privacy in determining their electronic commerce behaviors. The implementation of privacy-invasive or assurance mechanisms in a democratic country is related to how social commerce shoppers perceive the trustworthiness of a social commerce institution (Wang et al., 2022). However, in an authoritarian country like China, where free expression and information flow are often frowned upon by government officials, the state-mandated real-name registration and private/commercial Sesame Social Credit System requirements are likely to become a powerful surveillance instrument to discourage the political participation of Chinese citizens (Yang & Kang, 2016). In late November 2022, government agencies drafted a new law to establish the national social credit system to "codify past experiments on social credit and, theoretically, guide future implementation" (Yang, 2022, n.p.).

SOLUTIONS AND RECOMMENDATIONS

We employed a combination of case study and thematic content analysis methods to investigate the potential effects of the Sesame Social Credit System regime on social commerce in China. The case study method is a popular research technique in qualitative research (Rashid et al., 2019) and policy analysis (Pal, 2005). The case study approach is an appropriate method to enable researchers to develop "a deep understanding about a particular case, its features, and its impact" (Eltantawy & Wiest, 2011, p. 1209) and to study a broader phenomenon related to Internet governance (Pal, 2005). Baxter and Jack (2008) claimed that a qualitative case study helps explore "a phenomenon within a particular context, explored through various data sources, and undertaken through a variety of lenses to reveal multiple facets of the phenomenon (cited in Rashid et al., 2019, n.p.). On the other hand, thematic analysis has been a popular research method in privacy-related studies (Bandara et al., 2020). A thematic analysis approach has been claimed to "efficiently reduce the quantity of data to a realistic level and provide a bird-view perspective" (Hao, 2014, p. 346). Summarizing what other qualitative researchers have observed, Naeem et al. (2023) stated that "[t]hematic analysis is a research method used to identify and interpret patterns or themes in a data set; it often leads to new insights and understanding" (n.p.). Naeem et al. (2023) proposed a six-step approach to transcribe, create categories, and become familiar with the data, followed by keyword identification, code selection, theme development, conceptualization, and conceptual model development.

We employed a thematic (content) analysis method, a commonly used approach for categorizing and interpreting these discourse data (Wahl et al., 2005). The thematic analysis has been claimed to "efficiently reduce the quantity of data to a realistic level and provide a bird-view perspective" (Hao, 2014, p. 346). Following the procedures outlined by Wahl et al. (2005), the researchers have read, interpreted, and categorized the discourse data collected from microblog discussion forums by first identifying broad themes, then pinpointing sub-subthemes, and finally providing their names. To ensure the validity of a thematic analysis as a qualitative methodology (Braun & Clarke, 2023). As a methodology that varies in practices, thematic analysis often employs coding, thematic development, capturing latent and/or semantic meaning, and data induction or deduction (Braun & Clarke, 2023). To help identify broad themes, the researchers paid attention to forcefulness, recurrence, and repetition in the data (Wahl et al., 2005). Sub-themes were analyzed and identified when multiple meanings within a particular broad theme were found (Wahl et al., 2005). Both researchers discussed and debated the labelling and appropriateness of a theme and its related subthemes. Once both broad and sub-themes were identified, names were assigned to each theme and sub-theme to describe their meaning (Wahl et al., 2005).

Sampling Characteristics and Compilation of Discourse Corpus

To generate more representative data, we relied on discourse data collected from Chinese microblog discussions to identify the thoughts, reactions, and perceptions of Chinese social commerce users regarding the Sesame Social Credit System. These discourses were analyzed using a thematic (content) analysis method commonly employed in new media research (Hao, 2014; Yin, 2014; Zhou et al., 2008; Yang & Kang, 2016).

To collect narratives, texts, and media content for a thematic content analysis. To collect discourses for thematic content analysis, this study employed the following keywords and phrases to retrieve blog entries from the popular *Baidu* (site: tieba.baidu.com) and mass media sources. For example, from Lexis/Nexis Academic (English language media contents), "Sesame Social Credit System" [ ] (N=34), or "Sesame Credit" [ ] (N=36). From *The Global Times* (China), "Sesame Social Credit System" [ ] (N=0), or "Sesame Credit" [ ] (N=21). *Baidu* is an Internet Service Provider in China, offering a Chinese-language search engine that provides access to documents, multimedia, images, news, and webpages (*The New York Times*, n.d.). From *tieba.baidu.com* (Microblog), "Sesame Social Credit System" [ ] (N=218). From *Free Weibo* (https://freeweibo.com) & *Sina Weibo* (Microblog), "Sesame Social Credit System" [ ] (N=135). Ultimately, our corpus consisted of 411 items (see Table 1 for more details).

Table 1. Sample Characteristics

Databases or Media Search Keywords or Phrases Outlets	Lexis/Nexis Academic (English language media contents)	*The Global Times* (China) [环球时报] (English)	tieba.baidu.com (Microblog)	Free Weibo (https://freeweibo.com) & *S* (Microblog)
"Sesame Social Credit System" ["芝麻信用系统"]	49	0	218	135
(After removing duplicates and irrelevant items)	15	0	0	0
Subtotal	**34**	**0**	**218**	**135**
"Sesame Credit" ["芝麻信用"]	145	30		
(After removing duplicates and irrelevant items)	109	9		
Subtotal	**36**	**21**		

Source: The Authors

FINDINGS, DISCUSSIONS, AND CONCLUSION

We have answered our first research question in the previous background and introduction section. To answer our second research question about the reactions and discussions of Chinese netizens about the Sesame Social Credit System regime. We identified the following themes and subthemes to demonstrate how Chinese netizens and media perceived the Sesame Social Credit System. As Zhu et al. (2013) observed, verifying user identities and associating their credit scores with their real identities is likely to create a sense of trustworthiness and generate more followers and retweets. Consequently, government surveillance has become more convenient and easier to implement.

In terms of how the SSCS regime was framed by social media users in China, we followed the procedures outlined by Wahl et al. (2005), where two researchers, both fluent in Chinese, read, interpreted, and categorized the discourse data collected from microblog discussion forums and other media outlets. This process involved first identifying broad themes, secondly pinpointing sub-subthemes, and finally providing their names. To help identify broad themes, the researchers paid attention to forcefulness, recurrence, and repetition in the data (Wahl et al., 2005). Sub-themes were analyzed and identified when multiple meanings within a particular broad theme were found (Wahl et al., 2005). Once both broad and sub-themes were identified, names were assigned to each theme and sub-theme to describe their meaning (Wahl et al., 2005).

We identified the following themes about the Sesame Social Credit System:

Theme #1: A strong tendency toward utilitarian concerns about the Sesame Social Credit System. Under this common theme, several sub-themes also emerged. For example, many netizens were concerned about how the system works (sub-theme #1), how to manipulate the rules to enhance personal social credit scores (sub-theme #2), and how to learn the importance of a higher social credit score (sub-theme #3). Some complain about the SSCS system (sub-theme #4).

Sesame Credit hopes to provide new insights into creditworthiness by evaluating the spending and savings behavior of Ant Financial's more than 300 million real-name registered users - equivalent to nearly a quarter of China's population" (Gough, 2015, from The New York Times).

"Utilizing data from online shopping records and online financial behavior, Sesame Credit measures users' credit from five aspects - credit history, behavioral habits, ability to pay off debts, personal information and social networks. Each user can get a credit rating of between 350 and 950" (Asia News Network, July 15, 2015)

From the government's perspective, SSCS was discussed as a panacea for China's social and economic problems (Theme 2):

The Cyberspace Administration of China wants anyone demonstrating "dishonest" online behavior blacklisted, while a leading academic has argued that a media blacklist of "irresponsible reporting" would encourage greater self-discipline and morality in journalism. (Denyer, 2016, from The Washington Post)

At the heart of the social credit system is an attempt to control China's vast, anarchic and poorly regulated market economy, to punish companies selling poisoned food or phony medicine, to expose doctors taking bribes and uncover con men preying on the vulnerable. (Denyer, 2016, from The Washington Post)

China's social-credit backers want their system to be all-encompassing, to evaluate not just financial matters but anything that might speak to a person's trustworthiness. In modern China, "trust-keeping is insufficiently rewarded, the costs of breaking trust tend to be low," a 2014 Chinese government document describing the government's plans notes. The social-credit system aims to change that - raising the penalties for poor conduct and the rewards for deferential behavior. (Venderklippe, January 4, 2018, from The Globe and Mail, Canada)

SSCS is framed as Theme 3 by the Communist Party to "build a culture of 'sincerity" and a 'harmonious socialist society' where 'keeping trust is glorious" (Denyer, October 23, 2016, from *The Washington Post*).

A huge part of Chinese political theater is to claim that there is an idealized future, a utopia to head towards," said Rogier Creemers, a professor of law and governance at Leiden University in the Netherlands. (Denyer, October 23, 2016, from The Washington Post)

The fourth theme that emerged from our corpus is a strong emphasis on the many technical benefits of SSCS. For example, one article in *China Daily* (July 6, 2015) stated that:

The new service is part of Sesame Credit's broad efforts to expand the commercial application of credit in China. In May, the company inked a deal with baihe.com, a dating website in China, to add Sesame Credit to its users' resumes in the hope of helping people find true love online. Sesame Credit has also partnered with leading hotels and car-renting companies to provide better services to its users, enabling consumers with a certain level of credit score to check into hotels and rent cars without paying a guarantee deposit.

Those who have a sesame credit of 650 points or higher in Shanghai won't have to pay the 99 yuan ($14.4) deposit before unlocking a bike, Zhang Siding, ofo co-founder, said at a press conference in Shanghai....... Passing certain numerical benchmarks would entitle one to certain perks, like small loans, or in this case, waivers on deposits.

The fifth theme emerges from our corpus to show there is an increasing use of *SSCS* as a social control mechanism, as seen in the following two *China Daily* articles below:

Statistics showed that Sesame Credit has helped courts punish more than 1.21 million debt defaulters and over 126,000 of them have paid their debts as of the end of July. "We should reward those who keep their word and punish those who break their promises," said Chen Wenjin from Ant Financial. As authorities are working to establish a reliable nationwide credit rating system, Chinese courts are also exploring new ways to punish those who do not pay their debts (China Daily, October 4, 2017).

People with 600 points above can use a shopping-credit system called "Just Spend" which allows users to take out a loan of less than 5,000 yuan ($805.9) when shopping on Alibaba's online marketplace Taobao. Those with more than 666 points can take a cash loan of up to 50,000 yuan" (China Daily, June 9, 2017).

Another important theme (Theme #7) is to associate SSCS with China's leapfrogging into the digital dimension (*China Daily,* May 9, 2017) as seen below:

China has leapfrogged into the digital dimension to become the global center of financial technology innovation and adoption, outpacing the likes of New York, London and Singapore by a wide margin, according to a joint report by consultancy Ernst & Young and DBS in 2016......Through Sesame Credit, a credit-rating system embedded in Alipay, citizens of Hangzhou, capital of Zhejiang province, can freely borrow goods such as umbrellas and phone chargers throughout the city, based on their credit record.

Privacy concerns also emerged as our fifth theme when "IT watchdog slams tech firms over privacy" in the following articles below:

According to a post on the website of the Ministry of Industry and Information Technology (MIIT) on Friday, the regulator held a meeting with three tech firms - Ant Financial, the payment affiliate of Alibaba Group Holdings, China's search giant Baidu Inc and Beijing Bytedance Technology Co, which oversees Jinri Toutiao, one of the most popular mobile news apps in China - for their personal privacy breaches. The three firms failed to disclose sufficient information on why they collected personal data," said the ministry, requesting them to make rectifications immediately to guarantee users' right to know and freedom of choice" (The Global Times, January 12, 2018)

The Cyberspace Administration of China (CAC) had a meeting with Alipay and Sesame Credit on Saturday, regarding the Alipay yearly spending sharing incident, according to a post on its official website on Wednesday. The CAC official urged the platforms to comply with the requirements of the Network Security Act, conduct a thorough investigation and prevent personal privacy breaches from happening again, the post noted" (The Global Times, January 10, 2018)

Actually, if users don't agree to the service's terms and conditions, they can still view their bill. But the tricky thing is, most users cannot see the words because they are in such small font," a user surnamed Chen told the Global Times on Thursday. As a result, users "authorized Sesame Credit to collect their information without knowing," he said. (The Global Times, January 4, 2018)

Users were outraged and accused the company of infringing their privacy.......I will be more cautious when using other online services. I will make sure my personal information is safe before clicking a button on mobile payment platforms," said Zhang Menghan, who has just unsubscribed from Sesame Credit. (The Global Times, January 5, 2018)

China is moving towards a totalitarian society, where the government controls and affects individuals' private lives," said Beijing-based novelist and social commentator Murong Xuecun. This is like Big Brother, who has all your information and can harm you in any way he wants. (Denyer, 2016, The Washington Post).

The ambition is to collect every scrap of information available online about China's companies and citizens in a single place - and then assign each of them a score based on their political, commercial, social and legal "credit" (Denyer, 2016, The Washington Post).

A byproduct from all this heavy use is a torrent of rich data that reveal highly-detailed specifics about each individual user. But unlike the United States, which has laws - imperfect as they may be - about when and how the government can access this type of data, no such prohibitions exist in China. Tech companies routinely hand their data to the government which has made no secret about its efforts to integrate that data into its surveillance apparatus (PMS, August 22, 2017).

The final theme (Theme 8) pointed out the less transparent practices in calculating social credit scores, as seen below:

The creeping fear is that the Big Data cooperation between businesses and government has a tinge of moral policing. Alibaba is working on a credit scoring system where consumers could be rewarded for good behaviour on social media. Mr Weigend is looking at Alibaba's Sesame Credit rating with interest. (Lee, April 15,, 2017, The Business Times, Singapore)

Sesame Credit, however, also uses other data to calculate the scores, such as a person's hobbies, interaction with friends, shopping habits and lifestyle." (Asia News Network, June 9, 2015)

According to Ant Financial Services Group, "the system would take into consideration, among several factors, whether consumers are active Internet users, have a stable residential address and have been using the same mobile phone number for a long time. (Business Line, January 28, 2015)

Discussions

Electronic cyberspace is known for its anonymity and privacy-friendly environment (Lee & Liu, 2016). The assurance of anonymity and privacy protection contributes to a democratic decision-making process because individuals feel free to express themselves openly (Lee & Liu, 2016). As Lee and Liu (2016) argued, "[a]nonymity strengthens the expression of viewpoints while concealing the identity of the person expressing his or her viewpoints (p. 6). However, when the Chinese government introduced the real name registration regime, critics have pointed out its potential impacts on freedom of speech, civil liberty, and political freedom (Yang & Kang, 2016). However, when the Chinese government launched another surveillance regime, namely the Sesame Social Credit System, which associates a person's reputation with their political expressions, purchasing behaviors, and financial transactions, this regime hinders the human rights of many social commerce consumers (Lee & Liu, 2016). As A. Michael Froomkin has observed, "the debate about anonymity... is in effect a debate about the degree of political and economic freedom that will be fostered, or tolerated, in a modern society" (cited in Lee & Liu, 2016, p. 8). The deprivation of both political and economic freedom among many Chinese social commerce users, through a combination of the corporate Sesame Social Credit System and state real-name registration regimes, could easily violate the human rights of many Chinese netizens.

Although anonymity in the social commerce space can protect the privacy of Chinese consumers, Lee and Liu (2016) pointed out the potential negative impacts of "bad behaviors" because of the lack of accountability. The arguments (as demonstrated in Theme #3 and Theme #5) showed the government's stance of adopting the Sesame Social Credit System to develop a harmonious Chinese society to control better fraud, mistrust, and scams in the social commerce marketplace. The contestation between social order, law enforcement, and individual freedom is evident in the emerging themes between the Chinese government and netizens' perceptions of these surveillance regimes (Lee & Liu, 2016). The historical recount of the government's early attempt in 2003 to collect users' identities in local Internet cafes demonstrates how an authoritarian government attempted to curb the newly found individual political and economic freedoms ushered in by the Internet, social media, and social commerce, to better protect human rights among Chinese netizens. Li and Chin (2017) even made a bold claim that two major Chinese electronic commerce giants, Tencent and Alibaba, helped the Chinese government to spy on Chinese people. The negative impacts of these social control regimes were exacerbated by overlapping regulatory entities (Dong, 2012). For example, Dong (2012) identified five layers of regulatory bodies ranging from "the government, service and content providers to webmasters and individual users" (p. 403), which further complicated the technology's negative implications.

Although some have pointed out, critics of the Social Credit System did not accurately interpret the intention of its adoption (MERCIS, 2022) (Refer to Figure 1). It is worth noticing that in late 2016, the State Council formally referred to this corporate system as "the establishment of a personal integrity score management system" (MERCIS, 2022, n.p.). It should be noted that government public statements and stances did not necessarily reflect how the Social Credit System was implemented by different tiers of government agencies and even private entities in China.

A quick guide to the Social Credit System
The five most common Social Credit-related myths related to individuals

COMMON MISPERCEPTION	EXPLANATION
There is no score that dictates citizens' place in society	• **Some cities or companies have experimented with rating systems, but these are merely "loyalty rewards programs".** • Citizens cannot be penalized for low scores. • A national, all-encompassing Social Credit Score for citizens is highly unlikely to ever materialize.
The Social Credit System is not primarily a tool for mass surveillance of individuals	• **The Social Credit System primarily focuses on businesses and marketplace behavior.** • Individuals are primarily included concerning debt repayment and in their role as legal representatives of companies. • Not more than 0.2 percent of individuals receive Social Credit-related penalties annually.
The Social Credit System does not constantly monitor and assess individual behavior	• **Only violations of laws and regulations can serve as ground for punishments.** • Citizens cannot land on a blacklist for playing too many games, occasional jaywalking, having "untrustworthy" friends, etc. • Recent regulations have further restricted scope for the inclusion of individual behavior.
The Social Credit System is low-tech and fragmented	• **Virtually all Social Credit-related decisions are taken by humans, not AI.** • Digitization of the system remains limited and data sharing challenges hamper its implementation. • This will remain the case for the coming decade, even as attempts are made to slowly integrate and digitalize the system.
The Social Credit System will not be fully completed anytime soon	• **The Social Credit System has been worked on since 2001 and is still far from complete.** • 2020 was the end of a key construction phase, but the system will remain under development for at least the coming decade. • There is still dynamic debate on what the Social Credit System should become, even within China's administration. • The focus for the coming years will be to integrate information sharing systems, establish unified standards, and improve the legal basis.

Source: Drinhausen and Brussee (2021): *China's Social Credit System in 2021, from Fragmentation to Integration.*

© MERICS

Source: https://merics.org/en/comment/chinas-social-credit-score-untangling-myth-reality

Limitations

Our chapter identified and explored themes from China's microblog users, state-controlled media, and overseas media outlets to gain a deeper understanding of what Chinese netizens think about the Sesame Social Credit System regime. Despite strong utilitarian concerns, Chinese netizens increasingly began to pay attention to potential violations of their privacy, the accuracy of their credit scores, and the government's justifications. Methodologically, this chapter was limited by the amount and the scope of narratives collected for the thematic analyses. Recent debates and discussions on this issue were also not available. Additionally, due to meticulous monitoring and censoring of posts critical to the government, the identified themes and sub-themes could represent biased perspectives that need to be interpreted and evaluated carefully after considering China's social media space.

REFERENCES

Bandara, R., Fernando, M., & Akter, S. (2020). Privacy concerns in E-commerce: A taxonomy and a future research agenda. *Electronic Markets, 30*, 629–647. 610.1007/s12525-12019-00375-12526

Bischoff, P. (2015, February 5). A brief history of China's campaign to enforce real-name registration online. *TechInAsia,* https://www.techinasia.com/history-chinas-campaign-enforce-realname-registration-online/?utm_source=Read+Next&utm_medium=web&utm_campaign=readnext-posts

Blanc, S. (2015, June 4). China's propaganda machine is in overdrive after a cruise ship disaster that's left hundreds missing. *Business Insider,* http://www.businessinsider.com/afp-propaganda-machine-in-overdrive-for-china-shipwreck-2015-6#ixzz3caNWpED0

Braun, V., & Clarke, V. (2023). Toward good practice in thematic analysis: Avoiding common problems and be(com)ing a knowing researcher. *International Journal of Transgender Health, 24*(1), 1–6. DOI: 10.1080/26895269.26892022.22129597 PMID: 36713144

Burkell, J., Fortier, A., Yeung, L. L., Wong, C., & Simpson, J. L. (2014). Facebook: Public space, or private space? *Information Communication and Society, 17*(8), 974–985.

Caragliano, D. (2013, March 26). Why China's 'real name' internet policy doesn't work. https://www.theatlantic.com/china/archive/2013/03/why-chinas-real-name-internet-policy-doesnt-work/274373/

Carsten, P. (2015, February 4). China to ban online impersonation accounts, enforce real-name registration. *Reuters,* https://www.reuters.com/article/2015/2002/2004/us-china-internet-censorship-idUSKBN2010L2080ZF20150204

Chin, J. (2015, February 4). China is requiring people to register their real names for some internet services. *The Wall Street Journal,* https://www.wsj.com/articles/china-to-enforce-real-name-registration-for-internet-users-1423033973

Cooke, J. (2024). WPIC Perspectives: Exploring social commerce's impact on China's e-commerce sphere. *AmCham China Quarterly Magazine*, https://www.amchamchina.org/wpic-perspectives-exploring-social-commerces-impact-on-chinas-e-commerce-sphere/

Custer, C. (2015, January 14). Real-name system coming to Weibo, Tieba, and other Chinese websites (for real this time). *TechInAsia,* https://www.techinasia.com/realname-system-coming-weibo-tieba-chinese-websites/

Dalje.com. (2015, June 3). Chinese authorities censor questions about the Yangtze ship sinking. http://dalje.com/en-world/chinese-authorities-censor-questions-about-yangtze-ship-sinking/546073

daxueconsulting.com. (2023, November 15). How social commerce in China is transforming shopping and social media. *daxueconsulting.com*, https://daxueconsulting.com/social-commerce-in-china/

Dinulescu, C. C., Visinescu, L. L., Prybutok, V. R., & Sivitanides, M. (2021). Customer relationships, privacy, and security in social commerce. *Journal of Computer Information Systems*, *62*(3), 642–654. 610.1080/08874417.08872021.01975172

Dong, F. (2012). Controlling the internet in China: The real story. *Convergence (London)*, *18*(4), 403–425.

Drinhausen, K., Shi-Kupfer, K., & Sadeler, C. (2025, February 21). China's fragile online spaces for debate: Between entertainment and heavy state guidance, citizens raise social concerns and create new communities. *Friedrich Naumann Foundation for Freedom*, https://merics.org/en/report/chinas-fragile-online-spaces-debate

Eltantawy, N., & Wiest, J. B. (2011). Social media in the Egyptian Revolution: Reconsidering resource mobilization theory. *International Journal of Communication*, *5*, 1207–1224.

Fitzsimons, T. (2017, May 13). Study reveals Chinese censorship of Weibo. *The World*, https://theworld.org/stories/2017/2005/2013/study-reveals-chinese-censorship-weibo

Gow, G. A., & Parisi, J. (2008, February). Pursuing the anonymous user: Privacy rights and mandatory registration of prepaid mobile phones. *Bulletin of Science, Technology & Society*, *28*(1), 60–68.

Grifantiniarchive, K. (2009, August 13). China relents on censorship software. *MIT Technology Review*, https://www.technologyreview.com/2009/2008/2013/211018/china-relents-on-censorship-software/

Guan, Y., Guang, L., Li, L., & Liu, Y. (2025). The rally effect of the COVID-19 Pandemic and the White Paper Movement in China. *Journal of Contemporary China*, *34*(151). Advance online publication. DOI: 10.1080/10670564.10672024.12356863

Hao, J. (2014). "A real China": On user-generated videos audiovisual narratives of Confucianism. *TripleC, 12*(1), 342–355.

Hassid, J. (2012). Safety valve or pressure cooker? Blogs in Chinese political life. *Journal of Communication, 62*, 212–230.

Hatton, C. (2015, October 26). China "social credit": Beijing sets up huge system. *BBC News*, https://www.bbc.com/news/world-asia-china-34592186

He, W. (2017, March 16). Sesame Credit determines who can ride OFO bikes deposit-free. *China Daily*.

Huang, R., & Sun, X. (2014). Weibo network, information diffusion and implications for collective action in China. *Information Communication and Society, 17*(1), 86–104.

Jiang, M., & Schlæger, J. (2014, August 6). How Weibo is changing local governance in China. *The Diplomat,* https://thediplomat.com/2014/2008/how-weibo-is-changing-local-governance-in-china/

Kan, M. (2010, September 1). China demands real names from mobile phone users. *PC World*, https://www.pcworld.com/article/502854/article-502708.html

Kobie, N. (2019, June 7). The complicated truth about China's social credit system. *Wired*, https://www.wired.com/story/china-social-credit-system-explained/

Lancaster University. (n.d.). Privacy-deprived e-commerce: The efficacy of consumer privacy policies on China's e-commerce websites from a legal perspective. https://eprints.lancs.ac.uk/id/eprint/146046/146041/Privacy_deprived_E_commerce_the_efficacy_of_customer_privacy_policies_on_China_s_E_commerce_websites_from_a_legal_perspective.pdf

Langer, A. I., Wang, H., & Duckett, J. (2025). Social media and policy change: The Chinese government's strategic policy responsiveness during the COVID-19 Pandemic. *Political Studies*. Advance online publication. DOI: 10.1177/00323217251345776

Lee, J.-A., & Liu, C.-Y. (2016). Real-name registration rules and the fading digital anonymity in China. *Washington International Law Journal, 26*(1), https://digitalcommons.law.uw.edu/wilj/vol25/iss21/23/

Li, J., & Rao, H. R. (2010). Twitter as a rapid response news service: An exploration in the context of the 2008 China earthquake. [EJISDC]. *The Electronic Journal on Information Systems in Developing Countries, 42*(4), 1–22.

Lin, J., Li, L., Yan, Y., & Turel, O. (2018, February). Understanding Chinese consumer engagement in social commerce: The roles of social support and swift guanxi. *Internet Research*, https://www.emerald.com/insight/content/doi/10.1108/intr-1111-2016-0349/full/html

Ma, Y. (2024, October 9). Social commerce in China - statistics & facts. *Statista*, https://www.statista.com/topics/6718/social-commerce-in-china/#topicOverview

MERCIS. (2022). China's social credit score untangling myth from reality. https://merics.org/en/comment/chinas-social-credit-score-untangling-myth-reality

Ming, C. (2017, March 16). FICO with Chinese characteristics: Nice rewards, but punishing penalties. *CNBC*, https://www.cnbc.com/2017/2003/2016/china-social-credit-system-ant-financials-sesame-credit-and-others-give-scores-that-go-beyond-fico.html

Naeem, M., Ozuem, W., Howell, K., & Ranfagni, S. (2023). A step-by-step process of thematic analysis to develop a conceptual model in qualitative research. *International Journal of Qualitative Methods*, *22*. Advance online publication. DOI: 10.1177/16094069231205789

Pal, L. A. (2005). Case study method and policy analysis. In Geva-May, I. (Ed.), *Thinking Like a Policy Analyst*. Palgrave Macmillan., DOI: 10.1057/9781403980939_12

Ramzy, A. (2011, February 21). State stamps out small "Jasmine" Protests in China. *Time*, https://content.time.com/time/world/article/0,8599,2052860,00.html

Rashid, Y., Rashid, A., & Waseem, A. (2019, July 24). Case study method: A step-by-step guide for business researchers. *International Journal of Qualitative Methods*. Advance online publication. DOI: 10.1177/1609406919862424

Research and Markets. (2025, May 8). China Social Commerce Intelligence Report 2025: Market to Reach $769 Billion by 2030, Driven by Platform Innovations, Strategic Partnerships, and Significant Investments. *GlobeNewswire*, https://www.globenewswire.com/news-release/2025/2005/2008/3077093/3028124/en/China-Social-Commerce-Intelligence-Report-3072025-Market-to-Reach-3077769-Billion-by-3072030-Driven-by-Platform-Innovations-Strategic-Partnerships-and-Significant-Investments.html

Sandoval, G. (2009, March 24). China bans YouTube, Chinese officials confirm that they are blocking the Web's largest video site but haven't disclosed the reason. *The Wall Street Journal*, https://www.cnet.com/news/wsj-china-bans-youtube/

Storm, D. (2015, October 7). ACLU: Orwellian citizen score, China's credit score system, is a warning for Americans. *ComputerWorld*, https://www.computerworld.com/article/1648895/aclu-orwellian-citizen-score-chinas-credit-score-system-is-a-warning-for-americans.html

Sullivan, J. (2012, September). A tale of two microblogs in China. *Media Culture & Society*, *34*(6), 773–783.

Sullivan, J. (2014, February). China's Weibo: Is it faster different? *New Media & Society*, *16*(1), 24–37.

The Economist. (2012, January 28). Unrest in China, A dangerous year, Economic conditions and social media are making protests more common in China—at a delicate time for the country's rulers. *The Economist*, https://www.economist.com/node/21543477

The New York Times. (n.d.). Baidu Inc. http://topics.nytimes.com/top/news/business/companies/baiducom-inc/index.html

Thomala, L. L. (2025a, February 26). Most popular social media in China Q3 2024. *Statista*, https://www.statista.com/statistics/250546/leading-social-network-sites-in-china/

Thomala, L. L. (2025b, March 18). Internet usage in China - statistics & facts. *Statista*, https://www.statista.com/topics/1179/internet-usage-in-china/

Tindall, R. (2021, September 6). China's move towards e-chops and real name verification. *China Britain Business Council*, https://www.cbbc.org/news-insights/chinas-move-towards-e-chops-and-real-name-verification

Voice of America. (2012, May 29). China's Sina Weibo unveils new censorship system. http://www.voatibetanenglish.com/content/chinas-sina-weibo-unveils-new-censorship-system-155335335/1267399.html

Wahl, S. T., McBride, M. C., & Schrodt, P. (2005). Becoming "point and click" parents: A case study of communication and online adoption. *Journal of Family Communication*, *5*(4), 279–294.

Wang, L.-Y., Hu, H.-H., Wang, L., & Qin, J.-Q. (2022, July). Privacy assurances and social sharing in social commerce: The mediating role of threat-coping appraisals. *Journal of Retailing and Consumer Services*, *67*, 103028. https://www.sciencedirect.com/science/article/abs/pii/S0969698922001217

Wang, Q. (2015, June 22). Alibaba in partnership with Luxembourg Consulate in Shanghai to issue credit-based visas. *KaproAsia*, https://www.kapronasia.com/china-payments-research-category/alibaba-in-partnership-with-luxembourg-consulate-in-shanghai-to-issue-credit-based-visas.html

Xinhua News Agency. (2017, October 2). Debt defaulter fined for flying first-class. https://archive.shine.cn/nation/Firstclass-result-as-debts-paid/

Yang, K. C. C., & Kang, Y. W. (2016). Real-name registration regulations in China: An examination of Chinese netizens' discussions about censorship, privacy, and political freedom. In Orwenjo, D. O., Oketch, O., & Tunde, A. H. (Eds.), *Political Discourse in Emerging, Fragile, and Failed Democracies* (pp. 61–87). IGI-Global Publisher.

Yang, Z. (2022, November 22). China just announced a new social credit law. Here's what it means. *MIT Technology Review*, https://www.technologyreview.com/2022/2011/2022/1063605/china-announced-a-new-social-credit-law-what-does-it-mean/

Youn, S. (2009). Determinants of online privacy concern and its influence on privacy protection behaviors among young adolescents. *The Journal of Consumer Affairs*, *43*(3), 389–418.

Zhao, Y. (2016, December 4). Wide-ranging credit rating system aims to make society more trusting. *Global Times*, https://www.ecns.cn/2016/2012-2005/236416.shtml

Zhou, X., Chan, Y.-Y., & Peng, Z.-M. (2008, October). Deliberativeness of online political discussion: A content analysis of the GuangZhou daily website. *Journalism Studies*, *9*(5), 759–770.

ADDITIONAL READING

Agence France-Presse in Beijing. (2014, April 17). Chinese blogger jailed under crackdown on 'internet rumours'. *The Guardian,* https://www.theguardian.com/world/2014/apr/2017/chinese-blogger-jailed-crackdown-internet-rumours-qin-zhihui

Anderlini, J. (2015, January 20). Chinese GDP growth lowest in 24 years. *Financial Times,* http://www.ft.com/cms/s/10/760621a760628-760629fcf-760611e760624-aa760689-700144feab760627de.html#axzz760623cfdVq760624Kt

Associated Press in Beijing. (2013, September 18). Shi Tao: China frees journalist jailed over yahoo emails. *The Guardian,* https://www.theguardian.com/world/2013/sep/2008/shi-tao-china-frees-yahoo

Biao, T. (2012). Rights defence (*weiquan*), microblogs (Weibo), and the surrounding gaze (*weiguan*). *China Perspectives*, *2012*(3), 29–41.

Bischoff, P. (2015, February 5). A brief history of China's campaign to enforce real-name registration online. *TechInAsia,* https://www.techinasia.com/history-chinas-campaign-enforce-realname-registration-online/?utm_source=Read+Next&utm_medium=web&utm_campaign=readnext-posts

Bondes, M., & Schucher, G. (2014). Derailed emotions: The transformation of claims and targets during the Wenzhou online incident. *Information Communication and Society*, *17*(1), 45–65.

Bradsher, K., & Mozur, P. (2014, September 21). China clamps down on web, pinching companies like Google. *New York Times,* https://www.nytimes.com/2014/2009/2022/business/international/china-clamps-down-on-web-pinching-companies-like-google.html

Buckley, C. (2013, September 10). Crackdown on bloggers is mounted by China. *The New York Times,* https://www.nytimes.com/2013/2009/2011/world/asia/china-cracks-down-on-online-opinion-makers.html

Chen, W.-H. (2014). Taking stock, moving forward: The Internet, social networks and civic engagement in Chinese societies. *Information Communication and Society*, *17*(1), 1–6.

Chinese Internet Network Information Center (CNNIC). (2014, July). *Statistical report on Internet development in China*. Beijing: Chinese Internet Network Information Center. http://www1.cnnic.cn/IDR/ReportDownloads/201411/P020141102574314897888.pdf

Deutsche Welle. (2015, April 17). EU, US condemn Chinese journalist Gao Yu's prison sentence. *Deutsche Welle,* http://www.dw.de/eu-us-condemn-chinese-journalist-gao-yus-prison-sentence/a-18390975

Dong, F. (2012). Controlling the internet in China: The real story. *Convergence (London)*, *18*(4), 403–425.

Ducketta, J., & Wang, H. (2013, October). Extending political participation in China: New opportunities for citizens in the policy process. *Journal of Asian Public Policy*, *6*(3), 263–276.

Endeshaw, A. (2004). Internet regulation in China: The never-ending cat and mouse game. *Information & Communications Technology Law*, *13*(1), 41–57.

Feng, B. (2010, June 14). China's Internet censorship system. https://www.hrichina.org/en/content/3244

Flemming, S. (2015, June 3, 2015). The state of Chinese social media in 2015: What you need to know. *AdAge.com Magazine,* https://adage.com/article/guest-columnists/hold/298829/?utm_source=daily_email&utm_medium=newsletter&utm_campaign=adage&ttl=1433911133

Foucault, M. (1995). *Discipline & punish: The birth of the prison.* Vintage Books.

Frizell, S. (June 4, 2014). Here are 6 huge websites China is censoring right now. *Time,* https://time.com/2820452/china-censor-web/

Fu, K.-W., Chan, C., & Chau, M. (2013). Assessing censorship on microblogs in China: Discriminatory keyword analysis and impact evaluation of the 'real name registration' policy. *IEEE Internet Computing, 17*(3), 42–50.

Fukuyama, F. (2012). Interview with Francis Fukuyama (by with AFP Geopolitics Editor Marlowe Hood). https://www.afp.com/en/node/592898/

Fung, E., & Orlik, T. (2012, December 5). China tackles land grabs, key source of rural anger. *The Wall Street Journal,* https://www.wsj.com/articles/SB10001424127887324640104578160931049622330

Garrett, R. K. (2006). Protest in an information society: A review of literature on social movements and new ICTs. *Information Communication and Society, 9*(2), 202–224.

Göbel, C., & Ong, L. H. (2012). *Social unrest in China.* ECRAN: Europe China Research and Advice Network.

Gough, N. (2013, September 7). Chinese democracy advocate is freed after 8 years in prison. *The New York Times,* https://www.nytimes.com/2013/2009/2008/world/asia/shi-tao-chinese-democracy-advocate-is-released-from-prison.html?_r=2010

Herold, D. K., & Marolt, P. (Eds.). (2013). *Online society in China: Creating, celebrating, and instrumentalising the online carnival.* Routledge.

Huang, R., & Sun, X. (2014). Weibo network, information diffusion and implications for collective action in China. *Information Communication and Society, 17*(1), 86–104.

Human Rights in China. (2014, August 12). *China issues new regulations on mobile text and voice messaging services* (HRIC translation). Human Rights in China, https://www.hrichina.org/en/press-work/hric-bulletin/china-issues-new-regulations-mobile-text-and-voice-messaging-services-hric

Jacobson, T. (2008). Harmonious society, civil society and the media: A communicative action perspective. *China Media Research*, *4*(4), 31–38.

Jiang, M., & Schlæger, J. (2014, August 6). How Weibo is changing local governance in China. *The Diplomat,* https://thediplomat.com/2014/2008/how-weibo-is-changing-local-governance-in-china/

Jiang, S. (2015, April 17). China jails prominent journalist Gao Yu for leaking state secrets, https://www.cnn.com/2015/2004/2017/asia/china-gao-yu-jail/

Lapitskiy, I. (2015). China GDP growth forecast 2013-2015 and up to 2060, data and charts. http://cn.knoema.com/loqqwx/china-gdp-growth-forecast-2013-2015-and-up-to-2060-data-and-charts

Levin, D. (2014, June 2). China escalating attack on Google. *New York Times,* https://www.nytimes.com/2014/2006/2003/business/chinas-battle-against-google-heats-up.html

Li, J., & Rao, H. R. (2010). Twitter as a rapid response news service: An exploration in the context of the 2008 China earthquake. [EJISDC]. *The Electronic Journal on Information Systems in Developing Countries*, *42*(4), 1–22.

Li, N. (2009, March/April). Amid economic crisis, Beijing extends its legal and security arms to handle social instability. *ChinaScope*, 18-19.

Lubman, S. (2013, August 27). Document No.9: The party attacks western democratic ideals. *China Real Time Report,* http://blogs.wsj.com/chinarealtime/2013/2008/2027/document-no-2019-the-party-attacks-western-democratic-ideals/

MacKinnon, R. (2008). Flatter World and thicker walls? Blogs, censorship and civic discourse in China. *Public Choice*, *134*, 31–46.

Martinsons, M. G. (2005, April). The internet enlightens and empowers Chinese society. *Communications of the ACM*, *48*(4), 59–60.

Martinsons, M. G., Ng, S., Wong, W., & Yuen, R. (2005). State censorship of the Internet in China. *Communications of the ACM*, •••, 67.

Mbaku, J. M., & Yu, Z. (2013, March). Information communication technologies, transparency, and governance in China. *International Journal on World Peace*, *15*(1), 9–59.

Mbaku, J. M., & Yu, Z. (2013, March). Information communication technologies, transparency, and governance in China. *International Journal on World Peace*, *15*(1), 9–59.

O'Reilly, B. P. (2015, February 26). The implications of China's growth slowdown. *The Diplomat,* https://thediplomat.com/2015/2002/the-implications-of-chinas-growth-slowdown/

Orlik, T. (2011, September 26). Unrest grows as economy booms. *The Wall Street Journal,* https://www.wsj.com/articles/SB10001424053111903703604576587070600504108

Rayburn, J. M., & Conrad, C. (2004, December). China's internet structure: Problems and control measures. *International Journal of Management, 21*(4), 471–480.

Rodriguez, K. (2011, January). *Freedom of expression, privacy and anonymity on the Internet: Comments submitted to the United Nations special rapporteur on the promotion and protection of the right to freedom of opinion and expression.* San Francisco, CA: Electronic Frontier Foundation, https://www.eff.org/files/filenode/unspecialrapporteurfoe2011-final_3.pdf

Rudolph, J. (2015, January 13). 50 websites and WeChat accounts shut down. *China Digital Times,* https://chinadigitaltimes.net/2015/01/china-shuts-50-websites-social-media-accounts/

Sha, L. (2012, June 12). Environmental NGOs grow across China but still struggle for support. *The Global Times,* http://www.globaltimes.cn/content/714330.shtml

Strether, L. (2013, July 28). Global political risk: China "social unrest" numbers, the Chengguan and the watermelon seller, and the economic slowdown. https://www.nakedcapitalism.com/2013/07/some-datapoints-on-global-political-risk-3.html

Svensson, M. (2014). Voice, power and connectivity in China's microblogosphere: Digital divides on Sina Weibo. *China Information = Zhongguo Qing Bao, 28*(2), 168–188.

Tai, Z. (2007). *The Internet in China: Cyberspace and civil society* (1st ed.). Routledge.

The Liberty Times. (2015, June 4). Poster criticizing government's censorship of Yangtze cruise incident. https://news.ltn.com.tw/news/world/breakingnews/1339124

The World Bank. (2007). *Cost of pollution in China: Economic estimates of physical damage.* Washington, D.C.: Rural Development, Natural Resources and Environment Management Unit, East Asia and Pacific Region. http://www-wds.worldbank.org/external/default/WDSContentServer/WDSP/IB/2007/03/30/000090341_20070330141612/Rendered/PDF/392360CHA0Cost1of1Pollution01PUBLIC1.pdf

The World Bank, (2012). *China 2030: Building a modern, Harmonious, and creative high-income society*. International Bank for Reconstruction and Development & International Development Association or the World Bank.

The World Bank. (2015). *GDP growth (Annual %)*. https://data.worldbank.org/indicator/NY.GDP.MKTP.KD.ZG

Tibetan Review. (2009, July). PC sold in China from July 1 to be censorship-enabled. *Tibetan Review,* 30-31.

Tong, J., & Zuo, L. (2014). Weibo communication and government legitimacy in China: A computer-assisted analysis of Weibo messages on two "mass incidents.". *Information Communication and Society, 17*(1), 66–85.

Wang, H. (2011). *Protecting privacy in China: A research on China's privacy standards and the possibility of establishing the right to privacy and the information privacy protection legislation in modern China*. Springer.

Wong, B. (2003). A matter of trust: The internet and social change in China. *China Rights Forum, 3*, 41-43.

Yang, T. (2015). *Environmental problems in China*. Washington, D.C.: World Wide Fund for Nature (WWF). http://wwf.panda.org/who_we_are/wwf_offices/china/environmental_problems_china/

Yang, Y. (2014). *A new normal, but with robust growth: China's growth prospects in the next 10 years.* Paper presented at the THINK TANK 20: Growth, Convergence and Income Distribution: The Road from the Brisbane G-20 Summit, Brisbane, Australia. https://www.brookings.edu/~/media/Research/Files/Interactives/2014/thinktank20/chapters/tt20%20china%20growth%20prospects%20yao.pdf

Yao, Y. (2014, November). *A new normal, but with robust growth: China's growth prospects in the next 10 years.* Paper presented at the Think Tank 20: Growth, Convergence and Income Distribution: The Road from the Brisbane G-20 Summit, Washington, DC.

Yin, J. (2015, June). Social media and multinational corporations' corporate social responsibility in China: The case of ConocoPhillips Oil Spill Incident. *Professional Communication, IEEE Transactions on, 58*(2), 135-153.

Yu, M. (2015, June 11). The Chinese government's sinking credibility. *The Washington Times,* https://www.washingtontimes.com/news/2015/jun/2011/chinas-governments-credibility-sunk-over-yangtze-r/

Zhou, X., Chan, Y.-Y., & Peng, Z.-M. (2008, October). Deliberativeness of online political discussion: A content analysis of the GuangZhou daily website. *Journalism Studies*, *9*(5), 759–770.

Zhou, Y. M. (2006). *Historicizing online politics: Telegraphy, the Internet, and political participation in China*. Stanford University Press.

Zhu, X. (2012). Understanding China's growth: Past, present, and future. *The Journal of Economic Perspectives*, *26*(4), 103–124.

KEY TERMS AND DEFINITIONS

Anonymity: It refers to the state of being unknown, unrecognizable, and unacknowledged, where a person's real identity is concealed and their personal information is not disclosed to the public. An example of anonymity is that an individual's identity is protected by law when they vote freely. Some emerging legal frameworks to protect individual privacy include GDPR and CCPA.

Civil Society: The World Bank defined "civil society" as a term to refer to a variety of not-for-profit and non-governmental organizations or institutions (such as NPOs or NGOs) that facilitate the expression of the interests and values of the public as well as their members for cultural, ethical, political, philanthropic, scientific, and religious considerations. With the aim of social change, civil society organizations encompass a range of entities, including charitable organizations, community groups, faith-based organizations, foundations, labor unions, non-governmental organizations (NGOs), institutions, and professional associations.

Chinese Internet Network Information Center: Also known as CNNIC, it is the national center of service and administration organization responsible for regulating China's national information network in the public interest. CNNIC was established on June 3, 1997, to monitor and oversee the Internet infrastructure and ICT sectors in China. Additionally, CNNIC also provides research data and consultation to guide China's emerging ICT sectors. The center serves as an essential administrator, constructor, operator, and research branch of China's Internet infrastructure.

Chinese Jasmine Revolution: Also known as *the 2011 Chinese Pro-Democracy Protests, the Chinese Jasmine Revolution was a taboo term in China's* search engines and social network sites. As a civil rights and social movement organized and mobilized through Weibo to launch protests simultaneously in 13 major cities in China on February 20, 2011, the defunct Chinese Jasmine Revolution did not lead to widespread protests in China, despite garnering media attention and interest from the international community. After the mass incident, a large number of dissidents were arrested and detained by public security officers without due process.

China's Great Firewall: A content censorship and filtering mechanism that was designed, implemented, and launched by the Chinese government to facilitate the censorship of the Internet and social media platforms. Combined with other censorship mechanisms, the Golden Shield Project and the Green Dam Youth Escort Software program construct a metaphorical "wall" in China's borders in digital cyberspace.

Content Filtering Mechanisms: Censorship practices (either in hardware or software) that filter or block "inappropriate" and "sensitive" Internet content before it reaches users' end. The mechanisms function as a shield between the Internet and other service providers to block materials that are deemed "objectionable," "politically sensitive," and "undesirable."

Information and Communication Technologies (ICTs): Also abbreviated as ICTs, this popular term is commonly used as an umbrella to cover all communication devices, technologies, and their applications for creating, storing, and transmitting information. As a phenomenon of contemporary human experience, ICTs impact various dimensions of modern society, encompassing business and commerce, education, entertainment, politics, and other areas.

Internet Service Provider (ISP): Often abbreviated as ISP, this term gained popularity in the late 1980s and early 1990s and is commonly referred to as a company that provides Internet services to users through various platforms, including wired and wireless connections, such as cable, coaxial cable, fiber optic, and satellite.

Ministry of Industry and Information Technology (MIIT): A high-level state agency organization that was established in March 2008 under the State Council of the People's Republic of China (PRC) to regulate and develop the broadcasting, communication, digital media, postal service, Internet, social media, software, and mobile/wireless technologies.

Public Sphere: Developed by the renowned German sociologist Jürgen Habermas, who defined the concept of public sphere as "a realm of our social life in which something approaching public opinion can be formed" (p. 49). Known as "Öffentlichkeit" in German, Habermas's conceptualization of the public sphere emphasizes the importance of free and uncensored access to all citizens, enabling them to discuss and debate public affairs and thereby transform themselves from private individuals into a public body. The public sphere is considered an essential component of a modern democratic society; the concept was widely used in the study of new ICTs and has been extended to study phenomena in cyberspace.

Real Name Registration Regime: Also known as "real name authentication" in China, it is a regulatory regime that requires all information service providers and internet content providers to obtain the identity and personal information of their customers. This regulatory regime aims to eliminate possible anonymity in cyberspace, ensuring accountability, traceability, and prosecutability of individual users in China.

Social Media: Defined by Andreas Kaplan and Michael Haenlein (2010) as "a group of Internet-based applications that build on the ideological and technological foundations of Web 2.0, and that allow the creation and exchange of user-generated content." The social media ecosystem encompasses a diverse range of electronic communication platforms that facilitate the aggregation, creation, and sharing of information. The social media platforms range from collaborative projects (such as Wikipedia) to microblogs and blogs, content platforms (like YouTube), social networking services (like Facebook), virtual games, and virtual social life (such as *Second Life*).

Weibo **(Microblog):** Written as " " in Chinese, or *Weibo*, meaning microblog in English, is a Chinese version of then, Twitter (now, X), characterized by short and frequent user-generated posts. This social media platform was created by *Sinanet* in 2009. The Chinese microblog website, equivalent to Twitter (or X), is completely banned in China.

Compilation of References

Abbate, J. (2017). What and where is the Internet? (Re)defining Internet histories. *Internet Histories*, *1*(1–2), 8–14. DOI: 10.1080/24701475.2017.1305836

Abdulganiyu, O.H., Tchakoucht, T.A., Saheed, Y.K. (2023). A systematic literature review for network intrusion detection system (IDS). *International Journal of Information Security.*

Abdulkareem, H. K. K., Jimoh, S. O., Nofiu, T. T., & Akande, R. S. (2024). Leaving No One Behind: Examining the effect of financial, gender, and digital inclusion on sustainable development. *Sustainable Development*, *33*(2), 2519–2534. DOI: 10.1002/sd.3245

Abdullahi, M., Baashar, Y., Alhussian, H., Alwadain, A., Aziz N., Capretz, L.F. (2022). Detecting cybersecurity attacks in Internet of Things using artificial intelligence methods: A systematic literature review. *Electronics (Basel).*

Adetomiwa, F. (2021). Artificial intelligence and human rights. SSRN *Electronic Journal*. https://doi.org/DOI: 10.2139/ssrn.3964199

Afet ve Acil Durum Yönetimi Başkanlığı (AFAD). (2023). *Kahramanmaraş'ta Meydana Gelen Depremler Hk.*https://www.afad.gov.tr/kahramanmarasta-meydana-gelen-depremler-hk-36

African Union Commission. (2020). Digital transformation strategy for Africa (2020–2030). African Union. https://au.int/en/documents

Ağca, M. E. (2024). A study of disinformation on social media during disasters: The case of the dam burst. *Contemporary Issues of Communication*, *3*(1), 41–50. DOI: 10.5281/zenodo.10778108

Ağca, M. E. (2025). *Bilim iletişimi: Antik Uygarlıklardan Yapay Zeka Çağına.* Kriter Yayınevi.

Ahishakiye, D., & Nizeyimana, P. (2024). Enhancing digital literacy performance in Rwanda using machine learning: A case study of Irembo. *Journal of Intelligent Learning Systems and Applications*, *16*(04), 430–447. DOI: 10.4236/jilsa.2024.164022

Ahmad, N., Ali, A. W., & bin Yussof, M. H. B. (2025). The Challenges of Human Rights in the Era of Artificial Intelligence. *UUM Journal of Legal Studies, 16*(1), 150-169.

Akyıldız, M. (2023). Yalan Haber ve Dezenformasyonun Sosyal Medyada Yayılımı: Kahramanmaraş Depreminin Haarp Silahı Olduğu İddiası. *Türkiye Medya Akademisi Dergisi*, *3*(6), 523–543. DOI: 10.5281/zenodo.8378837

Alazab, M., Soman, K. P., Srinivasan, S., Venkatraman, S., & Pham, V. Q. (2023). Deep learning for cyber security applications: A comprehensive survey. *Authorea Preprints.*

Al-Billeh, T., Hmaidan, R., Al-Hammouri, A., & Makhmari, M. A. (2024). The risks of using artificial intelligence on privacy and human rights: Unifying global standards. *Jurnal Media Hukum*, *31*(2), 333–350.

Albris, K., Fast, K., Karlsen, F., Kaun, A., Lomborg, S., & Syvertsen, T. (2024). The Digital Backlash and the Paradoxes of Disconnection: An Overview

Alhassan, M. D., & Adam, I. O. (2024). Digital inclusion and sustainable development goals. *Journal of Science and Technology Policy Management*. https://doi.org/DOI: 10.1108/jstpm-09-2023-0152

Allcott, H., & Gentzkow, M. (2017). Social Media and Fake News in the 2016 Election. *The Journal of Economic Perspectives*, *31*(2), 211–236.

Alsamiri, J., & Alsubhi, K. (2019). Internet of Things Cyber Attacks Detection using Machine Learning [IJACSA]. *International Journal of Advanced Computer Science and Applications*, *10*(12), •••.

Altay, S., Berriche, M., & Acerbi, A. (2023). Misinformation on misinformation: Conceptual and methodological challenges. *Social Media + Society*, *9*(1). Advance online publication. DOI: 10.1177/20563051221150412

Amelicheva, L., Martyniuk, O., Pyroha, I., Qaracayev, C., & Myroshnychenko, V. (2021). Implementation of Constitutional Human Rights and Social Guarantees of Security in the Context of Digitalization. *Amazonia Investiga*, 10(45), 265-271. https://amazoniainvestiga.info/check/45/26-265-271.pdf

Amnesty International. (2023). Meta's dangerous algorithmic amplification in Ethiopia. Amnesty International. https://www.amnesty.org

Amnesty International. (2023, April 5). *Türkiye: Deprem bölgesinde polis ve jandarma ihlalleri - İşkence ve diğer türde kötü muamele yapıldı, şiddetli saldırılar önlenmedi.* https://www.amnesty.org.tr/icerik/turkiye-deprem-bolgesinde-polis-ve-jandarma-ihlalleri-iskence-ve-diger-turde-kötü-muamele-yapildi-siddetli-saldirilar-onlenmedi

Andersen, J., & Søe, S. O. (2019). Communicative actions we live by: The problem with fact-checking, tagging or flagging fake news – the case of Facebook. *European Journal of Communication, 35*(2), 126–139. DOI: 10.1177/0267323119894489

Arora, A., Chakraborty, P., & Bhatia, M. P. S. (2021). Problematic Use of Digital Technologies and Its Impact on Mental Health During COVID-19 Pandemic: Assessment Using Machine Learning. *Emerging Technologies During the Era of COVID-19 Pandemic pp.197-221*

ARTICLE 19. (2022). Content moderation and freedom of expression in Africa. ARTICLE 19. https://www.article19.org

Aslan, Ö., Aktuğ, S. S., Ozkan-Okay, M., Yilmaz, A. A., & Akin, E. (2023). A Comprehensive Review of Cyber Security Vulnerabilities, Threats, Attacks, and Solutions. *Electronics (Basel).*

Australian Human Rights Commission. (2025). Artificial intelligence and human rights. https://humanrights.gov.au

AVPN. (2024). *Harnessing the Power of Digital Technologies for Climate Adaptation in Asia-Pacific.* Asia Venture Philanthropy Network.

Avtalion, Z., Aviv, I., Hadar, I., Luria, G., & Bar-Gil, O. (2024). Digital infrastructure as a new organizational digital climate dimension. *Applied Sciences (Basel, Switzerland), 14*(19), 8592. DOI: 10.3390/app14198592

Ayhan, D. (2023, February 8). *Twitter'a 9,5 saat erişim engeli....* Sözcü. https://www.sozcu.com.tr/twitter-ve-tiktoka-erisim-engellendi-wp7584907

Aziz, L. A. R., & Andriansyah, Y. (2023). The Role Artificial Intelligence in Modern Banking: An Exploration of AI-Driven Approaches for Enhanced Fraud Prevention, Risk Management, and Regulatory Compliance. *Reviews of Contemporary Business Analytics, 6*(1), 110–132.

Babuta, A., Oswald, M., & Rinik, C. (2018). Machine Learning Algorithms and Police Decision-Making: Legal, Ethical, and Regulatory Challenges. *Whitehall Report 3-18.* https://researchportal.northumbria.ac.uk/ws/portalfiles/portal/21461394/Babuta_et_al_Machine_Learning_Algorithms_and_Police_Decision_Making_OA.pdf

Bag, A., Sharma, P., Khare, P., & Roy, S. (2024). Decentralized Data and Privacy: Exploring the Conflict Between Distributed Ledger Technology and the Right to Be Forgotten Under GDP. *IGI Global Scientific Publishing*, 74-104. https://doi.org/ DOI: 10.4018/979-8-3693-0472-3.ch006

Baker, D. J., & Robinson, P. H. (Eds.). (2020). *Artificial Intelligence and the Law: Cybercrime and Criminal Liability*. Routledge.

Banaji, S., & Bhat, R. (2022). *Social media and political misinformation in India and Brazil*. Routledge.

Bandara, R., Fernando, M., & Akter, S. (2020). Privacy concerns in E-commerce: A taxonomy and a future research agenda. *Electronic Markets*, *30*, 629–647. 610.1007/s12525-12019-00375-12526

Banisar, D. (2009). *ICT policies relating to privacy, freedom of expression and access to information: A briefing paper*. Human Rights and Peace Centre, Makerere University.

Bao, Y., Hilary, G., & Ke, B. (2022). Artificial intelligence and fraud detection. *Innovative Technology at the Interface of Finance and Operations*, *I*, 223–247.

Barocas, S., Hardt, M., & Narayanan, A. (2023). *Fairness and machine learning: Limitations and opportunities*. MIT Press.

Batool, A., Zowghi, D., & Bano, M. (2025). AI governance: A systematic literature review. *AI and Ethics*, *5*(3), 3265–3279. DOI: 10.1007/s43681-024-00653-w

Batta, H., Udousoro, N., & Abubakar, Y. (2015). Digital health technologies and implications for developing country media and health communication.

Bauman, Z., Bigo, D., Esteves, P., Guild, E., Jabri, V., Lyon, D., & Walker, R. B. J. (2014). After Snowden: Rethinking the impact of surveillance. *International Political Sociology*, *8*(2), 121–144. DOI: 10.1111/ips.12048

Baumüller, H. (2018). The little we know: An exploratory literature review on the utility of mobile phone-enabled services for smallholder farmers. *Journal of International Development*, *30*(1), 134–154.

BBC. (2022, August 11). Kenya elections: Disinformation campaigns flood social media. BBC News. https://www.bbc.com

Belyanskaya, O. V., Kazanovskaya, J. A., & Strutinskaya, T. A. (2022). Updating Human Rights and Freedoms in a Digitalized Society. In E.G. Popkova (Ed.), *Business 4.0 as a Subject of the Digital Economy: Advances in Science, Technology, & Innovation* (PP. 225-228). Springer. https://link.springer.com/chapter/10.1007/978-3-030-90324-4_37

Berners-Lee, T. (2019, November 24). I invented the World Wide Web. Here's how we can fix it. The New York Times. https://www.nytimes.com

Bianet. (2023, April 6). *Karaismailoğlu, "Depremde İnterneti kestik çünkü gerekliydi" dedi, nedenini açıklayamadı.* https://bianet.org/haber/karaismailoglu-depremde-interneti-kestik-cunku-gerekliydi-dedi-nedenini-aciklayamadi-276943

Bignami, F., & Resta, G. (2018). Human rights extraterritoriality: The right to privacy and national security surveillance. In E. Benvenisti & G. Nolte (Eds.), *Community interests across international law* (Forthcoming). Oxford University Press. GWU Law School Public Law Research Paper No. 2017-67; GWU Legal Studies Research Paper No. 2017-67. https://ssrn.com/abstract=3043771

Bilton, R. (2017). *Why don't people trust the news and social media? A new report lets them explain in their own words.* Niemanlab. https://www.niemanlab.org/2017/11/why-dont-people-trust-the-news-and-social-media-a-new-report-lets-them-explain-in-their-own-words/

Bin, R. A., & Kausik, M. A. K. (2024). *AI revolutionizing industries worldwide: A comprehensive overview of its diverse applications* (Vol. 7). Hybrid Advances.

Bischoff, P. (2015, February 5). A brief history of China's campaign to enforce real-name registration online. *TechInAsia,* https://www.techinasia.com/history-chinas-campaign-enforce-realname-registration-online/?utm_source=Read+Next&utm_medium=web&utm_campaign=readnext-posts

Blanc, S. (2015, June 4). China's propaganda machine is in overdrive after a cruise ship disaster that's left hundreds missing. *Business Insider,* http://www.businessinsider.com/afp-propaganda-machine-in-overdrive-for-china-shipwreck-2015-6#ixzz3caNWpED0

BMWK. (n.d.). Energiewende and Digitalization. Bundesministerium für Wirtschaft und Klimaschutz. https://www.bmwk.de/EN/Themen/Energy/Energiewende/energiewende.html

Bochkov, A. A. (2019). Modern State and Law in the Context of Digital Reality. *Law, Economics. Psychology (Irvine, Calif.), 1*(13), 3–9. https://rep.vsu.by/handle/123456789/17978

Bonini, T., & Treré, E. (2024). *Algorithms of resistance: The everyday fight against platform power*. The MIT Press.

Borges do Nascimento, I. J., Pizarro, A. B., Almeida, J. M., Azzopardi-Muscat, N., Gonçalves, M. A., Björklund, M., & Novillo-Ortiz, D. (2022). Infodemics and health misinformation: A systematic review of reviews. *Bulletin of the World Health Organization, 100*(9), 544–561. DOI: 10.2471/BLT.21.287654

Botan, M. (2023, April 23). *Tam 77 gün oldu: Depremlerden sonra hızla yayılan yağma haberleri fikri takip bekliyor*. Journo. https://journo.com.tr/deprem-yagma-haberleri

Boztepe Taşkıran, H. (2023). Afet İletişimi Nedir, Ne Değildir? *Yeni Medya*, (14), 359–363.

Branwyn, G. (1997). *Jamming the media: A citizen's guide; reclaiming the tools of communication*. Chronicle Books.

Braun, V., & Clarke, V. (2023). Toward good practice in thematic analysis: Avoiding common problems and be(com)ing a knowing researcher. *International Journal of Transgender Health, 24*(1), 1–6. DOI: 10.1080/26895269.26892022.22129597 PMID: 36713144

Brennen, J. S., & Kreiss, D. (2016). Digitalization. In *The International Encyclopedia of Communication Theory and Philosophy* (pp. 1-11). https://onlinelibrary.wiley.com/doi/epdf/10.1002/9781118766804.wbiect111

Bruns, A., Angus, D., Hurcombe, E., Harrington, S., & Tan, J. (2022). The dissemination of problematic news on Facebook: A large-scale, longitudinal study. *Digital Journalism (Abingdon, England), 10*(10), 1275–1299. DOI: 10.1177/20563051231196880

Bucher, T. (2020). Nothing to disconnect from? Being singular plural in an age of machine learning. *Media Culture & Society, 42*(4), 610–617.

Bucher, T., & Helmond, A. (2018). The affordances of social media platforms. In *The SAGE handbook of social media*. SAGE Publications Ltd., https://hdl.handle.net/11245.1/149a9089-49a4-454c-b935-a6ea7f2d8986

Bunce, M. (2019). Humanitarian communication in a post-truth world. *Journal of Humanitarian Affairs, 1*(1), 49–58. DOI: 10.7227/JHA.007

Burkell, J., Fortier, A., Yeung, L. L., Wong, C., & Simpson, J. L. (2014). Facebook: Public space, or private space? *Information Communication and Society, 17*(8), 974–985.

Büyük, G. (2023, February 11). *Ailesine ilaç götüren gençleri yağmacı diyerek linç ettiler*. Aydınlık. https://www.aydinlik.com.tr/haber/ailesine-ilac-goturen-gencleri-yagmaci-diyerek-linc-ettiler-367295

Cadwalladr, C., & Graham-Harrison, E. (2018). *Revealed: 50 million Facebook profiles harvested for Cambridge Analytica in major data breach*. The Guardian

Çakı, F. (2020). Afet Yönetişiminde Sivil Toplum ve Güven Algıları. [SKAD]. *Sosyal Ve Kültürel Araştırmalar Dergisi*, *6*(12), 1–45. DOI: 10.25306/skad.720617

Çakır, O. (2023, February 8). *Twitter erişimi neden kısıtlandı? Açıklama geldi*. Shiftdelete.net. https://shiftdelete.net/twitter-erisimi-neden-engellendi-resmi-aciklama

Calzada, I. (2022). Citizens' data privacy in China: The state of the art of the Personal Information Protection Law (PIPL). *Smart Cities*, *5*(3), 1129–1150. DOI: 10.3390/smartcities5030058

Camara, M. S. (2008). Media, civil society, and political culture in West Africa.

Cao, L., Yang, Q., & Yu, P. S. (2021). Data science and AI in FinTech: An overview. *International Journal of Data Science and Analytics*, *12*, 81–99.

Caragliano, D. (2013, March 26). Why China's 'real name' internet policy doesn't work. https://www.theatlantic.com/china/archive/2013/03/why-chinas-real-name-internet-policy-doesnt-work/274373/

Carah, N., & Brodmerkel, S. (2022). Regulating platforms' algorithmic brand culture: The instructive case of alcohol marketers on social media. In Flew, T., & Martin, F. R. (Eds.), *Digital platform regulation* (pp. 111–130). Springer International Publishing., DOI: 10.1007/978-3-030-95220-4_6

CarbonCredits.com. (2025). Are Nature-Based Solutions and Blockchain the Future of Carbon Credits?

Carsten, P. (2015, February 4). China to ban online impersonation accounts, enforce real-name registration. *Reuters*, https://www.reuters.com/article/2015/2002/2004/us-china-internet-censorship-idUSKBN2010L2080ZF20150204

Castro, C. A. D., O'Reilly, I., & Carthy, A. (2022). The evolution of the Internet and social media: A literature review. *International Journal of E-Education, e-Business, e-. Management Learning*, *12*(1), 30–41. DOI: 10.17706/ijeeee.2022.12.1.30-41

Centre for Law and Democracy. (2021). *Report of the Special Rapporteur on the promotion and protection of the right to freedom of opinion and expression*. https://undocs.org/A/HRC/35/22

Çetindemir, Ç. (2023, February 6). *Depremlerin Boğaz'daki ABD savaş gemisiyle alakalı olduğu" iddiası*. Anadolu Ajansı. https://www.aa.com.tr/tr/teyithatti/aktuel/depremlerin-bogazdaki-abd-savas-gemisiyle-alakali-oldugu-iddiasi/1815311

CFI. (n.d.). Mobile Banking. https://corporatefinanceinstitute.com/resources/wealth-management/mobile-banking/

Chalapath, R., & Chawla, S. (2019). Deep Learning for Anomaly Detection. *Survey (London, England).*

Chen, Z., Van Khoa, L. D., Teoh, E. N., Nazir, A., Karuppiah, E. K., & Lam, K. S. (2018). Machine learning techniques for anti-money laundering (AML) solutions in suspicious transaction detection: A review. *Knowledge and Information Systems, 57*, 245–285.

Chibita, M. B. (2016). Digital activism in Uganda. In Chibita, M. B. (Ed.), *Digital activism in the social media era* (pp. 119–136). Springer., DOI: 10.1007/978-3-319-40949-2_7

Chin, J. (2015, February 4). China is requiring people to register their real names for some internet services. *The Wall Street Journal,* https://www.wsj.com/articles/china-to-enforce-real-name-registration-for-internet-users-1423033973

Chirkov, D., Plohih, G., Kapustina, D., & Vasyukov, V. (2022). Opportunities for Using Digital Data in Evidence for Criminal Cases. *Revista Juridica*, 4(71), 364-380. https://revista.unicuritiba.edu.br/index.php/RevJur/article/view/5782/0

Chithaluru, P., AL-Turjman, F., Kumar, M., Stephan, T. (2023). Computational-Intelligence-Inspired Adaptive Opportunistic Clustering Approach for Industrial IoT Networks. *IEEE Internet of Things Journal.*

Çınarlı, İ. (2016). *Örnek vaka analizleri ile kriz iletişimi.* Beta Yayıncılık.

CIPESA. (2021). State of internet freedom in Africa 2021: The impact of COVID-19 on digital rights in Africa. Collaboration on International ICT Policy for East and Southern Africa. https://cipesa.org

Cobelli, N., & Chiarini, A. (2020). Improving Customer Satisfaction and Loyalty through m-Health Service Digitalization: New Challenges for Italian Pharmacists. *The TQM Journal*, *32*(6), 1541–1560. https://www.emerald.com/insight/content/doi/10.1108/tqm-10-2019-0252/full/html

Cohen, J. E. (2013). WHAT PRIVACY IS FOR. *Harvard Law Review*, *126*(7), 1904–1933. https://www.jstor.org/stable/23415061

Cooke, J. (2024). WPIC Perspectives: Exploring social commerce's impact on China's e-commerce sphere. *AmCham China Quarterly Magazine*, https://www.amchamchina.org/wpic-perspectives-exploring-social-commerces-impact-on-chinas-e-commerce-sphere/

Coombs, W. T. (2019). Crisis Communication. In J. Gephart, C. C. Miller, & K. S. Helgesson (Eds.), *The Routledge Companion to Risk, Crisis and Emergency Management.*[2]

Coombs, W. T. (2014). *Ongoing crisis communication: Planning, managing, and responding* (4th ed.). Sage Publications.

Council of Europe. (1950, November 4). European Convention for the Protection of Human Rights and Fundamental Freedoms, as amended by Protocols Nos. 11 and 14, ETS 5.

Council on Foreign Relations. (2022). *Ethiopia's Tigray conflict: Disinformation and social media*. CFR.

Creemers, R. (2018). *China's Social Credit System: An Evolving Practice of Control.* MERICS.

Cuervo-Cazurra, A., Dieleman, M., Hirsch, P., Rodrigues, S. B., & Zyglidopoulos, S. (2021). Multinationals' misbehavior. *Journal of World Business*, *56*(5), 101244. DOI: 10.1016/j.jwb.2021.101244

Cumhuriyet. (2023, February 7). *NTV canlı yayında arka plandaki depremzedelerin seslerini kestiler.* https://www.cumhuriyet.com.tr/turkiye/ntv-canli-yayinda-arka-planda-depremzedelerin-seslerini-kestiler-2049207

Cunningham, S., & Craig, D. (2021). *Creator culture*. New York University Press.

Custer, C. (2015, January 14). Real-name system coming to Weibo, Tieba, and other Chinese websites (for real this time). *TechInAsia,* https://www.techinasia.com/realname-system-coming-weibo-tieba-chinese-websites/

D'Alessio, F. A. (2021). *Computational propaganda: Challenges and responses*. Academia Letters., DOI: 10.20935/AL3468

D'Arma, A., Aslama Horowitz, M., Lehtisaari, K., & Nieminen, H. (2024). Introduction: The epistemic turn. In Aslama Horowitz, M., Nieminen, H., Lehtisaari, K., & D'Arma, A. (Eds.), *Epistemic rights in the era of digital disruption* (pp. 3–9). Springer International Publishing., DOI: 10.1007/978-3-031-45976-4_1

Dakroury, A. I., & Birdsall, W. F. (2008). Blogs and the right to communicate: Towards creating a space-less public sphere? In *2008 IEEE International Symposium on Technology and Society* (pp. 1–8). https://doi.org/DOI: 10.1109/ISTAS.2008.4559762

Dalje.com. (2015, June 3). Chinese authorities censor questions about the Yangtze ship sinking. http://dalje.com/en-world/chinese-authorities-censor-questions-about-yangtze-ship-sinking/546073

Dash, B., Sharma, P., & Ali, A. (2022). Federated learning for privacy-preserving: A review of PII data analysis in Fintech. [IJSEA]. *International Journal of Software Engineering and Its Applications*, *13*(4).

Dastyari, A., & Jose, C. (2024). Achieving inclusive and equitable quality education for all: The importance of digital inclusion. *Alternative Law Journal*, *49*(4), 282–287. DOI: 10.1177/1037969x241295798

daxueconsulting.com. (2023, November 15). How social commerce in China is transforming shopping and social media. *daxueconsulting.com*, https://daxueconsulting.com/social-commerce-in-china/

De Gregorio, G., & Radu, R. (2022). Digital constitutionalism in the new era of Internet governance. *International Journal of Law and Information Technology*, *30*(1), 68–87. DOI: 10.1093/ijlit/eaac004

de Vries, A. (2021). Bitcoin's growing energy problem. *Joule*, *2*(5), 801–805.

Dias, S. A. de J., & Sátiro, R. M. (2024). Artificial intelligence in the judiciary: A critical view. *Futures*, *164*, 103493. DOI: 10.1016/j.futures.2024.103493

Díaz-Rodríguez, N., Del Ser, J., Coeckelbergh, M., López de Prado, M., Herrera-Viedma, E., & Herrera, F. (2023). Connecting the dots in trustworthy Artificial Intelligence: From AI principles, ethics, and key requirements to responsible AI systems and regulation. *Information Fusion*.

Digital Green. (n.d.). Smart Farming for Climate Resilience. https://www.digitalgreen.org/

Diken. (2023, March 20). *Mahkeme, Twitter kısıtlamasının nedenini açıklamayan BTK'yı haksız buldu.* https://www.diken.com.tr/mahkeme-twitter-kisitlamasinin-nedenini-aciklamayan-btkyi-haksiz-buldu/

Dinulescu, C. C., Visinescu, L. L., Prybutok, V. R., & Sivitanides, M. (2021). Customer relationships, privacy, and security in social commerce. *Journal of Computer Information Systems*, *62*(3), 642–654. 610.1080/08874417.08872021.01975172

Djatmiko, G. H., Sinaga, O., & Pawirosumarto, S. (2025). Digital transformation and social inclusion in public services: A qualitative analysis of e-government adoption for marginalized communities in sustainable governance. *Sustainability, 17*(7), 2908. DOI: 10.3390/su17072908

Dobber, T., Metoui, N., Trilling, D., Helberger, N., & de Vreese, C. (2021). Do (microtargeted) deepfakes have real effects on political attitudes? *The International Journal of Press/Politics, 26*(1), 69–91. DOI: 10.1177/1940161220944364

Donahoe, E. (2014). Human Rights in the Digital Age. *Just Security*. https://www.justsecurity.org/18651/human-rights-digital-age/

Dong, F. (2012). Controlling the internet in China: The real story. *Convergence (London), 18*(4), 403–425.

Dow, B., Johnson, A., Wang, C., Whitson, J., & Menon, T. (2021). The COVID-19 pandemic and the search for structure: Social media and conspiracy theories. *Social and Personality Psychology Compass, 15*(9).

Dragu, T., & Lupu, Y. (2021). Digital Authoritarianism and the Future of Human Rights. *International Organization, 75*(4), 991–1017. DOI: 10.1017/S0020818320000624

Drinhausen, K., Shi-Kupfer, K., & Sadeler, C. (2025, February 21). China's fragile online spaces for debate: Between entertainment and heavy state guidance, citizens raise social concerns and create new communities. *Friedrich Naumann Foundation for Freedom*, https://merics.org/en/report/chinas-fragile-online-spaces-debate

Duan, Y., Edwards, J. S., & Dwivedi, Y. K. (2019). Artificial Intelligence for Decision-Making in the Era of Big Data—Evolution, Challenges, and Research Agenda. *International Journal of Information Management, 48*, 63–71. https://www.sciencedirect.com/science/article/abs/pii/S0268401219300581

Dufva, T., & Dufva, M. (2019). Grasping the future of the digital society. *Futures, 107*, 17–28. DOI: 10.1016/j.futures.2018.11.001

Dumas, J. (2019). General Data Protection Regulation (GDPR): Prioritizing resources. *Seattle University Law Review, 42*(3), 1115–1128.

Dwivedi, Y. K., Hughes, L., Baabdullah, A. M., Ribeiro-Navarrete, S., Giannakis, M., Al-Debei, M. M., & Wamba, S. F. (2022). Metaverse beyond the hype: Multidisciplinary perspectives on emerging challenges, opportunities, and agenda for research, practice and policy. *International Journal of Information Management, 66*, 102542.

Edelman. (2025). *2025 Edelman Trust Barometer*. https://www.edelman.com/trust/2025/trust-barometer

EDPB. 2023, EDPB binding decision on Meta. https://www.edpb.europa.eu/news/news/2023/12-billion-euro-fine-facebook-result-edpb-binding-decision_en

Ekwueme, M., & Folarin, S. F. (2017). Role of social media in electioneering: The case of the Nigerian 2015 presidential election.

Eltantawy, N., & Wiest, J. B. (2011). Social media in the Egyptian Revolution: Reconsidering resource mobilization theory. *International Journal of Communication*, *5*, 1207–1224.

Eubanks, V. (2019). *Automating inequality: How high-tech tools profile, police, and punish the poor* (Picador, F., Ed.). Picador St. Martin's Press.

European Commission. (2017). Digital4Development: Mainstreaming Digital Technologies and Services into EU Development Policy. https://digital-strategy.ec.europa.eu/en/library/digital4development-mainstreaming-digital-technologies-and-services-eu-development-policy

European Commission. (2022). The Digital Services Act: Ensuring a safer digital space. European Commission. https://digital-strategy.ec.europa.eu

European Commission. (2024). Regulation (EU) 2024/1689 of the European Parliament and of the Council on artificial intelligence (EU AI Act). EUR-Lex. https://eur-lex.europa.eu/eli/reg/2024/1689/oj

European Commission. (2024). State of the Digital Decade 2024: DESI indicators. https://digital-strategy.ec.europa.eu/en/policies/desi

European Environment Agency (EEA). (2023). *Climate-Adapt Platform*. https://climate-adapt.eea.europa.eu/

European Union. (2016). Regulation (EU) 2016/679 of the European Parliament and of the Council on the protection of natural persons with regard to the processing of personal data (GDPR). EUR-Lex. https://eur-lex.europa.eu/eli/reg/2016/679/oj

European Union. (2019). Directive (EU) 2019/790 on copyright and related rights in the Digital Single Market. EUR-Lex. https://eur-lex.europa.eu/eli/dir/2019/790/oj

Fallis, D. (2015). What is disinformation? *Library Trends*, *63*(3), 401–426. DOI: 10.1353/lib.2015.0014

Farraj, A. (2011). Refugees and the biometric future: The impact of biometrics on refugees and asylum seekers. *Columbia Human Rights Law Review*, *42*(3), 891–939.

Fekete, A., Tzavella, K., Armas, I., Binner, J., Garschagen, M., Giupponi, C., Mojtahed, V., Pettita, M., Schneiderbauer, S., & Serre, D. (2015). Critical Data Source; Tool or Even Infrastructure? Challenges of Geographic Information Systems and Remote Sensing for Disaster Risk Governance. *ISPRS International Journal of Geo-Information*, *4*(4), 1848–1869. DOI: 10.3390/ijgi4041848

Festl, R. (2020). Social media literacy & adolescent social online behavior in Germany.[3]. *Journal of Children and Media*, *15*(2), 249–271.

Fetzer, J. H. (2004). Disinformation: The Use of False Information. *Minds and Machines*, *14*, 231–240. DOI: 10.1023/B:MIND.0000021683.28604.5b

Finnis, J. (2015). Grounding Human Rights in Natural Law. *The American Journal of Jurisprudence*, *60*(2), 199–225. https://academic.oup.com/ajj/article-abstract/60/2/199/83306

Fitzsimons, T. (2017, May 13). Study reveals Chinese censorship of Weibo. *The World*, https://theworld.org/stories/2017/2005/2013/study-reveals-chinese-censorship-weibo

Fjeld, J., Achten, N., Hilligoss, H., Nagy, A., & Srikumar, M. (2020). Principled artificial intelligence: Mapping consensus in ethical and rights-based approaches to principles for AI. *Berkman Klein Center Research Publication*, (2020-1).

Floridi, L. (2020). What the near future of artificial intelligence could be. In Floridi, L. (Ed.), *The 2019 yearbook of the digital ethics lab* (pp. 127–142). Springer., DOI: 10.1007/978-3-030-29145-7_9

Fotiadis, A. (2025, January 24). The EU wants to scan every message sent in Europe. Will that really make us safer? *The Guardian*. https://www.theguardian.com/commentisfree/2025/jan/24/eu-digital-surveillance-child-protection

Freelon, D., & Wells, C. (2020). Disinformation as Political Communication. *Political Communication*, *37*(2), 145–156. DOI: 10.1080/10584609.2020.1723755

Fuchs, C. (2012). Dallas Smythe today: The audience commodity, the digital labour debate, Marxist political economy and critical theory. *TripleC*, *10*(2), 692–740. DOI: 10.31269/triplec.v10i2.443

Gandini, A. (2021). Digital labour: An empty signifier? *Media Culture & Society*, *43*(2), 369–380. DOI: 10.1177/0163443720948018

Garimella, K., & Eckles, D. (2020). Images and misinformation in political groups: Evidence from WhatsApp in India. *Harvard Kennedy School Misinformation Review*, *1*(2). Advance online publication. DOI: 10.37016/mr-2020-013

Ged & Schmidt, T. (2020). Integrating finance into the multi-level perspective: Technology niche-finance regime interactions and financial policy interventions. *Research Policy*, *49*(6), 103985.

Gellers, J. C., & Gunkel, D. J. (2023). Artificial intelligence and international human rights law: Implications for humans and technology in the 21st century and beyond. In *Handbook on the politics and governance of big data and artificial intelligence* (pp. 430–455). Edward Elgar Publishing.

Giest, S. (2025). The intersection of digital and social infrastructures in (a) spatial policymaking. *Policy Sciences*. Advance online publication. DOI: 10.1007/s11077-025-09516-3

Global Solutions Initiative. (2022). *Big Data Analytics for Safe*. Decarbonised and Climate-Resilient Infrastructure.

Gölbaşı, S. D., & Metintaş, S. (2020). COVID-19 pandemic and infodemic. *ESTUDAM Public Health Journal*, *5*, 126–137.

Goode, L. (2009). Social news, citizen journalism and democracy. *New Media & Society*, *11*(8), 1287–1305. DOI: 10.1177/1461444809341393

Gow, G. A., & Parisi, J. (2008, February). Pursuing the anonymous user: Privacy rights and mandatory registration of prepaid mobile phones. *Bulletin of Science, Technology & Society*, *28*(1), 60–68.

Grifantiniarchive, K. (2009, August 13). China relents on censorship software. *MIT Technology Review*, https://www.technologyreview.com/2009/2008/2013/211018/china-relents-on-censorship-software/

Grover, R. (2024, August 12). *The case for (meta)data privacy: Applying Carpenter to browser fingerprints*. Proceedings of the TPRC2024: The Research Conference on Communications, Information and Internet Policy. *SSRN*. https://ssrn.com/abstract=4923706

GSMA. (2022). The mobile economy: Sub-Saharan Africa 2022. GSMA Intelligence. https://www.gsma.com

Guan, Y., Guang, L., Li, L., & Liu, Y. (2025). The rally effect of the COVID-19 Pandemic and the White Paper Movement in China. *Journal of Contemporary China*, *34*(151). Advance online publication. DOI: 10.1080/10670564.10672024.12356863

Gultom, D. I. (2016). Community-based disaster communication: How does it become trustworthy? *Disaster Prevention and Management*, *25*(4), 478–491.

Günaydın, A. (2023, February 23). *Büyük sansür dalgası korkusu... Ekranlar karartıldı, meal toplatıldı, platformlara erişim engeli getirildi*. Independent

Hamelink, C. J., & Hoffmann, J. (2008). The state of the right to communicate. *Global Media Journal*, *7*(13).

Hao, J. (2014). "A real China": On user-generated videos audiovisual narratives of Confucianism. *TripleC*, *12*(1), 342–355.

Hariyani, D., Hariyani, P., & Mishra, S. (2025). Digital technologies for the Sustainable Development Goals. *Green Technologies and Sustainability*, *3*(3), 100202. DOI: 10.1016/j.grets.2025.100202

Hassid, J. (2012). Safety valve or pressure cooker? Blogs in Chinese political life. *Journal of Communication*, *62*, 212–230.

Hatton, C. (2015, October 26). China "social credit": Beijing sets up huge system. *BBC News*, https://www.bbc.com/news/world-asia-china-34592186

Havryliuk, O., Yakushev, O., Prodanova, L., Yakusheva, O., & Kozlovska, S. (2021). Digital Banking and E-commerce in the Context of Digitalization of Business Management. *Financial and Credit Activities: Problems of Theory and Practice*, 5(40), 4-15. https://fkd.net.ua/index.php/fkd/article/view/3465/3341

He, W. (2017, March 16). Sesame Credit determines who can ride OFO bikes deposit-free. *China Daily*.

Herrmann, C. F. (1963). Some consequences of crisis which limit the viability of organizations. *Administrative Science Quarterly*, *8*(1), 61–82.

Hilty, L. M., & Aebischer, B. (2015). *ICT innovations for sustainability*. Springer.

Hoijtink, M., & Planqué-van Hardeveld, A. (2022). Machine learning and the platformization of the military: A study of google's machine learning platform TensorFlow. *International Political Sociology*, *16*(2), olab036.

Homaei, M., Mogollón-Gutiérrez, O., Sancho, J. C., Ávila, M., & Caro, A. (2024). A review of digital twins and their application in cybersecurity based on Artificial Intelligence. *Artificial Intelligence Review*.

Ho, T. L., Ngoc, L. H., & Ho, T. H. (2025). Digital inclusion or exclusion? Exploring the moderating role of governance in digitalization's impact on income inequality in developing countries. *Research in Globalization*, *10*, 100283. DOI: 10.1016/j.resglo.2025.100283

Huang, R., & Sun, X. (2014). Weibo network, information diffusion and implications for collective action in China. *Information Communication and Society, 17*(1), 86–104.

Human Rights Watch. (2022). Meta's broken promises: Systemic failures in tackling hate speech in Ethiopia. HRW. https://www.hrw.org

Human Rights Watch. (2023, March 23). *Türkiye: Deprem bölgesinde polis ve jandarma ihlalleri.* https://www.hrw.org/tr/news/2023/04/05/turkey-police-and-gendarmerie-abuses-earthquake-zone

Human, S. (2024). Humans [plural] in the loop: The forgotten collective aspects of privacy, consenting, controlling, and digital protection. *Frontiers in Political Science, 6*, 1391755. DOI: 10.3389/fpos.2024.1391755

Iden, J., & Bygstad, B. (2025). Sociotechnical micro-foundations for digital transformation. *European Journal of Information Systems, 34*(2), 367–382. DOI: 10.1080/0960085X.2024.2404197

IJRPR. (2025). Blockchain for Secure Carbon Markets: Comprehensive Review. *International Journal of Research Publication and Reviews, 6*(6), 289–307.

İletişim Başkanlığı, T. C. (2023, March 7). *5-6 Mart 2023 tarihli Deprem Dezenformasyon Bülteni yayımlandı.* https://www.iletisim.gov.tr/turkce/haberler/detay/5-6-mart-2023-tarihli-deprem-dezenformasyon-bulteni-yayimlandi

ILO. (2016). *Guidelines for a just transition towards environmentally sustainable economies and societies for all.* International Labour Organization.

Imran, M., Castillo, C., Diaz, F., & Vieweg, S. (2014). Processing social media messages in mass emergency: A survey. ACM Computing Surveys, 47(4). *Article, 67*, 1–38.

Indar, I. N., Razi, D. F., Atmansyah, L., Yani, A. A., & Ismail, N. (2024). Digital transformation of public services: An analysis of the effectiveness of online services at the local government level. *Journal of Digital Sociohumanities, 1*(2), 92–101. DOI: 10.25077/jds.1.2.92-101.2024

Instituto Nacional de Pesquisas Espaciais (INPE). (n.d.). DETER: Real-time Deforestation Detection in Amazonia. http://www.obt.inpe.br/OBT/Assuntos/Satelites/DETER

International Energy Agency. (2024). Electricity 2024: Analysis and forecast to 2026. https://www.iea.org/reports/electricity-2024

International Fact-Checking Network. (2020). Code of principles. Poynter Institute. https://ifcncodeofprinciples.poynter.org

International Telecommunication Union (ITU). (2023). *Facts and Figures 2023.* ITU Publications.

International Telecommunication Union. (2022). Measuring digital development: Facts and figures 2022. ITU. https://www.itu.int

Iosifidis, P., & Nicoli, N. (2021). *Digital democracy, social media and disinformation*. Routledge.

IPCC. (2022). *Climate change 2022: impacts, adaptation, vulnerability*. Contribution of Working Group II to the Sixth Assessment Report. Cambridge University Press.

Islam, M. T. (2022). *A brief introduction to the right to privacy: An international legal perspective*. Hauser Global Law School Program, New York University. https://doi.org/DOI: 10.2139/ssrn.4154695

Jacobson, D. (2020). Dutch Anti-Fraud System Violates Human Rights, Court Rules. *UPI.* https://www.upi.com/Top_News/World-News/2020/02/05/Dutch-anti-fraud-system-violates-human-rights-court-rules/6051580914081/#google_vignette

Jakobson, R. (1996). Šest predavanj o zvoku in smislu. In *Lingvistični in drugi spisi* (pp. 9–85). ISH–Inštitut za humanistične študije.

Järvekülg, M., Ibrus, I., & Rohn, U. (2024). Shifting from Web2 to Web3: The adaptive creator experiences on blockchain-based video-sharing and streaming platforms. *Convergence*, *30*(3), 1290–1306. DOI: 10.1177/13548565231214184

Jiang, M., & Schlæger, J. (2014, August 6). How Weibo is changing local governance in China. *The Diplomat,* https://thediplomat.com/2014/2008/how-weibo-is-changing-local-governance-in-china/

Jobin, A., Ienca, M., & Vayena, E. (2019). The global landscape of AI ethics guidelines. *Nature Machine Intelligence*, *1*(9), 389–399.

Johansson, E. L., Brogaard, S., & Brodin, L. (2022). Envisioning sustainable carbon sequestration. *Environmental Science & Policy*, *134*, 198–207.

Journo. (2023, February 8). *Sansür, otosansür ve propaganda: Depremin ardından Twitter'dan medyaya dair 10 tespit*. https://journo.com.tr/deprem-medya

Kaiser, Z. R. M. A. (2024). Smart governance for smart cities and nations. *Smart Cities*, *7*(1), 35–48. DOI: 10.1016/j.smci.2024.100031

Kan, M. (2010, September 1). China demands real names from mobile phone users. *PC World*, https://www.pcworld.com/article/502854/article-502708.html

Kanalan, I. (2018). Extraterritorial State Obligations Beyond the Concept of Jurisdiction. *German Law Journal, 19*(1), 43–64. DOI: 10.1017/S2071832200022598

Kandemir, E. Z. (2024, February 6). *Yağmacı Sanılarak Dövülen Suriyeli Depremzede: "Allah Türkiye'den Razı Olsun"*. Perspektif. https://perspektif.eu/2024/02/06/yagmaci-sanilarak-dovulen-suriyeli-depremzede-allah-turkiyeden-razi-olsun/

Kaur, R., Gabrijelčič, D., & Klobučar, T. (2023). Artificial intelligence for cybersecurity: Literature review and future research directions. *Information Fusion, 97*, •••.

Kemper, J., & Kolkman, D. (2019). Transparent to Whom? No Algorithmic Accountability without a Critical Audience. *Information Communication and Society, 22*(14), 2081–2096. https://www.tandfonline.com/doi/epdf/10.1080/1369118X.2018.1477967?needAccess=true

Khallaf, A., Abdallah, A.-N., Zoubi, T., & Alnesafi, A. (2024). Blockchain-Driven Carbon Accountability in Supply Chains. *Sustainability, 16*(24), 10872.

Khare, P. & Raghuwanshi, V. (2025). Legal Frameworks Surrounding the Use of AI in Online Content Moderation. *IGI Global Scientific Publishing*, 235-260. https://doi.org/DOI: 10.4018/979-8-3693-9904-0.ch011

Khare, P. & Raghuwanshi, V. (2025). Navigating Emerging AI Technologies and Future Trends in Cybersecurity and Forensics. *IGI Global Scientific Publishing*, 321-346. https://doi.org/DOI: 10.4018/979-8-3373-0857-9.ch012

Khare, P. (2025). Investigating the Influence of AI in Social Media Governance. *IGI Global Scientific Publishing*, 365-388. https://doi.org/DOI: 10.4018/979-8-3693-9904-0.ch015

Khazieva, N. O., Khaziev, A., & Klyushina, E. (2018). Digital society: The experience of the philosophical understanding of a problem. *Tarih Kültür ve Sanat Arastirmalari Dergisi, 7*(4), 347–353. DOI: 10.7596/taksad.v7i4.1832

Kıyan, Z., & Özer, A. (2023). Kahramanmaraş merkezli 6 Şubat depremleriyle ilişkilendirilen bir komplo teorisinin düşündürdükleri: #HAARP hashtaginin analizi. In *İletişim Yönetiminde Hayaller* (pp. 21–22). Gerçekler ve Depremler.

KlimAdapt. (n.d.). Climate Adaptation Portal Germany. https://klimadapt.de/

Kobie, N. (2019, June 7). The complicated truth about China's social credit system. *Wired*, https://www.wired.com/story/china-social-credit-system-explained/

Kopf, S. (2020). "Rewarding good creators": Corporate social media discourse on monetization schemes for content creators. *Social Media + Society, 6*(4), 2056305120969877. DOI: 10.1177/2056305120969877

Korherr, P., Kanbach, D. K., Kraus, S., & Mikalef, P. (2022). From Intuitive to Data-Driven Decision-Making in Digital Transformation: A Framework of Prevalent Managerial Archetypes. *Digital Business*, 2(2), 100045. https://www.sciencedirect.com/science/article/pii/S2666954422000254

Kostka, G., & Antoine, L. (2020). Fostering model citizenship: Behavioral responses to China's emerging social credit systems. *Policy and Internet*, *12*(3), 256–289.

Kressbach, M. (2021). Period hacks: Menstruating in the big data paradigm. *Television & New Media*, *22*(3), 241–261. DOI: 10.1177/1527476419886389

Kshetri, N. (2021). Blockchain and sustainable supply chain management in developing countries. *International Journal of Information Management*, *60*, 102376.

Kudina, O., & van de Poel, I. (2024). A sociotechnical system perspective on AI. *Minds and Machines*, *34*(3), 21. DOI: 10.1007/s11023-024-09693-1

Kumar, V. (2019). Dynamics of the "right to privacy": Its characterization under the Indian Constitution. *Journal of the Indian Law Institute*, *61*(1), 68–96. https://www.jstor.org/stable/27097351

Kuo, R., & Marwick, A. (2021). Critical disinformation studies: History, power, and politics. *Harvard Kennedy School (HKS) Misinformation Review*, *2*(4).

La Rue, F. (2013). Report of the Special Rapporteur on the Promotion and Protection of the Right to Freedom of Opinion and Expression. *A/HRC/23/40*. https://www.right-docs.org/doc/a-hrc-23-40/

Lancaster University. (n.d.). Privacy-deprived e-commerce: The efficacy of consumer privacy policies on China's e-commerce websites from a legal perspective. https://eprints.lancs.ac.uk/id/eprint/146046/146041/Privacy_deprived_E_commerce_the_efficacy_of_customer_privacy_policies_on_China_s_E_commerce_websites_from_a_legal_perspective.pdf

Langer, A. I., Wang, H., & Duckett, J. (2025). Social media and policy change: The Chinese government's strategic policy responsiveness during the COVID-19 Pandemic. *Political Studies*. Advance online publication. DOI: 10.1177/00323217251345776

Latour, B. (2005). *Reassembling the social: An introduction to actor-network-theory*. Oxford University Press.

Lee, J.-A., & Liu, C.-Y. (2016). Real-name registration rules and the fading digital anonymity in China. *Washington International Law Journal*, *26*(1), https://digitalcommons.law.uw.edu/wilj/vol25/iss21/23/

Lee, S.M., Trimi, S,. (2016). Innovation for creating a smart future. *Journal of Innovation & Knowledge*

Lee, C.-C., Lou, R., & Wang, F. (2023). Digital financial inclusion and poverty alleviation: Evidence from the sustainable development of China. *Economic Analysis and Policy*, *77*, 418–434. DOI: 10.1016/j.eap.2022.12.004

Lee, N. M., & VanDyke, M. S. (2015). Set It and Forget It: The One-Way Use of Social Media by Government Agencies Communicating Science.[5]. *Science Communication*, *37*(4), 533–541. DOI: 10.1177/1075547015588600

Lepri, B., Oliver, N., Pentland, A,. (2021). Ethical machines: The human-centric use of artificial intelligence.

Li, J., & Rao, H. R. (2010). Twitter as a rapid response news service: An exploration in the context of the 2008 China earthquake. [EJISDC]. *The Electronic Journal on Information Systems in Developing Countries*, *42*(4), 1–22.

Lin, J., Li, L., Yan, Y., & Turel, O. (2018, February). Understanding Chinese consumer engagement in social commerce: The roles of social support and swift guanxi. *Internet Research*, https://www.emerald.com/insight/content/doi/10.1108/intr-1111-2016-0349/full/html

Liu, B. F., Fraustino, J. D., & Jin, Y. (2016). Social media use during disasters: A field experiment. *Communication Research*, *43*(5), 626–646.

Liu, H., Zhou, Q., & Liang, S. (2025). Digital inclusion in public services for vulnerable groups: A systematic review for research themes and goal-action framework from the lens of public service ecosystem theory. *Government Information Quarterly*, *42*(2), 102019. DOI: 10.1016/j.giq.2025.102019

Livingstone, S. (2004). Media literacy: Ambitions, policies and measures. *Intermedia*, 18–20.

Lütz, F. (2024). The AI Act, gender equality and non-discrimination: What role for the AI office? *ERA Forum, 25*(1), 79–95. https://doi.org/DOI: 10.1007/s12027-024-00785-w

Ly, B., Dem, T., Ly, R., Sorn, S., & Doeur, B. (2024). Exploring the nexus of digital inclusion and environmental sustainability: Insights from Cambodia. *Information Technology for Development*, *31*(1), 77–94. DOI: 10.1080/02681102.2024.2345381

Ma, Y. (2024, October 9). Social commerce in China - statistics & facts. *Statista*, https://www.statista.com/topics/6718/social-commerce-in-china/#topicOverview

Mahboubi, A., Luong, K., Aboutorab, H., Bui, H.T., Jarrad, G., Bahutair, M. (2024). Evolving techniques in cyber threat hunting: A systematic review. *Journal of Network and Computer Applications.*

Malfacini, K. (2025). The impacts of companion AI on human relationships: Risks, benefits, and design considerations. *AI & Society.*

Malgieri, G. (2025). Digital Dependency: Needs, Vulnerability, and Power in the Digital Society. *SSRN*

Mamidi, S.R. 2024. The Role of AI and Machine Learning in Cloud Cybersecurity, *Journal of Artificial Intelligence General Science.* Vol. 1 Issue 3

Manoharan, A., & Sarker, M. (2022). Revolutionizing Cybersecurity: Unleashing the Power of Artificial Intelligence and Machine Learning for Next-Generation Threat Detection. *International Research Journal of Modernization in Engineering Technology and Science.*

Martínez, J., Comesaña, C., & García-Nieto, P. J. (2019). Review: Machine learning techniques applied to cybersecurity. *International Journal of Machine Learning and Cybernetics.*

Martin, K. D., & Zimmermann, J. (2024). Artificial intelligence and its implications for data privacy. *Current Opinion in Psychology, 58*, 101829. DOI: 10.1016/j.copsyc.2024.101829 PMID: 38954851

Martynov, V. V., Shavaleeva, D. N., & Zaytseva, A. A. (2019). Information technology as the basis for transformation into a digital society and Industry 5.0. In 2019 International Conference on Quality Management, Transport and Information Security, Information Technologies (IT&QM&IS) (pp. 539–543). IEEE. https://doi.org/DOI: 10.1109/ITQMIS.2019.8928362

Mattelart, T. (2023). US digital platforms in the Global South. In P. Bouquillion, C. Ithurbide, & T. Mattelart, *Digital platforms and the Global South* (pp. 18–36). Routledge. https://doi.org/DOI: 10.4324/9781003391746-1

McIver, W. J.Jr, Merrilee, R., & Birdsall, W. F. (2003). The Internet and the right to communicate. *First Monday, 8*(12). https://firstmonday.org/issues/issue8_12/mciver/index.html

McKendrick, K. (2019). Artificial intelligence prediction and counterterrorism. *London: The Royal Institute of International Affairs-Chatham House, 9.*

McNamara, K. E., & Prasad, S. S. (2014). Coping with extreme weather: Communities in Fiji and Vanuatu share their experiences and knowledge. *Climatic Change, 123*(2), 121–132. DOI: 10.1007/s10584-013-1047-2

Medyascope. (2023, February 9). *Erdoğan: "Tefeciler, fitne grupları ve yağma olaylarına OHAL ile müdahale etme imkânı olacak"*. https://medyascope.tv/2023/02/09/erdogan-tefeciler-fitne-gruplari-ve-yagma-olaylarina-ohal-ile-mudahale-imkani-olacak/

Mendel, T. (2008). *Freedom of information: A comparative legal survey* (2nd ed.). UNESCO., https://law.yale.edu/sites/default/files/documents/pdf/Intellectual_Life/CL-OGI_Toby_Mendel_book_%28Eng%29.pdf

Méndez-Muros, S., Alonso-González, M., & Pérez-Curiel, C. (2024). Disinformation and fact-checking in the face of natural disasters: A case study on Turkey–Syria earthquakes. *Societies (Basel, Switzerland), 14*(4), 43. DOI: 10.3390/soc14040043

MERCIS. (2022). China's social credit score untangling myth from reality. https://merics.org/en/comment/chinas-social-credit-score-untangling-myth-reality

Merga, M. K. (2024). TikTok and digital health literacy: A systematic review. *IFLA Journal.* Advance online publication. DOI: 10.1177/03400352241286175

Meskic, Z., Albakjaji, M., Jevremovic, N., Omerovic, E., & Adams, J. (2022). Digitalization and Innovation in Achieving SDGs—Impacts on Legislation and Practice. *IOP Conference Series. Earth and Environmental Science, 1026*(1), 012061. https://iopscience.iop.org/article/10.1088/1755-1315/1026/1/012061

M-Farm. (n.d.). About M-Farm. https://mfarm.co.ke

Mhlanga, D. (2021). Financial inclusion in emerging economies: The application of machine learning and artificial intelligence in credit risk assessment. *International journal of financial studies, 9*(3), 39.

Mihaila, S., Bădicu, G., Codrean, V., & Dascălu, I. (2021). E-Commerce in the Context of Globalization and Digitalization: Opportunities, Challenges, and Perspectives. *European Journal of Accounting, Finance, &. Business (Atlanta, Ga.), 16*(26), 1–9. https://ibn.idsi.md/vizualizare_articol/202031

Miller, S. (2019). *Citizen Journalism.* Oxford Research Encyclopedia of Communication., DOI: 10.1093/acrefore/9780190228613.013.786

Milmo, D. (2023, January 24). Meta spends 87% of misinformation budget on US users, report finds. The Guardian. https://www.theguardian.com

Ming, C. (2017, March 16). FICO with Chinese characteristics: Nice rewards, but punishing penalties. *CNBC*, https://www.cnbc.com/2017/2003/2016/china-social-credit-system-ant-financials-sesame-credit-and-others-give-scores-that-go-beyond-fico.html

Mitra, B., Cramer, H., & Gurevich, O. (2024). Sociotechnical implications of generative artificial intelligence for information access. In Ekstrand, M. D., Potthast, M., & Ferro, N. (Eds.), *Information access in the era of generative AI* (pp. 161–200). Springer Nature., DOI: 10.1007/978-3-031-45432-5_8

Mohan, R., Saleem, F., Voderhobli, K., & Sheikh-Akbari, A. (2024). Ensuring sustainable digital inclusion among the elderly: A comprehensive analysis. *Sustainability*, *16*(17), 7485. DOI: 10.3390/su16177485

Mozilla Foundation. (2021). *Platform transparency: Why Africa is left behind.* Mozilla.

Mpinga, E. K., Bukonda, N. K., Qailouli, S., & Chastonay, P. (2022). Artificial Intelligence and Human Rights: Are There Signs of an Emerging Discipline? A Systematic Review. *Journal of Multidisciplinary Healthcare*, •••, 235–246.

Mühlhoff, R. (2021). Predictive privacy: Towards an applied ethics of data analytics. *Ethics and Information Technology*, *23*(4), 675–690.

Mujokoro, J. I. T. (2017). An analysis of the Sunday Times and Twitter's reporting of President Mugabe's state visit to South Africa.

Musa, N. S., Mirza, N. M., Rafique, S. H., Abdallah, A. M., & Murugan, T. (2022).. . *Machine Learning*.

Musoni, M., Domingo, E., & Ogah, E. (2023). *Digital ID systems in Africa: Challenges, risks and opportunities* (Discussion Paper No. 360). European Centre for Development Policy Management (ECDPM).

Naeem, M., Ozuem, W., Howell, K., & Ranfagni, S. (2023). A step-by-step process of thematic analysis to develop a conceptual model in qualitative research. *International Journal of Qualitative Methods*, *22*. Advance online publication. DOI: 10.1177/16094069231205789

Nagy, P., & Neff, G. (2015). Imagined affordance: Reconstructing a keyword for communication theory. *Social Media + Society*, *1*(2), 2056305115603385. DOI: 10.1177/2056305115603385

Nagy, S., & Somosi, M. V. (2022). The relationship between social innovation and digital economy and society. arXiv. https://arxiv.org/abs/2212.13840

Nakashima, D., McLean, K. G., Thulstrup, H. D., Castillo, A. R., & Rubis, J. T. (2012). *Weathering Uncertainty: Traditional Knowledge for Climate Change Assessment and Adaptation*. UNESCO & UNU.

Narayana, Y. V., & Sreedevi, M. (2023, October). DDCATF: Deep Learning Approach for Detection of Cybercrime Activities Based on Temporal Features. In *2023 International Conference on Self Sustainable Artificial Intelligence Systems (ICSSAS)* (pp. 462-469). IEEE.

Neuman, W. L. (2021). *Toplumsal araştırma yöntemleri: Nitel ve nicel yaklaşımlar*. Siyasal Kitabevi.

Nguyen, A. (2020). Digital inclusion: Social Inclusion in the Digital Age. *Springer International Publishing*, 1-15. https://doi.org/DOI: 10.1007/978-3-030-48277-0_14-1

Nieborg, D. B., Poell, T., & van Dijck, J. (2023). Platforms and platformization. In Flew, T., Holt, J., & Thomas, J. (Eds.), *The SAGE handbook of the digital media economy* (pp. 29–49). SAGE Publications Ltd., DOI: 10.4135/9781529757170.n4

Niranjanamurthy, M., Nithya, B. N., & Jagannatha, S. J. C. C. (2019). Analysis of Blockchain technology: Pros, cons and SWOT. *Cluster Computing*, *22*(Suppl 6), 14743–14757.

Nishnianidze, A. (2024). Surveillance in the digital age. *European Scientific Journal*, *20*(37), 1–25. DOI: 10.19044/esj.2024.v20n37p1

Nyale, D., Angolo, S.M. 2022. A Survey of Artificial Intelligence in Cyber Security, *International Journal of Computer Applications Technology and Research* Vol. 11–Issue 12, 474-477

Obijiofor, L. (2009). *Is bad news from Africa good news for Western media?* Marquette Books.

Ochoa-Dąderska, R., Ochoa-Dąderska, G., García, S., Callarisa-Fiol, L., Navikiene, Z., Demirci, M., Niemczyk, A., Gródek-Szostak, Z., Gasińska-Bańka, K., & Siguencia, O. (2024). Digital Inclusion To Improve People's Lives and Promote Sustainable Development: DigIN report III. *Zenodo*. https://zenodo.org/doi/10.5281/zenodo.10676614

OECD. (2020). *Digital economy outlook 2020*. OECD Publishing., DOI: 10.1787/2617653f-

OECD. (2024). *Digital Economy Outlook 2024* (Vol. 1). Organisation for Economic Co-operation and Development.

OECD–UNDP. (2025). Investing in Climate, Investing in Growth: Climate Action Monitor 2024.

Ogunyemi, O. (2011). Representation of Africa online: Sourcing practice and frames of reference. *Journal of Black Studies*, *42*(3), 457–478. DOI: 10.1177/0021934710378747

Okoli, U. L., Obi, O. C., Adewusi, A. O., & Abrahams, T. O. (2024). *Machine learning in cybersecurity: A review of threat detection and defense mechanisms*. World Journal of Advanced Research and Reviews.

Open Forest Protocol. (n.d.). Overview. https://openforestprotocol.org/

Ozturk, I., Alqassimi, O., & Ullah, S. (2024). Digitalization and SMEs development in the context of sustainable development: A China perspective. *Heliyon*, *10*(6), e27936. DOI: 10.1016/j.heliyon.2024.e27936 PMID: 38510016

Pal, L. A. (2005). Case study method and policy analysis. In Geva-May, I. (Ed.), *Thinking Like a Policy Analyst*. Palgrave Macmillan., DOI: 10.1057/9781403980939_12

Pangrazio, L., & Sefton-Green, J. (2021). Digital Rights, Digital Citizenship, and Digital Literacy: What's the Difference? *Journal of New Approaches in Educational Research*, *10*, 15–27. https://link.springer.com/article/10.7821/naer.2021.1.616

Panova, L., Gramartskyy, E., Kryvosheyina, I., & Makoda, V. (2022). Human Rights in the Context of Digitalization: International-Legal Analysis. *International Journal of Computer Science and Network Security*, *22*(5), 320–326. https://koreascience.kr/article/JAKO202221358522908.page

Papadopoulos, G., Arduini, S., Uyar, H., Psiroukis, V., Kasimati, A., & Fountas, S. (2024). Economic and Environmental Benefits of Digital Agricultural Technologies in Crop Production: A Review. *Smart Agricultural Technology*, *8*, 100441. https://www.sciencedirect.com/science/article/pii/S2772375524000467

Parliament, U. K. (2025). *Data (Use and Access) Act 2025*. UK Government.

Parviainen, P., Tihinen, M., Kääriäinen, J., & Teppola, S. (2017). Tackling the Digitalization Challenge: How to Benefit from Digitalization in Practice. *International Journal of Information Systems and Project Management*, *5*(1), 63–77. https://aisel.aisnet.org/ijispm/vol5/iss1/5/

Pearce, T., Ford, J., Willox, A. C., & Smit, B. (2015). Inuit traditional ecological knowledge (TEK), subsistence hunting and adaptation to climate change in the Canadian Arctic. *Arctic*, *68*(2), 233–245.

Pennycook, G., & Rand, D. G. (2021). The psychology of fake news. *Trends in Cognitive Sciences*, *25*(5), 388–402. DOI: 10.1016/j.tics.2021.02.007

Pérez-Escolar, M., & Canet, F. (2022). Research on vulnerable people and digital inclusion: Toward a consolidated taxonomical framework. *Universal Access in the Information Society*, *22*(3), 1059–1072. DOI: 10.1007/s10209-022-00867-x PMID: 35125988

Petrov, A., Kuraev, A., Mirzagitova, A., & Kirillova, E. (2024). Main Threats to Human Rights and Freedoms in the Context of Digitalization. *Jurídicas CUC*, 20(1), 343-357. https://revistascientificas.cuc.edu.co/juridicascuc/article/view/5330

Petryshyn, O. V., & Hyliaka, O. S. (2021). Human Rights in the Digital Ages: Challenges, Threats, and Prospects. *Journal of the National Academy of Legal Sciences of Ukraine*, *28*(1), 16–23. https://visnyk.kh.ua/web/uploads/journals_pdf/%D0%92%D1%96%D1%81%D0%BD%D0%B8%D0%BA%20%D0%9D%D0%90%D0%9F%D1%80%D0%9D%D0%A3_%D0%A2%D0%BE%D0%BC%2028(1)_2021.pdf#page=16

Piccone, T. (2018). Democracy and Digital Technology. *International Journal of Human Rights*, *15*(27), 29–38. https://sur.conectas.org/wp-content/uploads/2018/07/sur-27-ingles-ted-piccone.pdf

Platania, F., Toscano Hernandez, C., & Arreola, F. (2022). Social media communication during natural disasters and the impact on the agricultural market. *Technological Forecasting and Social Change*, *179*, 121594.

Pocher, N., Zichichi, M., Merizzi, F., Shafiq, M. Z., & Ferretti, S. (2023). Detecting anomalous cryptocurrency transactions: An AML/CFT application of machine learning-based forensics. *Electronic Markets*, *33*(1), 37.

Poell, T., Nieborg, D., & van Dijck, J. (2019). Platformisation. *Internet Policy Review*, *8*(4). Advance online publication. DOI: 10.14763/2019.4.1425

Pomeranz, J. L., & Schwid, A. R. (2021). Governmental actions to address COVID-19 misinformation. *Journal of Public Health Policy*, *42*(1), 1–15. DOI: 10.1057/s41271-020-00270-x PMID: 33510401

Premium Times. (2021, July 29). Nigeria's anti-fake news laws spark controversy. Premium Times.

Public Media Alliance. (2022). *Caribbean media and the politics of disinformation*. PMA.

Pūraitė, A., Adamonienė, R., & Žemeckė, A. (2020). Sustainable Digitalization in Public Institutions: Challenges for Human Rights. *European Journal of Sustainable Development*, *9*(3), 91–102. https://ecsdev.org/ojs/index.php/ejsd/article/view/1072/1054

Rahman, M., & Rashid, H. (2025). Bridging digital divides and sustainability imperatives: A systematic review of interoperability frameworks for sustainable development (2011–2025). *Journal of Cleaner Production*, *456*, 141239. DOI: 10.1016/j.jclepro.2025.141239

Rai, R., & Sahu, C. K. (2020). Driven by data or derived through physics? a review of hybrid physics guided machine learning techniques with cyber-physical system (cps) focus. *IEEE Access : Practical Innovations, Open Solutions*, *8*, 71050–71073.

Ramzy, A. (2011, February 21). State stamps out small "Jasmine" Protests in China. *Time*, https://content.time.com/time/world/article/0,8599,2052860,00.html

Rashid, Y., Rashid, A., & Waseem, A. (2019, July 24). Case study method: A step-by-step guide for business researchers. *International Journal of Qualitative Methods*. Advance online publication. DOI: 10.1177/1609406919862424

Reddy, S., Allan, S., Coghlan, S., & Cooper, P. (2020). A governance model for the application of AI in health care. *Journal of the American Medical Informatics Association : JAMIA*, *27*(3), 491–497. DOI: 10.1093/jamia/ocz192 PMID: 31682262

Reed, A., & Thompson, K. (2021). Never waste a crisis: Digital inclusion for sustainable development in the context of the COVID pandemic. *Library Journal*, *40*(2), 14–16. DOI: 10.13663/j.cnki.lj.2021.02.001

Renda, A. (2018). The legal framework to address "fake news": Possible policy actions at the EU level. CEPS Research Report. https://www.ceps.eu/ceps-publications

Research and Markets. (2025, May 8). China Social Commerce Intelligence Report 2025: Market to Reach $769 Billion by 2030, Driven by Platform Innovations, Strategic Partnerships, and Significant Investments. *GlobeNewswire*, https://www.globenewswire.com/news-release/2025/2005/2008/3077093/3028124/en/China-Social-Commerce-Intelligence-Report-3072025-Market-to-Reach-3077769-Billion-by-3072030-Driven-by-Platform-Innovations-Strategic-Partnerships-and-Significant-Investments.html

Reuters Institute for the Study of Journalism. (2024, June 17). *Sources for news consumption in selected major media markets worldwide as of February 2024, by type* [Graph]. In Statista. Retrieved June 10, 2025, from https://www.statista.com/statistics/262079/news-access-worldwide-by-media/

Reuters. (2025, January 12). Kenyan court allows Meta disinformation lawsuit to proceed. Reuters.

Reynolds, B., & Seeger, M. W. (2005). Crisis and emergency risk communication as an integrative model. *Journal of Health Communication, 10*(1), 43–55. DOI: 10.1080/10810730590904571

Richards, N., & Hartzog, W. (2019). The pathologies of digital consent. *Washington University Law Review, 96*(6), 1461–1528.

Roberts, J. (2025). Citizen Journalism. In Hobbs, R., & Mihailidis, P. (Eds.), *The International Encyclopedia of Media Literacy.*, DOI: 10.1002/9781118978238.ieml0027

Rodrigues, R. (2020). Legal and human rights issues of AI: Gaps, challenges and vulnerabilities. *Journal of Responsible Technology, 4*, 100005. DOI: 10.1016/j.jrt.2020.100005

Rolnick, D., Donti, P. L., Kaack, L. H., Kochanski, K., & Lacoste, A.. (2022). Tackling climate change with machine learning. *ACM Computing Surveys, 55*(2), 1–96.

Ruud, O. (2018). How to Succeed with Digital Transformation Projects in Public Sector with Focus on Municipalities (Research in Progress). *Central and Eastern European EDem and EGov Days*, 325, 425-436. https://ejournals.facultas.at/index.php/ocgcp/article/view/1575

Sætra, H. S. (2020). Privacy as an aggregate public good. *Technology in Society, 63*, 101422. DOI: 10.1016/j.techsoc.2020.101422

Sag, M., & Yu, P. K. (2025). The globalization of copyright exceptions for AI training. *Emory Law Journal, 74*(5), 1163–1218.

Salem, A.H., & Azzam, S.F, Emam., Abohany, A.A. (2024). Advancing cybersecurity: A Comprehensive Review of AI-driven Detection Techniques. *Journal of Big Data.*

Saltz, J., Skirpan, M., Fiesler, C., Gorelick, M., Yeh, T., Heckman, R., & Beard, N. (2019). Integrating ethics within machine learning courses. [TOCE]. *ACM Transactions on Computing Education, 19*(4), 1–26.

Sanders, C. K., & Scanlon, E. (2021). The Digital Divide is a Human Rights Issue: Advancing Social Inclusion through Social Work Advocacy. *Journal of Human Rights and Social Work, 6*, 130–143. https://link.springer.com/article/10.1007/s41134-020-00147-9 PMID: 33758780

Sandoval, G. (2009, March 24). China bans YouTube, Chinese officials confirm that they are blocking the Web's largest video site but haven't disclosed the reason. *The Wall Street Journal*, https://www.cnet.com/news/wsj-china-bans-youtube/

Schot, J., & Kanger, L. (2016). Deep Transitions: Emergence, Acceleration, Stabilization, Directionality. SWPS 2016-15.

Scott, M. (2023, March 8). Facebook ignored warnings over Ethiopia hate speech. Politico. https://www.politico.eu

Selçuk, S., Kurt Konca, N., & Kaya, S. (2025). AI-driven civil litigation: Navigating the right to a fair trial. *Computer Law &amp. Secourisme - Revue*, *57*, 106136. DOI: 10.1016/j.clsr.2025.106136

SellersCommerce. (2025). 51 e-Commerce [Global and U.S. Data] [. https://www.sellerscommerce.com/blog/ecommerce-statistics/.]. *Statistics in, 2025,* •••.

Sharma, A., Mansotra, V., & Singh, K. (2023). Detection of Mirai Botnet Attacks on IoT devices Using Deep Learning. *Journal of Scientific Research and Technology*, 174-187.

Shu, K., Bhattacharjee, A., & Alatawi, F.. (2020). Combating disinformation in a social media age. *Wiley Interdisciplinary Reviews. Data Mining and Knowledge Discovery*, *10*, e1385. DOI: 10.1002/widm.1385

Shyaa, M. A., Ibrahim, N. F., Zainol, Z., Abdullah, R., Anbar, M., & Alzubaidi, L. (2024). Evolving cybersecurity frontiers: A comprehensive survey on concept drift and feature dynamics aware machine and deep learning in intrusion detection systems. *Engineering Applications of Artificial Intelligence*.

Sigaut, F. (1995). Technology. In *Companion encyclopedia of anthropology* (pp. 420–459). Routledge.

Silverman, C. (2015). *Verification handbook for digital content: A definitive guide to verifying digital content for emergency coverage*. European Journalism Centre. https://verificationhandbook.com/

Sindakis, S., & Showkat, G. (2024). The digital revolution in India: Bridging the gap in rural technology adoption. *Journal of Innovation and Entrepreneurship*, *13*(1). Advance online publication. DOI: 10.1186/s13731-024-00380-w

Singh, H. (2024). Navigating the legal landscape of information governance. In Helge, K., & Rookey, C. (Eds.), *Creating and sustaining an information governance program* (pp. 217–235). IGI Global., DOI: 10.4018/979-8-3693-0472-3.ch012

Smith, P. S. (2013). Imprisonment and Internet-Access-Human Rights, the Principle of Normalization and the Question of Prisoners' Access to Digital Communications Technology. *Nordic Journal of Human Rights, 30*(4), 454–482. https://www.scup.com/doi/10.18261/ISSN1891-814X-2012-04-04

Smith, R. K. M. (2022). *International Human Rights Law* (10th ed.). Oxford University Press.

Solhaber. (2023, February 8). *Show TV muhabiri 'Ekipler asla gelmiyor' diyen depremzededen mikrofonu çekip uzaklaştı.* https://haber.sol.org.tr/haber/show-tv-muhabiri-ekipler-asla-gelmiyor-diyen-depremzededen-mikrofonu-cekip-uzaklasti-365067

Solove, D. J. (2025). *Privacy in authoritarian times: Surveillance capitalism and government surveillance. SSRN.* https://doi.org/DOI: 10.2139/ssrn.5103271

Sorce, G., & Dumitrica, D. (2023). From school strikes to webinars: Mapping the forced digitalization of Fridays for Future's activism during the COVID-19 pandemic. *Social Media + Society*. PMID: 38603442

South African Government. (2020). *Disaster Management Act: COVID-19 misinformation penalties*. Government Gazette.

Sözcü. (2023, February 11). *Hatay'da baraj patladı iddiası! Bakan Kirişçi'den açıklama.* https://www.sozcu.com.tr/hatayda-baraj-patladi-iddiasi-bakan-kirisciden-aciklama-wp7587984

Srinivasan, M., Mathew, G., Mathew, N., Kumar, M., Goyal, N., & Kamath, M. S. (2024). Technologies that empower women for better access to healthcare in India – A scoping review. *Global Public Health: An International Journal for Research, Policy and Practice, 19*(1). Advance online publication. DOI: 10.1080/17441692.2024.2318240 PMID: 38373725

Srinivasan, R., & San Miguel González, B. (2025). The role of empathy for artificial intelligence accountability. *Journal of Responsible Technology, 9*, •••.

Statista. (2024). Number of Internet of Things (IoT) connected devices worldwide from 2019 to 2030. https://www.statista.com/statistics/1183457/iot-connected-devices-worldwide/

Statista. (2025). Retail E-Commerce Sales Worldwide from 2022 to 2028. https://www.statista.com/statistics/379046/worldwide-retail-e-commerce-sales/

Stewart, H. (2025). Fostering interoperability of data, models, communication, and governance for disaster resilience through transdisciplinary knowledge co-production. *Natural Hazards and Earth System Sciences*, *25*, 3055–3073.

Stewart, R., Madonsela, A., Tshabalala, N., Etale, L., & Theunissen, N. (2022). Social media users' responses are important in tackling digital COVID-19 misinformation in Africa. *Digital Health*, *8*, 20552076221085070. DOI: 10.1177/20552076221085070 PMID: 35321021

Stilgoe, J. (2020). *Who's Driving Innovation?* New Technologies and the Collaborative State. Palgrave Macmillan.

Storm, D. (2015, October 7). ACLU: Orwellian citizen score, China's credit score system, is a warning for Americans. *ComputerWorld*, https://www.computerworld.com/article/1648895/aclu-orwellian-citizen-score-chinas-credit-score-system-is-a-warning-for-americans.html

Sullivan, J. (2012, September). A tale of two microblogs in China. *Media Culture & Society*, *34*(6), 773–783.

Sullivan, J. (2014, February). China's Weibo: Is it faster different? *New Media & Society*, *16*(1), 24–37.

Sun, M., Zhang, X., & Zhang, X. (2022). The impact of multilevel innovation networks and government support. *Sustainability*, *14*(12), 7334.

Su, Y., Lee, D. K., Xiao, X., Li, W., & Shu, W. (2021). Who endorses conspiracy theories? A moderated mediation model of Chinese and international social media use, media skepticism, need for cognition, and COVID-19 conspiracy theory endorsement in China. *Computers in Human Behavior*, •••, 106760.

Taddeo, M., & Floridi, L. (2025). Digital ethics. In Wareham, C. (Ed.), *A companion to digital ethics* (pp. 1–9). Routledge., DOI: 10.4324/9781003241297-1

Tandoc, E. C., Lim, Z. W., & Ling, R. (2017). Defining "Fake News": A typology of scholarly definitions. *Digital Journalism (Abingdon, England)*, *6*(2), 137–153. DOI: 10.1080/21670811.2017.1360143

Tatlı, İ. (2023, February 1). *Deprem üzerinden kışkırtılan nefret söylemi ve ayrımcılık deprem kadar yıkıcı olabilir.* Independent Türkçe. https://www.indyturk.com/node/611146/türkiyeden-sesler/deprem-üzerinden-kişkirtilan-nefret-söylemi-ve-ayrimcilik-deprem

Taylor, G., & Vink, S. (2021). Managing the risks of missing international climate targets. *Climate Risk Management*, *34*, 100379.

Tekeş, A. F. (2025, February 2). *6 Şubat depremlerinin ardından yüzlerce yanıltıcı içerik yayınlandı*. Anadolu Ajansı Teyit Hattı. https://www.aa.com.tr/tr/teyithatti/blog/6-subat-depremlerinin-ardindan-yuzlerce-yaniltici-icerik-yayinlandi-/1818720

Tekeş, A. F., & Sarsılmaz, M. (2023, February 11). *Hatay'da Yarseli Barajı'nın Patladığı İddiası*. Anadolu Ajansı. https://www.aa.com.tr/tr/teyithatti/aktuel/hatayda-yarseli-barajinin-patladigi-iddiasi/1815346

Temperman, J., & Quintavalla, A. (2023). *Artificial intelligence and human rights*. Oxford University Press., DOI: 10.1093/law/9780192882486.001.0001

Teo, S. A. (2024). Artificial intelligence and its 'slow violence' to human rights. *AI and Ethics*, *5*(3), 2265–2280. DOI: 10.1007/s43681-024-00547-x

Terren, L., & Borge-Bravo, R., & Open University of Catalonia. (2021). Echo chambers on social media: A systematic review of the literature. *Review of Communication Research*, *9*, 99–118. DOI: 10.12840/ISSN.2255-4165.028

Teyit.org. (2018, May 31). *Facebook'un doğrulama programı Türkiye'de Teyit iş birliğiyle hayata geçiyor*. Teyitpedia. https://teyit.org/teyitpedia/facebookun-dogrulama-programi-turkiyede-teyit-org-is-birligiyle-hayata-geciyor

Thapaliya, S., & Sharma, P. K. (2023). Optimized deep neuro fuzzy network for cyber forensic investigation in big data-based IoT infrastructures. [IJISP]. *International Journal of Information Security and Privacy*, *17*(1), 1–22.

The Economist. (2012, January 28). Unrest in China, A dangerous year, Economic conditions and social media are making protests more common in China—at a delicate time for the country's rulers. *The Economist*, https://www.economist.com/node/21543477

The New York Times. (n.d.). Baidu Inc. http://topics.nytimes.com/top/news/business/companies/baiducom-inc/index.html

Thoba, A. (2017). Human rights discourse and postcolonial Africa: The call for intervention in Darfur.

Thomala, L. L. (2025a, February 26). Most popular social media in China Q3 2024. *Statista*, https://www.statista.com/statistics/250546/leading-social-network-sites-in-china/

Thomala, L. L. (2025b, March 18). Internet usage in China - statistics & facts. *Statista*, https://www.statista.com/topics/1179/internet-usage-in-china/

Tindall, R. (2021, September 6). China's move towards e-chops and real name verification. *China Britain Business Council*, https://www.cbbc.org/news-insights/chinas-move-towards-e-chops-and-real-name-verification

Troeger, J., & Bock, A. (2022). The sociotechnical walkthrough: A methodological approach for platform studies. *Studies in Communication Sciences*, *22*(1). Advance online publication. DOI: 10.24434/j.scoms.2022.01.3064

Tüfekçi, Z. (2017). *Twitter and tear gas: The power and fragility of networked protest*. Yale University Press.

Türkçe. https://www.indyturk.com/node/612526/haber/büyük-sansür-dalgası-korkusu…-ekranlar-karartıldı-meal-toplatıldı-platformlara

Türkiye Cumhuriyeti İçişleri Bakanlığı. (2023, February 14). *Cumhurbaşkanımız Sn. Erdoğan: "Hiçbir Vatandaşımızı Maddi-Manevi Açıdan Sahipsiz Bırakmayacağız"*. https://www.icisleri.gov.tr/cumhurbaskanimiz-sn-erdogan-hicbir-vatandasimizi-maddi-manevi-acidan-sahipsiz-birakmayacagiz

Türkiye Cumhuriyeti İletişim Başkanlığı. (2023, February 8). *Depremden etkilenen 10 ilde kararlaştırılan OHAL ilanı, Resmî Gazete'de*. https://www.iletisim.gov.tr/turkce/haberler/detay/depremden-etkilenen-10-ilde-kararlastirilan-ohal-ilani-resmi-gazetede

Turkle, S. (1997). *Life on the screen: Identity in the age of the Internet.* Phoenix.

Tyagi, A. K., Aswathy, S. U., & Abraham, A. (2020). Integrating blockchain technology and artificial intelligence: Synergies perspectives challenges and research directions. *Journal of Information Assurance and Security*, *15*(5), 1554.

U.S. Congress. (2024). *Generative AI Copyright Disclosure Act of 2024*. U.S. Government Publishing Office.

UBS. (2022). The History of Digital Banking. https://www.ubs.com/ch/en/wealth-management/womens-wealth/magazine/articles/history-of-digital-banking.html

UNCTAD. (2024). Digital Economy Report 2024. *United Nations Conference on Trade and Development*.

UNESCO. (2021). *Media and information literacy: Policy and strategy guidelines*. UNESCO.

UNESCO. (2022). *Media in crisis preparedness and response: Case studies and lessons learned from the COVID-19 pandemic*. United Nations Educational, Scientific and Cultural Organization. https://unesdoc.unesco.org/ark:/48223/pf0000381736

UNESCO. (2023). Recommendation on the ethics of artificial intelligence. UNESCO Publishing. https://unesdoc.unesco.org/ark:/48223/pf0000381137

UNFCCC. (2021). *Just Transition of the Workforce, and the Creation of Decent Work and Quality Jobs*. UNFCCC Technical Paper.

United Nations Development Programme (UNDP). (2022). Bridging the digital divide for inclusive climate action.

United Nations Development Programme (UNDP). (2025). *The case for Nature ID: How digital public infrastructure can catalyze nature and climate action*. UNDP. https://climatepromise.undp.org/sites/default/files/research_report_document/undp-the-case-for-nature-id.pdf

United Nations. (1948). *Universal Declaration of Human Rights*. https://www.un.org/en/about-us/universal-declaration-of-human-rights

United Nations. (2015). *Transforming our world: the 2030 agenda for sustainable development*. United Nations.

United Nations. (2021). *The State of the World's Indigenous Peoples: Rights to Lands, Territories and Resources*. United Nations Publications.

Ünver, H. A. (2024). *Artificial intelligence (AI) and human rights: Using AI as a weapon of repression and its impact on human rights*. European Parliament, Directorate-General for External Policies, Policy Department for External Relations (PE 754.450).

Utami, S. H., Purnama, A. A., Hidayanto, A. N., Utami, S. H., Purnama, A. A., & Hidayanto, A. N. (2022). Fintech Lending in Indonesia: A Sentiment Analysis, Topic Modelling, and Social Network Analysis using Twitter Data. *International Journal of Applied Engineering & Technology*, *4*(1), 50–56.

Van Dijk, J. (2020). *The network society* (4th ed.). SAGE.

Van Stam, G. (2021). Appropriation, coloniality, and digital technologies: Observations from within an African place. arXiv. https://doi.org//arXiv.2108.10087DOI: 10.48550

Varma, P., Nijjer, S., Sood, K., Grima, S., & Rupeika-Apoga, R. (2022). Thematic Analysis of Financial Technology (Fintech) Influence on the Banking Industry. *Risks*, *10*(10), 186.

Vatikiotis, P. (2005). Communication theory and alternative media. *Westminster Papers in Communication and Culture*, *2*(1), 4–29.

Vicente, P. N. (2024). Artificial intelligence and freedom of speech. *European Journal of Communication*, *39*(2), 197–200. DOI: 10.1177/02673231241234766

Vincent, J. (2016). UN Condemns Internet Access Disruption as a Human Rights Violation.

Vinuesa, R.. (2020). The role of artificial intelligence in achieving the Sustainable Development Goals. *Nature Communications*, *11*, 233. PMID: 31932590

Voice of America. (2012, May 29). China's Sina Weibo unveils new censorship system. http://www.voatibetanenglish.com/content/chinas-sina-weibo-unveils-new-censorship-system-155335335/1267399.html

Vosoughi, S., Roy, D., & Aral, S. (2018). The Spread of True and False News Online. *Science*, *359*(6380), 1146–1151.

Vuolo, M., Schneider, L. E., & LaPlant, E. G. (2023). Surveillance and the experience of the COVID-19 pandemic for formerly incarcerated individuals. *Punishment & Society*, *25*(2), 386–406. DOI: 10.1177/14624745221080696 PMID: 38603030

Wagh, A. (2023). What's generative AI? Explore underlying layers of machine learning and deep learning. Medium. https://medium.com/@amol-wagh

Wagner, B., Bronowicka, J., Berger, C., & Behrndt, T. (2015). Surveillance and Censorship: The Impact of Technologies on Human Rights. European Parliament. https://www.europarl.europa.eu/RegData/etudes/STUD/2015/549034/EXPO_STU(2015)549034_EN.pdf

Wahl, S. T., McBride, M. C., & Schrodt, P. (2005). Becoming "point and click" parents: A case study of communication and online adoption. *Journal of Family Communication*, *5*(4), 279–294.

Wang, Q. (2015, June 22). Alibaba in partnership with Luxembourg Consulate in Shanghai to issue credit-based visas. *KaproAsia*, https://www.kapronasia.com/china-payments-research-category/alibaba-in-partnership-with-luxembourg-consulate-in-shanghai-to-issue-credit-based-visas.html

Wang, C., Zhan, J., Zhang, F., Liu, W., & Twumasi-Ankrah, M. (2020). Analysis of urban carbon balance. *Journal of Cleaner Production*, *281*, 125–138.

Wang, F. Y. (2020). Cooperative Data Privacy: The Japanese model of data privacy and the EU-Japan GDPR adequacy agreement. *Harvard Journal of Law & Technology*, *33*(2), 661–692.

Wang, L.-Y., Hu, H.-H., Wang, L., & Qin, J.-Q. (2022, July). Privacy assurances and social sharing in social commerce: The mediating role of threat-coping appraisals. *Journal of Retailing and Consumer Services*, *67*, 103028. https://www.sciencedirect.com/science/article/abs/pii/S0969698922001217

Wang, X., Chen, M., & Chen, N. (2024). How artificial intelligence affects the labour force employment structure from the perspective of industrial structure optimisation. *Heliyon*. PMID: 38434398

Ward, S. J. A. (2015). *Ethics and the media: An introduction*. Cambridge University Press.

Watanabe, S., Ogura, E., & Oikawa, K. (2025). *Current status of ASEAN data governance and its implications for the Digital Economy Framework Agreement (DEFA)* (ERIA Discussion Paper Series No. 360). Economic Research Institute for ASEAN and East Asia (ERIA).

We Are Social. Meltwater. (2025). *Digital 2025*. https://wearesocial.com/wp-content/uploads/2025/02/GDR-2025-v2.pdf

West, J. C. (2011). *Without a Net: Librarians Bridging the Digital Divide*. Libraries Unlimited. *The Verge*. https://www.theverge.com/2016/7/4/12092740/un-resolution-condemns-disrupting-internet-access

Wiederhold, B. K. (2013). When more is actually less: The rise of social media misinformation during disasters [Editorial]. *Cyberpsychology, Behavior, and Social Networking*, *16*(11), 783–784.

Wilkinson, M. D., Dumontier, M., Aalbersberg, I. J., & Mons, B. (2016). The FAIR Guiding Principles for Scientific Data Management and Stewardship. *Scientific Data*, *3*, 160018. https://www.nature.com/articles/sdata201618 PMID: 26978244

Wilson, C., Grizzle, A., Tuazon, R., Akyempong, K., & Cheung, C. K. (2011). *Media and information literacy curriculum for teachers*. UNESCO.

Wong, B. (2020). Data localization and ASEAN Economic Community. *Asian Journal of International Law*, *10*(1), 158–180. DOI: 10.1017/S2044251319000250

World Bank. (2019). *Digital Agriculture Profile*. World Bank Group.

World Economic Forum. (2024). Climate Adaptation: Unlocking Value Chains with the Power of Technology.

World Health Organization. (2025a). Misinformation and disinformation. WHO. from https://www.who.int/news-room/misinformation-and-disinformation

World Health Organization. (2025b). Infodemic. WHO. Retrieved August 5, 2025, from https://www.who.int/health-topics/infodemic

Wu, L., Morstatter, F., Carley, K. M., & Liu, H. (2019). Misinformation in social media. *SIGKDD Explorations*, *21*(2), 80–90. 10.1145%2F3373464.3373475

Xie, Y., Fadahunsi, K. P., Kelleher, C., Tarn, D., Grace, A., & O' Donoghue, J. (2025). Towards an inclusive digital health ecosystem. *Bulletin of the World Health Organization*, *103*(02), 170–173. DOI: 10.2471/blt.24.292020 PMID: 39882496

Xinhua News Agency. (2017, October 2). Debt defaulter fined for flying first-class. https://archive.shine.cn/nation/Firstclass-result-as-debts-paid/

Xue, L., & Pang, Z. (2022). Ethical governance of artificial intelligence: An integrated analytical framework. *Journal of Digital Economy*, *1*(1), 44–52. DOI: 10.1016/j.jdec.2022.08.003

Yang, Z. (2022, November 22). China just announced a new social credit law. Here's what it means. *MIT Technology Review*, https://www.technologyreview.com/2022/2011/2022/1063605/china-announced-a-new-social-credit-law-what-does-it-mean/

Yang, H., & Chen, Y. (2022). China's Data Security Law: Governance, regulation, and global implications. *Journal of Cyber Policy*, *7*(2), 163–182.

Yang, J., & Zhang, M. (2023). Beyond structural inequality: A socio-technical approach to the digital divide in the platform environment. *Humanities & Social Sciences Communications*, *10*(1), 1–12. DOI: 10.1057/s41599-023-01640-9

Yang, K. C. C., & Kang, Y. W. (2016). Real-name registration regulations in China: An examination of Chinese netizens' discussions about censorship, privacy, and political freedom. In Orwenjo, D. O., Oketch, O., & Tunde, A. H. (Eds.), *Political Discourse in Emerging, Fragile, and Failed Democracies* (pp. 61–87). IGI-Global Publisher.

Yerkinbayeva, L., Nurmukhankyzy, D., Kalymbek, B., Ozenbayeva, A., & Kalymbekova, Z. (2022). Digitalization of Environmental Information in the Republic of Kazakhstan: Issues of Legal Regulation. *Journal of Environmental Management and Tourism*, *13*(1), 115–127. https://journals.aserspublishing.eu/jemt/article/view/6815

Youn, S. (2009). Determinants of online privacy concern and its influence on privacy protection behaviors among young adolescents. *The Journal of Consumer Affairs*, *43*(3), 389–418.

Zaagsma, G. (2013). On digital history. *Bijdragen en Mededelingen Betreffende de Geschiedenis der Nederlanden*, *128*(4), 3–29. DOI: 10.18352/bmgn-lchr.9353

Zajc, M. (2000). *Tehnologije in družbe.* ISH Fakulteta za podiplomski humanistični študij.

Zajc, M. (2015). Social media, prosumption, and dispositives: New mechanisms of the construction of subjectivity. *Journal of Consumer Culture, 15*(1), 28–47. DOI: 10.1177/1469540513493201

Zarocostas, J. (2020). How to fight an infodemic. *Lancet,* •••, 395.

Zeng, J., Abidin, C., & Schäfer, M. S. (2021). Research perspectives on TikTok and its legacy apps: Introduction. https://doi.org/DOI: 10.5167/UZH-205427

Zhang, B., Chen, C., Lee, I., Lee, K., & Ong, K.-L. (2025). A survey on security and privacy issues in wearable health monitoring devices. *Computers & Security, 155*, 104453. DOI: 10.1016/j.cose.2025.104453

Zhang, X., Liu, L., Lan, M., Song, G., Xiao, L., & Chen, J. (2022). Interpretable machine learning models for crime prediction. *Computers, Environment and Urban Systems, 94*, 101789.

Zhang, Y., Zhao, W., & Chen, L. (2024). From narrow AI to AGI: Technical, ethical, and governance perspectives. *AI & Society*. Advance online publication. DOI: 10.1007/s00146-024-01712-5

Zhang, Z., Al Hamadi, H., Damiani, E., Yeun, C. Y., & Taher, F. (2022). Explainable artificial intelligence applications in cyber security: State-of-the-art in research. *IEEE Access : Practical Innovations, Open Solutions.*

Zhang, Z., Ning, H., Shi, F., Farha, F., Xu, Y., & Xu, J. (2022). Artificial intelligence in cyber security: Research advances, challenges, and opportunities. *Artificial Intelligence Review.*

Zhao, Y. (2016, December 4). Wide-ranging credit rating system aims to make society more trusting. *Global Times*, https://www.ecns.cn/2016/2012-2005/236416.shtml

Zhou, X., Chan, Y.-Y., & Peng, Z.-M. (2008, October). Deliberativeness of online political discussion: A content analysis of the GuangZhou daily website. *Journalism Studies, 9*(5), 759–770.

Zivic, P. (2023, February 23). *HAARP: Kahramanmaraş depremleriyle yeniden gündeme gelen komplo teoriler*. BBC. https://www.bbc.com/turkce/articles/c72l07yln1qo

Zuboff, S. (2019). *The age of surveillance capitalism: The fight for a human future at the new frontier of power*. PublicAffairs.

Zuboff, S. (2022). "We make them dance": Surveillance capitalism, the rise of instrumentarian power, and the threat to human rights. In *Human rights in the age of platforms* (pp. 73–93). The MIT Press.

About the Contributors

Maja Pucelj is an assistant professor and Head of research at EMUNI. She graduated from the Faculty of Public Administration in Ljubljana and the Faculty of Management in Koper, with a master's degree from the Faculty of Government and European Studies at the New University and the European Faculty of Law. She completed her first doctorate degree at Alma Mater Europaea - ISH in the humanities and her second doctorate degree at the Faculty of Government and European Studies of the New University in the field of international studies with an emphasis on human rights. She began her career as a police officer, where she was a member of a special police unit, continuing her career path as a risk manager, head of the legal department in the field of leasing and banking, as a director of marketing in the economy and as an auditor in an audit company. Prior to joining EMUNI and FOŠ, she worked as an advisor to the Minister of Education, Science and Sport in the field of pre-school education, primary education, secondary and higher education, adult education, and the quality of education and as an undersecretary in the Service for the Implementation of Cohesion Policy at the Ministry of Education, Science and Sport. She teached or co-teached the following courses: Fundamentals of Law in Organizational Studies, Organizational Behaviour and Seminar for Doctoral Dissertation. In 2024 she received reward from Slovenian Ombudsman for the best PhD research in the field of human rights in Slovenia. In the same year she also finished International Post-doctoral programme in Globalisation and Human rights in Mediterranea International Centre for Human Rights Research. Her research interest focuses on human rights, law, social responsibility and gender equality.

***

Saquib Ahmed is a legal professional and accomplished academic, currently a Research Scholar at the Sharda School of Law, Sharda University, Greater Noida, India. He has a strong educational background and a bachelor's degree.

from Aligarh Muslim University and Master of Law from Jamia Millia Islamia, where he developed his knowledge in Corporate Law, Intellectual Property Rights, Competition law etc.. He has a robust portfolio of publications in esteemed journals and books, reflecting his dedication to contributing to the body of knowledge in his fields of interest. His research has been recognized on various platforms, as evidenced by his participation in national and international conferences, seminars, webinars, and symposiums. Also, in his academic and research pursuits, Saquib is a skilled editor, having successfully overseen the editorial process of several publications and he is also editorial team member of the Sharda Law Review. Mr Ahmed has been active in organizing various programs like Moot Court Competition, Conferences, Faculty Development Programs and Quiz Competitions.

Jipson Joseph has a PhD in Ethics from DVK Bangalore. Currently, he is a Research Scholar at School of Law, Christ University, Bangalore, India. His research interests are in the fields of ethics, gender studies, constitutional law, human rights, human security, environmental justice, SDGs, developmental policies, and global poverty. He has published 6 books, co-edited one book, and contributed scholarly articles to many international and national journals and edited volumes including IGI Global Scientific Publishing's edited books.

Yowei Kang is an Assistant Professor at the Department of Communication and Theatre, Auburn University at Montgomery, USA. His research focused on new media design, digital game research, and visual communication. His work has been published in the International Journal of Strategic Communication, Howard Journal of Communication, and Creative Communication. He also co-edited Asian histories and heritages in videogames.

Mumtaz Khan Experienced and result-oriented Assistant Professor (Law) at Rayat law college (Affiliated to Panjab University) Railmajra (Punjab) with 8 years 03 months of experience in teaching criminal/civil and family law. Proficient in classroom management and using various teaching pedagogies like e- learning and case study method for preparing versatile lesson plan and curriculum. Focused on student learning outcomes and assessment tools. Skilled in academic-administrative management of law school towards establishing productive relationship among students and faculty members, through organizing various national & international seminars & other competitions. UGC-NET certified with Doctorate in Law (Ph.D.) From Panjab University, Chandigarh

Pranjal Khare is a distinguished corporate lawyer and is currently working as a law faculty at O.P. Jindal Global University, India. He specializes in Property Law, Corporate laws, Intellectual Property Rights, and International law. Mr. Pranjal is a highly regarded scholar and has published on numerous issues related to international affairs, economy, politics, data & privacy, artificial intelligence and IP disputes. He is also a frequent speaker at legal conferences and has served as a consultant to numerous law firms and corporations.

Saurabh Kumar is a distinguished Assistant Professor in Law at The Neotia University, Kolkata, with over seven years of teaching experience and an equally robust tenure as an Advocate before the Supreme Court of India. His academic journey is marked by a PhD (draft thesis submitted) from MUIT, an LL.M. with Grade A from MUIT, Delhi, and an LL.B. (Hons.) from Banaras Hindu University. Further enriching his credentials, he qualified the National Eligibility Test (NET) in 2019 and completed a specialized course in Public International Law at The Hague Academy of International Law, Netherlands. Saurabh's professional expertise spans legal education and practice, having served as an Assistant Professor at GNSU, Bihar,His scholarly contributions include peer-reviewed publications such as "Women In Indian Prisons: Rights And Challenges", "Women's Rights in India: A Contemporary Challenge*, alongside paper presentations at national and international conferences on human rights and gender justice. A passionate advocate for lifelong learning, Saurabh has completed an impressive array of international certifications from prestigious institutions like the Asian Development Bank, Open University UK, UNITAR, and WIPO, covering topics from climate change and human rights to criminology and sustainable development. His commitment to professional growth is evident in his participation in numerous Faculty Development Programs (FDPs) and webinars on emerging legal trends. Based in Delhi NCR, Saurabh blends academic rigor with practical insights, making him a dynamic educator and legal professional. His interdisciplinary approach, global perspective, and dedication to advancing legal scholarship position him as a valuable asset to any academic or legal institution. Contact him at Saurabhmishralawbhu@gmail.com or 9818012429 for collaboration or inquiries.

Anitha Kumari is an Assistant Professor in the Department of Information Systems at GITAM School of Business, GITAM (Deemed University), Bengaluru, Karnataka. She earned her PhD in Information Systems under the Faculty of Management, Hindustan Institute of Technology and Science, where she was actively engaged in teaching and research. She holds a Bachelor's degree in Computer Applications and a Master's degree in Business Administration, specializing in Systems and Finance. Her research interests include information systems, digital transformation, public governance, fintech, blockchain, business analytics, big data analytics, artificial intelligence, machine learning and deep learning. She has presented at conferences and published research articles in academic journals. With eight years of teaching experience, she brings extensive knowledge and expertise to her field.

Ajitabh Mishra Working as an Assistant Professor of Law at Rayat College of Law, Railmajra, affiliated with Panjab University, Chandigarh. With a strong academic and research background, he has been actively engaged in teaching Constitutional Law, Criminal Law, Evidence, and Administrative Law, along with mentoring students for moot courts and debates. His research interests include constitutional governance, criminal justice reforms, and the evolving role of law in contemporary society. Apart from teaching, he has coordinated several academic and cultural initiatives, published scholarly papers

Hemendra Singh is a Lecturer of Law at Jindal Global Law School, situated within O.P. Jindal Global University, Sonipat. He pursued his LL.M. in Intellectual Property Rights from National Law University, Jodhpur, following his graduation with a B.A. LL.B. (Hons.) from Rajiv Gandhi National University of Law, Punjab. With a focus on corporate law, intellectual property law, criminal law, and constitutional law, he has authored numerous research articles and book chapters published in both national and international journals and books.

Wafaa Taleb is a lecturer and researcher at the University of Oran 2 Mohamed Ben Ahmed, specializing in postcolonial studies, African civilizations, and feminist theory. She teaches courses on African, British, and American history and civilization. Her scholarly work focuses on neo-colonialism, ethnic diversity, and human rights in Africa, with a particular emphasis on gendered narratives and digital activism in Algeria. Dr. Taleb has participated in several international conferences and has published on topics such as feminist resistance in North Africa. She serves as Editor-in-Chief of the IMAGO Interculturality and Didactics journal, which promotes interdisciplinary studies in the humanities, languages, and social sciences.

Kenneth C.C. Yang is a Professor in the Department of Communication at the University of Texas at El Paso, USA. He has edited or co-edited four books, Asia.com: Asia Encounters the Internet (2003), Multi-Platform Advertising Strategies in the Global Marketplace (2018), Cases on Immersive Virtual Reality Techniques (2019), and Asian histories and heritages in videogames (2024). His works have been published in Cyberpsychology, Journal of Strategic Communication, International Journal of Consumer Marketing, Journal of Marketing Communication, and Telematics and Informatics.

Index

A

C

D

E

G

H

I

M

www.ingramcontent.com/pod-product-compliance
Lightning Source LLC
LaVergne TN
LVHW081533300926
849161LV00006B/1403
* 9 7 9 8 3 3 7 3 3 6 8 5 5 *